ASIAN DEFENCE REVIEW 2016

ASIAN DEFENCE REVIEW 2016

Edited by

Air Marshal

Vinod Patney

SYSM PVSM AVSM VrC (Retd)

KNOWLEDGE WORLD

KW Publishers Pvt Ltd

New Delhi

in association with

Centre for Air Power Studies

New Delhi

The Centre for Air Power Studies is an independent, non-profit, academic research institution established in 2002 under a registered Trust to undertake and promote policy-related research, study and discussion on the trends and developments in defence and military issues, especially air power and the aerospace arena, for civil and military purposes. Its publications seek to expand and deepen the understanding of defence, military power, air power and aerospace issues without necessarily reflecting the views of any institution or individuals except those of the authors.

Vinod Patney
Director General
Centre for Air Power Studies
P-284, Arjan Path
Subroto Park
New Delhi 110010

Tele: (91-11) 25699131

E-mail: capsnetdroff@gmail.com
capsoffice@capsindia.org
website: www.capsindia.org

ISBN 978-93-83649-90-7

Published in India by Kalpana Shukla

KNOWLEDGE WORLD
KW Publishers Pvt Ltd
4676/21, First Floor, Ansari Road, Daryaganj, New Delhi 110002
✆ +91 11 23263498 / 43528107 ✉ knowledgeworld@kwpub.com • www.kwpub.com

2011 FIPBA BEST PUBLISHERS AWARD (ENGLISH)

Printed and bound in India

Contents

Contributors

Air Marshal Vinod Patney SYSM PVSM AVSM VrC (Retd)

Air Marshal Vinod Patney—a decorated veteran of the 1965 and the 1971 Wars; and the recipient of the Sarvottam Yudh Seva Medal (SYSM) for exceptional leadership during the Kargil War—is the Director General of the Centre for Air Powers Studies. He is a graduate of the Royal Air Force Staff College and a founder member of the premier Tactics & Air Combat Development Establishment of the IAF. He has been a member of the National Security Advisory Board and was a part of the study on Global Security. He lectures regularly at security seminars and participates in Track 2 dialogues. He has authored a book titled, *Essays on Aerospace* and edited several others. He has contributed a number of articles on national security issues and aerospace affairs to eminent journals and periodicals.

Air Vice Marshal Manmohan Bahadur VM (Retd)

Air Vice Marshal Manmohan Bahadur is a Distinguished Fellow at the Centre for Air Power Studies, New Delhi. He is an Experimental Test Pilot from France, a graduate of the Air Command and Staff College, USA and a post graduate in Defence and Strategic Studies from Madras University. He has been Head of Training (Air) at Defence Services Staff College, Wellington and as Assistant Chief of Air Staff was the operational head of Transport and Helicopter Operations. His core interests concern Air Power and Strategic Affairs, on which he writes in leading periodicals and lectures in India and abroad.

Dr Manpreet Sethi

Dr Manpreet Sethi is a Senior Fellow at the Centre for Air Power Studies, New Delhi where she heads the project on nuclear security. An expert on a range of nuclear issues, she has published over 80 papers. Her recent books include *Code of Conduct for Outer Space: Strategy for India* (Knowledge World, 2015), *Nuclear Power: In the Wake of Fukushima* (Knowledge World, 2012) and *Nuclear Strategy: India's March Towards Credible Deterrence* (Knowledge World, 2009). She is recipient of the K Subrahmanyam award conferred for excellence in strategic and security studies.

Dr Sitakanta Mishra

Dr Sitakanta Mishra is currently an Assistant Professor of International Relations in the School of Liberal Studies (SLS), Pandit Deendayal Petroleum University (PDPU), Gandhinagar, Gujarat. Till recently, he was a Research Fellow at the Centre for Air Power Studies, New Delhi. Dr Mishra has authored three books and many national and international research papers on foreign policy, missile and nuclear proliferation, India-Pakistan relations. He is also involved in Indo-Pak track-2 dialogue.

Dr Temjenmeren Ao

Dr Temjenmeren Ao is an Associate Fellow at the Centre for Air Power Studies (CAPS), New Delhi. He is working on a project titled, China's Aerospace Sector: A Study on its Rise through Transfers of Technology. His area of interests includes US-China relations, China's economic and military engagements, and China's dual-use technology transfers. He has completed his Masters of Arts in Economics from Centre for Economics Studies and Planning, School of Social Sciences, Jawaharlal Nehru University (JNU), Delhi, and holds a PhD in International Relations from School of International Studies, Jawaharlal Nehru University, Delhi.

Ms Swati Arun

Ms Swati Arun is currently a PhD scholar with China Division of Centre for East Asian Studies, School of International Studies, Jawaharlal Nehru University (JNU), New Delhi. She also finished her MPhil from the same, where she wrote her desertion on 'China's Strategy Towards the US in East Asia'. She was an Associate Fellow with Centre for Air Power Studies, where she worked on the project titled *Geopolitics in East Asia, China-US Relations and Challenges for Indian Foreign Policy*. Her areas of interests include China's Security Policy, China-US Relations, East Asian Geopolitics, International Security and Balance of Power. Swati has also published with various think tanks and magazines.

Ms Chandra Rekha

Ms Chandra Rekha is an Associate Fellow in Centre for Air Power Studies (CAPS). This year she launched her first book titled *India- Russia Post Cold War Relations: A New Epoch of Cooperation*. Presently, she is working on *Shifting Trends in Russia-China Relations in Contemporary International Geopolitics*. Three of her published articles are indexed in the Parliamentary Documentation. She is also pursuing her PhD on *Revival of Russia's Defence Industrial Complex, 2000-2014* from the Centre for Russian and Central Asian Studies in Jawaharlal Nehru University. She has presented papers in conferences both in India and abroad.

Group Captain Rajiv Kumar Narang

Group Captain Rajiv Kumar Narang is a Senior Fellow at the Centre for Air Power Studies (CAPS), New Delhi. He is a helicopter pilot and an alumnus of Defence Services Staff College, Wellington, India. He is currently working on a project on Unmanned Aerial Vehicles. His areas of interests include Aerospace Sector, Strategic Affairs and Indian Military History. He has published articles in *Defence and Diplomacy*, *Air Power Journal* and online journals.

Ms Manisha Chaurasiya

Ms Manisha Chaurasiya is a Research Associate at the Centre for Air Power Studies, New Delhi. She is pursuing a project on India's Nuclear Diplomacy: The Challenges of the New 'Exceptional Status'. She is a Research Scholar at the Centre for International Politics, Organization and Disarmament (CIPOD), Jawaharlal Nehru University, New Delhi. Nuclear Security, the Indo-US Nuclear Deal and Bilateral Civilian Nuclear Cooperation are some of her broad interest areas. She has written several articles for the CAPS journals and the website on a variety of nuclear issues. She is also in-charge and member of the editorial team of 'Nuclear Security' the fortnightly newsletter from CAPS.

Group Captain Ashish Gupta

Group Captain Ashish Gupta, a Senior Fellow at Centre for Air Power Studies (CAPS) is a prolific reader and has an intense and professional yearning to explore the nuances of today's cyber zeitgeist. An alumnus of the Defence Services Staff College and Post Graduate in Communication stream from IIT Delhi, he avidly follows the developments taking place in cyber security realm. His lucid articulation and incisive insights on the subject of Cyber Security has fructified in authoring many seminal papers and posting of online literary contributions. His has also authored peer reviewed articles on cyber-related issues which have been published in various reputed journals.

Mr E Dilipraj

Mr E Dilipraj is an Associate Fellow at the Centre for Air Power Studies (CAPS), New Delhi. He is also pursuing his Ph.D from Centre for Latin American Studies, School of International Studies, Jawaharlal Nehru University. His academic area of interest includes global cyber security, future warfare technologies like Robotics, 3D printing, Nano technology, supercomputers, Brazilian Studies and South American Studies.

1

Indian Air Force: Persuasive in Peace, Effective in War

Vinod Patney

Introduction

The Indian Air Force (IAF) is today a well-balanced air force with some state-of-the-art attributes. It is the fourth largest air force in the world and capable of performing, adequately and satisfactorily, most missions that an air force could be tasked with, throughout the spectrum of conflict. The spectrum of conflict is forever widening and the IAF has so far managed to keep abreast of increasing requirements and possible tasks. It is a characteristic of the IAF that it has a penchant for innovativeness; making best use of available resources, howsoever limited they may be; and working for mission accomplishment is an article of faith. Its capabilities are sufficient to ward off any regional threat and it is better equipped and manned than almost all air forces in neighbouring countries. The IAF lays great stress on human resource development, with particular emphasis on training, both *ab initio* and continued training. It is a mature and confident Service. IAF pilots have won the admiration of pilots of many developed countries during joint peace-time exercises.

In 2012, the IAF essayed a doctrine for itself titled "The Basic Doctrine of the Indian Air Force". The 'vision' spelt out in the doctrine reads, "To acquire strategic reach and capabilities across the spectrum of conflict that serve the ends of military diplomacy, nation building and enable force projection within India's strategic area of influence". Implicit in the vision statement is the commitment to be ever ready to safeguard national security and promote national interests. National interests go beyond mere security needs and the IAF commits itself to be the instrument of deterrence, and to wage wars successfully, if so needed. It must also be prepared to showcase its capabilities in acts of coercion if that requirement ever comes to pass. More importantly, the IAF has to train and equip itself to provide operational options to the government; options that can then be considered to formulate national policies. The IAF also recognises that it is more than likely that it will be the first to enter the fray and that high readiness levels have to be maintained. This must be done as in air wars, the side that successfully attacks first secures a tremendous advantage and seizes the initiative for further actions. All air forces recognise this truism and the IAF is no exception. It is far easier to seize and retain the initiative than to have to win it back and then to try and retain it. In addition, the inherent characteristics of air power of speed of action and reaction; flexibility; and the ability to more readily ratchet up or down the intensity of conflict make the IAF the prime Service to effect deterrence and coercion. The IAF has to be prepared for all such tasks.

An air force is essentially an offensive arm and offensive action is its metier. Yet, it has the important role of inhibiting, if not prohibiting, offensive action by the other side; a mission given the title Air Defence (AD). Air defence of the Indian skies is the axiomatic responsibility of the IAF. Air defence and offensive action are both important and it is always a complex calculation as to which mission must get more resources. All air forces try and balance these competing requirements and, again, the IAF is no exception. It is a balanced air force.

The progress of the IAF from a small fledging force to a universally well respected Service has been slow but replete with notable achievements. The history of the IAF is worthy of examination.

Brief History

Within a mere seven to eight years of the historic first flight of the Wright Brothers in 1903, India was home to aviation and aircraft. The interest in aviation continued to grow and many Indians took part in World War I, flying with the Royal Flying Corps, and with distinction. One name, amongst many others, that merits mention is that of Lt Indra Lal Roy who was awarded the Distinguished Flying Cross (DFC) for his exploits over Europe. Such exploits were the fillip for a growing voice in India for the establishment of an air arm. Finally, on October 8, 1932, the Indian Air Force Act came into being and the first flight, comprising 4 Westland Wapiti aircraft, became operational on April 1, 1933. The IAF started as an independent Service and its personnel were recruited directly and not seconded from any other Service. On formation, it became the fifth independent air arm. Almost immediately, it was operationally tasked against the tribal fighters in Waziristan in northwest India.

Soon after the start of World War II in September 1939, the IAF was again pushed into action. Gradually, the strength also grew to the planned strength of 10 squadrons by 1946. The 'Indian' squadrons performed very creditably and won laurels. Many pilots of those times are recognised icons of the IAF. Twenty-four pilots were also sent to Europe and participated in the Battle of Britain and on bombing missions in Europe. By the end of the war, the IAF was battle tested and battle hardened.

The inadequate strength of the IAF was depleted when India gained independence in August 1947 and the assets were divided between India and the newly created Pakistan. India was left with only six squadrons. Within two months of independence, Pakistan started a covert war in Kashmir, soon followed by overt military action. The resilience of the IAF and its innovativeness was soon tested. When the Maharaja of Kashmir signed the Instrument of Accession to India and requested military support, troops were airlifted to Srinagar to ward off the raiders who were already on the outskirts of the city. For this, civil aircraft were requisitioned as the IAF had only one transport aircraft squadron equipped with Dakota aircraft. This squadron did yeoman service and carried troops and even guns to the area, often landing at small airfields at night. Even Leh, an airfield at a height of 10,000 ft, was activated. Tempest aircraft also provided firepower support to the army. Some tremendous work was done by the fledgling air force and professional expertise and innovativeness were much in evidence. Though the start of the war was under trying circumstances, the tables were soon turned. The fourteen-month war ended with a ceasefire but Kashmir was saved.

The 1950s comprised a period of consolidation and near state-of-the-art fighter jet aircraft were inducted. By the end of the decade, the IAF could boast of a position amongst the foremost air forces in the world and was certainly the strongest air force in the region. Then came the Chinese attack in 1962. The debacle of the Indo-China conflict was a sad period in our history where strategically we miscalculated and our tactics and approach to the conflict were decidedly questionable. In the east, the Chinese intruded to a considerable distance and then withdrew. However, in the Ladakh region, they occupied large tracts of our territory that they continue to hold. The ignominy still rankles and we cannot but think that we could, and should, have acquitted ourselves more creditably. Unfortunately, combat air power was not used and conventional wisdom suggests that had we used our air force energetically, the course of the conflict could have been very different. It is a fact that in all the wars or conflicts we have been engaged in since independence, the 1962 conflict was the only time we lost the war. This was also the only occasion when combat air power was not used. The inference is obvious.

Our poor performance in the 1962 War probably emboldened Pakistan to launch yet another war against India in 1965. The curtain raiser was Pakistan's moving into the desolate area of Kutch in western India in April 1965. No air action was carried out apart from a few reconnaissance missions, but Pakistan soon withdrew. Once again,

Pakistan had taken the initiative and again Pakistan's designs were effectively thwarted. In August of the same year, Pakistan infiltrated 8,000 raiders into Jammu and Kashmir (J&K) with the idea of creating pockets of revolt and widespread destruction of civilian and military targets. This was followed in September 1965 by an armed attack into our territory supported by the Pakistan Air Force (PAF). We retaliated in force. This was the first major air war for the IAF and essentially it was a war of attrition. A number of infrastructural and training limitations were highlighted but in spite of these, the IAF's performance was satisfactory. The Pakistani designs once again failed miserably.

Immediate action was taken to rectify the shortcomings noticed with special reference to security of air bases and improvements in ground infrastructure. The serious problems of inter-Service cooperation were also addressed. As a result, we were soon better prepared. In 1971, there were mass scale killings in the then East Pakistan and over 10 million refugees moved into India. The situation was patently untenable and then Pakistan launched another air attack on December 3, 1971. This time, we were better prepared as there was adequate warning of an impending attack. The riposte was swift and effective. Inter-Service cooperation was also better. The war in the east ended precipitously when, on December 12, 1971, the governor's residence was attacked and the governor decided to surrender. As a result, East Pakistan was dismembered and a new country, Bangladesh, was created. In addition, over 93,000 POWs (Prisoners of War) were captured. After that, India announced a unilateral ceasefire that was accepted by Pakistan. The IAF's performance was good and a number of new measures were adopted; two that merit mention are the use of lumbering heavy transport aircraft for carpet bombing; and the use of fighter aircraft for attacking enemy airfields by night. The fighter aircraft had little to go on except a clock and a compass. The fact that these missions were successful indicates the high level of training and expertise.

The 1971 War was followed by a long period of relative peace that was used by both India and Pakistan to modernise their forces. However, although no major conflict occurred till 1999, Pakistan started sending terrorists into India and this state sponsoring of terrorism has continued till date. For Pakistan, this is cost-effective aggression. India, on its part, in 1984, deployed forces in the Siachin area to obviate Pakistan's designs to create a presence there. This came as a surprise to Pakistan but there was little that it could do about it. Moreover, legality was on the side of India. Other instances and disagreements can be cited. There have also been many attempts to bring about a lasting peace or at least make some progress towards that end, but to no avail.

Possibly, Pakistan was emboldened once again when in May 1998, both countries became declared nuclear powers. In early 1999, Pakistan launched a bold plan to occupy strategic locations on the Indian side in the general area of Kargil with the explicit purpose of cutting off the supply link to Siachin. India got wind of the intrusion somewhat late by which time the intruders were firmly entrenched. The IAF went into action on May 26, 1999, but was severely limited as there was an unequivocal government diktat that we were not to cross the Line of Control (LoC). The area of operations was at heights of 12,000 to 16,000 ft, and it represented the highest battlefield where air power was ever used. No aircraft has been specifically built to operate at such altitudes, either before or since. Under these limitations, the IAF had to work afresh on the optimum utilisation of air power. In this, the IAF succeeded and delivered many telling blows. There were also many innovative ideas that were put into play. Slowly, our army advanced to capture lost ground but it is a feather in the cap of the IAF that there were no fratricidal attacks and every location recaptured by our army was first visited by the air force. In time, the inevitable occurred. Spurred by President Clinton's categorical intervention, Pakistan had to agree to a withdrawal. The intrusion was totally vacated and, once again, Pakistan had to eat humble pie. This was the fourth occasion when Pakistan attacked India and was unable to achieve its objective. Will there be a fifth or a sixth occasion? Is there a likelihood of another conflict with China? These are difficult questions but such conflicts can be obviated if our armed forces are strong. We just have to ensure that we have adequate strength to deter any adversary and for this, the IAF has to play the leading role. In an uncertain or trying environment, the IAF has time and again shown great initiative and innovativeness; attributes that will continue to yield decided benefits in future as well.

Since 1999, Pakistan has continued with its policy of state sponsored terrorism and the attempts are also becoming bolder. We have to find ways to ensure that there is some cost that Pakistan must bear for such activities. There can be many options but if it is decided to use the military option, the IAF is bound to play the leading role.

This brief history of the IAF cannot be restricted to the wars thrust on us. Many other notable events also occurred and these are covered in the paragraphs to follow.

Major Activities Other Than War

Apart from the Kargil conflict where combat air power was used inside our own territory, there were four other such instances. The first was the air action against Hyderabad and its annexation in September 1948. The IAF ably supported the army and it was a short operation. One interesting aspect was that Dakota aircraft were modified to carry bombs. Similarly, Goa was liberated from the Portugese in December 1961. This was a more extensive operation starting with the bombing of the airfields to obviate outside support.

In this operation, the IAF was in the vanguard and later supported the army when it was activated. At around the same time, combat air power was used against the Nagas in northeast India. One mission involved the lifting of a blockade when our troops were surrounded. Well placed firing helped lift the blockade. During this operation, armed reconnaissance missions were also flown to cover the move of our army columns. In all these instances, air power played a significant role even though the aircraft of those times had many limitations. One other instance bears mention. In April 1984, our army took over control of the Siachin glacier. This had become essential as there were indications that Pakistan would attempt to do so. It was a difficult task as the only helicopters that could get to the high altitudes nearing 20,000 ft could take a load of just two or three soldiers. The conditions were testing and in five and a half hours of continuous activity, only 30 troops and about a tonne of load could be airlifted. These troops were then required to stamp down the snow and create makeshift helipads. Similarly, all the earmarked posts were manned and thereafter, till the present day, have to be maintained by air. Pakistan made many attempts to dislodge us, but failed every time.

The IAF has also participated in peace-keeping operations under the UN flag. Three such deployments can be quoted and all of them were in difficult locations. The first was in 1961-63 when our Canberra aircraft operated in Congo. The second occasion was in Somalia from October 1993 to December 1994, and the third, probably the most difficult, was in Sierra Leone in the year 2000. In this last deployment, the IAF detachment helped break a 75-day siege of UN troops. The troops were de-inducted with the help of our helicopters, including attack helicopters.

On two occasions, the IAF was used in aid of a foreign power. The ethnic divide in Sri Lanka between the Sinhalese in the south and the Tamils in the north led to the Tamils arming themselves. The faction titled Liberation Tigers of Tamil Eelam (LTTE) became the dominant force. The Tamils of India strongly supported their brethren in Sri Lanka. To provide succour to the Sri Lankan Tamils, the IAF resorted to air-dropping of supplies often called the "rice bombing of Jaffna". The transport aircraft were escorted by Mirage aircraft. The message was clear. Soon thereafter, on July 29, 1987, a pact was signed between India and Sri Lanka. The IAF was part of the Indian Peace-Keeping Force (IPKF) despatched to Sri Lanka thereafter. The object was to disarm the LTTE but when the LTTE refused to do so, the conflict soon degenerated into a battle to forcibly defeat and disarm them. Hence, a detachment for two weeks became a 32-month-long deployment. It was a unique experience for the IAF to operate in some other land with all the attendant limitations. The air activity involved rapid and large-scale lifting and maintenance of troops and their equipment, reconnaissance, casualty evacuation, and use of helicopters in special operations supported by attack helicopters. Tanks and artillery guns were also airlifted and the operations were conducted over hostile areas. This was the first out of country contingency and many lessons were learnt.

Whilst the IPKF was busy in Sri Lanka, another emergency arose. At 0815 hr on November 3, 1988, the IAF was informed that a coup was underway in Maldives to depose President Gayoom. It was reported that the rebels were fighting near the Presidential Palace. Government and army/air force machinery was put into gear. There was scant information about the progress of the rebels and, more importantly, as to whether the airfield was safe. In spite of this, it was decided to airlift troops to the island. The first IL-76 aircraft, with a company of troops, landed at the Hulule airport at 2156 hrs. The president was secured by 0235 hrs on November 4, and the island was under complete control by 0450 hrs. A difficult task had been accomplished with aplomb and the speed of action and commitment won the appreciation of many other nations.

The IAF was also tasked to evacuate our nationals from the war-torn Middle East during the First Iraq War in 1991. As many as 117,000 nationals were brought home to safety. A phenomenal task was successfully completed.

India is in an area prone to natural calamities. Earthquakes, floods, landslides, etc. are frequent occurrences. The IAF has been called upon to provide succour on every such occasion. Relief operations have been mounted rapidly and effectively. Many lives have been saved, sometimes involving rescues where a high level of professional expertise was called for to rescue the injured and incapacitated under very difficult conditions. Many of the saviours remain unsung heroes but have the undying gratitude of those rescued. In many cases, tremendous initiative was used. The annals of the IAF are full of such heroism combined with professional expertise of a very high order. Three events of the many disasters that merit mention are the January 26, 2001 earthquake in Gujarat, the tsunami of December 26, 2004, the ravaging floods in Uttaranchal in 2013 and the more serious floods in J&K in 2014.

The short description of the activities of the IAF over the years would have given a flavour of what was accomplished. The range of missions and tasks was very extensive and often stretched the resources of the IAF. It can be stated with certitude that no other air force in the world has the experience of the diverse operations that the IAF has performed or performs routinely. The entire ambit of air power missions have been flown and are regularly practised. The positioning of our troops in Siachin in 1984 and thereafter maintaining them since then by air is a feat without parallel in the annals of global air power. Undoubtedly, the IAF will continue to be extensively tasked in peace and war and will be required to meet future challenges effectively.

Future Challenges

Is there a likelihood of a change in the operational utilisation of the IAF in the near future? The answer must be a negative. The roles and missions are classic and will remain constant. What could alter is the manner of use of air power to meet the demands of the moment. The flexibility or strategic agility of air power is well appreciated and will have to come into play to an increasing extent. Thus, whilst joint operations will be the norm, the salience and participation of individual Services will depend on the planned objectives. Also, with the ever increasing cost of aircraft assets, possibly, close support missions will increasingly give way to interdiction and attacks on targets that are further inland. Much will depend on the diplomatic and political imperatives, but close support missions will remain an important operation of war. What could change is the use of better stand-off precision weapons. It is tempting to state that armed helicopters and Unmanned Aerial Vehicles (UAVs) will fit the bill better, but we have to be careful about their use in a contested air space. A helicopter is a versatile machine and will have increasing relevance but its utilisation in an attack mode is likely to be limited. However, it will be prudent to retain the capability and build on the expertise so as to be ready when their use is the best or only viable option.

The use of unmanned systems will become more prevalent. Although they could have an attack role, their major contribution will be towards intelligence gathering. Intelligence collection, collation, analysis, and timely dissemination is a continuous requirement that can never be over-emphasised. The demand is also increasing and we will have to use all possible means, including use of space assets, aircraft, UAVs and human intelligence. In the opinion of the author, intelligence is the foremost requirement for success in a conflict.

The modern battle arena is becoming more complicated and complex. The degree of automation will increase, and we will have to contend with cyber war, use of cruise missiles, weaponisation of space and much more. The 'wish list' is long, and moneys difficult to come by. That begs the question as to how we should approach modernisation requirements.

Modernisation: Modernisation of the armed forces is an essential requirement. This is more significant in the case of air forces because of two reasons. Firstly, air forces by their very nature operate at the cutting edge of technology. Secondly, in the air battle, superiority in a given attribute could have an impact far greater than the intrinsic value of the attribute. It could be war winning. Hence, the IAF has to be equipped with near state-of-the-art capabilities at least when compared to our possible adversaries. Some modernisation has been effected in the IAF during the last decade or so but much more needs to be done. Modernisation must be a continuous process.

Modernisation is expensive and as much of our equipment is imported, continued imports at ever increasing costs will soon become unsustainable. Indigenisation is the only way out. This aspect needs urgent attention. Our own industry is not yet mature enough for the demands of the air force. It is also necessary that we alter or introduce procedures to ensure that the user becomes the driver of our procurement programmes. Our Defence Procurement Procedure (DPP) has been revised nearly on an annual basis to facilitate greater indigenisation but we are still floundering. The Foreign Direct Investment (FDI) limits for defence have been recently raised to 49 percent. Hopefully, this will help but FDI limits may have to be raised to levels that will encourage foreign enterprises to set up manufacturing facilities in India. Our rules and procedures must also be appropriately amended. At this stage, we need the foreign vendors at least as much as they need us. Our experience with our state owned Defence Public Sector Units (DPSUs) and the Research and Development (R&D) organisations has been less than happy. It is time to put the government owned agencies in competition with the private sector. The private sector's entry into the defence equipment manufacturing sector should be facilitated with required advances and government commitments. Export restrictions should be eased and, in time, the private sector should be encouraged to carry out its own R&D. Are such ideas utopian? In the opinion of the author, they are doable. We need to make a concerted effort to ensure rapid indigenisation and increase defence exports. The concept of indigenisation should change from 'made by Indians' to 'made in India'. We should set ourselves a target to ensure that defence exports reach some 25-30 percent of our defence budget in the not too distant future.

Defence Budgets: For some years, the defence budget has been restricted to under 2 percent of the Gross Domestic Product (GDP). Some Indian strategic analysts believe that the defence budget should be increased to 3 percent of the GDP. It is mentioned by them that the declared Chinese budget is some three times our budget, and the real budget is likely to be considerably higher. That is probably true but each country has specific needs and plans and the size of budgets alone is not indicative of present or future capabilities. In the budget presented to our Parliament on July 10, 2014, the defence budget was pegged at 1.74 percent of the GDP. To examine the defence budget as percentage of the GDP has limited value. Far more important is the absolute value and the defence budget as percentage of total government expenditure. The current budget is Rs 230,000 ($38.33 billion approximately) or 13.0 percent of government expenditure but as 'plan' expenditure should not be reduced, the defence budget is 18.85 percent of non-plan expenditure. If we were to set aside the amounts for subsidies and interest and loan repayments, the defence budget is 26 percent of the remaining non-plan expenditure. For a developing country, this figure is substantial and not much more can be expected. In fact, the total amount spent by the government on security is much greater if one were to include the expenditure on the police, paramilitary forces, etc. We can only hope that the country grows at a rapid rate and more moneys are then available for a higher defence budget.

If the defence budget is likely to stay below the perceived requirements, it behoves us to spend it as wisely as we can. This is one area where much can be done. The obvious answer lies in an assessment of the requirements of national security involving all the players. However, this article will be restricted to the need for a joint inter-Service analysis of future requirements on the basis of likely availability of funds. In other words, the need is for effective jointmanship.

Effective Jointmanship

In the Indian armed forces, jointmanship has remained elusive. Joint thinking has not taken root. There are two prerequisites to effective jointmanship. They are: the recognition that some individual Service interests must be sacrificed for the common good; and respect for each other's core competencies. The discussions on jointmanship, and there are many, are often led by the need for a suitable organisational structure and then that leads on to the requirement for joint procurement procedures. This is akin to putting the cart before the horse. The primary need is to jointly determine our extant operational capabilities, how best to use them, and the capabilities we must have in the near and mid-terms. We do not require an organisation for the purpose.

It follows that the first step must be to examine our capabilities in response to the furtherance of our national interests. A joint study should determine how best to meet the likely contingencies with what we have. A dispassionate analysis may suggest that a single Service should be the lead Service in the the stated circumstances. It is also possible, indeed probable, that a contingency can be best met by a single Service, say, the air force. This is likely to be the optimum solution in many cases given the essential attributes of an air force and the nature of likely conflicts in the near future. There is a continuing evolution in the nature and intensity of conflicts and in the expanding capabilities of air power. This is often not appreciated by non-practitioners. Joint planning will bring home such capabilities. The IAF is ideally suited to interface with the army and navy and influence the land or sea battle. Air power is expensive but it is also cost-effective and often a wiser option. Again, it is not necessary that we must respond to the adversary's actions in like manner. In fact, that would seldom be the option of choice. What is essential is that all three Services are aware of the operational planning and the roles required of them. True jointmanship does not imply that all three Services must operate together in all cases. What it does imply is that the Services must plan together and develop a system for such planning on a regular, even continuous basis. Far more important than 'planning for joint operations' is 'joint planning for operations'. A joint effort is also needed to decide on technologies that we should invest in for our future requirements. Joint planning for future procurements for all three Services based on the operational planning first undertaken should be the next step. Such a procurement plan will have a solid basis and not be a mere wish list. Sound joint operational planning will, in its wake, ensure that the prioritisation of purchases is based on good operational logic. A worthy objective. In the opinion of the author, we should begin to examine organisational issues only when the planning processes are understood and adhered to, and the detailed plans of how to prosecute a conflict(s) are decided. Such a system will then automatically throw up the organisation needed to best serve the purpose. Organisational issues can never be more important than operational planning. The requirements of operations and the manner of their conduct should determine the optimum organisation for the tasks.

To bring about effective jointmanship is a future challenge for the IAF but three other issues merit examination, namely our space capabilities, the cyber domain and the collection, collation, analysis and timely dissemination of intelligence information.

Space Capabilities

Use of space assets is becoming increasingly important in all walks of life and the armed forces are no exception. In fact, the efficiency and effectiveness of the armed forces is acutely dependent on the availability and accessibility of space assets. This requirement is particularly acute for air forces. Space systems aid in better and surer communications, accuracy of weapon delivery, analysis of weather, navigation, search and rescue, etc. The challenge, therefore, is two-fold. Firstly, we must ensure the development of our space assets to stay ahead of our adversaries in terms of both extent and nature of use. Better and more reliable systems are needed. The challenge is to ensure that we are not found wanting at any time. The second challenge is to ensure that our systems are not interfered with, jammed, damaged or destroyed. Any side that is able to do so, and preferably covertly, will be at a distinct advantage. The above highlights that whilst militarisation of space implying military use of space is already widely prevalent, weaponisation of space is probably inevitable. Space is no longer a distant frontier. Seeking space situational awareness and control whilst attempting to deny the same to the adversary is becoming a valid operation of war. Space is now the fourth dimension of war.

In the commercial field as well, space is becoming increasingly important. Space is now a $ 300 billion industry and growing rapidly. As it so often happens, increasing competition often degenerates into conflict and nations have to be prepared for such eventualities either by defensive means or by the ability to adopt a strong dissuasive posture. The IAF believes that space is only a vertical extension of air power and there is considerable merit in the term 'aerospace power' entering the military lexicon. The IAF should lead the other Services in the planning and utilisation of space assets. Such an approach has been adopted by many countries.

Cyber Domain

Hacking of computers, extracting information and infiltrating bugs are threats that are both widely prevalent and becoming more powerful. Considerable resources are being allocated for cyber war, both the defensive and offensive aspects. Legality and morality issues are being ignored. It is conjectured that soon it may become possible to interfere with civilian plants and industries, command and control of different agencies, civil and military, as well as interfere with the weapon systems themselves. It is a frightening thought to imagine that when after a nuclear weapon is released for use, the response does not occur as the controlling computers have been affected. What is worse is that the attacker may assume, with supreme confidence but erroneously, that he has impaired the functioning of all adversary weapons and a full-fledged nuclear war results. The menace of cyber war has to be curtailed but as long as the deniability factor remains, the advantages of a cyber attack are far too compelling. In cyber war, so much can be achieved with relatively modest investments. The world has been seized of the danger but may be the danger has not reached a level where the world becomes keen to seriously deal with it. Attempts at the acceptance of a 'code of conduct' are inadequate. A verifiable binding commitment is needed.

A cyber war will impact the air force more than the other Services as aircraft, weapon systems and communication nodes are susceptible to cyber attacks. Indeed, computers and data processing are at the heart of air force functioning. Hence, the overriding requirement to ensure that our systems are impervious to cyber attacks. A tall order but one that cannot be ignored. Cyber is now the fifth domain of warfare and possibly, in the next conflict, the first shots will be fired in the cyber sphere.

Intelligence Inputs

The IAF has had to often wrestle with the problem of inadequate, sparse, inaccurate and late intelligence information. In modern warfare, this must be unacceptable. The IAF has the capability to carry out blind bombing with a great deal of accuracy but the results can only be as good as the accuracy of the coordinates supplied by the intelligence agencies. Far more effort has to be devoted to the means of acquiring good intelligence inputs, not only about target coordinates but also the planning, training, equipment serviceability, capabilities, etc. of the adversary. Intelligence will also be required in the broader framework of national activities on the other side. Good and reliable intelligence supports the planning and conduct of war. Indeed, it is a prerequisite for sound planning. Planning must be based on facts rather than educated guesswork.

Conclusion

The IAF is now only 82 years young, far younger than the other two Services. However, it is in the nature of modern warfare that the air force has to be always prepared and ready to fire the first shots in war. This the IAF has learnt to do. It is now a mature force with considerable battle experience in different types of conflicts. The IAF work culture is to be persuasive in peace and effective in war. The confidence level to meet this requirement is high.

During the last 82 years, there have been major improvements in the capabilities of aerospace power. In fact, real and meaningful transformations in capabilities have occurred every 10 years or less. The trend is likely to continue. As these transformations occur, the real challenges will be assimilation of technologies and acquisition of knowledge. Human resource development will also become increasingly important and could well be the lynchpin of operational effectivenesss.. The capabilities of the IAF a mere 16 years hence, when it will be 100 years old, will be a transformation or two ahead of today. More importantly, the IAF would have travelled a long road well and will remain a confident and dedicated Service.

Note: The article was first published in Harsh V Pant ed., *Handbook of Indian Defence Policy: Themes Structures and Doctrines*, published by Routledge (2016). Reproduced here with permission.

2

India's Security Environment

Manmohan Bahadur

Introduction

South and Southeast Asia are the 'happening' places in world politics today. India finds itself in a turbulent region that is a challenge to its government as it endeavours to improve the well-being of its masses. Indians find themselves in a milieu that has to be seen in the context of the aspirations of a proud people who have a rich heritage and whose influence in yesteryears extended a great distance beyond the shores of their country. In early times, time and distance were big buffers to intercourse between societies and nations, but the past 50 years have seen these being removed and/or being limited to the time taken to click a mouse. So, geographical regions may have lost relevance in terms of time and distance but they remain valid entities for a nation when its span of influence is analysed.

South Asia as a region is in the news for many reasons, most importantly as one in which resident nations, as also extra-regional powers, are vying for influence. The motives of each country are varied, as is to be expected, but what is of greater salience is the geographical span over which these arch. As time passes, the span changes depending on the political, diplomatic, security and commercial requirements of a nation and its leadership. This is being seen so clearly in the conflict of interests between countries bordering the East China and South China Seas as also in China's attempts to overcome its Malacca Dilemma by finding overland links to the Bay of Bengal and the Persian Gulf. The lure of petrochemical resources of the Arctic, post the increased rate of melting of the Arctic ice cap, and the subsequent opening of the Northern Sea route is changing the geo-political dynamics as nations reevaluate their interests in the Gulf and African regions and reassess the costs of transportation of oil, gas and other trade via traditional routes.

In this setting, what is India's span of interest that needs to be included in a regional security scan? India's Ministry of Defence (MoD) issues a report every year in which it lays out the nation's area of strategic interest. In the 2002-03 annual report, it defined it as "…from the Persian Gulf in the West to the Straits of Malacca in the East and from the Central Asian Republics in the North to near the equator in the South...."[1] This has been modulated over the years, as is to be expected, and the 2012-13 report stated that "India's size and strategic location…….links its security environment with the extended neighbourhood, particularly with neighbouring countries and the regions of West Asia, Central Asia, South-East Asia, East Asia and the Indian Ocean."[2] The latest annual report, of 2014-15, discusses relations with immediate neighbours and adds, "India's geo-strategic location makes it sensitive to developments beyond its immediate neighbourhood, in West Asia, Central Asia, in the Indian Ocean Region and the Asia Pacific region. Major geo-political and geo-economic developments are currently transforming the global security scenario into one of uncertainty and volatility."[3] The 'vastness' is, thus, expanding year on year as India tries to cement its rightful place in the comity of nations. An indicator to this is the fact that with a long-term view to laying claim to the natural resources of the Antarctic and Arctic regions, India has a permanent base in the former and has become an observer in the Arctic Council of the latter (as indeed, has China). What is of interest is that both are non-Arctic nations!

This analysis will study India's security concerns in six sections. The importance of Asia would first be debated followed by the contours of security that a nation needs to evaluate in order to plan its security strategy. Next, the underpinnings of conflict in the world would be looked into followed by the present status of India's relations with its neighbours. Global threats, that influence all nations and need to be factored into any security appreciation, would then be evaluated, followed by an appreciation of the security outlook for India before a summation is done of the regional security scenario.

Importance of Asia

The 21st century has been termed an Asian Century as it has the four largest economies of the world — China, Japan, India and some put the United States (US) also in this grouping due its all round presence, and hence, influence, in the region. More than half the world's population resides in this area and it is a region of history's biggest socio-economic changes and associated challenges. Asia has many nuclear weapon states; India, Pakistan, China and North Korea are the overt nuclear nations while Israel is widely accepted to have such weapons. In addition, there are the likes of Iran, Japan and South Korea that clearly have the capability but due to a variety of reasons have not gone nuclear. The region is also one of proven nuclear proliferation, with North Korea and China having given nuclear and missile knowhow to Pakistan; in turn, Pakistani scientist AQ Khan's proliferation activities through his 'nuclear Wall-Mart' are well known. The Afghanistan-Pakistan (Af-Pak) region has been christened the epicentre of global terrorism as a multitude of terrorist organisations have spawned in the area during the past three decades. It is also a hub of the narcotics trade, with Afghanistan accounting for 85 percent of the world's opium being grown and processed there.[4] Whoever governs in Kabul has a big dilemma on his hands, as putting a stop to its farming would spell disaster for small-time farmers for whom it is the only source of income; this would only make them anti-government and, in turn, strengthen the insurgency. It is a Catch-22 situation since narcotics comprise the fund raiser for the militants to continue their war against the Afghan government.

The conflict in Afghanistan adds to the statistics that show Asia being a region with the most unresolved disputes in the world. Recent history attests to the fact that all long wars since 1945 have taken place in Asia: Korea in the 1950s, Vietnam in the 1960s and 1970s, Afghanistan's invasion by the USSR was in 1979 and the seven-year Iraq-Iran conflict took the better part of the 1980s. The 1990s saw the short but sharp Gulf War but the end of the last century and the first decade of the 21st saw Afghanistan and Iraq embroiled in conflict with the US and the West for very different reasons, and with different players involved. Crimea and Ukraine, technically in Europe, but abutting Asia, are the latest friction points between the Western groupings and Russia, as they jostle for preeminence in the region. As this goes to the press, the conflict in Syria, already in its fifth year, has become a vexed cauldron with the presence of Russia in support of President Assad, who has ranged against him an opposition aided by a coalition that includes Turkey, the US and a host of European and Gulf countries. While Iran, the Hezbollah and the Peshmarga of the Kurds side with Assad, the so-called Islamic State of Iraq and Syria (ISIS), while being ranged against him, is opposed by the Western alliance as well as the Russians. The shooting down of a Su-24 Russian fighter jet by Turkey on November 24, 2015, just added to the mélange of confusion and made the situation worse. How this will pan out and how long it will take to subdue the threat of the ISIS is anyone's guess. What is sure is that the world is in for another long drawn out conflict in Asia – true to the trend of the past seven decades or so.

Asia is also the region through which the energy trade lines of many developing and developed economies pass. Presently, 80 percent of the oil and gas imports of China pass through the Malacca Strait,[5] with the figure being identical for Japan.[6] India imports 60 percent of its oil requirements from the Gulf region.[7] This makes the maritime routes very strategic passages, mandating their protection to ensure freedom of navigation. Adding to the fact that many nations have intractable territorial disputes amongst them

(India-Pakistan, India-China, China with all countries bordering the South and East China Seas *et al*), security in Asia is a challenge to strategists of all hues. Before the challenges facing India's security with its neighbours are analysed, it will only be right to run through the basic ingredients of 'national security,' the contours of which have expanded manifold over time.

Contours of Security

The ingredients of security have increased over the ages, even as man is supposed to have become more 'civilised' and the world more integrated over the past century. The combinations are many but can broadly be classified into four sub-sets, as follows:

Sovereignty: Sovereignty has many contours, ranging from the physical security of a nation's territory to a nation's independence and its ability to exercise its power to govern. Gbenga Oduntan has written, "Sovereignty in law is often considered to be the essence of the state. It explains the powers of a state over its entire territories and its inhabitants."[8] Another way to define it is "…supreme and independent power or authority as possessed or claimed by a state or community in a defined territory."[9] Thus, any infringement in these two overarching domains – spatial and authority over that space – has led to conflict.

Societal: Societal factors have gained in importance in determining how 'secure' a nation is since these internal variables have a corresponding effect on the sense of safety a citizen experiences. They also have an effect on the internal and external policies of the government as it goes about addressing the associated issues. Thus, food, energy, water and internal peace are ingredients that have gained in salience, with increase in population, industrialisation, urbanisation, increase in life expectancy and their corresponding effects on the geo-political equations of a region.

Technology: Technology is now omnipresent in nearly all aspects of human existence (the area of defence all the more so) and technological advancement has increasingly become a factor to be reckoned with. When evaluating the societal security environment, one cannot but emphasise the absolutely vital importance of cyber in today's age. Availability of technology has another dimension, which is technological asymmetry in today's world. Technological asymmetry is an added disadvantage for the technologically handicapped nations, and the advanced countries, through denial regimes, are ensuring that they retain the exclusivity of their progress and retain an upper hand.

International Activism: The responsibility to protect the global commons (which have become integral parts of everyday life) is slowly but surely assuming an important place in the security dialogue. In the near future, the aspect of universality of the global commons could become a very potent tool for proponents of international intervention whose activism is becoming ominous for established Westphalian states and impinges on their sovereignty.

All these points have a bearing on the strategic autonomy of a state, which permits a nation's leadership to plan for the future, build friendships and alliances with other nations and move on a path of development for its people without fear and pressure of any other nation. A nation with its strategic autonomy intact is the master of its own destiny and if conflict comes its way, then its freedom to prosecute violence is unhindered.

Underpinnings of Conflict

Down history, conflicts between nations and empires have arisen due varied reasons ranging from the abduction of a regent's spouse to expansionist forays for empire building. With the advent of 'modernity' and acceptance of the Westphalian system of governments, the reasons for discord between nations have crystallised to the following few:

Territory: A reason that will never go into oblivion, the importance of territory has as its base the quintessential desire of some nations to expand their sphere of influence by coveting and/or attempting to acquire another nation's territory due to economic necessity, a geo-political requirement, or to correct a perceived injustice of yesteryears. Thus, Hitler's *lebensraum* was for a desire to satisfy the perceived requirement for additional space (read territory) for Germany's economic and political growth, while Saddam Hussein invaded Kuwait for reasons of perceived 'pilferage' of oil by the latter through its slant oil wells that presumably tapped into oil deposits reaching into Iraq.[10]

Ideology: During the Cold War, it was the stated policy of the US to further the cause of democracy and stop the expansion of Communism; in the case of the erstwhile USSR, it was just the opposite. Thus, the Soviet Union invaded Hungary and Czechoslovakia in November 1956 and August 1968 respectively when it thought that the leadership in those nations was drifting away from the path of Communism and taking their nations towards democracy. The US went to war in Korea and Vietnam to avoid a southward expansion of Communist ideology in Southeast Asia. Similarly, Angola, Mozambique, Honduras, Nicaragua and many other sovereign states became proxy battlegrounds for the two superpowers that wanted their ideological influence to expand in Africa and South America.

Economic Rationale: It is widely accepted, and Paul Kennedy has written about it in his magnum opus *The Rise and Fall of Great Powers*, that history is witness to the fact that as nations improve the lot of their people, they have to go offshore in search of raw materials, which brings them in conflict with other countries. The European powers colonised much of Asia and Africa in their drive to get raw materials for their development post the industrial revolution. The Great Game was played out in Afghanistan with the British opposing the southwards expansion of the Russians in the 19th century.[11] While Russia's move was more to do with its need to expand its influence in Central Asia, the British saw it as an incoming threat to their empire in India from an expansionist Russia.[12] In the present times, there is no greater example than China's outreach to the world for raw materials. As an example, China has oil interests in almost every part of the world[13] and has told the world at large that it considers the East China and South China Seas as its backyard. The large scale reclamation work in progress in the area and building of proper 3,000-metre-long runways (capable of operating combat aircraft) on reclaimed islands attest to its assertion that it considers the oil and other resources of the area to be its own. All other nations bordering these seas have also laid claim to these waters and have embarked on strengthening diplomatic and military cooperation with the US to give them a sense of security. One sees greater interaction among India, Japan, the US and Australia as they review their policies and outlook to the so-called 'peaceful' rise of China – which slowly seems to be becoming ominous.

Religion: Down the ages, man has gone to war for his religious beliefs. History has been replete with stories of the Crusades, pressures brought on by the Inquisition and competing factors amongst civilisations. As Samuel P Huntington wrote in 1993 in an article in the magazine *Foreign Affairs*, *"Civilizations are differentiated from each other by history, language, culture, tradition and, most important, religion. The people of different civilizations have different views on the relations between God and man, the individual and the group…….liberty and authority, equality and hierarchy. These differences are the product of centuries. They will not soon disappear……. Differences do not necessarily mean conflict, and conflict does not necessarily mean violence. Over the centuries, however, differences among civilizations have generated the most prolonged and the most violent conflicts."*[14]

Governance Model: Homogeneity of race, religion, culture and other societal attributes is no guarantee of peace since the orientation of the governing structure of a country plays an important part in the fulfillment of the political ambitions of its population. Thus, the world has been witness to the manifestation of the Arab

Spring in North Africa. Tunisia led the way, followed by Egypt, Libya, Yemen and Bahrain. Except for Tunisia, where the 'spring' is holding, the security situation has been pretty volatile after the initial success. In Bahrain, the protests were put down with a heavy hand, while Libya and Yemen are in a lawless state now. These nations did not have issues with a religious divide or an economic imbalance in society but what irked the populace was the dictatorial leadership that was at the helm, severely suppressing the political aspirations of the lay people.

Human Rights: In the past few decades, proponents of human security have attempted to usurp the mantle of protection of the individual when pitted against the views of the state. It is essentially a Western concept that "...brings into confrontation the political foundations of an institutional state versus the legal unaccountability of ideologues and institutions who work the masses and the media to 'topple' a stable, albeit perhaps a dictatorial, system, which could result in an even more appalling end state."[15] Their work is not just limited to autocratic systems but they operate in democracies too, leading to disaffection between the masses and the ruling dispensation. The net result is an entanglement of views between two or more governments which can spiral into a conflict situation. The root cause is the application of similar yardsticks of 'human security' to cultures and societies that have different ideologies and are at varying stages of societal development.[16] With power and geo-political groupings prevalent in the world, mutual assistance agreements come into the act when a conflict situation arises due these interventions, leading to a lateral spread of conflict.[17]

Power Blocs

In the Cold War era, besides the two power groupings of NATO and the Warsaw Pact, China maintained its own aspirations by not being part of any group, as did India, which was a leader of the Non-Aligned Movement (NAM). Post the Cold War and the upheavals in the constituents of the erstwhile Soviet Union which has left the US as the sole superpower, is it a polycentric world today, with the USA being the main power broker, China being a distant second and a large number of smaller powers to complete the picture? What is certain is that China is fast emerging as the main competitor to the US, with Russia making determined efforts to recover lost ground. Elsewhere, power remains defused amongst a host of other nations too, to include India, South Korea, Japan and Iran in the Asian region. In this milieu, India's relations with its neighbouring states would be studied as this essay proceeds to make a recommendation of what India's future posture should entail in international relations.

India-China

In India's attempted power sphere, China looms as a large competitor for many and varied reasons; these will be examined briefly.

Territorial Issues: Leading the list is the territorial dispute between the two Asian giants, which seems intractable given the rigid stands taken by the two countries. What makes the issue difficult is that India bases its claims on historical facts, while China pegs it on a desire to, as it sees it, right historical wrongs that were inflicted on China when it was not politically and militarily strong to resist such moves So, while there has been a flurry of visits of the top leaders to each other's nations (accompanied with a lot of pomp and cultural pageantry on display), the Confidence Building Measures (CBM) instituted by the heads of states have not prevented the stand-offs on the northern and northeastern borders. The Border Dispute Cooperation Agreement signed during the October 2013 visit of Prime Minister Manmohan Singh was supposed to be the panacea to prevent further Daulat Beg Oldie type of face-offs between the two armies, but a similar incident occurred at Chumar in September 2014 even as President Xi Jinping was meeting Prime Minister Modi in Ahmedabad.[18] When Prime Minister Modi visited the state of Arunachal Pradesh in February 2015, the reaction from China was very hostile,[19] though prior to his May 2015 visit to Beijing the rhetoric from China was mellowed down to create an agreeable environment. Whether this portends a change in China's attitude to one of greater accommodation on the vexed boundary issue, is difficult to state, but the past behavioural profile would suggest that China will continue to play hard ball on the issue.

Technological Asymmetry: It is a cliché that in politics there are no permanent friends but only permanent interests. China is moving in a focussed manner to advance its technological capabilities and in the bargain achieving technological asymmetry of an order that should be considered a security challenge to India. Technological asymmetry gives a country the capability to advance to a position of relative dominance in most aspects of daily life due to the ubiquitous dependence on it. It is in India's interest that this gap (in pure sciences, defence knowhow, space technology and manufacturing capability) which has developed during the three decades, is not allowed to widen any further. The asymmetry is clearly visible in China's advancement in cyber warfare and its space prowess, besides a fast developing military industrial complex that is moving to make it self-sufficient in modern military hardware for its three Services.[20]

Economic Asymmetry: India and China achieved independence around the same time in the 20th century and had similar issues of insufficiency of food, industrial laggardness and rural poverty. Their economic indicators were also similar in the 1960s.[21] In fact, the *Business Standard* wrote in April 2014 that "CRISIL's latest study showed India's economy was 1.75 times bigger than China's in 1960. In fact, by 1980 as well, India's economy was $0.3 trillion, while the Chinese was only $0.2 trillion on a Purchasing Power Parity (PPP) basis."[22] The opening of the Chinese economy in 1979 preceded a similar act by India that happened a decade later in 1991. The two nations are now in an economic competition as they modernise. The bilateral trade is expected to reach US$ 100 billion by this year but the worrying factor is the massive trade deficit that has been built up over the years. The trade deficit in 2008 was US$ 11.18 billion which increased to US$ 15.87 billion by 2009 and to US$ 20 billion by 2010. In the financial year 2013-14, the deficit increased to US$ 36.21 billion and thereafter rose by a whopping 34 percent to US$ 48.43 billion in 2014-15 as per a government report tabled in India's Parliament![23] Besides the sheer imbalance in terms of cost, an additional worry, and an important one at that, is that India's exports are basically of raw materials but the imports are finished products.[24]

Strategic Encirclement: As part of its 'peaceful' rise, China has developed strategic ties with most nations in India's vicinity, mainly through its economic clout which it has used to great effect. While no sovereign power can be denied this right, the pattern of engagement, its geographical spread and areas of engagement (all around India's vicinity and in the Indian Ocean) has been disconcerting as it gives a picture of attempted encirclement of India.[25]

Military Ambitions: The Defence White Papers that China started issuing a decade plus ago, are clear indicators of the direction that its foreign and defence policies are taking in international affairs. From an earlier stated intent of a "national defence policy defensive in nature" it stated, for the first time in its 2004 White Paper, that in "local border wars" (the type India would most likely be engaged in) it would aim for command of the air. The world knows well by now what it means by a defensive security policy; Andrew Scobell, a noted Sinologist, has characterised it as born of its strategic culture of offensive defence.[26] This has been further articulated, and in fact, has charted a new direction in the 2015 National Security Review, wherein China has said that one of the strategic tasks of the Chinese armed forces "...is to safeguard Chinese overseas interests."[27] The open allusion to 'overseas' has startled observers and made its neighbours fearful of the ambition of the Dragon as it is an indication of a doctrinal declaration of use of force by Chinese armed forces abroad in the protection of Chinese interests; something so overt had never been declared earlier. The changed philosophy is evident in the Anti-Access and Area Denial (A2/AD) strategy with respect to its defence of the first and second island chains. The development of the DF 21A anti-ship ballistic missile, aimed primarily to counter American sea power that is centred on its carrier battle groups, has moved the US to devise its Air-Sea battle concept. India too is in the South China Sea for oil as well as to build its relations with Japan and countries in that region as part of the Look East policy. Though not aimed at China, the Look East policy is sufficiently 'imaginative' to inject an element of concern to keep the Chinese engaged.

So, India's perceptions about China are influenced by considerations of the economy, border dispute, technological asymmetry that it has built up, its military ambitions as enunciated in its 2015 White Paper, its engagement with countries in India's neighbourhood that is leading to its strategic encirclement, its fast growing cyber warfare capability as part of its technological asymmetry, and if one may say, its propensity to use it, and its fast developing maritime capability and space prowess. However, the rise of China presents both countries with a historical tryst which depends on how their rivalry is perceived—as a mutual challenge or as an emerging threat. It must be remembered that in multilateral meetings, India and China are friends but there is discord in bilateral fora. Both countries have a shared interest in a just and stable order through a multipolar world.[28]

India-Pakistan

Pakistan's presence in India's calculations and daily life conversations is a good exercise in enhancing one's patience! The bilateral problems are based on territorial disputes, Kashmir and the proxy war that Pakistan is waging in Jammu and Kashmir (J&K); it is as if there is an almost visceral opposition to India and anything Indian. While Pakistan's policy of trying to 'bleed India through a thousand cuts' through terrorist action has been in force for the past few decades, the 26/11 Mumbai attacks brought the problem up front for the world to sit up and take note of the duplicity in its statements and actions. The lack of progress in action against the perpetrators (in Pakistan) of the Mumbai carnage has upset many peace initiatives that have been taken by every political dispensation in power in Delhi – only to see the momentum break down after some symbolic progress in programmes aimed at enhancing people-to-people contact. Increased contact among certain sections of the populace is only ephemeral in geo-politics and international relations, and hoping for such popular sentiments to facilitate a drive towards lasting peace is as fallacious as what

Shekhar Gupta, a noted Indian journalist said in a television interview on the same subject, "If the Iranians love Michael Jackson for his music, it doesn't mean that they love America as a corollary!" Strong, and may be unpopular, initiatives by the political establishments on both sides are the need of the hour to break the impasse and the latest initiatives by the Modi and Nawaz Sharif governments to start a comprehensive dialogue process would be watched with interest, albeit with a touch of *déjà vu*, as many such initiatives have not brought any substantial progress. The withdrawal of American troops from Afghanistan, now deferred from 2014 to 2016 and possibly even later, is a cause for further suspense on how Indo-Pak events and politics progress. While a stable Afghanistan, friendly to India, would be welcome, it is perhaps naïve to expect that Pakistan would accept this scenario to play out in this fashion. The history of the Indo-Pak relationship has been a simmering pot of hostilities which can only be solved with statesmanship and firm political handling on both sides.

India-Sri Lanka

India and Sri Lanka have a traditionally friendly relationship which has come under a lot of strain post the LTTE wipe-out and the ending of the Tamil insurrection in the island nation. Obviously, the complicating aspect for India is the Tamil factor in its own internal politics. As is well known, Sri Lankan armed forces personnel undergoing courses of instruction were sent back from Indian training establishments in Tamil Nadu. In fact, when this writer went to the Defence Services Staff College in 2013, he was surprised to find the Sri Lankan officers not on the list of foreign participants (traditionally two to three officers have been attending the Staff Course). When queried about their absence, the response was that they had been sent back, and further, they soon moved to the Pakistani Staff College in Quetta within a week of their return. Thereafter, however, things have taken a turn for the better, with India abstaining in the UN Human Rights Commission vote against Sri Lanka in March 2014, showing that it values its relationship with that country.[29] Events after the January 2015 election in Sri Lanka have been more positive with a change of government and installation of Mr. M Sirisena as President. The attempt of China to get a foothold in the strategically located Trincomalee oil farm has been thwarted and the contract awarded to Indian Oil Corporation to develop it. In April 2015, Sri Lanka refused permission to a Chinese submarine to dock in Colombo (after India had protested against an earlier such visit in end 2014) which finally had to go to Pakistan for replenishment.[30] Will India's cultural pull hold Sri Lanka back with it, as some observers claim? One cannot say for sure, but Prime Minister Modi's visit to the island country in March 2015 seems to have retrieved some lost ground, as events enumerated earlier testify to.[31] Thus, India has to play its cards well to ensure that Pakistan and China do not get a chance to get a foothold in its southern flank.

India-Myanmar

India did some good forward thinking, and despite international (read Western) criticism, it engaged with the military junta in Myanmar in the late 1990s; that engagement is now paying dividends. The putting on hold of the China aided Myitsone Dam project in 2010 was a good indication of a partial weaning away of Myanmar from the Chinese path; that the military junta had heeded local protests was a good sign of a move away from China.[32] The cross-border special forces action by the Indian Special Forces on June 9, 2015, was reportedly done in coordination with the Myanmarese government. Later, on October 15, 2015, when the government there signed a peace pact with eight militant groups that operate in the Indo-Myanmar border, the Indian national security adviser was also present;[33] this is, indeed, a sign of increasing cooperation between the two countries. The 2015 elections have brought Aung San Suu Kyi's National League for Democracy to power and it is hoped that her India connection would further improve bilateral relations. One, however, has to be pragmatic considering China's heavy investment in Myanmar towards the oil and gas pipelines and road links built by it, which would help it have considerable leverage with any Yangon government. Continuous engagement with the new government and enhancing people-to-people contact is the need of the hour to have a pro-India Myanmar.

India-Bangladesh

Indo-Bangladesh relations have had a yoyo journey, depending on the political party in power in Dhaka. Presently, the Awami League government which is seen as pro-India, has been alive to India's concerns on matters of security. There have been some proactive steps from the Indian side to keep the eastern neighbour on its side, notable among them being the Land Boundary Agreement wherein the long pending issue of 'enclaves' was settled amicably.[34] The non-fulfillment of the Teesta water accord is the next sticking point but indicators are that this too would get settled with the active involvement of the state government of West Bengal. Support to the northeast insurgents has waned, as seen from the 'extradition' of Anup Chetia and Rajkhowa who were spearheading the insurgency in Assam.[35] However, the present Bangladesh government has fundamentalist forces ranged against it and pro-Pakistan elements are still active in the country, as seen from the violent protests that have always followed the sentencing of people in the ongoing

1971 War trials. The insidious involvement of Pakistan in support of such elements can be seen from its "…deep concern and anguish" expressed following the recent hanging of the Bangladesh National Party and Jamaat-e-Islami leaders for genocide and war crimes.[36] One has to be wary of the future as political sentiments in the subcontinent are very fickle and can affect the positive India-Bangladesh relations. The biggest threat, however, is the continuing illegal migration from Bangladesh; it is a waiting social time bomb for India due to changes in the demographic structure in the northeast[37] and the associated political fallouts.[38]

India-Nepal

Hitherto, India has had a very cozy relationship with Nepal but, for a variety of reasons, this has soured at present to a certain extent. The almost two-decade-long Maoist insurgency led to a breakdown of internal institutions and a tilt towards China,[39] which stepped in with massive aid to offset the traditional ties with India.[40] It is indeed a paradox that despite close historic, cultural and religious ties, India is being seen more as a big brother, resulting in the elites and government functionaries moving closer to their northern neighbour. The common man, on the other hand, still has deep-rooted relations with the Indian society due to the open borders and issues of employment and ties based on a common Hindu culture.[41] Prime Minister Modi's visit to Nepal in April 2014 was a determined attempt to bridge fissures that had opened up in the relations and the subsequent prompt response to the devastating April 2015 earthquake only helped add to the goodwill. [42] However, the enactment of the new controversial Constitution by the Nepalese Parliament has resulted in a piquant situation for India where it is being blamed by the native populace for a blockade of essential commodities; the blockade has been enforced by the marginalised Madhesi community that lives in the Indo-Nepal border Terai region. The fact is that despite vehement denials from the Indian establishment that it has no hand in the shortage of essential commodities (due to the blockade), the prevalent sentiment in Nepal is to the contrary.[43] Meanwhile, China has stepped in by opening an oil supply route through emergency trans-shipment.[44] This move is a sure indicator of China continuing to drive a wedge in Indo-Nepal relations. Thus, India has to play its cards well so as not to have an unfriendly populace just north of its strategic northern frontier, which otherwise is a buffer with China.

India-Bhutan

Bhutan is pro-India though the withdrawal of the fuel subsidy by India created some fissures in the relationship in 2013, prior to the second ever elections held there — wise sense prevailed and the fuel subsidy has been reinstated;[45] one only hopes that this has not dented the Indian image too much. Prime Minister Modi's visit, the first by him to any country after assuming office, conveyed the importance India attaches to its relations with Bhutan. It is important that India's Foreign Office and political leadership impart due significance to nurturing this vital relationship as already there are warning signals that statesmanship exercised by New Delhi has been conspicuous by its absence.[46]

Island Nations

The island nations of Mauritius, Maldives and Seychelles are important for India and it needs to be alive to China's moves in the Indian Ocean where it has already obtained, what it euphemistically calls, support bases for its ships. Prime Minister Modi's visit to Mauritius in March 2015 has helped India get permission for joint development of its Agalega Island (situated 1,100 km north of Port Louis); with Seychelles too, a similar agreement has been signed for the Assumption Island.[47] These two islands are strategically located but are just too small for a military base or facilities to be developed. Agalega Island is in two parts – the bigger one being 12.5 km long and 1.5 km wide, while the southern one is just 7 km long and 4.5 wide at the broadest point. Similarly, Assumption Island has an area of only 11 sq km. Possibly, India would use them as listening posts, as some press reports indicate, as also provide more coastal surveillance radars in these island states (in Sri Lanka too) so as to have greater maritime domain awareness in the Indian Ocean Region (IOR).[48] The visit of Prime Minister Modi has seen a reversal of India's hands-off policy in the IOR. As C Raja Mohan, a noted writer on strategic affairs comments, "….India is no longer hesitant about taking a larger responsibility for securing the Indian Ocean and promoting regional mechanisms for collective security and economic integration. It is confident enough to collaborate with the US in self-interest and engage China on maritime issues with greater self-assurance."[49] So, the 'game' is heating up and it is good that India has got its foot in. However, nearer home, the traditionally friendly Maldives is turning out to be unfriendly. What started as the forced jettisoning of the GMR Infrastructure Group from the Male International Airport project, snowballed, such that Prime Minister Modi's trip to the island, which was part of his four nation tour to the IOR island nations, was cancelled.[50] With the new government in place in Male, India seemed to be (and may be still is) on the back foot vis-à-vis China's entry in the archipelago but India's Foreign Minister Ms Sushma Swaraj's October 2015 visit has apparently succeeded in bringing the relations back on line.[51]

For India, thus, the possible scenarios in the region depend on how China plays its cards and how intrepid and sharp India is in playing its own. Would China coerce its neighbours and in the process try and undermine the influence of the Americans in the region or would it be openly assertive and create its own space at the expense of the US? Would issues essential to its stated sovereignty like Taiwan, Tibet and the Uighur militancy force its hand internally, resulting in an external fall-out for its neighbours? These are all questions that Indian policy planners need to ponder over as India goes about its task of improving the lot of its people in a world that has undergone upheavals in power equations. As long as the Cold War was on, the two superpowers, despite their own power tussle, ensured a modicum of world order by exerting pressures where and when required. After the demise of the USSR as a power node, only the US has been executing the role of a security referee in most parts of the world.

US interest in Asia

The US has been the security provider in the Gulf due its dependence on the region for oil, but this is tending to change as there are other issues that would impinge on the amount of interest that America would have in the area. Central to this is the fact that its dependency on Gulf oil will reduce drastically as it exploits its own substantial shale oil and gas reserves in the decades to come. It has the second largest shale oil reserves in the world while its shale gas reserves are the fourth largest. Interestingly, China and Pakistan also figure high on the list. As per an International Energy Agency's 2012 report, "... the US' need for oil imports from the Middle East will fall to almost zero in the next 10 years" and by 2020, it will be an oil exporter![52] The predictions for melting of the Arctic cap have been advancing with every new forecast. The resultant opening of the Arctic sea route from the Chinese coast to Western Europe, which is 4,000 nautical miles (nm) shorter than the traditional one through the Suez Canal, will change the geo-politics of the region. With 13 percent of the world's oil reserves and 30 percent of gas reserves, it's a bonanza that's waiting to be exploited. The US is also an Arctic nation, due its state of Alaska and one would expect it to exploit its share too. This would add to the surplus of the oil that America would possess, further adding to reduced American interest in the Gulf; a power vacuum would occur, and if this happens it would most likely be filled in by China due to its already established outposts as part of its String of Pearls strategy and also born of its need to be the security provider for its own oil imports (which would continue to be very large in 2030). India's thrust back into the area, with Prime Minister Modi being the first prime minister in 34 years to visit the UAE, is, thus, a good step to safeguard its interests. Much more needs to be done on the global scene to have an all round safety net to safeguard Indian national interests.

Global Threats

In the present-day inter-connected world, a regional security scan would be incomplete without a word on global threats as these would have a spin-off into India's security region too. These can be classified into four broad heads and their sub-parts:

- Technology, which is an aid in normal times, would be a threat in the case of asymmetry. Cyber attacks could cripple a nation – the examples of Estonia and the Stuxnet strike on the Iranian nuclear centrifuges are vivid examples of the insidious nature of such attacks.
- Societal challenges in the form of differences in ideology and/or religion and spilling over of such intra-state imbalances into other countries would be threats with their own unique dynamics. It must be remembered that the Buddhist-Rohingya Muslim conflict in Myanmar spilt into India with a bomb blast on July 7, 2013, at Bodh Gaya (the place of the enlightenment of the Buddha) in the state of Bihar.[53] The burning of religious books in some corner of the world has resulted in turbulence many a time in India. Added to these threats with religious intonations is the menace of the so-called Islamic State in Iraq and Syria (ISIS) that has reared its head in the Syria-Iraq conflict zone; with its menacing ideology and brutal methods, the ISIS is drawing recruits from all over the world as also creating franchises in other countries. While India may be relatively free from such ideological fanatics at present, the permeation of such thinking in the unemployed youth in trouble prone areas cannot be ruled out – the danger from ISIS can be neglected at one's own peril.
- A new phenomenon in the form of 'international activism' and interventionism in other countries on the basis of 'human security' has gained in salience. While interventionism by the so-called 'international community' has taken place in Iraq, Afghanistan, Libya, Egypt and Syria in various overt and covert forms, India should not be smug, in the belief that attempts at such interventions cannot be made in India due a multitude of problems that exist in its society – it would be wise to tackle the problems resolutely for solutions. Stretching this thought further, the global commons could also be used by powerful countries that have their own agendas to progress, to further own interests.
- Migration due to disparity in the GDP or wealth of neighbouring countries, as is being seen from Bangladesh to northeast India, would result in serious economic and social tensions; this would have repercussions on the internal security of the receiving nation.

Security Outlook

In this security environment in Asia, what would be the stance of the major players? Would America engage China or try to contain it? Would it be even possible to contain it, given the momentum its economy and the associated political clout has gathered? What about China itself? Would it engage the US and, thus, undermine its power by showing itself as an equal? And what about its relations with India? Would China try to engage it as an equal or undermine its standing by hyphenating it with other countries of the region? And what should India's role be? While staying non-aligned, should it engage China, cooperate with the USA and maintain a finely balanced relationship with these two nations so as to insure against any reversals that may happen in any of the bilateral relationships? These are many questions that would engage the thought process of the political leadership in these countries.

While the Indian national leadership evaluates and tackles the external security environment, there are many daunting challenges in the internal security ambit too. Issues of law and order, economic disparity amongst the masses, unemployment, low literacy levels *et al* have to be addressed as also the lack of a defence industrial base that strangles India's strategic autonomy. In the final analysis, India would have to ensure comprehensive national development, achieve self-reliance and maintain a credible deterrence by engaging with its neighbours in a relationship of cooperative peace to move forward in its *primary* aim of improving the living standards of its people.

Summation

The national security canvas of India is vast, with many ingredients of diverse hues affecting policy-making by the political leadership. India's physical location itself is in an area where its relations with its immediate neighbours are fraught with uncertainties due to disparate political governance, varied religious beliefs, unequal economic development and lingering historical legacies. The 'peaceful' rise of China is taking on an ominous tinge, due its expansionist policies and a tendency to ride roughshod over the claims of other nations. It has established an asymmetry with India in almost all fields and it is imperative that the present challenges be addressed, lest at a later date they become uncontrolled threats. The India-China boundary dispute is not going to be settled in a hurry and would be an irritant to be milked by China to try and unhinge India at a time of its choosing. Pakistan is, and would continue to be, a test for India's diplomacy; the Kashmir issue is vexed and the challenge is to counter the 'bleeding through a thousand cuts' strategy with reasoning and postures short of war so that the primacy of the task of internal economic development is sustained. Relations with other neighbours have to be based on foresight and statesmanship so that the 'big brother' syndrome does not bring in anti-India feelings; recent history has shown that China and Pakistan have stepped in whenever this has happened.

Historically, all developing nations have had to go offshore for raw materials as no country is self-sufficient in all its needs. As one sees China's presence in this endeavour in almost all parts of the world, India's forays would bring it in competition with it. It is indeed timely that Prime Minister Modi has reengaged India's neighbours, both on the subcontinent and in the IOR, to impart the necessary impetus to dormant relationships which once were thriving to India's advantage. Traditionally, India has had a positive image, especially in the underdeveloped, but resource rich, nations; this diplomatic advantage must be used to good effect to build economic relationships to enhance India's standing. At the same time, the military capability and capacity needs to be built up to deter any misadventures from China, as also Pakistan.

India has a demographic dividend presently with 65 percent of its population being below the age of 35; this will start becoming negative by 2035. The next two decades, thus, are critical for India's polity to resolve the myriad socio-economic disparities and law and order problems that afflict the Indian nation. Internal security issues are being, and will be, used to advantage by interests inimical to India, and these can be neglected at the nation's peril. India has many good things going for it now, the most important being that the central government has a stable majority, the absence of which in the past decade was a bane for national development due, as the then Prime Minister put it, to "compulsions of coalition politics." Not grabbing the opportunity with both hands would only vitiate the security scenario to the detriment of India's economic development.

Notes

1. Ministry of Defence, Government of India *Annual Report 2002-2003*, p. 2, available at http://mod.nic.in/writereaddata/MOD-English2003.pdf. Accessed on December 19, 2015.
2. Ministry of Defence, Government of India *Annual Report 2012-2013*, p. 2, available at http://mod.gov.in/writereaddata/AR_2013/Eng/ch1.pdf. Accessed on December 19, 2015.
3. Ministry of Defence, Government of India *Annual Report 2014-2015*, p. 2, available at http://mod.nic.in/writereaddata/AR1415.pdf. Accessed on December 19, 2015.
4. Dania Ahmed, "Heroin and Extremism in Pakistan," *Foreign Policy,* August 17, 2015, available at http://foreignpolicy.com/2015/08/17/heroin-and-jihad-in-pakistan/. Accessed on December 20, 2015. The article says, "There has been much discussion of the Afghan Taliban using the drug trade as a source of funding. In fact, the mafia and terrorists receive $70 billion from narcotics in Afghanistan, $2 billion of which goes to the TTP, the Taliban in Pakistan. Profits of that magnitude are significant considering drug busts are on the rise. Recently, 232 packages of heroin worth an estimated $92 million were seized on a Pakistani boat off the coast of India."

5 Eric Meyer, "With Oil And Gas Pipelines, China Takes a Shortcut Through Myanmar," available at http://www.forbes.com/sites/ericrmeyer/2015/02/09/oil-and-gas-china-takes-a-shortcut/. Accessed on December 19, 2015.
6. Robert D Kaplan, "Why the South China Sea is so Crucial," Excerpt from the author's book *Asia's Cauldron,* available at http://www.businessinsider.com.au/why-the-south-china-sea-is-so-crucial-2015-2. Accessed on December 20, 2015.
7. As per a speech given by India's petroleum minister in a conference in Pune, "Link West: India and the Gulf Session: The Gulf Region in India's Energy Security Landscape," available at http://www.irconference.in/assets/Symbiosis%20Pune%20-%20Minister's%20Speech%20-%2010.10.2015%20-%20For%20printout.pdf. Accessed on December 20, 2015.
8. Gbenga Oduntan, *Sovereignty and Jurisdiction in the Air Space and Outer Space: Legal Criteria for Spatial Delimitation* (Oxon: Routledge:2012), p. 21.
9. Kal Raustila, "Rethinking the Sovereignty Debate in International Law," *Journal of International Economic Law 6(4)* (Oxford University Press: 2003), p. 842.
10. "Saddam States Reasons for Kuwait Invasion," *Gulf News*, July 21, 2009, available at http://gulfnews.com/opinion/thinkers/saddam-states-reasons-for-kuwait-invasion-1.502105. Accessed on December 21, 2015.
11. David Fromkin, "The Great Game in Asia," *Foreign Affairs*, Spring 1980 issue, available at https://www.foreignaffairs.com/articles/south-asia/1980-03-01/great-game-asia. Accessed on December 20, 2015.
12. Owen Bennett Jones, "Pakistan and Afghanistan: The New Great Game," available at http://www.bbc.com/news/world-asia-34503849. Accessed on December 20, 2015.
13. Suisheng Zhao, "China's Global Search for Energy Security: Cooperation and Competition in the Asia-Pacific," available at http://www.japanfocus.org/-Suisheng-Zhao/2978/article.html. Accessed on December 20, 2015. The author states that, "…the Chinese search for overseas energy supplies has played a more and more important role in shaping China's foreign relations. To secure overseas energy supplies, China has intensified its efforts to deepen economic and political relationships with energy producing countries around the world. The main focus of this diplomatic drive is the Middle East. But a diversification strategy has led to a Chinese search for energy supplies in every part of the globe, including Africa, Latin America, and the Asia-Pacific."
14. Samuel P Huntington, "The Clash of Civilizations," an essay originally published in the Summer 1993 issue of *Foreign Affairs*, available at https://www.foreignaffairs.com/articles/united-states/1993-06-01/clash-civilizations. Accessed on December 5, 2015. Further, expounding the tensions that arise between religious leanings of people, Huntington says, "..Even more than ethnicity, religion discriminates sharply and exclusively among people. A person can be half-French and half-Arab and simultaneously even a citizen of two countries. It is more difficult to be half-Catholic and half-Muslim."
15. Manmohan Bahadur, "Interventionism and Human Security," *Strategic Analysis*, vol 38, no.1, 204, p. 7.
16. Ibid. The author, speaking of the driving spirit of human security activists, adds, "Is anything wrong with the spirit of desired freedom? Most certainly not, but it is unrealistic if applied in equal measure across all strata of society and in all regions of the world, irrespective of the stage of development or the cultural background of the country or region being addressed. All cultures do not have the same 'sense' to follow up on rebuilding their societies after the toppling of the 'evil' dispensation in power. How many takers... for a future Western-style stability scenario in countries that have seen external intervention (in any form) in the recent past?"
17. In the ongoing crisis in Syria, Turkey went to NATO after it shot down a Russian Su-24 fighter on November 24, 2015, presumably to invoke Article 5 of the NATO Charter that considers an

attack on one country of the alliance as an attack on all, enjoining other member states to come to the aid of the member state.

18. Gurmeet Kanwal, "Border Tensions with China Can Flare: India Needs to Resolve Them Now," available at http://www.dailyo.in/politics/india-china-border-lac-ladakh-arunachal-dispute-incursion/story/1/2661.html. Accessed on December 15, 2015.
19. "China Warns PM Narendra Modi Against Visiting Arunachal Pradesh," available at http://indiatoday.intoday.in/story/narendra-modi-arunachal-visit-china-warns-india/1/421324.html. Accessed on December 15, 2015.
20. "Making up Asymmetric Deficit vis-à-vis China," available at http://www.indiandefencereview.com/news/making-up-asymmetric-deficit-vis-a-vis-china/ Accessed on December 17, 2015.
21. "China Beats India by a Huge Margin," available at http://www.business-standard.com/article/economy-policy/china-beats-india-by-a-huge-margin-114042000193_1.html Accessed on December 17, 2015.
22. Ibid.
23. "India-China Trade Deficit Swells 34 percent to $48 Billion" available at http://www.thehindu.com/news/national/indiachina-trade-deficit-swells-34-to-48-billion/article7201545.ece Accessed on December 17, 2015.
24. "Top 20 Items that India, China Trade," available at http://www.rediff.com/business/slide-show/slide-show-1-top-20-items-india-china-import-export/20110916.htm#10. Accessed on December 17, 2015. Though the data in the website is for 2010, the trends have not changed.
25. "Chinese Plans in Seychelles Revive Indian Fears of Encirclement," available at http://www.theguardian.com/world/2012/mar/22/china-seychelles-indian-fears-encirclement. Accessed on December 20, 2015.
26. Andrew Scobell, "China and Strategic Culture," Strategic Studies Institute, Carlisle, PA, May 2002, available at http://www.globalsecurity.org/military/library/report/2002/ssi_scobell.pdf. Accessed on December 17, 2015. The author says, "The two main strands are a Confucian-Mencian one that is conflict averse and defensive minded; and a Realpolitik one which favors military solutions and is offensive oriented. Both strands are operative and both influence and combine in dialectic fashion to form a 'Chinese Cult of Defense.' This cult paradoxically tends to dispose Chinese leaders to pursue offensive military operations as a primary alternative in pursuit of national goals, while rationalizing these actions as being purely defensive and last resort."
27. Anthony H. Cordesman and Steven Colley, "Chinese Strategy and Military Modernization in 2015: A Comparative Analysis," p. 3. CSIS paper available at http://csis.org/files/publication/150901_Chinese_Mil_Bal.pdf Accessed on December 17, 2015.
28. VR Raghavan, "How India and China See Each Other", *The Hindu*, March 24, 2014, available at http://www.thehindu.com/books/books-reviews/how-india-china-see-each-other/article5827120.ece. Accessed on December 18, 2015.
29. Indrani Bagchi, "India Abstains on Human Rights Vote on Sri Lanka, Rescues Foreign Policy," March 27, 2014, available at http://timesofindia.indiatimes.com/world/south-asia/India-abstains-on-human-rights-vote-on-Sri-Lanka-rescues-foreign-policy/articleshow/32793377.cms. Accessed on December 20, 2015.
30. "Chinese Naval Ships to Use Gwadar Port After Colombo Snub," Press Trust of India report, available at http://www.ndtv.com/world-news/chinese-naval-ships-to-use-pakistans-port-after-colombo-snub-755291. Accessed on December 20, 2015.
31. N Sathiya Moorthy, "Sri Lanka: 'Re-vitalising' India Relations Even More After the Polls," August 18, 2015, available at http://www.orfonline.org/cms/sites/orfonline/modules/analysis/AnalysisDetail.html?cmaid=86903&mmacmaid=86904. Accessed on December 20, 2015.
32. Marcia G Yerman, "The Myanmar Election and the Myitsone Dam," November 11, 2015,

available at http://www.huffingtonpost.com/marcia-g-yerman/the-myanmar-election-and-_b_8506220.html?ir=India&adsSiteOverride=in. Accessed on December 20, 2015.
33. "Myanmar Inks Peace Pact with Ethnic Rebels in India's Presence," *The Hindu*, October 15, 2015, available at http://www.thehindu.com/news/international/myanmar-inks-peace-pact-with-ethnic-rebels-in-indias-presence/article7766332.ece. Accessed on December 20, 2015.
34. "Land Boundary Agreement Done, PM Modi to Meet Mamata Banerjee to Discuss Teesta," *Economic Times,* August 3, 2015, available at http://economictimes.indiatimes.com/news/politics-and-nation/Land-boundary-agreement-done-PM-Modi-to-meet-Mamata-Banerjee-to-discuss-Teesta/articleshow/48325038.cms. Accessed on December 19, 2015.
35. "Anup Chetia's Extradition has Broken Ulfa's Spine," *Hindustan Times,* November 13, 2015, available at http://www.hindustantimes.com/editorials/anup-chetia-s-extradition-has-broken-ulfa-s-spine/story-7XtL6CTYcd3CltiFg1nmNK.html. Accessed on December 19, 2015.
36. "Pakistan Deeply Disturbed by Bangladesh Executions: FO", *Dawn*, November 22, 2015, available at http://www.dawn.com/news/1221498. Accessed on December 19, 2015.
37. Bhadra Sinha, "Illegal Bangladeshi Migrants Influx Changing Assam's Demography," *Hindustan Times,* October 27, 2015, available at http://www.hindustantimes.com/india/illegal-bangladeshi-migrants-influx-changing-assam-s-demography/story-MYSsEWQHBsaa4Pg4KLyDOJ.html. Accessed on December 19, 2015.
38. Jaikhlong Basumetry, "Implications of Demographic Change in the Security Environment of Assam," available at http://www.claws.in/958/implications-of-demographic-change-in-the-security-environment-of-assam-jaikhlong-basumatry.html. Accessed on December 19, 2015.
39. "Insurgency in Nepal," available at http://www.globalsecurity.org/military/world/war/nepal_insurgency.htm. Accessed on December 19, 2015.
40. Saibal Dasgupta, "China Raises Nepal Aid 5-fold to Compete with India," *The Times of India,"* December 26, 2014, available at http://timesofindia.indiatimes.com/world/south-asia/China-raises-Nepal-aid-5-fold-to-compete-with-India/articleshow/45652472.cms. Accessed on December 19, 2015.
41. Tsering Shakya and Ashok Gurung "Was Nepal a Soft Power Victory for China?" *Foreign Policy,* May 1, 2015 available at http://foreignpolicy.com/2015/05/01/nepal-china-earthquake-aid-taiwan-power/. Accessed on December 19, 2015.
42. "Modi Concludes Historic Visit to Nepal," August 4, 2015, available at http://timesofindia.indiatimes.com/india/Modi-concludes-historic-visit-to-Nepal/articleshow/39628843.cms. Accessed on December 19, 2015.
43. "Nepal Border Blockade 'Threatens the Future of the Country Itself', says UN," available at http://www.theguardian.com/global-development/2015/nov/18/nepal-border-blockade-india-threatens-future-un-unicef. Also see Kunda Dixit, "India and Nepal Have No Choice but to End Their Border Dispute and Move On," available at http://time.com/4115801/nepal-india-border-blockade-madhesh/Both. Accessed on December 19, 2015.
44. "China Says to Channel Fuel Aid to Nepal Amid Deepening Crisis," available at http://in.reuters.com/article/china-nepal-oil-idINKCN0SN10L20151029 Accessed on December 19, 2015.
45. Jyoti Malhotra, "India Breathes Sigh of Relief as with Elections, Bhutan Returns to the 'Fold,'" July 15, 2013, available at http://www.business-standard.com/article/opinion/india-breathes-sigh-of-relief-as-with-elections-bhutan-returns-to-the-fold-113071500056_1.html. Accessed on December 20, 2015.
46. Omair Ahmad, "Losing the Dragon — India-Bhutan Relations One Year After Modi's Historic Visit," July 30, 2015 available at http://www.thehindu.com/opinion/op-ed/prime-minister-narendra-modis-historic-visit-to-bhutan/article7480714.ece. Accessed on December 20, 2015.
47. Kanwal Sibal, "Modi Should Have Shown Interest Toward the Indian Ocean a Lot Earlier,"

available at http://www.dailyo.in/politics/modi-saarc-indian-ocean-visit-seychelles-sri-lanka-mauritius/story/1/2726.html. Accessed on December 21, 2015.

48. C Raja Mohan, "Modi and the Indian Ocean: Restoring India's Sphere of Influence," available at http://amti.csis.org/modi-and-the-indian-ocean-restoring-indias-sphere-of-influence/ Accessed on December 21, 2015.
49. Ibid.
50. N Sathiya Moorthy, "Maldives: When Will Modi Follow Suit After Sushma's Visit – Analysis," October 17, 2015, available at http://www.eurasiareview.com/17102015-maldives-when-will-modi-follow-suit-after-sushmas-visit-analysis/. Accessed on December 21, 2015.
51. Ibid. Also see Suhasini Haidar, "India-Maldives Ties at a Peak, says Envoy," available at http://www.thehindu.com/news/national/indiamaldives-ties-at-a-peak-says-envoy/article7793555.ece. Accessed on December 21, 2015.
52. Benoît Faucon and Sarah Kent, "IEA Pegs US As Top Oil Producer by 2020," *The Wall Street Journal,* November 12, 2012, available at http://www.wsj.com/articles/SB10001424127887323894704578114492856065064. Accessed on December 21, 2015.
53. Abhishek Bhalla, "Bodh Gaya Temple Attack was Revenge for Rohingyas," *Mail Online India,* January 6, 2014, available at http://www.dailymail.co.uk/indiahome/indianews/article-2534250/Bodh-Gaya-temple-attack-revenge-Rohingyas.html. Accessed on December 21, 2015.

3

No First Use of Nuclear Weapons: Sane Logic, Sound Doctrine

Manpreet Sethi

What deters? Is it the threat of use of nuclear weapons in a scenario which is at a critical conventional level? Or is it the threat of retaliation with nuclear weapons after the first use/strike[1] by the adversary? Indeed, from the time of the first demonstration of the destructive power of the nuclear weapon in 1945, there has been considerable soul searching on how to deter by credibly projecting the actual use of the weapon for national security. In 1950, George Kennan pithily articulated this crucial question. Though he was addressing this to the then US secretary of state, it is pretty much relevant for every country with nuclear weapons:

> Are we to rely upon weapons of mass destruction as an integral and vitally important component of our military strength, which we would expect to *employ deliberately, immediately, and unhesitatingly* in the event that we become involved in a military conflict with the Soviet Union? Or are we to retain such weapons in our national arsenal only as a deterrent to the use of similar weapons against ourselves and as a *possible means of retaliation* in case they are used?[2]

All countries that have acquired nuclear weapons have faced this dilemma. In order to project credible deterrence, when, and the related question of where (on which targets) should one employ nuclear weapons? Does the threat of a first strike on military targets evoke better deterrence or does it work better as a counter-strike to impose punitive retaliation over cities? Each country has settled for an answer for itself based essentially on two parameters. First, its individual and unique threat perceptions arising from, among other factors, a sense of its conventional capability vis-a-vis the adversary. Second, from the role that it ascribes to its nuclear arsenal – to deter conventional war or only nuclear use by the adversary.

So, it is that a country that finds itself conventionally inferior feels the need to use its nuclear arsenal as a shield against the possibility of conventional aggression (whether provoked or otherwise) and, hence, tends to adopt a first use strategy? Today's Russia and Pakistan are good examples of this. On the other hand, countries that perceive themselves as being capable of handling conventional eventualities at the conventional level and look upon their nuclear weapons as being necessary only to deter nuclear use of the adversary, find greater prudence in deterring through the threat of nuclear retaliation or No First Use (NFU). India and China fall in this category.

When India first announced a nuclear doctrine in the form of a draft in 1999, and subsequently made an announcement on operationalisation of the doctrine in 2003 through a Press Note, the attribute of NFU was a prominent part of both. The draft doctrine described its policy as "retaliation only", in its clause 2.3 whose section (b) further elaborated "any nuclear attack on India and its forces shall result in punitive retaliation with nuclear weapons to inflict damage unacceptable to the aggressor."[3] The Press Note of January 4, 2003, issued by the Cabinet Committee on Security (CCS) reiterated the same. Clause 2 (ii) clearly mentioned acceptance of a "posture of 'no first use': nuclear weapons will only be used in retaliation against a nuclear attack on Indian territory or on Indian forces anywhere".[4]

However, not all strategic analysts or military strategists have wholeheartedly accepted this doctrine. In fact, debate over the matter reached a crescendo in 2014 after the party manifesto of the Bharatiya Janata Party (BJP) put it out that if elected into government, it would "study in detail India's nuclear doctrine and revise and update it to make it relevant to the challenges of the current times." Many analysts who were always dissatisfied by the aspect of NFU were quick to lend their weight to this call. This was also the time by when Pakistan had already tested its very short range ballistic missile, the Nasr, and declared it as nuclear capable. Seemingly, the dreaded tactical nuclear weapon had entered the adversary's arsenal and this was projected by Pakistan as a lowering of its nuclear use threshold and seen as reason enough by some Indians to unbind the country's hands too and reevaluate the wisdom of retaining no first use in the changed circumstances. Many opined that credible deterrence demanded the threat of first use against an adversary who was doing the same and that a country like Pakistan could only be deterred through such a threat.

The clamour over NFU finally died down only after Narendra Modi, the projected prime minister of the BJP, spoke up in its favour and against any revision of the doctrine in April 2014. He described NFU as a "great initiative" and as a "reflection of our cultural inheritance."[5] It certainly is that, but much more. It makes military and political sense too. Yet, rumblings of discontent over the wisdom of NFU continue under the surface. The apparent loss of initiative by allowing the enemy to use his nuclear weapons first causes great angst, especially in some quarters of the military and strategic community. NFU is criticised for leaving India open to a nuclear strike and projecting the country as passive. The allegations against NFU are that it is a pacifist, idealist and Gandhian strategy that has no role to play in the modern context.

This, however, is a complete misreading of NFU. A considered and detailed assessment of the NFU strategy reveals that it is far more credible and useful in the contemporary context. This essay explores the value of NFU as a meaningful deterrence strategy. It briefly analyses why militaries tend to be inclined in favour of offensive strategies, but then highlights the limitations – both logistically and politically – of executing a militarily useful nuclear offence in a situation where secure second strike capabilities are available with the adversary. And, this is the case with at least eight out of the nine nuclear armed states today, even if one was to be sceptical about the robustness of the North Korean (Democratic People's Republic of Korea – DPRK) nuclear arsenal to a first strike by a country like the USA. But even in this scenario, one cannot discount the possibility of China stepping in to support the DPRK, thereby bringing its own secure second strike capability into play.

Therefore, in the current state of nuclear relations, what is the value of first use, even if it were a well considered first strike, when nuclear retaliation is a certainty? Can any rational actor find circumstances compelling enough to use the weapon first, suffer nuclear retaliation, and yet feel that it has come out better in a conflict? If the answer to this is in the negative, which it should be, given that the damage caused to modern megacities by even modest fission weapons would be unimaginable, then is the threat of first use credible at all?

In fact, there is an inherent paradox of nuclear deterrence that gets magnified with first use. It is believed that it may be rational to make a first use threat, but it would not be rational at all to carry it out. If it is not rational to carry it out, then how can the threat be credible? And if it is not credible, then why should it deter? But, if it does not deter, why do states retain first use strategies and are dismissive of NFU? Does not the presence of secure retaliatory capabilities make NFU credible and first use incredible? Are there any other benefits of an NFU that can better address contemporary challenges? These are some of the questions that this essay seeks to address. Towards this end, it offers three hypotheses:

- There is value in no first use as a potent and viable deterrent strategy that is more credible than first use in the present times.
- NFU can help in lessening existential nuclear risks and serve the cause of strategic stability.

- NFU can be an effective tool of non-proliferation and disarmament and, thus, contribute to international security.

Militaries Prefer Offence... But Lessons from the Cuban Missile Crisis

A good starting point for assessing the credibility of deterrence is the Cuban missile crisis of 1962. In October that year, US President Kennedy was confronted with the surprise deployment of Soviet nuclear tipped missiles on the tiny island of Cuba, only 144 km away from the state of Florida on the US mainland. Rattled to find the missiles so close to the country, the Executive Committee that he immediately constituted of hand-picked advisers was categorical in stating their resolve of getting the USSR to remove these missiles. But, how was this to be achieved without escalating the situation into a wider conflict? President Khruschev appeared to be in no mood to reverse his action and Cuban President Fidel Castro was actually egging him on not to back down. At that moment, the US had significant superiority in its strategic bombing forces. According to one estimate, when the crisis ended, "a total of 1,306 American bomber planes were deployed with the ability to deliver 2,962 nuclear weapons. By the time the Strategic Air Command (SAC) reached its maximum strength on November 4, these weapons were either continually in the air or on a fifteen minute alert. The equivalent Soviet force at the time consisted of just 138 bombers."[6] According to the estimates of the Natural Resources Defence Council, the USA had a total of 27,000 nuclear warheads compared to a mere 3,000 of the USSR, a 10:1 differential.[7] Did these figures matter?

President Kennedy was presented with a set of alternative courses of action to handle the situation. These included undertaking military strikes on the missile bases in Cuba; complete invasion of the island; or a naval blockade of the country. The American president chose the last option because it was considered the least destabilising. The understanding provided to him by his security advisers was that any of the options employing US military force would eventually—and there were more chances of it being sooner rather than later—lead to Moscow retaliating by overrunning Berlin. The US would then have to get into a "general war" which would, at some stage, require Washington to use nuclear weapons in a first strike. This was conceived as a large scale use of nuclear weapons against Soviet targets.

It may be recalled that at the time Washington had a professed strategy of first use with an elaborate targeting plan. In 2015, the US National Archives and Records Administration released a detailed list of the US targets in the USSR called "Atomic Weapons Requirements Study for 1959". It was produced by the Strategic Air Command in 1956, identifying bombers as the primary means of delivery.[8] This information is relevant in this context only to make the point that despite so much nuclear preponderance and a well planned comprehensive targeting strategy, the idea of having to use nuclear weapons first in a situation that could develop out of escalation of a conventional military strike by the US was unpalatable to the US president. When Kennedy asked his generals for an assurance that there would be no nuclear retaliation from the Soviet end, he could not be given that guarantee. The prospect of loss of even one American city even at the cost of destroying several Soviet cities, stayed Kennedy's hand from authorising a military response to the Soviet deployment. However unacceptable the Soviet action was to the US, Kennedy was yet not prepared to risk the prospect of nuclear retaliation despite a well considered military strategy of nuclear first strike. In fact, he dismissed every option that could bring the US to that brink, and described such choices as "a hell of an alternative"[9].

2012 marked 50 years of the Cuban missile crisis. The occasion was subject to some deep analysis of the lessons learnt from that episode. Amongst these was the debate over what constitutes credible deterrence. Can the threat of first use by a country that has the capability and wherewithal to execute such a first strike actually make sense? Militaries tend to believe it does since they are trained on a diet that believes in seizing the initiative and inflicting damage rather than suffering it. But does the same logic apply in the case of nuclear weapons too? A well thought out analysis is long overdue.

Militaries like to function according to Standard Operating Procedures (SOPs) – whether in peace-time or war operations. This preference leads to a propensity for offensive doctrines where the armed forces have thought through their strategy and devised SOPs to address pre-meditated scenarios. Offence allows the military to stay with its pre-deliberated course of action while denying the adversary the advantage of being able to play out his moves. As argued by Barry Posen, "A military organization prefers to fight its own war and prevent its adversary from doing so... An organisation fighting the war it planned is likely to do better than one that is not."[10]

With conventional weapons, this may be a prudent approach. The armed forces can concentrate on the first phase of war to be initiated by them at the time and place of their choice to thereby either increase the chance of their victory or lessen the damage of war on themselves. But the equation gets skewed with the entry of nuclear weapons. In a situation where both sides have secure second strike capabilities (hardened, concealed, dispersed, mobile nuclear assets), even if it is not a situation of mutual assured destruction, a nuclear first strike, however splendid it might be, cannot rule out the possibility of nuclear retaliation. Before the nuclear capabilities became secure, there might have been an incentive to strike first and quickly to destroy the enemy's retaliatory forces before they were launched. At such times, the advantage of striking first was evidently huge and could be a decisive factor in making nuclear doctrines tilt towards first use. But once a level of survivability has been attained, it should disincentivise strategic nuclear attack at any time since a return wave of nuclear destruction cannot be ruled out. With retaliatory forces becoming less vulnerable and more robust, the military logic and political sense in going first has declined considerably. So, moral and political inhibitions are supported by cold military calculations of not gaining any advantage in using nuclear weapons first. As explained by one analyst in a well researched article, "The presumed value of nuclear weapons has become psychological and political: the knowledge that they might be used can deter potential adversaries…."[11] And the irony of contemporary times is that there is greater credibility in the threat of nuclear retaliation than first nuclear use.

In fact, the calculation of the first user cannot be limited to the damage that will be caused by his first strike, but must also take into account the damage that will have to be endured from the adversary's nuclear response. Therefore, even an elaborate offensive nuclear strategy can neither assure victory nor help escape an extent of damage, owing to the very nature of the weapon. Is it then useful, and more importantly, credible, to threaten first use of nuclear weapons?

Those who persist in believing that first use is a better deterrent strategy often argue that this works especially so in two circumstances. The first of these is identified as a situation where the country faces the prospect of large scale conventional attrition and defeat. It would then be left with no option but to use the nuclear weapon. After all, what is the sense in keeping this weapon and letting the country face the prospect of defeat in the form of loss of territory or occupation? While this question appears logical, a nuclear response can be anything but rational. Even in such a dire situation, how does a country gain by using its nuclear weapon because once it has done so, its fate shifts from being defeated-now-but-living-to-fight-another-day to one of severe damage/annihilation depending on the state of its geographical, material and human capacities. Jonathan Schell explained this dilemma well when he questioned, "For how can it make sense to 'save' one's country by blowing it to pieces? And what logic is there in staving off a limited defeat by bringing on unlimited, eternal defeat? Nuclear deterrence is like a gun with two barrels, of which one points ahead and the other points back at the gun's holder."[12] In dodging conventional defeat, a country would have brought untold nuclear ruin upon itself. Can this make sense?

Robert McNamara tried to answer this question based on his experience of more than 40 years in the field of nuclear strategy and war plans. He wrote, "During that time [when in office], I have never seen a piece of paper that outlined a plan for the United

States or NATO to initiate the use of nuclear weapons with any benefit for the United States or NATO… To launch weapons against a nuclear-equipped opponent would be suicidal. To do so against a non-nuclear enemy would be militarily unnecessary, morally repugnant, and politically indefensible."[13] Though McNamara might have expressed this in writing only in 2005, he claims that he, as well as President Kennedy understood this in the 1960s itself but never made any such statements since they were "totally contrary to established NATO policy." He categorically stated that there was no way to effectively contain a nuclear strike and that there can be no guarantee against unlimited escalation once the first nuclear strike occurs. Those who point to the US to argue in favour of first use overlook the fact that retaining such a strategy is a compulsion for Washington owing to its extra-territorial security commitments. The fear that countries under the US nuclear umbrella will be driven to acquiring their own nuclear weapons if deprived of the cover, leading to uncontained nuclear proliferation, makes it necessary for the US to remain wedded to the first use strategy.

A second situation which is believed to merit first use is when a country gets to know that the adversary is preparing for a nuclear strike. Should not nuclear preemption then be the right step? The answer to this lies in understanding that even knowledge of preparation is no guarantee of a nuclear strike. Rather, it may well be part of a strategy of 'coercive diplomacy'. As brought out by Black, "To maximize the perceived psychological advantages conveyed by possession of nuclear weapons, national leaders have sometimes issued statements or authorized actions to remind adversaries of the potential for a nuclear war."[14] It is not a coincidence that nearly all of the more than 50 incidents of threat of use of nuclear weapons until now have actually intended coercion.[15] A summary of nuclear threats and threat targets compiled by Samuel Black indicates that India was subjected to such a threat 16 times between 1991 and 2000.[16] Therefore, despite the apparent show of readiness, there will, more likely than not, still be a chance that nuclear weapons would not actually come into use. In fact, the military utility of nuclear weapons has reduced over time even as the political utility of nuclear threat-making has steadily risen. If an instance of such threat-making was misread, leading to striking first in the face of apparent readiness on the other side, the first user country would end up inviting retaliation for certain. A country even with a first use doctrine may or may not use its nuclear weapons despite the projected preparedness, but after having been struck and where the first strike has not been disarming or decapitating (which is well nigh impossible with the kinds of arsenals states with nuclear weapons today have), retaliation would be a certainty.

Projection of First Use Far Easier than its Execution

Countries that adopt a first use strategy tend to project a low nuclear threshold suggesting that the use of nuclear weapons would be an inevitability, literally a *compulsion* for them, in case a conventional conflict turns unfavourable. However, can it be that easy a decision to opt for using nuclear weapons? Analysis proves otherwise.

The actual act of using the nuclear weapon first cannot be as easy as it is made out to be since the country that uses nuclear weapons first has to take into account not just what would happen in the first phase of war, but also on how it would proceed and end, scenarios which are not easy to coherently contemplate in the presence of robust retaliatory nuclear weapons. And, hence, despite having a first use strategy, most nations not only find it very difficult to actually execute it, but also politically limiting to do so. This is a thought worth considering since conventional wisdom has us believe that first use is more liberating compared to a counter-strike strategy. But serious thought to actual execution of first use reveals the complexities involved in doing so. After all, the purpose of first use should be to convey deterrence through communication of four essential messages:

- I will not hesitate to use the weapon first.
- By doing so, I would be able to substantively improve my situation.
- My first strike will interfere with, and degrade, your second strike capability.
- I will be able to come out of the crisis looking better after the use of the nuclear weapon than without its use.

Such communication can carry weight where there is a nuclear monopoly in an adversarial equation. But in a situation where the adversary has a survivable nuclear force, retaliation can seriously complicate the calculations of the first user on how it would 'look better' after suffering nuclear damage itself. As graphically explained by a strategist, "Engaging in a nuclear war with a nation with which one is in a condition of mutual vulnerability would be like running a red light across a high speed, heavily travelled, multilane highway under conditions of near zero visibility. One might make it safely across, but one could not form a reasonable expectation that one would."[17]

Therefore, the essential question that the first user has to ask and answer is whether in a state of mutual vulnerability, the initiator can be in a better position than the one that retaliates? Or can NFU convey its own set of messages more convincingly:

- I will not be the first to use nuclear weapons.
- But any first strike against me would trigger an assured retaliation to cause damage of a kind that you would find unacceptable.

- My counter-strike will ensure that your material situation is worse off after your using the weapon first.
- I might suffer losses, but you will not escape either and you would have brought it upon yourself.

As is clear from the above, a no first use strategy offers to concede the onus of escalation to the adversary and, in that sense, becomes more liberating. This concept is not easy to understand since militaries always tend to favour retaining the initiative rather than conceding it. It is difficult for them to believe that it could make sense to let the other side make the first move. But in the case of use of nuclear weapons, by letting the adversary decide to be the first user, the military with a no first use strategy can actually adopt a more relaxed posture rather than straining the nuclear leash of a hair-trigger alert system that can easily fall prey to misadventure. Neither does it have to perfect the logistics of first use which is not easy considering that it would involve coordinating a nuclear attack on a diversified arsenal with speed and surprise to hit the adversary's forces before they can be launched or dispersed. Conceiving and executing a first strike involves addressing several basic but deep questions such as whether to launch aircraft first or missiles, how many to launch in the first wave, on which targets, etc. It also requires an intelligence system of a very high order so that the storage sites and movements of the nuclear assets are regularly monitored and clearly known. Unless such information is available, a first strike meant to disarm or decapitate the adversary would be less than optimum and even more dangerous.

Besides the logistics pressures, the political leadership is also freed from the psychological strain of making the difficult choice of being the first to use a weapon of mass destruction. This is sure to weigh on him/her personally given the long standing norm of nuclear non-use that is today in place. Indeed, except for the use in 1945, the nuclear weapon has never ever been physically used. Moreover, not only would the damage caused to a section of humanity weigh on his conscience, but to cause such damage in the knowledge that his own country's vulnerability to retaliation can yet not be escaped would be onerous. In democracies, the limits on the political leadership when called upon to make this decision are well understood. But even in the more autocratic systems, this cannot be an easy choice given that today's societies are relatively invigorated by the modern means of communication enabled by the information revolution and these do influence national choices. Even the DPRK, a really 'isolated' country by today's standards, could go only so far with its nuclear brinkmanship.

The decision to use the nuclear weapon first is made even more difficult by the knowledge that unlike in the case of conventional weapons, the nuclear forces that inflict the damage on the adversary will not really protect own state either. Rather, they would end up inviting retaliation. This moral issue is not insignificant. Drawing upon the lessons of the Cuban Missile Crisis, one analyst correctly pointed out,

> Missiles and other modern weapons do not require tedious preparations but rather can be deployed at the push of a button. Accordingly, leaders must consider morality carefully before choosing military action as a first response…. to ensure that military action does not abandon the human element… This is especially true when there is seemingly less time to consider non-lethal options before media and politics drown out sober and patient approaches to resolution.[18]

In the face of such logic, NFU appears far more sensible and credible. While a country would find it very difficult to use the weapon first, the decision of retaliation would be far easier, seemingly legitimate, and more guilt free to make. Therefore, rather than having the first strike option, it would be better to take measures to deter the adversary from reaching for his nuclear trigger. Deterrence is, in fact, the only real defence against nuclear weapons. In fact, by projecting assured retaliation, a nation displays greater confidence, and, hence, greater deterrence credibility. By placing the onus of escalation on the adversary, while retaining the initiative of punitive nuclear retaliation, a country with a no first use strategy steers away from nuclear brinkmanship. And, by establishing the nuclear weapon as an instrument of punishment through retaliation, the country lessens the possibility of deterrence from breaking down, and, thus, aims to minimise, if not prevent, the very use of the nuclear weapon. NFU actually encourages the possibility of 'no use' instead of 'sure use'. This is clearly demonstrated in Table 1.[19]

Table 1

Nuclear Posture Country 1	**Nuclear Posture Country 2**	**Nuclear Threshold**	**Chance of Nuclear War**
First Use	First Use	Low	Very High
No First Use	No First Use	High	Very Low/Nil
First Use	No First Use	Relatively High	Relatively Low

As is evident from the table, through NFU, coupled with assured retaliation, a country can rein in the initiative more in favour of no use of nuclear weapons. Unless the adversary is completely irrational, has suicidal tendencies or is utterly unmindful of national survival and international public opinion, the possibility of a nuclear war should not arise. But in the case of having to deter a rational actor, projection of assured retaliation while maintaining NFU can enforce effective deterrence. This validates the first hypothesis that a credible retaliatory strategy deters effectively and, in fact, better, than a first use strategy given the contemporary nuclear capabilities.

NFU Promotes Strategic Stability

First use postures based on projection of nuclear war-fighting require large arsenals of first strike weapons (such as accurate missiles with multiple independently retargetable vehicles), nuclear superiority to carry out counter-force attacks against the adversary's retaliatory forces, elaborate and delegated command and control structures to handle launch on warning or launch under attack postures to coordinate simultaneous nuclear attacks from, and over, dispersed forces. None of this is conducive to strategic stability, especially in the present nuclear realities where many nuclear adversaries do not enjoy the luxury of being geographically apart. Rather, in some cases, such as India-China and India-Pakistan unsettled boundary issues and border skirmishes are routine events. In such a situation, maintaining nuclear forces in a state of hair-trigger readiness for first use not only raises the possibility of an accidental nuclear war based on a miscalculation, but also lowers the threshold of a nuclear war in a crisis situation.

It may be recalled that in the early years of the Cold War, the warheads of the two superpowers were not routinely mated, nor necessarily co-located with delivery systems. It was the subsequent development of advanced safety features designed into modern warheads and the advent of sophisticated administrative controls on nuclear weapons that made higher alert levels possible. Ironically, however, after keeping their nuclear missiles on hair-trigger alert for years, the two superpowers found the best nuclear risk reduction and confidence building in de-alerting these and separating warheads from delivery systems! These form a natural part of the NFU posture.

In fact, an NFU requires building nuclear forces which need not be necessarily in large numbers, but which are ensured survivability through a mix of measures that include hardening of nuclear storage sites, deception, mobility, dispersal over different delivery vectors, and a level of defence. The core of this strategy lies in projecting the invulnerability of a sufficient part of the arsenal to even a worst case first strike and incorporation of automaticity to retaliation which can cause damage that the adversary is unlikely to find acceptable in lieu of the gains made through the first use.

By virtue of the nature of its force structure and posture requirements, an NFU naturally eliminates the need for forward deployment of nuclear systems, and, thus, reduces the likelihood of accidental or unauthorised use. Force postures required to cater for launch on warning or launch under attack require pre-delegation of authority to launch nuclear weapons down a clearly defined chain of command and this can never be a risk free option. The US and USSR experienced this first-hand with their Tactical Nuclear Weapons (TNWs). Battles where use of TNWs was envisaged were described as "battles of great confusion". Even when the authority of launch was delegated, it was equally realised that in situations where the use of nuclear weapons was involved, it "could never be a purely 'tactical' decision, taken by the local commander according to the state of battle. It would be a strategic decision to be taken at the highest level and with reference to the prevailing overall political and military situation."[20] But whether this could be effectively enforced posed a huge challenge given that in times of crisis, lack of information, misinformation and misjudgments could often become causes of confrontation without either side having the intention to precipitate one. As Robert McNamara once said, "It is correct to say that no well informed, coolly rational political or military leader is likely to initiate the use of a nuclear weapon. But political and military leaders, in moments of severe crisis, are likely to be neither well informed nor coolly rational."[21]

NFU eases this dilemma considerably. In fact, NFU goes to alleviate the adversary's insecurity, which, in turn, is beneficial by relieving pressure on its leaders for launching a preemptive strike. If the adversary was constantly under the fear that a nuclear strike was imminent, his own temptation to use his nuclear force would be higher. But NFU helps to mitigate the 'use or lose' pressure and thereby lessens crisis instability since it sends a message that does not place the adversary on the edge at all times. Rather, it makes it feel more secure, a condition that enhances deterrence stability. To that extent, actions taken by nations to strengthen the survivability of their arsenal can be stabilising and reassuring. The logic of this was aptly explained by Robert McNamara in the context of the Soviets hardening their missile sites. He wrote,

> In a period of tension, I wanted the Soviet leaders to have confidence that those forces would survive an American attack and would be capable of retaliating effectively. Then they would not feel a pressure to use them preemptively… I had no desire to face, in a period of tension, an adversary who felt cornered, panicky and desperate and who might be tempted to move irrationally.[22]

In fact, reassurance is a critical aspect of deterrence based on no first use and it significantly reduces strategic instability. The nuclear situation is at ease when both nations do not feel the need to go after the other's nuclear weapons for fear of losing own and where neither feels the need to go after the other with nuclear weapons since the costs of assured destruction that neither could escape would be too high.

Managing bilateral superpower nuclear relations was not easy and history recounts many a tense moment. In the contemporary world where nuclear-armed nations are many, several sharing common and in some cases even contested borders, the challenge of creating strategic stability is exacerbated manifold. In such a scenario, the adoption of no first use doctrines would have many benign implications for strategic stability. It has the potential to lessen inter-state tensions, increase mutual confidence and, thus, reinforce a cycle of positives.

NFU Promotes Non-Proliferation and Disarmament

As of now, countries do not appear ready to give up their nuclear arsenals and, in fact, the role of nuclear weapon seems to be expanding beyond the basic purpose of nuclear deterrence. The challenge for non-proliferation as arising from this increasing sense of the value of the nuclear weapon is well evident today. And why not? Why should countries be expected to eschew a weapon that is perceived as effective for deterrence, including deterring conventional weapons, allowing blackmail, and earning monetary and political benefits? In fact, two countries have well shown the multi-role utility of nuclear weapons. North Korea and Pakistan harbour strong security suspicions and perceive their nuclear weapons as 'strategic equalisers' as well as potent bargaining chips. The DPRK has never been shy of brandishing its nuclear capability to drive a hard bargain with a country as powerful as the United States. Nuclear and missile tests, including in the garb of satellite launches, have been a regular feature. Islamabad, meanwhile, has intelligently used its nuclear weapons to deter a conventional war with a superior Indian military even as it has actively pursued a policy of terrorism. Projection of easy use of short range, low yield nuclear weapons in the battlefield has been one plank of this strategy.

Examples such as these tend to add value to the nuclear weapon and indirectly promote proliferation. It is another matter that Pakistan has even been involved in direct proliferation, but the point here is about the spread of the sentiment of the nuclear weapon being a worthwhile possession. As long as this impression is not removed, non-proliferation can never hope to be a sustainable proposition.

One way, however, of reducing the salience of the nuclear weapon can be through the universal adoption of NFU by the states possessing these weapons. If every country was to commit not to be the first to use the weapon, there would be no use – leading to a drop in the stock value of the weapon over a period of time. In turn, this would encourage non-proliferation by sending a strong signal of the diminishing utility of the weapon. At the same time, it would lessen the drive of each Non-Weapon State (NWS) for new and modernised nuclear arsenals. Rather, as the weapons fall into a state of disuse, they would lose their salience and, hence, become dispensable, aiding the move towards their eventual elimination.

A case for convincing/compelling states to accept a universal NFU may be made on three grounds. Firstly, the NFU would allow the NWS to retain the notional sense of security that they derive from their national nuclear arsenals. The NWS would only pledge not to be the first to use nuclear weapons, but could always retaliate to inflict unacceptable damage. They would have the freedom to possess the weapons but would pledge not to use them first. Gradually, the desire to possess, or improve an unusable weapon would lessen, making it easier to give up the weapon. Therefore, this step would work towards enhancing the gradual irrelevance of the nuclear weapon, especially when reinforced by a ban on use or threat of use of the weapon, quite as on the pattern and experience of the 1925 Geneva Convention. Secondly, an international consensus on, and acceptance of, NFU would put pressure on all countries. A united approach could provide the necessary firmness to the international community to deal with possible holdouts. Thirdly, as explained in the first section of this essay, no country can hope to come out better after the first use of nuclear weapons against another nuclear state with a robust second strike force. Therefore, first use against a nuclear adversary that also happens to have superior conventional and substantive nuclear capability is nothing short of suicidal for the first user. The admittance of this reality would demonstrate the futility of retaining a first use posture.

The NFU actually challenges a long held nuclear theology of first use. Until now, this has been largely considered the most effective deterrent posture in the service of national security. But, the adoption of NFU by China and India, the two most populous countries of the world that collectively comprise about a third of humanity, has opened up another possibility at the other end of the spectrum. It offers a counter-view to the traditional aggressive and arms race generating doctrine of first use. If NFU were to be accepted by all the NWS, then the world might find itself on its way to a diminishing salience of nuclear weapons, their delegitimisation, redundancy and eventually their abolition.

Conclusion

McNamara wrote in 2005, "I know from direct experience that US nuclear policy today creates unacceptable risks to other nations and to our own."[23] And yet, nuclear first use has been the predominant doctrine over the last six decades that the nuclear weapons have been around. Only two countries maintain an NFU strategy and the general tendency has been to be dismissive of these declarations since it has been believed that it is the threat of first use that establishes credible deterrence. Questioning this conventional wisdom in the face of the current nuclear realities where nearly all nuclear armed states (with the possible exception of North Korea) have a secure second strike capability, this essay explores the value of no first use as a meaningful and credible deterrence strategy. Besides, it also offers two other benefits of NFU. One, since it is premised on communication of threat of punishment, the nature of the required arsenal reduces existential nuclear risks, and by relieving the adversary of the 'use or lose' pressure, it enhances strategic stability. Secondly, by *de facto* making the nuclear weapon unusable, NFU brings down its salience and helps in promotion of non-proliferation and disarmament, thereby making a contribution to international security.

Most nuclear literature tends to be dismissive of NFU as a declaratory statement. Indeed, given that the USA, the trendsetter of nuclear fashion, has never seriously considered the adoption of NFU, the prolific writings that emanate from the country have largely been devoted to enhancing the credibility of deterrence based on first use.[24] The Soviet Union briefly adopted NFU from 1982 for about a decade but the fact that it gave it up in the face of reduced conventional capability in 1992 led the proponents of first use to further their argument that NFU was a posture that could possibly be adopted only by conventionally superior nuclear armed nations and could not be sustained in situations where a nuclear armed nation was faced with the prospect of conventional defeat.

This argument, however, ignores or dismisses the fact that the two nations that have consistently adopted a declared NFU doctrine—China and India – have done so at times when both have been conventionally wanting against their perceived adversaries. In the case of China, it announced its NFU doctrine in 1964 at a time when it counted the conventionally far superior USA and Russia amongst its adversaries. In the case of India, NFU was put down as its doctrine in 1999 when China, its declared adversary and the stated reason for its nuclear test, was rapidly undergoing conventional modernisation. Unfortunately, however, nuclear strategists and scholars in neither China nor India have laboured to explain the logic of NFU as a viable deterrent strategy.[25] In India, the critics of the doctrine have been louder, and claimed its validity as arising only from India's pacifist attitude and a historical experience that laid stress on non-violence. This, however, is only part of the story.

The initial makers of India's nuclear doctrine were not naïve babes in the nuclear woods. In fact, they understood far better the nuances of nuclear deterrence.

Given the lack of military utility of nuclear weapons and in order to handle the strategy of nuclear brinksmanship adopted by Pakistan, India has, in fact, helped the cause of its own security by following NFU. A wrong impression has been allowed to gain ground in the suggestion that Pakistan's first use strategy offers it better protection while leaving India open to damage. The fact of the matter is that India's NFU, accompanied by a strong message of assured retaliation, actually puts Pakistan in a quandary. Its credibility is seriously in doubt since it would amount to suicide. A first use strategy, when faced with the prospect of assured retaliation, amounts to tilting at windmills. Ours would too, if we were to have one. NFU, on the other hand, reflects a quiet, calming confidence.

Challenging the current conventional wisdom that tends to favour nuclear first use as a militarily meaningful deterrent strategy, this essay has established the value of NFU on three grounds: for national security, for strategic stability, and for international security premised on nuclear non-proliferation and disarmament. All three dimensions enhance India's security interests.

No doctrine is cast in stone. It reflects national political, economic and technological realities and could change as these parameters transform. But, for the time that it exists, a nuclear doctrine performs the crucial task of providing a window to how a country perceives its nuclear weapons. It explains why it needs these Weapons of Mass Destruction (WMDs) and how it plans to use them in the achievement of those objectives. India has premised its need for nuclear weapons on safeguarding itself against nuclear coercion or blackmail. Accordingly, New Delhi has enunciated a nuclear doctrine that perceives a political role for its nuclear weapons. It ascribes to NFU since it holds that the weapon has no role in enforcing compellence or staging aggression, but will only be usable in a situation where an adversary has first used such a weapon. In such a situation, the doctrine prescribes assured retaliation to inflict unacceptable damage. In order to carry out this exercise, the doctrine aspires for a minimum number whose credibility resides in its survivability.

The operational nuclear strategy as flows from India's nuclear doctrine provides the least risk option in the presence of nuclear weapons. It premises nuclear deterrence on a small arsenal that is not on hair-trigger alert, and, hence, less open to the possibilities of miscalculation or accidental use. At the same time, given its own orientation towards counter-strike to impose punishment, the strategy seeks to minimise the chances of nuclear use in the first place.

Indeed, as President Kennedy had concluded, a nuclear first use could hardly be an alternative less than hell. This may have been said in the context of the Cold War bipolar confrontation, but the same universally applies to all nations possessing nuclear weapons.

Notes

1. In nuclear literature, as it evolved over the Cold War, nuclear first use and first strike have different connotations. A first use amounts to any use of the nuclear weapon, of a small or high yield, in battlefield or on civilian targets. A first strike, on the contrary, involves a coordinated large scale use of the nuclear weapon largely to destroy the retaliatory assets of the adversary.
2. As cited in Lawrence Freedman, *The Evolution of Nuclear Strategy*, Third Edition (New York: Palgrave Macmillan, 2003), p. 63.
3. Draft Report of the National Security Advisory Board on the Indian Nuclear Doctrine, August 17, 1999, as available on http://meaindia.nic.in.
4. "The Cabinet Committee on Security Reviews Operationalisation of India's Nuclear Doctrine," January 4, 2003, as available on http://meaindia.nic.in.
5. "Narendra Modi Says Committed to No First Use of Nuclear Weapons", http://www.ndtv.com/elections-news/narendra-modi-says-committed-to-no-first-use-of-nuclear-weapons-557628, April 16, 2014. Accessed on January 29, 2016.
6. Rachel Dobbs, "What Was at Stake in 1962", *Foreign Policy*, October 19, 2012.
7. NRDC, "Table of Global Nuclear Weapons Stockpile 1945-2002", http://www.nrdc.org/nuclear/nudb/datab19.asp. Accessed on February 3, 2016.
8. Scott Shane, "1950s US Nuclear Target List Offers Chilling Insights", *The New York Times*, December 22, 2015.
9. Cited by Daryl G Press, *Calculating Credibility: How Leaders Assess Military Threats* (New York: Cornell University Press, 2005), p. 120.
10. Barry R Posen, "The Sources of Military Doctrine", in Robert Art and Kenneth Waltz, eds., *The Use of Force: Military Power and International Politics* (Boulder, Colorado: Rowman and Littlefield Publishers, Inc., 2004), p. 24.
11. Samuel Black, "The Changing Political Utility of Nuclear Weapons: Nuclear Threats from 1970 to 2010", Stimson Paper, August 2010.
12. Jonathan Schell, *The Abolition* (Stanford, CA: Stanford University Press, 2000), p. 54
13. Robert McNamara, "Apocalypse Soon", *Foreign Policy*, May-June 2005.
14 Black, n. 11, p. 2.
15. For a comprehensive list of incidents until 1996, see Jasjit Singh, "Why Nuclear Weapons", in Jasjit Singh, ed., *Nuclear India* (New Delhi: Knowledge World, 1998), pp. 12-13.
16. Black, n. 11, p. 9.
17. Steven P Lee, Morality, *Prudence, and Nuclear Weapons* (Cambridge: Cambridge University Press, 1993), p. 16.
18. Lois Farrow Parshley, "The Nine Most Important Lessons from the Cuban Missile Crisis", *Foreign Policy*, October 19, 2012.
19. Manpreet Sethi, *Nuclear Strategy: India's March Towards Credible Deterrence* (New Delhi: Knowledge World, 2009), p. 134.
20. An assessment of William Kaufmann as cited by Freedman, n. 2, p. 105.
21. Robert McNamara, *Blundering into Disaster: Surviving the First Century of the Nuclear Age* (London: Bloomsbury, 1987), pp. 13-14.
22. Ibid.
23. McNamara, n. 13.

24. To some extent, this can be explained on the basis of the fact that the Americans have crafted their war strategies on the Pearl Harbour experience where acting first and maintaining surprise has been critical. The same has been transposed onto the nuclear field too with Washington maintaining a nuclear first use doctrine and subscribing to a launch on warning and launch under attack force posture. This has been premised on the belief that unless the US was able to undertake a preemptive/surprise strike, it stood little chance of being able to destroy all Soviet targets as required by its war plans.
25. China, in fact, has seen greater prudence in maintaining nuclear opacity and ambiguity in its nuclear strategy and, hence, has never provided any explanations. Meanwhile, India has been engaged in operationalising its nuclear deterrent over the last decade and a half. However, though there prevails a general consensus in favour of a counter-strike doctrine in both countries, one can find rumblings of discontent too, especially among the military establishments.

4

Security of Pakistan's Nuclear Assets

Sitakanta Mishra

The spectre of Pakistan's nuclear weapons falling into terrorist and extremist hands, as suspected for the last few decades, has risen once more in December 2015 with the remarks by the US Congress members Bill Keating and Ted Poe who opposed any US-Pakistan civil nuclear cooperation, for, among other factors, the fear that "Pakistan's nuclear weapons...could fall into the hands of terrorists."[1] Five years ago, WikiLeaks had exposed US Embassy cables containing warnings about Pakistan's rapid expansion of its nuclear stockpile and the American, British and Russian diplomats' fear of these falling into terrorist hands.[2] While the major Western powers share concerns over the security of Pakistan's nuclear stockpile,[3] the Pakistani establishment vehemently rejects such apprehensions, claiming that "their fears are misplaced"[4] and the "country's nuclear assets are in safe hands, and that Pakistan's command and control system is invincible."[5]

Notwithstanding, the contention over the safety of Pakistan's nuclear assets brings forth two broad conceptual paradoxes involving nuclear weapons: (1) the question of 'safe custody' of nuclear weapons – *democracy vs. guardianship*?[6] – as the nuclear weapons discourse seems to be moving from an era of *security by* nuclear to *security of* nuclear; and (2) the true source of nuclear risk in Pakistan now is the *insecurity of Pakistan itself*. On the basis of these two paradoxes, this study looks into the complex debate and issues involving the safe-keeping of Pakistan's nuclear infrastructure.

A Complex Case

Conceptually, the issue of custody of nuclear weapons has been linked to the form and functioning of the political set-up of the concerned nation. Paradoxically, nuclear resources in the hands of a democratic country are generally viewed as non-threatening as opposed to those in a non-democratic country. Pakistan's nuclear weapons programme, though it was started by a civilian government, is under the control of the Pakistan Army and the military has taken the major decisions on the country's nuclear weapons policy over the years. Why, then, the apprehension about their misuse? The majority view is that a prolonged period of political instability, turbulence and infighting among Pakistan's president, prime minister and army could jeopardise the army's unity of command which is essential for the security of its nuclear assets.[7]

If the domestic political situation of a country is the prime indicator of the degree of safety of its nuclear assets, why then were there no such apprehensions when China was in deep political, economic turbulence during the Cultural Revolution (1966-76) that lasted for almost one decade? On the other hand, there was expression of widespread fear, particularly by the West, about the safety of nuclear weapons and orphan nuclear materials of the Soviet Union when it got disintegrated. A brazen attack on the highly secured Pelindaba nuclear facility of the politically stable South Africa that took place in November 2007 has strangely been overlooked. Pakistani writers often cite the reported loss of six US Air Force (USAF) advanced cruise missiles armed with 150-kiloton nuclear warheads for 36 hours in August 2007.[8] Is Pakistan's present political situation, and the status of its nuclear assets, different from these cases? In fact, mere political stability may not suffice to ensure absolute safety of nuclear assets as physical security arrangements are subject to human error and manipulation. The Inter-Services Intelligence (ISI) and Pakistan Army that play major roles in protecting Pakistan's nuclear weapons are professional organisations but known to have maintained contacts with, and extended support to, militant organisations as a matter of state policy. Large portions of the ISI's officer corps have been seconded to the ISI from the mainline army for rotation, and the ISI leadership has been thoroughly a product of the mainline army.

At the outset, Pakistan's case seems complex owing to the existence of all the variables – political instability, splintering of terrorist groups, probable existence of fundamentalist-*jihadist* elements within the defence forces, and a record of clandestine proliferation networks, suspected to be still alive. However, any conclusion on the basis of the face value of these variables would lead to doomsday scenarios. Given this scenario, the sections that follow, attempt to examine if the threat to Pakistan's nuclear assets is exaggerated, under-estimated, or are we being complacent?

Threat Prognosis

The apprehension on the threat to, and security of, Pakistan's nuclear assets has many facets. Firstly, who pronounced the threat and in what way? According to the WikiLeaks expose, in a September 2009 meeting between UK and US officials on the margins of the P-5 Conference, these officials expressed concern about Pakistan's nuclear programme.[9] Mariot Leslie, Britain's permanent representative to the North Atlantic Treaty Organisation (NATO), was quoted as saying that "the UK has deep concerns about the safety and security of Pakistan's nuclear weapons", and added that China could play a "big role" in "stabilising Pakistan".[10] Also Anne Patterson, the US ambassador to Islamabad, cabled to Washington that the "major concern is not having an Islamic militant steal an entire weapon but rather the chance that someone working in Government of Pakistan facilities could gradually smuggle enough material out to eventually make a weapon".[11] In 2009, US Secretary of State Hillary Clinton had described the Islamic militants in Pakistan as a "mortal threat" to global security. According to her, the "US could not contemplate the possibility of the Taliban taking control of Pakistan's nuclear assets".[12]

The Russian Foreign Ministry reportedly expressed to US officials that "Islamists are not only seeking power in Pakistan but are also trying to get their hands on nuclear materials".[13] In addition, Russia has the impression that the general educational and cultural levels in Pakistan are falling, and it has had to hire people of a religious bent to guard its nuclear facilities. Due to these facts, extremist organisations have more opportunities to recruit people working in the nuclear and missile programmes.[14]

On the other hand, in 2008 Adm Michael Mullen was saying that he is "comfortable that the nuclear weapons in Pakistan are secure" and that their coming under the control of terrorists is not going to happen, "but it is a strategic concern that we all share".[15] Similar concern was expressed by the head of the US Central Command Gen David Petraeus saying that he has confidence in Pakistan's security procedures and the security of those sites is adequate.[16] US President Barack Obama has been quoted saying, "Pakistan's nuclear arsenal is safe" and its "military is equipped to prevent extremists from taking over those arsenals".[17] The Americans perceive that there is a substantial threat to Pakistan's nuclear assets, but they are equally confident of the security arrangements and capability of the army to safeguard them. All the major powers share the concern regarding the safety of Pakistan's nuclear assets, and the US has been more vocal on the issue, perhaps for the reason that it has more information on the ground reality as NATO forces are present in and around Pakistan.

India, that could be the immediate victim of any such scenario because of its proximity to, and enmity with, Pakistan, has expressed a cautious view. In an interview with PTI, the former Indian Army Chief Gen V.K. Singh said, "I don't think there is any reason to say things are not secure". Pakistan's nuclear arsenal and weapons are secure and probably Pakistan also is taking extra measures to keep them safe.[18] India's former National Security Adviser M.K. Narayanan too has said that the Pakistani nuclear arsenal is safe and has adequate checks and balances.[19] Even China, the all-weather friend of Pakistan, has not expressed any such grave concerns so far.

In the wake of the 9/11 attacks, the United States and Pakistan have reportedly initiated a bilateral dialogue on improving nuclear security. The scope of the talk includes export and commodity controls, personnel reliability programmes, training of security personnel and provision of equipment.[20] However, it is claimed that this cooperation does not extend to the "safety" of nuclear weapons because of the limitation of US law as well as Pakistan's insistence on non-intrusiveness and on maintaining secrecy related to its nuclear weapons and their locations.[21] The funding level has been reported to be around $100 million and the cooperation has been of a "basic nature".[22] But Seymour M Hersh, in an article in *The New Yorker* (November 2009) said that the Obama Administration has been negotiating highly sensitive understandings with the Pakistani military.[23] These would allow specially trained American troops to provide added security for the Pakistani arsenal in case of a crisis. In an article in NTI (November 9, 2011), Jeffrey Goldberg and Marc Ambinder highlight US officials' public hints about the Pentagon's secret plan of a 'render-safe mission' to secure Pakistan's nuclear arsenal in the event of a Pakistani nuclear emergency.[24] These assertions, however, are negated vehemently in Pakistan Foreign Office pronouncements. On November 8, 2009, the Foreign Office spokesman said Pakistan "does not require any foreign assistance in this regard." Pakistan will never "allow any country to have direct or indirect access to its nuclear and strategic facilities" the spokesperson said, adding that "no talks have ever taken place on the issue of the security of Pakistan's nuclear arsenal with US officials.[25]

It is widely speculated that the US has a contingency plan in place to secure Pakistani nuclear weapons in case of a loss of control by the Pakistani government. This was addressed during former Secretary of State Condoleezza Rice's confirmation hearing in January 2005. Responding to press reports about this contingency, the Pakistan Foreign Office spokesperson said, "Pakistan possesses adequate retaliatory capacity to defend its strategic assets and sovereignty"; Pakistan's nuclear weapons have been under "strong multi-layered, institutionalised decision-making, organisational, administrative and command and control structures since 1998".[26] A similar response was advanced in the spokesman's briefing of the Foreign Office on March 26, 2009, to the question of whether America had gained access to Pakistan's nuclear facility on the pretext of providing an effective command and control system. The briefing said, "These reports are totally conjectural and baseless to say the least. … the Pakistan armed forces are fully capable to take care of our strategic assets and facilities".[27]

There could be many reasons for Pakistan's declining the US offer, or deliberately concealing that it had ever accepted such help. In fact, "many Pakistanis believe that America's true goal is not to keep their weapons safe but to diminish or destroy the

Pakistani nuclear complex".[28] The world's reaction to the hypothetical fear of loss of control over Pakistan's nuclear assets certainly diminishes the image of Pakistan, and more so of the capability of its army, which has claimed to be the proud guardian of national sovereignty. Moreover, any such technical cooperation in nuclear weapon matters is not permitted between a party and a non-party of the nuclear Non-Proliferation Treaty (NPT). Third, the issue is a grave one as it is not only a question of the safety and security practice (system) in Pakistan, but also involves the state (government), non-state (terrorists), the constituents of the state (officials, army, or scientific community) and precedents that have earned for Pakistan an image of a proliferator. A critical interplay among all these factors has begot a vicious circle of apprehensions, scepticism and doubts to rectify which even the stringent effort by Pakistan fall short.

The fountain of all apprehensions on its capability to safe-keep nuclear assets is the nature of the functioning of Pakistan as a nation-state. Repeated military takeovers, bitter civil-military relationship, clandestine nuclear proliferation networks, splintering *jihadist* groups and an off-on alliance with the US has culminated in a vicious circle of confusion in which Pakistan is struggling. Suspicion over Pakistan's capability to guard its nuclear assets seems to have been compounded owing to many other factors like (1) the legacy of A.Q. Khan's proliferation network; (2) Pakistan's proximity to the region of Al Qaeda and Taliban remnants; (3) religious conservatism in Pakistani society; and (4) deadly terrorist incidents.[29] Therefore, the threat to Pakistani nuclear assets has been interpreted along these fault lines. The studies that have been conducted on the issue by different scholars and officials during the last few years are symptomatic. For example, a Landau Network report suggests that "the risks of nuclear proliferation in Pakistan may be more significantly linked to the acquired nuclear expertise combined with pro-radical political attitudes, than with the actual risk of leakage of fissile material or of nuclear weapons".[30] Despite President Obama assurance in 2009 that Pakistan's nuclear materials "will remain out of militant hands," US Ambassador Anne W. Patterson was deeply worried about the stockpile of highly enriched uranium, which was enough to build several "dirty bombs" and if it was all in skilled hands, possibly enough for an actual nuclear bomb.[31]

These assertions hold some truth as two Pakistani nuclear scientists, Sultan Bashiruddin Mahmood and Abdul Majeed, are known to have met Osama bin Laden and Ayman al-Zawahiri in August 2001.[32] Michael Krepon, co-founder of the Stimson Centre, argues that "a prolonged period of turbulence and infighting among the country's president, prime minister, and army chief" could jeopardise the army's unit of command, which "is essential for nuclear security".[33] Graham T Allison, taking a broader view, says "political instability, a burgeoning Islamic insurgency, a demoralised army and an intensely anti-American population, puts Pakistan's nuclear weapons at risk".[34] According to Allison, what made it possible for A.Q. Khan to run the nuclear network "was an extended period of instability in the country". He fears that uncertainty and instability in Pakistan today provide similarly propitious opportunities for mini-Khans to proliferate.

The political instability in Pakistan is viewed as the major source of all insecurities. Seymour M. Hersh assumes "the principal fear is mutiny – that extremists inside the Pakistani military might stage coup, take control of some nuclear assets, or even divert a warhead".[35] Rolf Mowatt-Larssen, a former Central Intelligence Agency (CIA) official, points to the "lethal proximity between terrorists, extremists, and nuclear weapons insiders" in Pakistan. It is well-known how "insiders" from the Pakistani defence forces have been involved in terrorist attacks and suicide bombings many times.[36] Considering the splintering of fundamentalist groups and incidents, Bruce Riedel says Pakistan "has more terrorists per square mile than any place else on earth, and it has a nuclear weapons programme that is growing faster than any place else on earth".[37] In a similar tone, Pervez Hoodbhoy argues that "Pakistan's 'urban Taliban', rather than illiterate tribal fighters, pose a nuclear risk. There are indeed more than a few scientists and engineers in the nuclear establishment with extreme religious views".[38]

The deadly terrorist incidents – mainly three suicide attacks near vital installations of Pakistan during 2007-08 – have drawn international attention. On November 1, 2007, a suicide attack on a Pakistan Air Force bus in Sargodha killed seven; a suicide attack on a school bus carrying children of Pakistan Air Force employees at Kamra Air Force Base on December 10, 2007 injured five children and three adults; and on August 20, 2008, an attack near the Ordnance Factories in Wah cantonment killed at least 63 people. The Air Weapons Complex at Kamra is believed to be involved in a variety of tasks relating to air munitions and may have played a role in adapting Pakistan's air delivery vehicles for nuclear missions. Also because of Wah's extensive explosive-related infrastructure, it is commonly considered to be an assembly site for Pakistan's nuclear weapons.[39] The Pakistani Taliban also claimed responsibility for the attack near Wah.[40] Besides, there are numerous instances of military bases being targeted, including the 2009 Taliban siege of the Army Headquarters (HQ) in the garrison town of Rawalpindi, and in 2011, a major attack unleashed by the Taliban on a naval base in Karachi. All these incidents, though they were not directly on the nuclear installations and it is unknown whether they are in any way related to Pakistan's nuclear weapons, have, however, raised eyebrows.

More importantly, Pakistan's plan for expansion of its nuclear weapons and nuclear energy programmes has raised concerns the world over. The dimensions of the Pakistani nuclear weapons build-up are not fully understood yet but they are "scaling up their centrifuge facilities," said David Albright of the Institute for Science and International Security.[41] Worrisome is Pakistan's continued procurement of nuclear materials from the black market, and the two new plutonium reactors are located less than 100 miles from where Pakistani forces are fighting the Taliban.[42] Pakistan's Mid-Term Development Framework 2005 has planned for the installation of an additional 8,500 Mega Watt electric (MWe) of nuclear capacity by the year 2030, expecting a growth rate of 13 percent.[43] To achieve this target, it has to install at least 14 new units,[44] the first two of which are already planned for the Karachi Nuclear Power Plant (KANUPP) site near Karachi. This rapid expansion rate envisaged may pose some safety risks, given the persisting volatile security environment. Even if the expansion programme kicks off, there would be an urgent need to hire and train at a fast rate, an additional 18,000 technical staff in the next 20 years that may create vulnerabilities for the nuclear programme in terms of operation by inexperienced crews and the emergence of terrorist supporters within the system.[45] It is viewed that the future safety related events, in turn, might cause severe social and economic implications on their own, and might precipitate further national security related actions by the government, or terrorist attacks by capitalising on the general unrest created.[46]

Threat Interrogation

The question of safe-keep of Pakistan's nuclear assets has devolved into a binary argument of "are they or aren't they". Undoubtedly, the risks to Pakistan's arsenal are high due to the prevailing internal turbulence but what is important is to assess whether the safety-regulatory measures Pakistan claims to have undertaken so far are true in spirit, and adequate. Moreover, how imminent and real is the threat? Is Pakistan, which was determined to have nuclear weapons even if it needed to "eat grass and leaves", really incapable of protecting its prized-possessions from being misused today?

In the endeavour to diagnose the phenomenon of security of Pakistan's nuclear assets, it is crucial to examine, first, the nature of the threat. What are the potential sources of the threats? Are the terrorists really looking for, and capable of, acquiring them? If the Islamic fanatics within the army and terrorists operating within Pakistan are a cause of concern, how effective is the Pakistani security arrangement in and around the facilities? How effective are the measures implemented leading to the promulgation of the Pakistan Nuclear Regulatory Authority Ordinance in January 2001?

The 'implosion' or failing of Pakistan has been in the air for the last few decades. How probable is the reality of Pakistan becoming a "failed state"? Pakistan has failed in many respects as a stable or normal nation-state, but has survived and will continue to survive, despite all odds. Is the Pakistan Army, which proclaims to be, and has behaved as, the ultimate protector of the Pakistan nation, not capable now of playing the same role? What is the probability of a closet fundamentalist in the army rising to a position of much influence, or causing an internal coup, to misappropriate the nuclear arsenal and to pass it on to the terrorists? Moreover, what is the convincing base of the assumption that Pakistan would be taken over by radical Islamists, a scenario many, including Bruce Riedel, advance? What is the probability of a fundamentalist party coming power with a majority vote, when no Islamist party has ever garnered more than 11 percent of the vote in any election so far?

On the other hand, is the Pakistani nuclear infrastructure completely safe? Radiological materials are used for innumerable civilian purposes and at innumerable locations. According to the PNRA Report 2009, the Pakistan Nuclear Regulatory Authority (PNRA) has not been able to bring all X-ray facilities into the licensing net.[47] Terrorists, instead of attempting development of a full-fledged nuclear weapon, which is extremely difficult, may attempt to capture radiological materials from the civilian sector to produce a 'dirty bomb'. Then how safe are Pakistan's radiological materials used in various locations? Above all, why has such a scenario not yet taken place despite the prevalence of an unstable political situation in Pakistan for the last few decades? Are the terrorists finding it difficult to carry out such a design, or are the apprehensions baseless? To examine these critical questions, a realistic assessment of the evolving internal security situation and the security arrangement in and around Pakistan's nuclear facilities would help explain the degree and nature of the threat and the preparedness of the Pakistani establishment to mitigate it.

Fathoming the Contagion

Available literature on Pakistan's nuclear safety and security highlights issues relating only to its nuclear arsenal and it safe-keep. Whereas Pakistan's nuclear complex constitutes the nuclear weapon component storage sites, nuclear power plants, research reactors, heavy water reactors, reprocessing plants, radioactive waste facilities, uranium mines, medical applications (therapeutic and diagnostic radiography and irradiators for sterilisation of medical equipment), industrial applications (industrial radiography, irradiators and scanners, oil well logging and nuclear gauges), etc. scattered all over the country. The Pakistan Atomic Energy Commission (PAEC) is working actively in the field of agriculture, employing nuclear techniques at its agriculture centres at Faisalabad, Peshawar and Tandojam.[48] The PAEC manages a total of 14 nuclear medical centres across the country (another four centres were under construction till September-October 2010) that cater to half a million patients per year.[49] The total number of radiological units/sources in Pakistan is not clear. According to Kenneth N. Luongo and Naeem Salik, 65 percent of the sources are claimed to be stored and only 34 percent of them are in use.[50] Of the amount in use, 49 percent is under the PAEC, of which 26 percent is for medical use, 74 percent for non-medical use, and 51 percent is non-PAEC, of which 12 percent is for medical use and 88 percent is for non-medical use.[51]

The exact size of Pakistan's nuclear arsenal or fissile material production capability is a matter of speculation. It is assumed that "all fissile material has been machined into the warhead, even if the reality is that some fraction of fissile material remains in a form not easily usable for military purposes".[52] In 2008, the International Panel on Fissile Material (IPFM) estimated that Pakistan had "perhaps 65-80 weapons and may be increasing its stock by the equivalent of about six weapons worth per year".[53] The assessment of the Natural Resources Defence Council (NRDC) and the Federation of American Scientists (FAS) in 2009, had concluded that Pakistan may possess fissile material sufficient for 80-130 warheads, though the actual number of warheads was likely less than 100.[54] The *SIPRI Yearbook 2010* estimates Pakistan's nuclear weapons at 70–90.[55] According to the IPFM 2015 report, "As of the end of 2014, Pakistan is estimated to have a stockpile of 3.1 ± 0.4 tons of HEU (Highly Enriched Uranium) and continues to produce HEU for its nuclear weapon program."[56] Many other media reports place Pakistan's current weapons stockpile at 110-130; however, all the estimates seem unable to discern what portion of fissile material has been converted into warheads.

For fissile materials production, Pakistan follows both plutonium and HEU programmes. The IPFM baseline estimate of 2006 assumes four weapons worth of material from Pakistan's HEU programme (100 kg of HEU per year, 20 kg of HEU per weapon) and an additional 2 weapons worth of material from the plutonium route (10 kg per year, 5 kg of plutonium per weapon).[57] The two new reactors at the Khushab site could increase Pakistan's plutonium production capacity by an additional 20 kg a year (10 kg per reactor), or about four warheads equivalent per year.[58] Though questionable, the Institute for Science and International Security (ISIS) 2006 study estimated that one of the reactors at Khushab could have the capacity to produce a staggering 200 kg of weapon-grade plutonium per year (40-50 weapons equivalent).[59]

Determining Pakistan's HEU production is equally difficult. The IPFM baseline estimate assumes 100 kg per year of HEU production from the centrifuges at Kahuta but

Pakistan may also have centrifuge facilities at Gadwal, Golra, and Sihali with unknown enrichment capacities.[60] Pakistan seems to have employed four types of centrifuge designs (P-1, P-2, P-3 and P-4). The IPFM study assumes it as 65 weapons worth of material, say around 1,400 kg of HEU, the amount which the P-2s at Kahuta could produce. If Pakistan has used P-3s after 1998 (the IPFM estimate assumes 120 kg of HEU was used in the six tests in 1998), the upper end IPFM estimate reaches as high as 2,800 kg of HEU – or around 135 weapons worth of materials as of 2008.[61] According to Thomas Cochran of the NRDC, Pakistan has around 70-85 weapons worth of fissile material with an additional rate of perhaps 6 new additional weapons worth a year, which will increase to perhaps 10 new weapons worth a year by the completion of all three Khushab reactors in the 2011-14 time-frame.[62]

The general perception is that Pakistan's nuclear warheads are kept disassembled – de-mated from delivery vehicles implying a "geographical separation between them".[63] But it is unclear if these de-mated warheads are also stored in a partially disassembled state, with fissile cores perhaps stored separately from their triggers. The US Defence Department report (2001) states that "Islamabad's nuclear weapons are probably stored in component form" and that "Pakistan probably could assemble the weapons fairly quickly ...."[64]

Scanning the Nature of Threats

Given the upward trajectory of Pakistan's nuclear assets and domestic political instability, the concern factors for their safety and security are broadly three: (1) non-state actors or terrorists/insurgents operating in and around Pakistan; (2) the Pakistan Army officers with a fundamentalist-Islamic bent; and (3) personnel inside the Pakistani nuclear research establishment.

First, the issue of non-state actors' or terrorists' interest in nuclear arsenal/materials needs careful examination. According to Bruice Riedel, "Pakistan today is a country in the intensive care ward of the global state system".[65] What Ridel presumed (in 2009) was "a *jihadist* state would come to power through some combination of violence and intimidation" mainly by the Pakistani Taliban coalescing with the Punjab-based Lashkar-e-Tayyeba (LeT) and some Islamist political parties. The new regime would quickly take control of the nuclear arsenal and welcome Osama bin Laden and Ayman al Zawahiri.[66] This hypothetical situation brings forth three imminent questions: (a) can the Pakistan Army not defend its homeland against the *jihadist*-terrorist-insurgent groups? (b) are the *jihadist*-terrorist-insurgent groups really looking for nuclear arsenals? and (c) how invincible are Pakistan's nuclear facilities for the *jihadist*-terrorist-insurgent groups?

Undoubtedly, many of Pakistan's nuclear-related facilities are located in and around the tribal insurgency, Al Qaeda-Taliban active regions. Many nuclear facilities in the northwestern region, mostly around the Federally Administered Tribal Areas (FATA) like Mianwali, Sargodha and in the Northwest Frontier Province (NWFP) such as Kohat and the Wah Cantonment Ordnance Complex in Kamra, can be easy targets.[67] The Taliban-insurgents' incursion into Buner, a key region 60 miles from Islamabad, in April-May 2009 heightened the fear of terrorist intrusion into a nuclear facility.

Fig 1

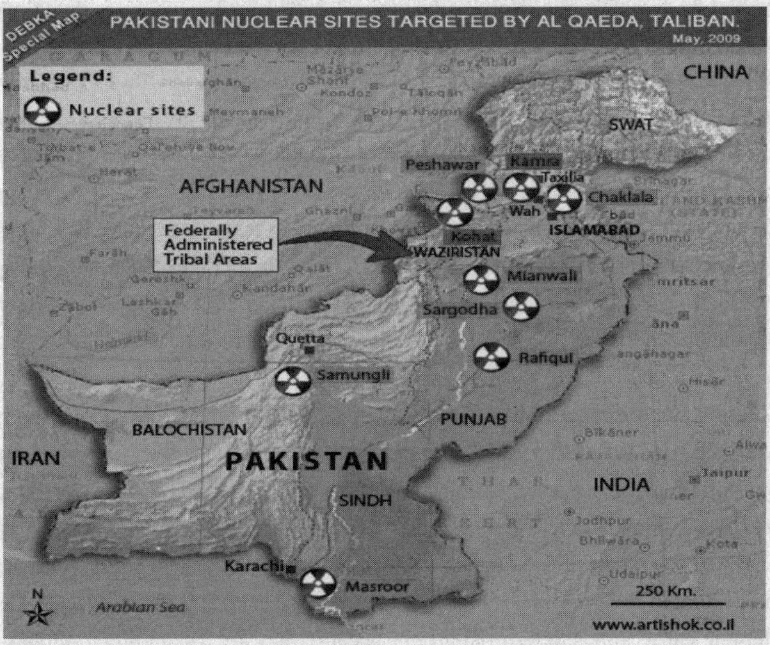

Source: Debka Special Map, www.artishok.co.ll

Since August 2008, Pakistani forces have launched offensive operations against the Al Qaeda-Taliban groups. The first phase (17-month campaign) that ended in March 2009 with the seizure of tunnels and caves frequently visited by Al Qaeda operatives in Damadola area, saw the killing an estimated 2,200 militants.[68] As the Taliban began to push into northern Punjab in 2009, along with the US pressure, Pakistani forces launched a concerted and sustained military operation. Islamabad seems determined to pursue its fight, though the operation has been selective and the pace or scope of its efforts greatly varies.[69] In a worst case scenario, the Pakistan Army, which has been the proclaimed guardian and protector of Pakistan, will not allow these *jihadi* forces to capture the nation.

As far as the *jihadists'* intention for nuclear weapons is concerned, it is doubtful whether they would be capable of developing or handling a nuclear device. Are they really looking for nuclear weapons? The Al Qaeda and LeT being strong and spread out terrorist outfits might have considered the nuclear option. But why have they not yet been able gain possession of, or used, such a device? Either they found it difficult or it doesn't suit their purpose. Or, they may be planning to capture/ sabotage a nuclear facility within their area of operation. If they are aware of the radiation consequences, they would not resort to such an act of destroying a plant as their own operation in the area would be affected, and the consequent government high-handedness would put the group's survival at stake.

Are the series of attacks from 2003 to 2006 near sensitive facilities not causes of concern? Among all the nuclear weapon states, Pakistan certainly provides the most fertile environment for non-state actors. A few virulent attacks in the past around sensitive defence facilities, particularly at the Dera Ghazi Khan PAEC facility and uranium mine (Baghalchur site, apparently used for storage of nuclear waste[70]) in April 2003 and May 2006 respectively, and an explosion at Wah in 2008, bring the impression that Pakistan's nuclear facilities could be their targets. However, none of the attacks could breach the perimeter security of the facilities. Rather, they occurred near the facilities or on personnel en-route.

Secondly, the apprehension of fundamentalist-oriented Pakistan Army or intelligence (ISI) officers rising to the highest level of authority and staging a coup, leading to misappropriation of the arsenal, is, in fact, a serious concern raised on the leadership of the Pakistan Army and the efficacy of its personnel reliability programme. Theoretically, the Pakistan Army could decide to transfer nuclear weapons to a terrorist group. As described in Philip Bobbitt's *Terror and Consent*, states can be pressurised or 'incentivised' to transfer nuclear weapons to terrorist groups because they are responding to threats from an external power but fear the consequences of being identified as the origin of a nuclear strike.[71] In an apocalyptic scenario, if Pakistan is pushed to a corner by India and the United States in a time of its political instability, the humiliation and frustration of being left behind, may result in an 'implosion' on ethnic lines, and the Pakistan Army may be tempted to use or hand over its nuclear arsenal to the extremists as a form of *national suicide*. However, such a situation is not likely, as a stable Pakistan is in the interest of all.

It needs to be kept in mind that the Pakistan military has been an ardent advocate of nuclear weapons and these are now its prized possessions. An internal coup within the Pakistan Army resulting in lower level officers with an Islamist bent overthrowing the top army leadership is theoretically plausible. But a scrutiny of the culture of the Pakistani rank and command suggests that such a situation would not take place given the robust internal intelligence, personnel reliability programme and strict scrutiny of promotion of senior or important officers. It is viewed that while some of the officers were recruited and groomed during the conservative reign of President Gen. Zia-ul Haq, the last three army chiefs – Karamat, Musharraf, and Kayani – have all been moderates.[72] What is conceivable is an attempt by a lower level officer of an Islamic bent resorting to a localised mutiny, together with local ethnic leaders angered by the support of the political leadership to the US-backed counter-insurgency operations. But the question is: are these splinter groups strong enough to overpower the Strategic Plans Division (SPD) security system guarding the concerned nuclear facility?

Pakistan's Inter-Services Intelligence (ISI) has been known for its close contacts with, and providing support to, militant groups. The ISI leadership has been drawn from the mainline army. It also plays a major role in securing Pakistan's nuclear assets. The probability of ISI agents involved in nuclear matters passing on information to militant groups cannot completely be ruled out. Therefore, Pakistan's personnel reliability programmes involving the ISI, the nuclear establishment and the military need serious introspection.

Thirdly, the issue of proliferation of nuclear technology by insiders (scientists) to rogue states, or the scientist-terrorist nexus, has been a major concern. The A.Q. Khan proliferation network and the Majeed-Mahmood episode has unfolded how "Pakistan's 'urban Taliban', rather than illiterate tribal fighters, pose a nuclear risk".[73] It is also found that engineers are over-represented among the Islamic terrorists.[74] Pervez Hoodbhoy, the chairman of the Physics Department at the Quaid-e-Azam University, has been widely quoted as saying that "secret institutions are seized with religious fervour".[75] Political and religious attitudes in the Pakistani scientific community may be diversified but there seems to be a growing influence of Islamic radicalism. A few people with some critical knowledge may decide to help a terrorist organisation to build a crude nuclear device. A physicist with 'cold implosion' expertise (implosion of spheres possibly with U238 that will not create a nuclear detonation) will be very useful in preparing a plutonium implosion bomb for any organisation that can acquire plutonium.[76] There are physicists in Pakistan having such knowledge as well as a bent towards Islamic radicalism, who could be hired by terrorist organisations.

Fourthly, the chances of all these plausible scenarios could be high depending on the political state of Pakistan. Theoretically, prolonged political instability leading to a complete breakdown of governance will put the nuclear arsenal in jeopardy. Many view Pakistan as a 'failing state', and the perpetual political "instability in Pakistan", owing to the power tussle among the president, prime minister, army, and fundamentalist insurgents, "could make its nuclear weapons and stocks of nuclear explosive material dangerously vulnerable to theft".[77]

However, the issue of state failure in Pakistan has been in the air for the last few years. The view is that radical Islamist parties/ groups would come to power. But there is little evidence that there is anything close to a majority support for the Islamists. In no Pakistani election have the Islamists garnered more than 5-8 percent of the vote, except in 2002, when these parties scored 11.10 percent because of the degree of anti-US sentiment as well as procedural rulings that favoured religious parties over mainstream parties.[78] Also, factors like the situation in Afghanistan, and internal divisions within parties have sufficiently conditioned the popular perception. Moreover, at that time, the issue of educational qualification was put in place for the National Assembly candidature and the religiously influenced politicians with a degree from a religious educational institution were permitted to compete.[79] As Frederich Grare says, "No objective observer believes that Pakistan's Islamic parties have a chance to seize power through elections in the foreseeable future".[80]

Undoubtedly, Pakistan has seen a great deal of ruin, and for the next few decades, it will remain a "troubled state", but the rumours of Pakistan's demise seem greatly exaggerated. The Pakistani state faces profound challenges but, at the same time, it has, and will continue, to endure. In any case, the army which is the strongest and most stable institution, would promptly intervene, as it has done before for whatever pretext, if the situation warrants.

Lastly, owing to Pakistan's proliferation record, insurgency, terrorism, troubled civil-military relations, etc., all its effort to ensure security through sweeping reforms have failed to appeal to the international community. This is the prism through which the entire world looks at Pakistan and its integrity to protect its nuclear assets.

The Compartmentalised Programme

Activities related to the promotion of the use of nuclear energy were initiated in Pakistan as early as 1955.[81] But the attempt for a framework to regulate radiation protection and manage occupational exposure dates back to 1965 when the first research reactor PARR-1 was commissioned.[82] During that time, the Pakistan Atomic Energy Commission Ordinance was promulgated, under which the PAEC became a statutory body. According to this ordinance, all nuclear installations were owned and operated by the federal government through the PAEC. For more than a decade since Pakistan started its nuclear weapons programme in the 1970s, not much was known of the status and structure of its nuclear safety and security policy. With the promulgation of the Pakistan Nuclear Safety and Radiation Protection Ordinance (PNSRP) in 1984, the Directorate of Nuclear Safety and Radiation Protection (DNSRP) was established within the PAEC. During the 1990s, Pakistan has promulgated a number of PNSRP ordinances for safe management of radioactive materials.

In 1994, in pursuit of its obligation under the International Convention on Nuclear Safety, the Pakistan Nuclear Regulatory Board (PNRB), an independent nuclear regulatory board, was established to implement the legislative and regulatory framework governing nuclear power and radiation use in the country. This attempt separated the regulatory functions from the promotional aspects of the nuclear programme. Theoretically, the process of complete separation was achieved in 2001 with the promulgation of the Pakistan Nuclear Regulatory Authority Ordinance that created the PNRA for the regulation of nuclear safety and radiation protection.

On the other hand, Pakistan's effort to control and secure its strategic nuclear assets before 1998 is unclear as Islamabad followed a clandestine programme until then. According to Mushahid Hussain, a senator close to Musharraf, from 1975 to 1991, the nuclear programme was supervised by a committee headed by G.I. Khan, who became the President of Pakistan in 1988.[83] But according to Gen Beg, there was a "National Nuclear Command Authority" from 1975 headed by the chief executive.[84] After the 1998 nuclear tests, Pakistan's nuclear weapons policy became much clearer and overt though Islamabad had not yet formulated a national nuclear doctrine. However, since 1998, Pakistan's nuclear control infrastructure, according to an International Institute for Strategic Studies (IISS) study, has gone through "four phases".[85] During the first phase from 1998-99, Pakistan began to consider a formal command-and-control system for the first time. In the second phase, during 1999-2001, Gen Pervez Musharraf, in his capacity as Chief of the Army Staff (CoAS) implemented his initial reforms. A third phase of reform during 2001-03 took place mainly because of the September 11 attacks that fundamentally changed Pakistan's security relationships. During this period, nuclear oversight and control got further consolidated under the leadership of Musharraf as the head of the government. A fourth phase of tight export control began at the end of 2003, especially in response to the US pressure and the exposure of the A.Q. Khan nuclear proliferation network.

One assertion often made is that if A.Q. Khan could manage to run his network and other personnel could have links with the terrorist groups, despite some controls in place, what is the guarantee that a similar event will not recur? This study believes that the Khan network was never entirely an individual design, without the backing and knowledge of the Pakistani authorities. Rather Khan's activity was a result of, and sanctioned by, the clandestine and 'compartmentalised' Pakistani national nuclear weapons programme which lacked a central oversight. This would be amply clear if one scrutinises the Pakistani nuclear policy-making organisation prior to 1998.

Fig 2: Evolution of Pakistan's Nuclear Command Pre-1999

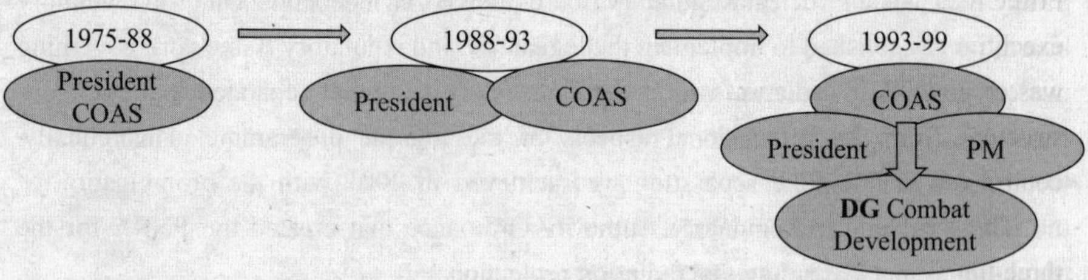

From 1975 until 1988, nuclear decision-making was under the tight control of one man (Bhutto, Zia); from 1988 until 1993, it was shared between the president and the COAS; from 1993 until 1999, the latter became the central figure, while prime ministers were involved in a limited way.[86]

It is known that Z.A. Bhutto took direct charge of the nuclear programme after the 1974 Indian nuclear test, abolishing the inter-ministerial committee in charge of nuclear issues.[87] During Zia's time (July 1977 to August 18, 1988) the office of the president and COAS was one and the same. After him, Ghulam Ishaq Khan took over as a civilian president who brought COAS Gen Beg into the nuclear loop to handle the weaponisation aspects. In July 1993, when both the president and the prime minister left simultaneously and an interim government emerged, G.I. Khan was known to have transferred all responsibilities and relevant documents to the COAS, Gen Abdul Waheed Kakar. Waheed, in turn, lengthened the chain of command by appointing a major-general as director general of combat development to be the nuclear policy contact point. However, the COAS was not formally considered the authority over all nuclear organisations, especially Kahuta Research Laboratory (KRL). More importantly, after G.I. Khan's resignation, the role of the president became weaker. Also, prime ministers had only a limited knowledge of nuclear matters and were only involved in some policy decisions through the Defence Committee of the Cabinet. It was within this politico-military organisational compartmentalisation and absence of a single oversight apparatus, that the Khan network had evolved.

Latest Reforms: The Command-and-Control

The current Pakistani nuclear command-and-control apparatus, restructured from 1999 to 2001, on the basis of the past experience and loopholes, is expected to streamline Pakistan's nuclear security and safety oversight. The formation of the Strategic Plans Division (SPD) by merging the poorly coordinated and competitive nuclear establishments like the Combat Development Directorate, the Operations and Plans Directorate, and the Command and Control and Intelligence Directorate was Gen Musharraf's plan which Prime Minister Nawaz Sharif approved. After Musharraf assumed the powers of chief executive by ousting Nawaz Sharif in October 1999, the National Security Council was created which later in 2000 consolidated Pakistan's nuclear command and control structure. This process brought all nuclear laboratories, including the KRL, under military control and formalised the role of the military in Pakistan's nuclear policy-making.

The command and control system, called the Strategic Command Organisation is a three-tier structure comprising the National Command Authority (NCA), the SPD, and the strategic force commands of the three defence forces. It is the highest decision-making authority for both conventional and nuclear security matters. All organisations involved in the missile and nuclear programmes were put under the NCA from November 2000. The SPD is responsible for formulating standard operating procedures for the regulation of, and code of conduct for, strategic organisations, like contact with the media, travelling abroad, financial expenditure reporting, etc. The operational control of the separate strategic force commands in the army, navy and air force remains with the NCA.

Fig 3: Pakistan's Nuclear Command and Control

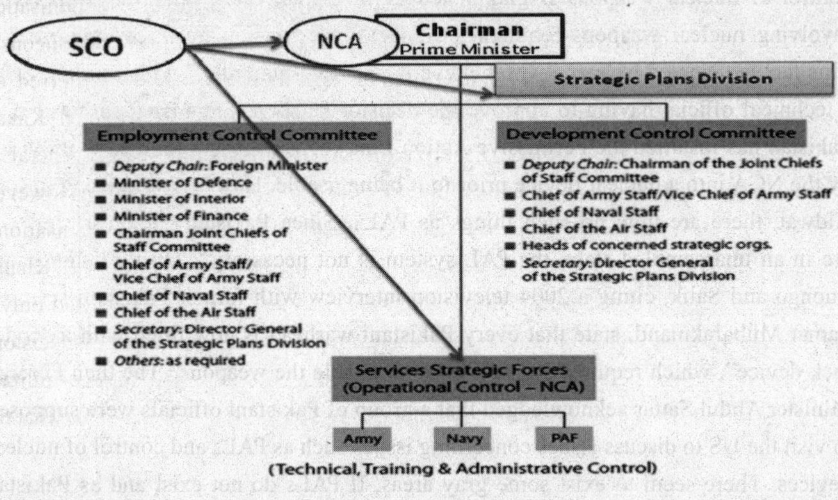

As far as the physical security of the nuclear installations is concerned, the 1999-2001 reforms put in place a three-level arrangement. At the immediate level, each facility has its own security procedures. At the second level, the SPD, having its own intelligence system, follows the 'perimeter multi-layered security' which is responsible to check all pilferages by coordinating with other intelligence agencies. At the third level, the ISI Directorate forms the outer ring of security and its Security Division comprising over 20,000 specially trained military personnel, is responsible for technical vigilance upgradation, including infrared and motion sensors, locks, video cameras and communication devices.

According to the former Director-General of the SPD, Lt Gen Khalid Ahmed Kidwai (Retd), Pakistan's multi-layered physical protection system for the nuclear programme is based on the 5Ds: Deter, Detect, Delay, Defence, and Destroys. Naeem Ahmed Salik, former director, Arms Control and Disarmament Directorate of the SPD, asserts that Pakistan's physical security architecture, based on multi-layered perimeter security, is an integral element of all nuclear installations, civilian or military.[88] The SPD's Security Division also has a Quick Reaction Force and a Site Protection Force to ensure physical security of the nuclear sites and facilities.

According to open source information, "to preclude any possibility of inadvertent or unauthorised use of nuclear weapons, Pakistan has developed physical safety mechanisms and firewalls both in the weapon systems themselves and in the chain of command. No single individual can operate a weapon system, nor can one individual issue the command for nuclear weapons use".[89] According to Gen Kidwai, the safe control of nuclear weapons is guaranteed by a "3-man rule" where any procedure involving nuclear weapons requires the concurrent decision by three authorities.[90] This fact is disputed by many who believe it is a "two-man rule," with a military and a technical official having to approve the decision.[91] These designated authorities, if Pakistan has installed the Permissive Action Link (PAL), must input a code provided by the NCA into a nuclear device prior to it being usable. However, according to Gen Kidwai, there are now no such things as PALs. Since Pakistan's nuclear weapons are in an unassembled state, the PAL system is not necessary.[92] On the other hand, Luongo and Salik, citing a 2004 television interview with former Pakistani scientist Samar Mubarakmand, state that every Pakistani warhead is now fitted with a "code-lock device", which requires a proper code to enable the weapon.[93] The then Foreign Minister Abdul Sattar acknowledged that a group of Pakistani officials were supposed to visit the US to discuss issues concerning issues such as PALs and control of nuclear devices. There seem to exist some gray areas. If PALs do not exist and as Pakistan claims, its weapons can be assembled very quickly in a crisis situation and they are also disassembled and dispersed, then the components must be stored in nearby places to reduce the response time. Therefore, the question is how effective would the control of nuclear weapons be in moments of crisis?

The Tactical Nuclear Weapons (TNWs) with Pakistan have been a major cause of concern, for the very nature of the TNWs, and the fact that they need to be deployed on the battlefields or stored close to the battlefield and away from the central command and control chain, substantially increases the risks of "accidental, unauthorised or mistaken use."[94] Pakistan maintains that it will continue to exercise centralised control over battlefield nuclear weapons during possible deployment. It is also asserted that these weapons won't need to be deployed prematurely or unnecessarily exposed to security risks or to the enemy, due to the relatively short distances between the storage sites and potential deployment areas (given Pakistan's lack of strategic depth).[95] However, given the politico-security situation in Pakistan, the smaller the nuclear weapon and its means of delivery, the more susceptible it is to loss of central control.

According to a growing number of statements by both Pakistani and US officials, the US has quietly assisted in Pakistan's efforts to strengthen its nuclear security. Adm Mullen commented in May 2009 that "the United States have invested fairly significantly over the last three years, to work with them, to improve that security. And we're satisfied, very satisfied with that progress".[96] Richard Armitage has the same view, "We have spent considerable time with the Pakistani military, talking with them and working with them on the security of their nuclear weapons. …They have pretty sophisticated mechanisms to guard the security of those".[97] According to a report in *The New York Times*, the US has provided around $100 million worth of training, equipment and other aid to Pakistan for this purpose.[98] But according to Feroz Hassan Khan, when the US Secretary of State Colin Powell offered nuclear security assistance to Pakistan President Musharraf in 2001, the SPD carefully examined the offer and accepted only training, but declined any technology transfers as it was perceived that it may be intrusive and compromise their secrecy.[99]

Radiation Safety: How Prepared is Pakistan?

Theoretically, the organisational arrangement for safe-keep of Pakistan's nuclear weapons seems very professional, notwithstanding its real capability and the existence of some gray areas involving the politico-strategic instability in and around Pakistan. Slippage of a full-fledged nuclear device, though it cannot be completely disregarded, will not be easy. Also, non-state actors fabricating a nuclear weapon does not seem possible as it requires state-level resources. But how prepared Pakistan is to contain a radiological terror incident if terrorists manage to prepare a 'dirty bomb', using orphan or smuggled radiological material, is a moot point.

Pakistan has 2,000 miles of open borders where illicit trafficking and smuggling takes place. In April 2000, the Uzbek state customs committee intercepted radioactive scrap travelling to Pakistan from Kazakhstan. An official statement said that the gamma rays emanating from the load had radiation levels which exceeded the safety level by over 100 times.[100] Even inside Pakistan, traces of orphan radioactive sources are being increasingly reported. Pakistani authorities dug up two radioactive sealed containers at the state-run Oil and Gas Development Corporation in Karachi.[101] Reportedly, the site at which the radioactive materials were unearthed was used by a Soviet oil company until the late 1960s when there was no nuclear regulatory authority in Pakistan. Also, the issue of shut down of the nuclear mine at Baghalchur in 2000, and making it a nuclear waste dumping site was widely criticised as 1,000 barrels of waste was dropped off and left outside for many weeks.[102] Repeated advertisements in Pakistani newspapers, urging the public to inform officials if they found any "lost or stolen" radioactive material,[103] highlight the concern for tracing orphan materials which could be confiscated by non-state actors. Moreover, radioactive materials are used in numerous places in Pakistan for various purposes but the security around them is rather lax.

According to official pronouncements, Pakistan follows a cradle to the grave concept of radioactive material management where records are kept of any radioactive source entering the country until its final disposal. The PNRA is empowered to control, regulate and supervise all matters related to nuclear safety and radiation protection in Pakistan. It regulates the radiation safety aspects of nuclear installations, e.g. nuclear power plants, nuclear research centres, etc. and radiation facilities such as diagnostic radiology and radiotherapy centres, nuclear medicine facilities, irradiators, industrial and agricultural radiography, etc. Starting from the 1990s, many regulatory instructions have also been promulgated and mechanisms for their implementation have been established.

Table 1: Legislative Regulatory Framework in Pakistan

Sl.	Regulations		Purpose
1	Regulations on radiation protection	PAK/904	No practice shall be licensed or authorised unless it produces sufficient benefit to individuals to be exposed or to society to offset the radiation harm that it might cause, taking into account social, economic and other relevant factors.

2	Regulation for licensing of radiation facilities other than nuclear installations	PAK/908	
3	Regulations for licensing of nuclear installation(s) in Pakistan	PAK/909	Establish a system of licensing for the nuclear installations which sets requirements for site registration, construction licence, fuel load permit, operation licence, licence beyond design life, inspections and submission of the radiation protection programme from the licence.
4	Regulations on safety of nuclear power plants – design	PAK/911	Establish requirements for the safe design of nuclear installations.
5	Regulations on safety of nuclear power plants – quality assurance	PAK/912	
6	Regulations on safety of nuclear power plants – operations	PAK/913	Deal with the safety aspects of the management, commissioning, operation and decommissioning of nuclear power plants. To provide assurance that operational activities are carried out without undue radiological hazards to the general public and to individuals on site.
7	Regulations on management of a nuclear or radiological emergency	PAK/914	Establish the requirements for an adequate level of preparedness and response for a nuclear or radiological emergency. To minimise the consequences for people, property and the environment of any nuclear or radiological emergency.
8	Regulations on radioactive waste management	PAK/915	
9	Regulations for safe transport of radioactive material	PAK/916	

With increasing concern in the post-9/11 period regarding the smuggling and misuse of radioactive materials, and a lack of awareness among the public officers and law enforcing agencies on how to respond to a radiological emergency, a comprehensive action plan was considered necessary. On the advice of the Government of Pakistan, the PNRA initiated the Nuclear Security Action Plan (NSAP) project in July 2006.[104] The focus areas of the NSAP are multifarious:

- **Management of Radioactive Sources**: The PNRA carries out physical protection inspections of radiation facilities to assess their security level, weaknesses, propagate a security culture, and upgrade security efforts. In the pursuit of strengthening the effectiveness of its management, the capacity of the three existing Regional Directorates has been enhanced, and two additional Nuclear Security Inspectorates have been established at Peshawar and Quetta.
- **Locating and Securing Orphan Radioactive Sources**: Rigorous searches for orphan radioactive materials have been carried out and a media campaign for the awareness of the general public about such orphan sources was launched by the PNRA in 2008. The PNRA has undertaken special efforts to locate, recover, and monitor the entry of radioactive sources through scrap metal. Till 2009, 31 non-physical and physical searches were conducted at the target locations, including airports cargo terminals, dry ports, seaports, scrap yards, steel mills and exploration sites. Three orphan sources were recovered and reported to the International Atomic Energy Agency (IAEA).[105]
- **Installation of Radiation Detection Equipment:** The PNRA signed a Memorandum of Understanding (MoU) with the Federal Board of Revenue in 2008 to provide radiation detection equipment to be installed at some important entry/exit points. It also provides training, maintenance facility and technical assistance to Pakistan Customs officials to seize or confiscate smuggled materials. Under the first phase, eight entry/exit points were selected: Torkham, Chamman (Pak-Af border), Sost (Pak-China border), Taftan (Pak-Iran border), Wagah (Pak-India border) and the sea ports of Gwadar, Karachi and Bin Qasim. In the second phase, international airports and dry ports were equipped.
- **Nuclear Security Emergency Coordination**: For effective and prompt coordination of efforts among government agencies for containing any radiological emergency situation, the Nuclear Security Emergency Coordination Centre (NuSECC) has been established. The NuSECC has set up a network of six emergency mobile labs at Islamabad, Kundian, Karachi, Peshawar, Quetta and Multan. Equipped with state-of-the-art radiation detection equipment to search and measure radiation hazards, it would be able to respond within four to six hours. The NuSECC is manned round the clock and can be accessed from anywhere toll free.

Fig 4: NuSECC Structure and Functions

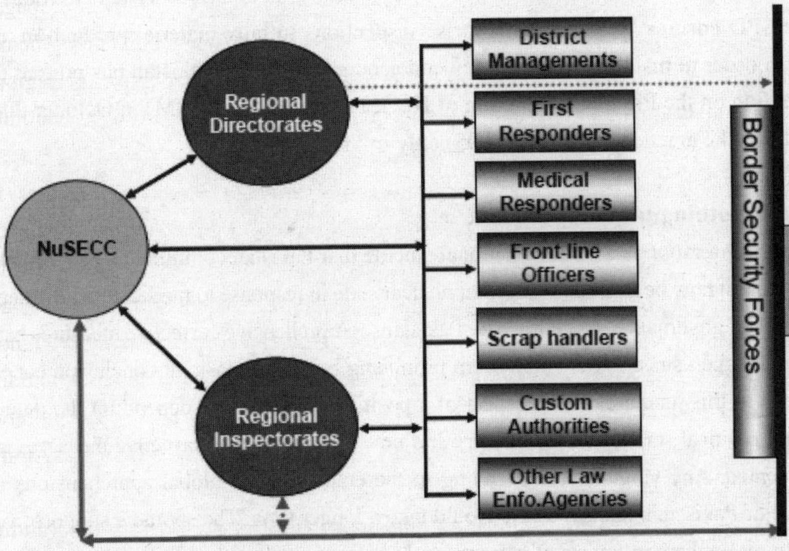

Source: Muhammad Khaliq, Project Director, NSAP

- **Nuclear Security Training**: With the aim of capacity building and skill, a large number of personnel from different national organisations have been trained through numerous training courses at the Nuclear Security Training Centre (NSTC) established in collaboration with the IAEA. For strengthening the physical protection and the nuclear security programme, the PNRA is in the process of establishing physical protection labs. More than 600 persons have been trained so far through 27 training courses till 2008. To ensure long-term nuclear security expertise from the graduate level, the PNRA-NSAP, in collaboration with the Pakistan Institute of Engineering and Applied Sciences (PIEAS), has introduced the specialised subject of nuclear security in the MS Nuclear Engineering Programme.

The PNRA is in charge of ensuring adequate physical protection of all nuclear facilities and materials with support from the SPD which has about 10,000 specially trained troops, of whom about 1,000 form a special unit having their own intelligence capability to ensure security at nuclear sites.[106] Over the past one decade, the SPD has reportedly screened all relevant personnel, granted levels of security clearances and determined the requisite degree of access for those handling sensitive nuclear materials. It is claimed that a stringent personnel reliability programme, with the help of the US is in place and the four agencies – the ISI, Military Intelligence, Intelligence Bureau, and SPD – screen and control the key people involved.[107] The current system introduced by the SPD ensures "regular and surprise inspections to tally material production and waste in order to maintain transparency and accountability".[108] Pakistan has ratified the Convention on the Physical Protection of Nuclear Materials (CPPNM) in October 2000 but ratified the amended CPPNM (2005) only in March 2016.

Is There Nothing to Worry About?

Nuclear proliferation is a form of national suicide that Pakistan committed a few decades ago. It cannot now be treated as a normal nuclear state in response to modicum adjustments in its nuclear governance. As claimed by Pakistan, comprehensive corrective measures have been undertaken since 2001 which seem promising but an all-positive conclusion cannot be drawn at this juncture. The prospect of a positive outcome will depend on the degree of future political stability in the country and how effectively the corrective measures are implemented. Any tangible result leading to the eradication of global apprehensions on the state of Pakistan's nuclear assets would take a longer time. The sporadic support from Western researchers in favour of offering an India-type nuclear deal to Pakistan will be a mockery of the non-proliferation order. However, the US Administration does not seem to be overlooking the apprehensions on the Pakistani behaviour and track record.

Meanwhile, is there nothing to worry about? What is the surety that the new administrative-security programmes in place and the political situation at present would continue in the desired direction? The Pakistani nuclear issue is *not just one of nuclear* security; it encompasses the nuances of its national psyche, its Islamic identity, its regional and global personality, and, more importantly, the nature of functioning of its political and military apparatus. Pakistan's pursuit of a nuclear weapons inventory and nuclear energy expansion in recent days will lead to increasing nuclear activities in the country. Taking into account the nascent nuclear regulatory framework, mismanagement and misappropriation of nuclear technology and resources is more likely.

The threat to Pakistan's nuclear assets emanates both from the loose ends of its national societal-political spectrum and its mainstream security governing apparatus which are also the causes of insecurity of Pakistan itself. Therefore, the insecurity of the Pakistani state, in fact, is the source of the nuclear risks in Pakistan. The domestic political reconciliation among warring groups, consolidation of the central political leadership, efficient counter-insurgency operations, and Pakistan's open-mindedness to seek or accept best practices would determine the level of safety-security of the nuclear assets in Pakistan.

Notes

1. "Civil Nuclear Cooperation With Pakistan: Prospects and Consequences", Hearing Before the Subcommittee on Terrorism, Non-proliferation, and Trade of the Committee on Foreign Affairs House of Representatives one Hundred Fourteenth Congress, December 8, 2015, Serial No. 114–124, http://docs.house.gov/meetings/FA/FA18/20151208/104258/HHRG-114-FA18-Transcript-20151208.pdf
2. David Leigh, "WikiLeaks Cables Expose Pakistan Nuclear Fears", guardian.co.uk, November 30, 2010.
3. "US, UK, Russia Share Concerns Over Pak Nuclear Stockpile, Proliferation: WikiLeaks", Karachi News.Net, December, 1, 2010.
4. "Pak Dismisses Fears Over Safety of its Nuke Weapons", *The Hindu*, December 2, 2010.
5. "Pakistan's Nuclear Weapons in Safe Hands: Nawaz", *Daily Times*, January 6, 2016.
6. Robert Dahl, *Controlling Nuclear Weapons: Democracy Versus Guardianship* (New York: Syracuse University Press, 1985).
7. "US-Pakistan Strategic Relations", Statement before the Committee on Senate Homeland Security and Government Affairs Subcommittee on Federal Financial Management Government Information, Federal Services and International Security, June 12, 2008.
8. Richard Weitz, "Repercussions from Air Force Nuclear Weapons Incident Continue", September 25, 2007, http://www.hudson.org/index.cfm?fuseaction=publication_details&id=5177
9. "New Leaks from WikiLeaks: UK, US Concerned over Pakistan's Nukes", http://tribune.com.pk/story/84305/new-leaks-from-wikileaks-uk-us-concerned-over-pakistans-nukes/
10. "US-UK Share 'Deep Concerns' over Pakistan's Nuke Weapons Programme: Wikileaks", *The Economic Times*, December 1, 2010.
11. "US Embassy Cables: Scene Setter for Washington Visit of Pakistan Military Boss", http://www.guardian.co.uk/world/us-embassy-cables-documents/192895
12. Quoted in Ron Synovitz, "Rising Tide of Militancy Feeds Fears about Pakistan's Nukes", April 24, 2009, http://www.rferl.org/content/Rising_Tide_Of_Militancy_Feeds_Fears_About_Pakistans_Nukes/1615403.html
13. "US Embassy Cables", November 30, 2010, http://www.guardian.co.uk/world/us-embassy-cables-documents/250573
14. Ibid.
15. Michael Mullen, "Defense Department Briefing Transcript", Federal News Service, May 4, 2009; Michael Mullen, "Remarks to the L.A. World Affairs Council", Federal News Service, September 22, 2008.
16. Gen David Petraeus, "Interview with Chris Wallace", *Fox News Sunday*, May 10, 2009.
17. Quoted in Jon Meacham, "A Highly Logical Approach: A Conversation with Barack Obama", *Newsweek*, May 16, 2009.
18. "Army Chief Feels Pak N-Arsenals are Secure", Press Trust of India, October 24, 2010.
19. "Pak Nukes Safely Guarded, Says Narayanan," Press Trust of India, December 16, 2007.
20. "Nuclear Security in Pakistan after Musharraf", *WMD Insights*, October 2008, http://www.wmdinsights.com/I27/I27_SA1_NucSecinPakistan.htm
21. Statement of the Pakistan Ministry of Foreign Affairs (Office of the Spokesman), November 19, 2007
22. Ibid.
23. Seymour M Hersh, "Are Nuclear Weapons Safe in Pakistan?", *The New Yorker*, November 16, 2009.
24. Jeffrey Goldberg and Marc Ambinder, "The Pentagon's Secret Plans to Secure Pakistan's Nuclear Arsenal", Global Security Newswire, www.nti.org, November 09, 2011.
25. "Pakistan Foreign Office Rejects U.S. Media Report on Nuclear Arsenal", Associated Press of

Pakistan, November 9, 2009.

26. "Strategic Assets Are Safe, Says FO", *Dawn*, November 12, 2007.
27. "Record of the Press Briefing on 26 March 2009", Spokesman Briefing, March 26, 2009, www.mofa.gov.pk/Spokesperson/2009/March/Spokes_26_03_09.htm
28. Hersh, n. 23.
29. Zafar Ali, "Pakistan's Nuclear Assets and Threats of Terrorism: How Grave is the Danger?", The Henry L. Stimson Centre, July 2007, p. 9.
30. "Nuclear Safety, Nuclear Stability and Nuclear Strategy in Pakistan: A Concise Report of a Visit by Landau Network", http://www.centrovolta.it/landau/content/binary/pakistan%20Januray%202002.pdf, p. 5.
31. "Jane Perlez, David E. Sanger and Eric Schmitt", "Nuclear Fuel Memos Expose Wary Dance With Pakistan", http://www.nytimes.com/2010/12/01/world/asia/01wikileaks-pakistan.html?pagewanted=all&_r=0
32. Graham T Allison, *Nuclear Terrorism: The Ultimate Preventable Catastrophe* (New York: Henry Holt, 2004), p. 20.
33. "Pakistan Enhances Second Strike N-Capability: US Report", http://news.dawn.com, May 30, 2009
34. Graham Allison, "What About the Nukes?", http://www.newsweek.com/2007/12/27/what-about-the-nukes.html
35. Hersh, n. 23.
36. Military personnel were involved in perhaps two assassination attempts against Musharraf – one in mid-December 2003 and another in late September 2006. In the December 14, 2003 attack, a number of low-ranking air force personnel as well as a handful of army troops were involved in emplacing and detonating explosives on a bridge in Rawalpindi regularly crossed by Musharraf. See "Junior Officers Tried to Kill Me: Musharraf", *Daily Times*, Pakistan, May 28, 2004; "Musharraf Attack Fugitive Was PAF Man", *The Nation*, (Pakistan), January 12, 2005.
37. David E. Sanger, "Pakistan Overshadows Afghanistan on US Agenda", *New York Times*, May 6, 2009.
38. Pervez Hoodbhoy, "Whither Pakistan? A Five-Year Forecast", *Bulletin of the Atomic Scientists*, June 3, 2009, www.thebulletin.org/web-editon/features/whither-pakistan-five-year-forecast
39. "Wah – Pakistan Special Weapons Facilities", www.globalsecurity.org/wmd/world/pakistan/wah.htm
40. Amjad Iqbal and Mohammad Asghar, "Taliban 'Claim' Credit for Wah Carnage", *Dawn*, (Pakistan), August 22, 2008.
41. Thom Shanker and David E. Sanger, "Pakistan Is Rapidly Adding Nuclear Arms, U.S. Says", http://www.nytimes.com/2009/05/18/world/asia/18nuke.html
42. Ibid.
43. John Stephenson and Peter Tynan, "Is Nuclear Power Pakistan's Best Energy Investment? Assessing Pakistan's Electricity Situation", http://www.npolicy.org/files/20081107-Dalberg-Pakistan.pdf
44. Chaim Braum, "Security Issues Related to Pakistan's Future Nuclear Power Program", in Henry D. Sokolski, ed., *Pakistan's Nuclear Future: Worries Beyond War*, January 2008, US Government Title 17, United Code, Section 101, p. 298.
45. Ibid., pp. 303, 321.
46. Ibid., p. 299.
47. "Message from the Chairman", in *Report 2009*, Pakistan Nuclear Regulatory Authority, www.pnra.org
48. Pakistan Atomic Energy Commission, "Agriculture", http://www.paec.gov.pk/paec-agrim.

htm

49. "PakAtom", http://www.nti.org/media/pdfs/36_4.pdf?_=1316819692, September-October, 2010.
50. Kenneth N. Luongo and Naeem Salik, "Building Confidence in Pakistan's Nuclear Security", http://www.armscontrol.org/act/2007_12/Luongo
51. Ibid.
52. Christopher Clary, "Thinking about Pakistan's Nuclear Security in Peace Time, Crisis and War", www.idsa.in/system/files/OP_PakistansNuclearSecurity.pdf, p. 7.
53. Zia Mian and A.H. Nayyar, "Pakistan", in *Banning the Production of Fissile Materials for Nuclear Weapons: Country Perspectives on the Challenges to a Fissile Material (Cutoff) Treaty* (International Panel on Fissile Materials, 2008), p. 196, www.ipfmlibrary.org/gfmr08cv.pdf
54. Robert S. Norris and Hans Kristensen, "Nuclear Notebook: Pakistan Nuclear Forces 2009", *Bulletin of the Atomic Scientists*, September-October 2009, p. 82.
55. "VIII. Pakistani Nuclear Forces", *SIPRI Yearbook Online*, http://www.sipriyearbook.org/view/9780199581122-gill/sipri-9780199581122-div1-77.xml#sipri-9780199581122-tableGroup-43
56. IPFM, "Global Fissile Material Report 2015", http://fissilematerials.org/library/gfmr15.pdf, p. 16.
57. Zia Mian, et al, *Fissile Materials in South Asia: The Implications of the US-India Nuclear Deal* (International Panel on Fissile Materials, September 2006), pp. 14-15, http://www.fissilematerials.org/ipfm/site_down/rr01.pdf
58. Ibid.
59. David Albright and Paul Brannan, "Commercial Satellite Imagery Suggests Pakistan is Building a Second, Much Larger Plutonium Production Reactor: Is South Asia Headed for a Dramatic Buildup in Nuclear Arsenals?", *ISIS Report*, (Washington, DC: ISIS, July 24, 2006), http://isis-online.org/publications/southasia/newkhushab.pdf
60. Mian, et al, n. 57, p. 15.
61. Ibid.
62. Thomas B. Cochran, "What is the Size of Khushab II?", http://docs.nrdc.org/nuclear/files/nuc_06090801A.pdf
63. According to Musharraf's statement in January 2003, "There is no button in our case. The missiles and warheads are not permitted together. There is a geographical separation between them". Secretary of State Hillary Clinton told Congress in April that Pakistan's nuclear weapons are "widely dispersed in the country – they are not at a central location". See Nicholas Kralev and Barbara Slavin, "Clinton Warns of Pakistan Nuke Risk", *Washington Times*, April 24, 2009.
64. Office of the Secretary of Defence, *Proliferation: Threat and Response* (GPO, Washington, DC, January 2001), p. 27.
65. Bruce Riedel, "Armageddon in Islamabad", *The National Interest*, June 23, 2009, http://nationalinterest.org/article/armageddon-in-islamabad-3148
66. Ibid.
67. Kamra is roughly 180 km northeast of the Kohat air base. It is home to the Pakistan Wah Cantonment Ordnance Complex, which consists of three armament facilities in Wah (Pakistan Ordnance Factories - POF), Kamra (Air Weapon Complex - AWC), and Taxila (Heavy Industries-HIT).
68. "Pakistan Army Claims 29 Insurgents Killed in Tribal Region – Summary", May 3, 2010, http://www.earthtimes.org/articles/news/321804,pakistan-army-claims-29-insurgents-killed-in-tribal-region--summary.html

69. "U.S.: Pakistan Vows to Keep Fighting Insurgents", http://www.cbsnews.com/stories/2010/08/25/world/main6804701.shtml
70. Zofeen Ebrahim, "Pakistan: Villagers Pay the Price of Nuclear Ambitions", Inter Press Service, May 31, 2006.
71. Philip Bobbitt, *Terror and Consent* (London: Allen Lane, 2008).
72. Clary, n. 52, p. 29.
73. Pervez Hoodbhoy, "Whither Pakistan? A Five-Year Forecast", *Bulletin of the Atomic Scientists*, June 3, 2009, www.thebulletin.org/web-edition/features/whither-pakistan-five-year-forecast
74. Diego Gambetta and Steffen Hertog, "Engineers of Jihad", *Sociology Working Papers,* no. 2007-10, Department of Sociology, University of Oxford, Oxford, U.K. 2007.
75. Peter Wonacott, "Inside Pakistan's Drive To Guard Its A-Bombs", http://www.wsj.com/articles/SB119629674095207239
76. "Nuclear Safety, Nuclear Stability and Nuclear Strategy in Pakistan", http://www.pugwash.org/septmeber11/pakistan-nuclear.htm
77. David Albright, "Securing Pakistan's Nuclear Weapons Complex", http://www.isis-online.org/publications/terrorism/stanleypaper.html
78. Ali, n. 29, p. 14.
79. Clary, n. 52, pp. 28-29.
80. Frederic Grare, "Pakistan: The Myth of an Islamic Peril", Carnegie Endowment for International Peace, Policy Brief No 45, February 2006.
81. "Report of the International Regulatory Review Team (IRRT) Mission to Pakistan", 1-12 December 2003, *IAEA-TCR-02028, IAEA/NSNI/IRRT/04/01*, January 2004, http://www.pnra.org/IRRT.pdf, p. 2.
82. Muzzammal Hussain, Rizwan Ali Khan, Bushra Nasim, "Regulatory Framework for Occupational Exposure Management in Pakistan", Presented in ISOE Symposium 2009, Vienna, Austria. http://www.isoe-network.net/index.php?option=com_docman&task=doc_download&gid=1304&Itemid=122
83. Mushahid Hussain, "Media Off Target with Pakistan Nuclear Scare", *Asia Times*, November 7, 2001.
84. "Pakistan's Nuclear Oversight Reforms", in *Nuclear Black Markets: Pakistan, A.Q. Khan and the Rise of Proliferation Networks*, (London: International Institute for Strategic Studies), p. 108.
85. Ibid., p. 107-108.
86. Ibid., p. 109.
87. Farhatullah Babar, "Bhutto's Footprints on Nuclear Pakistan", *The News*, April 4, 2006.
88. Luongo and Salik, n. 50.
89. Khalid Banuri and Adil Sultan, "Managing and Securing the Bomb", *Daily Times*, May 13, 2008, http://www.dailytimes.com.pk/default.asp?page=2008/05/30/story_30-5-2008_pg3_6
90. "Nuclear Safety, Nuclear Stability and Nuclear Strategy in Pakistan: A Concise Report of a Visit by Landau Network – Centro Volta", n. 27, p. 4.
91. Feroz Hassan Khan quoted in Martin Schram, *Avoiding Armageddon: Our Future, Our Choice* (New York: Basic Books, 2003), p. 54.
92. Ibid.
93. Luongo and Salik, n.50.
94. Samuel R. Berger, Steve Andreasen, "The Final Failure," *Foreign Policy*, September 8, 2011.
95. Mark Fitzpatrick, "Overcoming Nuclear Dangers," *Adelphi Paper* 443 (London: International Institute for Strategic Studies, March 2014), p. 90, https://www.iiss.org/en/publications/adelphi/by%20year/2014-de9e/overcoming-pakistan-nuclear-dangers-7ef0
96. Mike Mullen, "Defence Department Briefing Transcript", May 4, 2009, quoted in Clary, n. 52, p. 16.

97. Richard Armitage, "A Conversation with Richard Armitage", *The Charlie Rose Show*, November 6, 2007.
98. David Sanger and William Broad, "US Secretly Aids Pakistan in Guarding Nuclear Arms", *New York Times*, November 18, 2007.
99. Feroz Hassan Khan, "Nuclear Security in Pakistan: Separating Myth From Reality", Arms Control Association, http://www.armscontrol.org/print/3725
100. "Uzbeks Seize Truck Carrying Radioactive Materials", *Reuters*, April 4, 2000, also see "Radioactive Scrap Metal", http://www.nuclearpolicy.info/publications/scrapmetal.php
101. Zeeya Merali, "Pakistan Finds Two Radioactive Containers", http://www.nature.com/news/2008/080716/full/454258b.html
102. Paul Vos Benkowski, "Pakistan: Friend or Foe? Nuclear Menace", *Nukewatch Pathfinder-5*, Fall 2006.
103. "Pakistan Downplays Radioactive Ad", *BBC News*, http://www.bbc.co.uk/go/pr/fr/-/2/hi/south_asia/6616225.stm
104. "Nuclear Security Action Plan (NSAP)", http://www.pnra.org/nsap.asp
105. PNRA, Report 2009, Pakistan Nuclear Regulatory Authority, 2009, p. 29.
106. Jayshree Bajoria and Sharon Otterman, "Controls on Pakistan's Nuclear Technology", http://www.cfr.org/publication/7742/controls_on_pakistans_nuclear_technology.html
107. Luongo and Salik, n. 50.
108. Khan, n. 99.

5

China's Economic Downward Spiral: Impact on Comprehensive National Power

Temjenmeren Ao

This paper is based on the premise that economics is the foundation for a state to build its national power through advances in its military and high-technology industries. The paper would attempt to analyse the economic growth story of China that was marked by a downward trend in the year 2015 and how this could impact its long-term Comprehensive National Power (CNP). At the outset, it should be stated that China's comprehensive national power is a term that encapsulates all elements of state power, including economic capacity, military might and diplomacy. The prediction of a slowdown in China's economic growth and the bearish nature in its equity markets that dominated the news in the year 2015 has shaken the confidence of foreign investors who see China as an engine for global commerce. This could spell trouble for China's quest for achieving Comprehensive National Power and could prove ominous for perpetuating the rule of the Chinese Communist Party (CCP). In the paper, it has been argued that the speculations on the slowdown in China's economic growth are attributed not only to the existing external factors but are a result of the switch to a new model of economic growth being undertaken by China.

"Zonghe guoli" or Comprehensive National Power

It would be pertinent to define the Chinese concept of *Zonghe guoli* or Comprehensive National Power (CNP) before going any further. CNP refers to the combined overall conditions and strengths of a country in numerous areas. During the Cold War and the US-Soviet confrontation, a nation's power was largely determined by military force, but in the current transition period, as the world moves towards multipolarity, military might is no longer the defining factor of strength. Instead, elements such as economics and science and technology have become increasingly important in the competition for power and influence in the world. An evaluation of current and future strength requires the inclusion of a variety of factors such as territory, natural resources, military forces, economic power, social conditions, domestic government, foreign policy and international influence. CNP is the aggregate of all these factors, as Deng Xiaoping stated: “In measuring a country’s national power, one must look at it comprehensively and from all sides”. Deng Xiaoping modified Chairman Mao’s Party line that “world war was unavoidable”, by instead predicting that “world war probably can be avoided”. Deng’s new assessment of the security environment was that the growth of the world’s forces of peace exceeds the growth of the forces of war. As the international environment was changing and the importance of economic issues and conflicts was growing, military force was no longer the main index for judging a country’s strength. Numerous other factors contributed to a country’s power and were playing a greater role in warfare, such as economics, science and technology and popular will[1].

In his book *Grand Strategy,* Wu Chunqiu of the Academy of Military Science (AMS) of the People’s Liberation Army (PLA), attributes the early version of CNP to ancient Chinese military strategists who stated, “China’s wise ancient strategists never advocated relying only on military power to conquer the enemy, but emphasised combining military power with non-military power related to war in order to get the upper hand”. Huang Shuofeng of the PLA’s AMS, describes CNP as a complex system composed of four major index sub-systems: the material power (hard) index sub-system, the spirit power (soft) index sub-system, the coordinated power index sub-system and the environmental index sub-system. The material power and spirit power indices reflect the strength a country needs for survival and development. The coordinated power index reflects the leadership’s organisation, command, management and decision-making levels. The environmental index reflects the restricting conditions of comprehensive national power. Material power includes hard factors such as natural resources, economics, science and technology and national defence. It also includes soft factors such as national defence ideology and military theory. According to Hu Angang and Men Honghua, CNP means “the sum total of the powers or strengths of a country in the economy, military affairs, science and technology, education and resources and its influence. It combines all the powers possessed by a country for the survival and development of a sovereign state, including material and ideational ethos and international influence”. CNP stresses on comprehensiveness, measuring the basic national conditions and resources of a country’s economic, political, military and technical power[2].

Tong Fuquan and Liu Yichang analysed CNP by keeping economics at the core. They divided CNP into four major parts– economic, politics, science and technology and military affairs – placing economics in the most crucial position. According to them, actual economic strength is a major component of CNP since a country with strong economic power will have powerful political influence and a nation with unsubstantial economic strength will not have major political influence. A similar relationship exists between the extent of a country's economic strength and the level of its scientific and technological development. The importance of military power cannot be underscored in determining a country's CNP. However, there is the size of the military budget/expenditures which, in turn, would determine whether a country's actual military strength is strong or weak. The size of a country's military budget would be dependent on the country's economic strength and the level of its scientific and technological strength. Therefore, it could be stated that military strength, which is a strong symbol of a country's powerful CNP, is determined through its economic strength[3]. China's three strongest components of CNP are its natural resources, rapid growth rate, military manpower and weapons. China has had the good fortune of achieving a high economic growth rate for a sustained period of time. However, its road towards achieving comprehensive CNP has witnessed an offset due to its low science and technology levels. Realising its limitations, China has brought a shift in its economic model of growth and has emphasised on Research and Development (R&D) in order to make it an enabling power through its indigenous innovative capacity stimulated through its economic growth. According to Greg Autry, author of the book, *Death by China*, China's economy feeds its military growth and this in a way is being done through the Foreign Direct Investment (FDI) that goes into China from the West; enabling China to rapidly transform and modernise its defence industries. In the post-Cold War period, China has been increasing its expenditure on its military budget, mainly due to its hyper economic growth[4].

Emergence of China as an Economic Giant in the 21st Century

The emergence of China as an economic power and the sheer speed with which it has been able to achieve this can be comprehended by US Senator Dan Sullivan's (R- Alaska) statement in the US Senate's House of Representatives, that in the 1980s, China's economy was smaller than the economy of the Netherlands, and in 2014, China's incremental economic growth rate was larger than the economy of the Netherlands[5]. Three competing visions emerged in the Chinese discourse on the modern economy: an economy of absolute egalitarianism (radical populism), a competitive private economy with public guidance, and a mixed economy with private, cooperative and public enterprises coexisting. While an economy of absolute egalitarianism was the rallying cry of all poor peasant rebellions, it was most vigorously articulated by Hong Xiuquan in the midst of social suffering unprecedented since the Opium War. According to Hong, the root of all social upheavals lay in the great gap between the rich and the poor. His economic blueprint emphasised on the government's role in enforcing an egalitarian society. On the other hand, according to Liang, Kang and other constitutionalists, a modern Chinese economy must be a private economy, with public guidance. They argued that public enterprises had too often been ineffective and unproductive, as proved by the corrupt state enterprises of the 1860s and the 1870s. These constitutionalists stressed that in a competitive private economy, the emergence of one big corporation could not stop competition from others. If the government became the sole monopoly, then no one would ever have the power to compete against a government owned enterprise. Thus, according to Liang and Kang, both market competition and state intervention were necessary in the modern economy. Whether there should be more state intervention or market competition would depend on the specific situation in China[6]. The revolutionary nationalists put great emphasis on the principle of social justice in China's modern economy. Their leader, Sun Yat-sen, after World War I, proposed coexistence among private, cooperative and public enterprises in the modern economy. He emphasised that the mixed economy, or the principle of people's livelihood, was neither a capitalist free-enterprise economy nor a socialist planned economy. In his view, while the free-enterprise system was effective for increasing wealth, it lacked the concept of fair distribution; and if the socialist planned economy emphasised fair distribution of wealth, it was not effective for rapid industrial growth. Therefore, a combination of both, according to Sun would be the best economic system for China. Sun particularly accentuated on the concept of fair distribution that, unlike redistribution of wealth, opposed class warfare and embraced class reconciliation[7].

China's economic reforms, launched by Deng Xiaoping in 1978, have turned the country into the fastest growing economy in the world. With the growth of its Gross Domestic Product (GDP) in double digits for much of the 1980s and the 1990s, China had already become an economic power. Using measures of Purchasing Power Parity (PPP), the World Bank, in 1993, estimated that China was the world's third largest economy after the United States and Japan. China's economic achievements have not been confined solely to growth; from 1994 to 1995, its inflation rate dropped from 24 percent to 17 percent and continued to fall. Further, its trade balance was reversed from a total trade deficit of $12.2 billion in 1993 to a trade surplus of $ 5.3 billion in 1994 which further increased to $ 16 billion in 1995. China's growing trade surplus, coupled with a strong inflow of foreign investment, made it the economic breakthrough nation of the 1990s. In 2010, China overtook Japan to become the second largest economy in the world; many predict that it would overtake the US by 2030, and according to an International Monetary Fund (IMF) paper, it might reach the number one position as early as 2016. China's economy has been experiencing a continual growth of 10.6 percent in its annual average GDP since 2000.In the year 2007, China broke through the $3 trillion barrier and the scale of its economy, which was less than one-fourth of Japan's in 2000, reached two-thirds. China's total trade amount in 2007 was $ 2,177 billion with its foreign currency reserve exceeding $ 1,500 billion[8].

During the last 30 years, China's economy has changed from a centrally planned system that was largely closed to international trade to a more market-oriented one that has a rapidly growing private sector. A major component supporting China's rapid economic growth has been its exports growth with the US which is its largest importer. Furthermore, China is also looked at by the US and other Western multinational corporations as a very attractive market. A Gallup Poll of China, the first of its kind, concluded that a billion Chinese want to become rich and buy televisions, washing machines, and refrigerators, and so on. The Chinese also desired Western consumer staples such as McDonald's and Coca-Cola, Marlboros and Proctor and Gamble products. This made the Chinese market with its large size (probably the largest in the world) very attractive to the American and other Western entrepreneurs. US companies have made investment commitments in approximately 20,000 projects, focussing on long-term, fixed, high-tech investment projects. With over 1.3 billion citizens, China represents approximately one-fifth of the world's population. It has a population roughly five times larger than that of the US and nearly twice that of all Western countries combined that also makes it an attractive export and investment destination for the US as well as for other nations[9]

Table 1: Investment and Consumption in China, 1980, 1990, 2000 and 2005[10]

Measure	1980	1990	2000	2005
Investment (billion $)	106.8	141.1	420.9	971.0
Consumption (billion $)	200.8	252.8	743.0	1,182.8
Ratio of Investment to Consumption	0.53	0.56	0.57	0.82

High rates of investment have accelerated capital formation, which has been a key contributor to China's rapid growth. From 1980 to 2000, the investment rate averaged about 35 percent of the GDP. In recent years, it has accelerated to more than 40 percent, reaching 43.5 percent in 2005. Table 1 gives an account of China's investment and consumption from 1980 to 2005. It can be seen that the investment to consumption ratio in China has remained a little over point half percent and nearing the equal ratio in 2005. China's external trade began to grow after the economic reforms in the late 1970s, accelerating gradually during the 1980s and 1990s. Trade growth has been more rapid since China's accession to the World Trade Organisation (WTO) in 2001. The total of imports and exports reached $ 1.4 trillion in 2005, making China the world's third largest trader, after the United States and Germany, accounting for 7.3 percent of the world exports and 6.1 percent of the world imports. By 2013, China became the largest exporter of merchandised goods with a global share of 11.7 percent followed by the US, Germany and Japan. China also emerged as the second largest importer after the United States with a share of 12.3 percent. Fig 1 below highlights China's growth as a global exporter since 1948. As can be seen, its share towards world export was a mere 0.9 percent in 1948 and remained almost stagnant. However, in the 1990s, China's percentage share in global exports had a take-off and it further made huge gains after its accession to the WTO in 2001.

Fig 1: China's Merchandise Exports, 1948-2013[11]

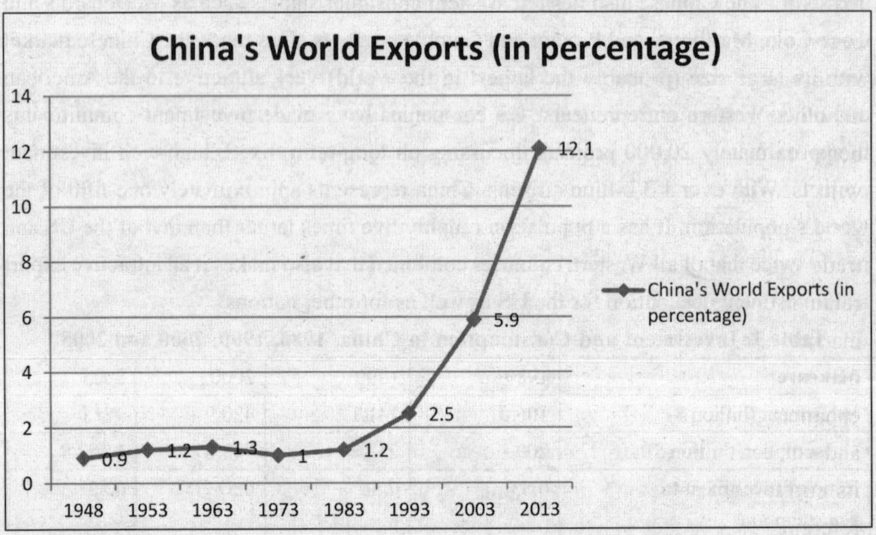

Conflicts as a Result of China's Economic Growth

China's global grand strategy amplified the need to maintain political stability and ensure the continued rule of the Chinese Communist Party (CCP). The CCP leaders have tried to build new sources of political support by raising living standards through rapid economic growth and by appealing to nationalist sentiments. Throughout the reform era, Chinese leaders have focussed on maintaining a stable international environment that supports economic modernisation. Much of China's economic success can be attributed to the operations of multinational companies that import components from Asia, assemble goods using Chinese workers, and export the finished products to markets in the US,

Europe and elsewhere. Although this has enabled China to gain its economic prominence globally, at the same time, it has also created major issues –one such being its increasing demand of energy to fuel its growth. This, in turn, has led to China's maritime expansion, which has caused major global concerns[12].

The emergence of China as an economic power in the 21st century has also created numerous conflicts. These conflicts are a result of China's own doing, one being its use of unfair trade practices in order to gain an edge over its rivals. It can be stated that China has used the 19th century mercantilist trade policy aggressively, where production is undertaken in excess of domestic demand in order to export, thus, enabling China to have an export surplus against its trading partners. The positive side of this strategy is that it enables the customers of the importing country to have goods at a relatively cheaper cost. On the negative side, this has ensured that the importing countries' manufacturing sector diminishes and, therefore, they become overly dependent on China's imports. China, like other developing nations, imposed numerous trade barriers such as high import tariffs, making imported goods unable to compete in the domestic market. However, since the mid-1990s, things began to change substantially with China's trade policy becoming more compatible with US trade demands and China's accession to the World Trade Organisation in 2001. This was done mainly because of Beijing's own calculation, that a more liberal trade policy was in its own self-interest and partly in recognition of the need to retain full access to the large, relatively accessible American as well as other Western markets. Furthermore, currency intervention undertaken by the Chinese government makes its exports more competitive as compared with its competitors, thereby enhancing its exports. Its currency until 2005 was artificially pegged to the US dollar and not determined by the market forces. In 2006, the Chinese government allowed its currency to float in a narrow margin around a fixed base rate determined with reference to a basket of world currencies. The Chinese government has announced that it will gradually increase the flexibility of the exchange rate, and as of 2013, China's yuan has emerged as the eighth most traded currency in the world[13].

All this enabled an annual hyper-growth; however, this has also led to an unsustainable strain on China, such as its huge and growing energy needs, its environmental degradation and pollution and a mounting income inequality. Investment in manufacturing has expanded from 1980-2005, although it has fluctuated and been concentrated in certain industries, including steel, aluminium, cement, textiles and automobiles. Excessive investment in some industries has led to excess productive capacity and less investment efficiency. As China's investment has risen, the share of consumption as a portion of GDP has fallen. There is the huge Chinese current account surplus that has resulted from too much savings as a result of less domestic consumption. China is still a low consumption economy because the per-capita income is still low and the people do not have welfare protection[14].

China's dependence on foreign trade as a driver of its economy has also increased sharply in recent years, from a ratio of total imports and exports to GDP of 43.8 percent in 2000 to 63.9 percent in 2005. Furthermore, there is also the evolving issue of an unfavourable demographic profile that China would witness in the future because of its 'one child policy'. Starting in the mid-1970s, China began to implement an aggressive birth control policy. As the smaller cohorts born under this policy began moving through the demographic structure of the country, the percentage of children in the overall population declined while the percentage of working age individuals (that is, 15 to 64 years) increased. From 1980 to 2000, the average annual growth rate for the total population was about 1.3 percent, while the working-age population grew at an average of over 2 percent. The working-age population ratio was projected to continue increasing until about 2010, reaching a high point of about 72 percent of the total population. After 2015, both the ratio and the absolute size of the labour force will likely decrease gradually due to continued small cohorts of children. In parallel, the share of the aged in total population was projected to keep rising, especially after 2010. From a share of 7 percent in 2000, the aged are projected to constitute 11.9 percent of the population by 2020.[15] Fig 2, on the following page, gives China's population and age composition from 2010-14. From the figure, it can be seen that the population in the age group between 0-14 and 14-64 has remained more or less constant, however, there has been a steady rise in the age group constituting 65 years and over. From the figures given in Fig 2, we can make a rough estimate of the gross dependency ratio which comes to about 36.1 percent in 2014, up from 34.2 percent in 2010. More specifically, the children dependency ratio has remained almost constant around the 22 percent mark. However, if we look into the old dependency ratio, it can be seen that it has risen continuously from 11.9 percent in 2010 to 13.7 percent in 2014, and with the growth in life expectancy, this ratio will continue to grow.[16]

Fig 2: China's Population and Age Composition, 2010-2014[17]

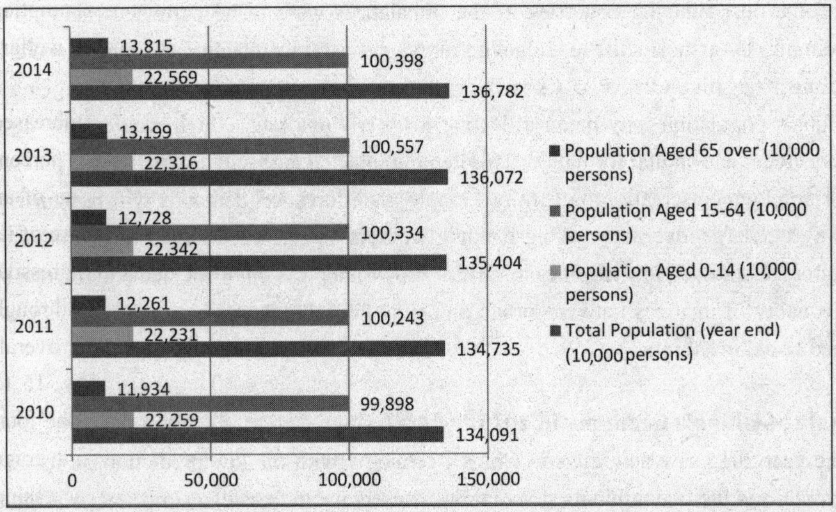

According to a 2015 World Bank report, changes in the demographic profile will lead to a decline in the labour market participation rate. China's working age population is expected to decline, and labour's contribution to growth will turn negative. This would also lead to an ageing population which would cause a shortage of not only the human resource but also a fall in the rate of savings which, in turn, would cause a fall in China's capital formation. There is also the concern that China like other developing countries such as South Africa, Brazil, and so on, might fall into the 'middle income trap', where it remains just a manufacturer for the big Multinational Corporations (MNCs) and is unable to achieve the required stimulus to get out of this trap in order to become a high income economy. The Total Factor Productivity (TFP) growth—a measure of improvements in economic efficiency and technological progress– has also declined, in part because the economy has exhausted gains from first generation policy reforms and the absorption of imported technologies. Implementation of much needed structural reforms will not reverse a moderation of economic growth over the next decade. Furthermore, it is also clear that many second generation reforms are likely to have a significantly smaller impact on growth than the first generation reforms that led to rapid technological absorption in the manufacturing sectors.[18]

The overall prospects of China's continued growth and development over the medium term are positive, although there are several reasons for concern, in both the international and national contexts. At the international level, there are serious imbalances in some countries' trade, most notably current account deficits in the US and surpluses in China and the oil-producing countries. If the imbalances were to be corrected rapidly– for example, by a short shift in exchange rates or a rise in protectionism– there could be stronger negative effects on China's export sector. At the national level, the ageing of China's population may mean a decline in its savings rate, which would slow down investment and capital formation. This demographic change will gradually ease pressure for employment creation, but overall employment creation demands will remain high until the large overhang of agriculture workers is absorbed into more productive sectors. Continued low incomes in rural areas will depress domestic demand. Increasing inequality of incomes between urban and rural households and between regions could feed social instability.[19]

State of China's Economy in 2015

The year 2015 saw new lows in China's economy with the low prediction on its GDP growth, and the free fall in its stock market caused due to fears of a slowdown of China's economy as well as speculation on the policy of the US Federal Reserve. To show the extent of the equity outflow from China, the trend in one of China's major stock markets has been considered. Fig 3 gives a trend of the Shanghai Stock Exchange (SSE). Taking a time period from 2006 till September 2015 of the SSE's Composite Index, it is found that from a high of almost 6,000 points in 2007, the SSE Composite Index has continued to decline since 2009. Post-2014, the SSE index has shown an upward trend crossing the 5,000 point mark. However, this steep rise in the stock prices due to massive inflows of Foreign Institutional Investors (FII) in 2014 was followed by a corresponding outflow in the year 2015.

Fig 3: Stock Trends of Shanghai Stock Exchange (SSE) Composite Index: 2006-2015[20]

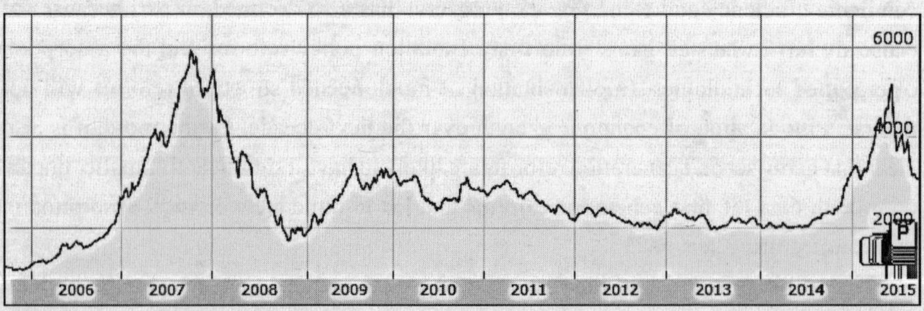

Fig 4: Stock Trends of Shanghai Stock Exchange (SSE) Composite Index: July- September 2015[21]

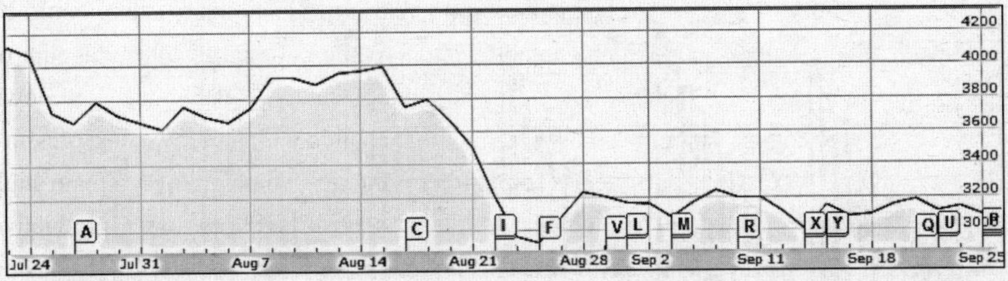

Fig 4 above shows the SSE index from July onwards till the month of September in 2015. It can be seen from the graph that between August and September, the SSE index tanked nearly one thousand points due to a massive outflow of FII. This huge outflow of equity from the stock markets resulted in China's central bank, the People's Bank of China, lowering the reserve rate and the devaluation of its currency by the government. Furthermore, the Chinese government had to pump about Yuan 800 to 900 billion into the stock market, according to estimates by Goldman Sachs, in order to stabilise the stock markets. Since the second quarter of 2014, portfolio and other capital outflows have been high, with the net non-FDI capital outflows reaching an estimated $ 295 billion in 2014. According to the World Bank, the trend would continue into 2015 with an estimated capital outflow of $ 209 billion in the first quarter of 2015, after an outflow of $ 168 billion in the previous years. However, despite a slowdown in economic activity, China's overall fiscal position remains strong. The huge outflow of capital in 2014 has been offset with a record high Foreign Direct Investment (FDI) inflow into services. It can be seen from the histogram in Fig 5 that since 2010, FDI inflow into China has reached close to the 1,200 hundred million dollar mark, and in 2015 as well, FDI inflow has been steady in line with the usual trend. The aggregate fiscal deficit of the public finance budget was also slightly lower than the original budget estimate. The annual fiscal deficit came to 1.8 percent of the GDP in 2014, slightly lower than in 2013.

Fig 5: Foreign Direct Investment into China, 2010-2015[22]

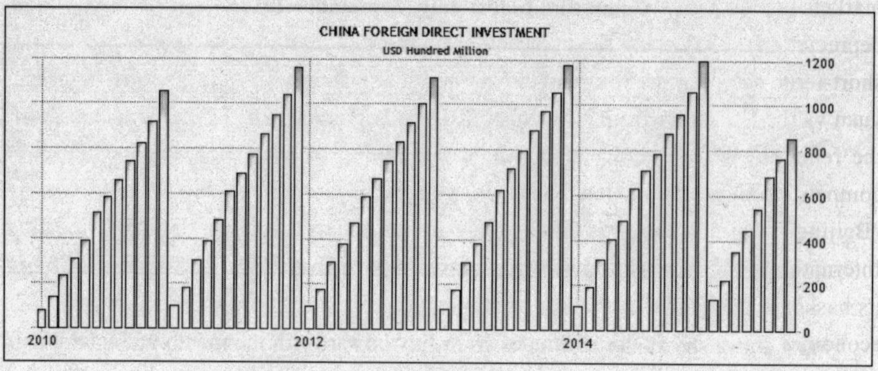

It should be stated that the Chinese economy is more insulated from stock market fluctuations than those of the developed countries like the US. The stock market just isn't a huge driver of economic activity in China. According to *The Economist*, in China, less than 15 percent of overall household assets are invested in the stock markets. The country's national savings rate remains extremely high, protecting it from a US-like debt crisis, and the government could still encourage more investment by lowering interest rates. The real problem with China's stock market fluctuation isn't that it will plunge China into a depression but that it could act as an irritant, as it would interrupt the country's long-term economic strategy. The Xi Administration wanted the equity markets to be a meaningful channel for Chinese companies and didn't want to rely too much on bank loans, and rather wanted to use the stock markets to accrue money for capital investments[23].

It is true that the stock market does not represent the entire health of an economy; however, it is a strong indicator of the market sentiments which is again based on the expected health of the economy. Furthermore, a serious cause of concern emerges with reports from the US Federal Reserve which tends to increase the interest rate –currently nearing zero percent post the global financial crises in 2008. On December 16, 2015, the US Federal Reserve did announce a raise in its key interest rate from a range of 0 percent to 0.25 percent to a range of 0.25 percent to 0.5 percent, with market analysis coalescing with the idea that the Federal Reserve will glide its benchmark interest rate higher two to three times in 2016[24]. The ramification, as a result of the intent of the US Federal Reserve, could lead to a further outflow of equity from the Chinese stock markets as well as other stocks markets in other developing economies; this could lead to a further downward spiralling of the Chinese economy in 2016.

On August 11, 2015, Beijing changed the way it values the yuan, allowing markets to play a greater role in the exchange rate. Market pressure has long been for depreciation, so allowing the currency to be more market-determined would, in the short-term, naturally see the yuan move lower. Fig 6 shows the devaluation of China's yuan vs the US dollar from November 2014 to September 2015. The devaluation of the renminbi isn't because of Beijing's scrambling to save the economy through competitive devaluation. Ian Talley, in a piece in the *Wall Street Journal,* wrote, "Beijing's depreciation was likely more about addressing a key concern for the International Monetary Fund as it considers whether to include the Chinese Yuan in its basket of currencies that comprise its lending reserves than it was about reviving economic growth by juicing exports"[25].

Fig 6: Devaluation of China's Yuan Vs the US Dollar[26]

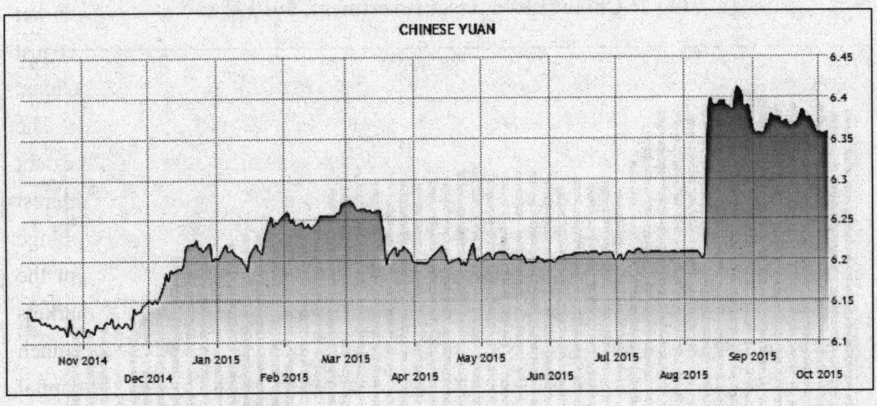

The slow growth rate experienced is also due to the slower Fixed Asset Investment[27] (FAI) growth China has witnessed. Chinese FAI measures the change in the total spending on non-rural capital investments such as factories, roads, power grids and property[28]. Table 2 shows China's fixed asset investment in 2015. As would be seen from the table, China's FAI since January 2015, except in the month of July, has been below the forecast estimate, indicating a slowdown in the economic growth. A higher than expected reading should be taken as a positive sign for economic growth, while a lower than expected reading should be taken as a negative sign for economic growth. Fig 7 on the following page, further elaborates on the downward trend in China's FAI in the last five years.

Table 2: China: Fixed Asset Investment, 2015[29]

Month	Actual	Forecast
January	15.7%	15.8%
February	-	-
March	13.9%	15%
April	13.5%	13.8%
May	12%	13.5%
June	11.4%	12%
July	**11.4%**	**11.2%**
August	11.2%	11.5%
September	10.9%	11.1%

Fig 7: China: Fixed Asset Investment, 2010-2015[30]

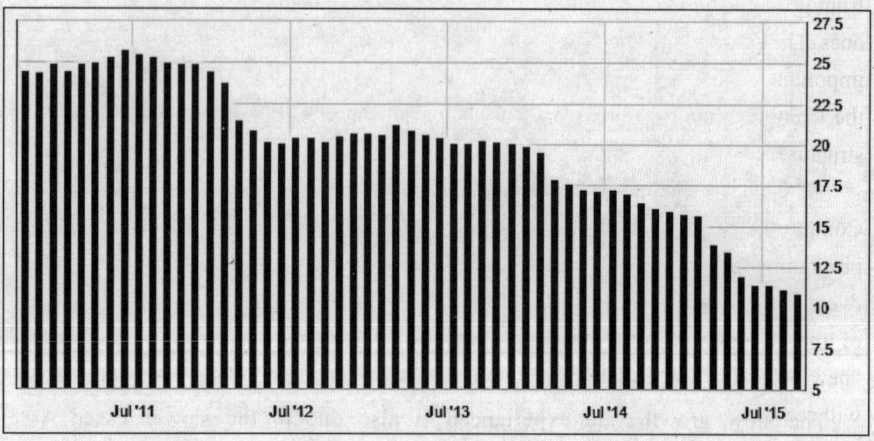

According to Damien Ma from the Paulson Institute, the year 2015 has been a year of transition for China. Once a high-octane growth machine, China would be shifting into the so-called "new normal" gear of development, in which top line GDP will be deemphasised. In addition, according to Ma, 2015 marks the end of the 12th Five-Year Plan cycle and the beginning of the 13th –which would end in 2020, the year by which China is supposed to have become a "moderately well-off society[31]. "During 2015, China will try to keep its economic growth and policies steady and adapt to the 'new normal' of slower speed but higher quality", read a statement released during the Central Economic Work conference held in December 2014.[32]

China's New Model of Economic Growth

China is pursuing a new model of economic growth which focusses on internal consumption rather than exports. In an interview to *C-Span,* Prof Bottelier stated that China's accelerated economic growth in the last few decades had resulted in a lot of problems, one being a huge trade export deficit with other nations. Therefore, in 2006, the central leadership decided to switch to a new model of growth which is focussed on domestic demand rather than export demand. This will be a new kind of shift in China's economic policy which is keen to develop its domestic manufacturing capacity and transition to a new model of growth which is less dependent on exports and more dependent on domestic demand[33]. The concept of "new normal" being propagated by China is characterised by a shift from high speed growth to a medium-to-high one, a shift from focussing on quantity and speed to quality and efficiency in the growth model, a shift from stressing production expansion to improving current production, and a shift from growth being driven by conventional engines to increasingly being driven by new ones. The concept does not necessarily change the fact that China is still in a strategically important period with great prospects, nor does it change the positive fundamentals of the Chinese economy—it calls for a change in the development mode and economic structure.[34]

At the Third Plenum of the Central Committee of the 18th Party Congress of the Communist Party of China in November 2013, the government set out an ambitious programme of 15 key reform areas covering 60 economic and social reforms, with the overarching objective of giving "the market a decisive role in resource allocation" and of improving government efficiency[35]. In May 2014, President Xi Jinping used the term "new normal" to describe an evolving economy of slower growth and new risks that will require a more efficient and effective bureaucracy, the rule of law, as well as other reforms. His premise is that upgraded economic structures and innovation will be the core of a strategy for sustainable, although moderate, growth over the next two decades. President Xi acknowledged the risks and challenges flowing from the new paradigm, and reiterated the collective will to "comprehensively deepen reform" to benefit from this new normal. According to a World Bank report, this transition to the "new normal" would require a better allocation of credit and indigenous capacity for innovation. The report further adds that China's economy will shift from rapid to moderate growth, with an average annual growth of around 5 percent. According to World Bank staff estimates and projections, in 2015, gross capital formation is expected to contribute 44.4 percent points of the GDP, and aggregate consumption, 52.7 percent points. Economic growth will continue moving from an industrial to a service base. A transition from capital and resource-intensive industries to services will remain rapid, facilitated by policies to ease business regulations in the services sector and tighten excess capacity in the industrial sectors. Growth in services is expected to outpace that in manufacturing, contributing more than half of GDP growth by 2017.[36]

Therefore, the new economic model of growth that China is switching towards is consumption-led growth rather than the investment-led growth that is currently happening in China. According to a piece in *The Economist*, on October 3, 2015, "...after three decades in which the country averaged double-digit growth, it is now growing by just over seven percent... until now, the Chinese growth has been powered by investment. But it is shifting towards a greater reliance on consumption…."[37]

Critics on China's economic decline are really overlooking the fact that the growth model has changed in China and the services sector is now the driver of growth. So the fact that industrial growth has slowed down quite a bit does not matter as much today as it would have 10 years ago. Fig 8 below shows China's Purchasing Managers Index (PMI)[38] for its non-manufacturing industries. It should be noted that non-manufacturing PMI tracks the business activities of the services and construction sectors. PMI reading above 50 points indicates that the manufacturing economy is generally expanding and the economy is generally declining when the reading falls below 50 points.

Fig 8: China PMI for its Non-Manufacturing Sector, 2010-2015[39]

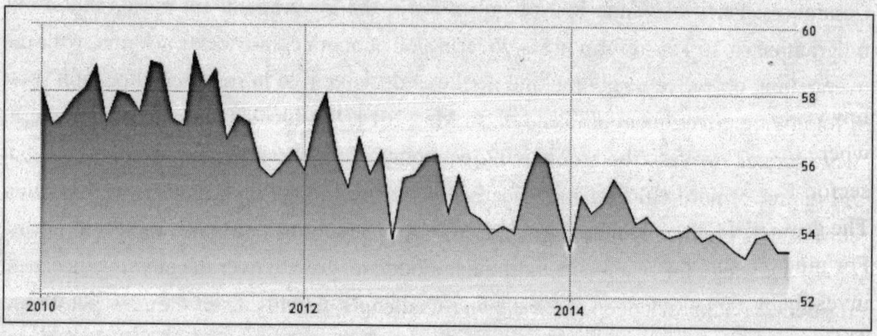

The data presented in Fig 8 highlights the PMI in China's non-manufacturing sector for the last five years. From the figure, it can be seen that there has been a downward trend in China's non-manufacturing PMI. However, it has remained above the 50 point mark, indicating that there has been a continuous expansion and growth in this sector. In 2015 the non-manufacturing PMI has been more on the border with a point of 53.9 in July, up from 53.8 in June and falling to 53.4 points in August, according to reports released jointly by the National Bureau of Statistics and the

China Federation of Logistics and Purchasing (CFLP)[40]. Another indication of China switching towards the services sector is the data from the State Administration of Foreign Exchange (SAFE) on August 31, 2015 which showed an emerging deficit in China's foreign service trade. For instance, service trade deficit in the month of July 2015 stood at Yuan 107.6 billion ($ 16.8 billion) as compared to Yuan 90.9 billion in June[41].

Fig 9: China's FDI Breakdown by Industry, 2010-2014 (in percentage)[42]

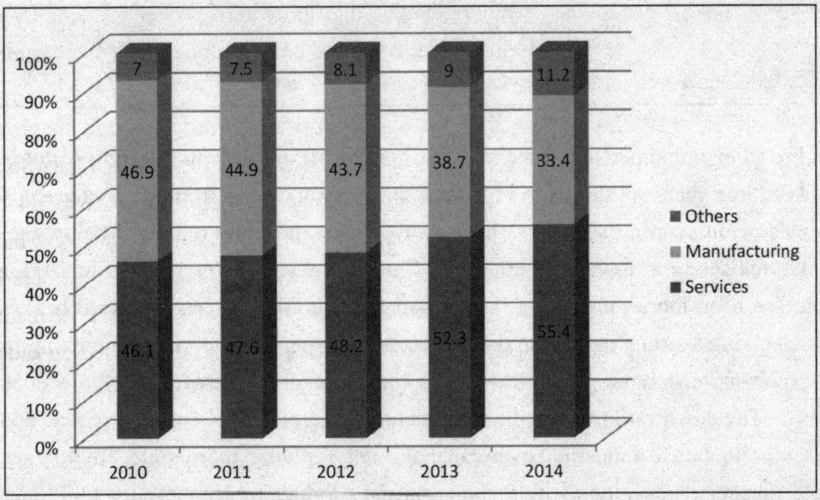

Perhaps the most significant development in the FDI inflow into China in the past few years has been the growth in FDI in the services sector, as can be seen from Fig 9, where the percentage FDI inflow into China has continued to increase in the services sector. In 2014, services attracted $ 66.2 billion in FDI, up 7.8 percent year-on-year. The growth of the services sector FDI reflects an underlying shift in China's economy. For much of the past 30 years, China's economic policies have tended to emphasise investment activities and export-led manufacturing over domestic consumption. This economic model generated high rates of growth, but also led to an economy in which consumption accounted for a relatively smaller part. The emergence of a sizeable middle class has helped to spur the development of the services sector. China's consumers today have increased disposable income and higher demand for quality services, ranging from health care and education to financial services. At the same time, China's government has in recent years been actively encouraging the shift towards a consumption-led economy and the development of a vibrant services sector.[43]

Fig 10: China PMI for its Manufacturing Sector, 2012-2015[44]

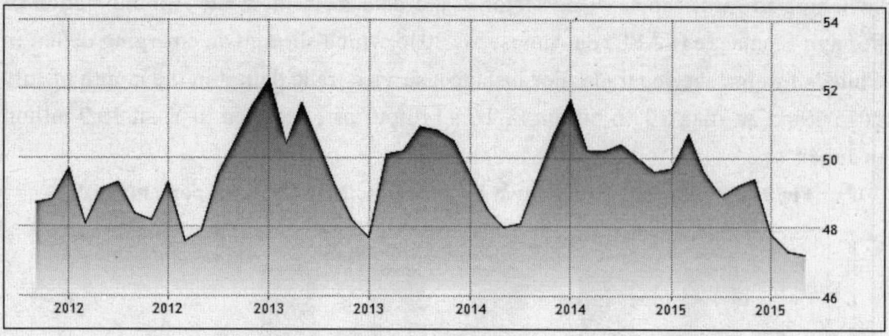

For a better comparison, if we look at China's PMI in the manufacturing sector over the last three years, as shown in Fig 10, it can be seen clearly from the area graph that China's manufacturing sector has been more erratic and often remained below the 50 points, indicating a downward trend in its manufacturing sector growth. In 2015, the trend has been more prevalent as China's manufacturing PMI has remained below 50 points, giving a strong indication that the economic orientation is strongly moving from an export-led economic growth towards a consumption-led, services-driven economic growth. The downward trend in the manufacturing sector is also a result of China taking measures to tackle industrial over-capacity, and applying more rigid environmental protection standards, along with rising costs and a tightening labour market; these have also contributed towards the manufacturing activities' decline[45].

Fig 11 shows the GDP of China in percentage terms over the last decade to highlight how this new economic model adopted by China could have impacted its growth. From the figure, it can be seen that from a GDP of over 14 percent in 2007, the GDP in China has witnessed a downward trend. The past decade that saw China grow in double digit figures has taken a dip and this may well have been as a result of its shift towards a new model of economic growth. The first quarter of 2015 has shown a further dip in its GDP to 7 percent and according to the forecast made by Goldman Sachs, the GDP in 2015 could be about 6.8 percent. Furthermore, in forecasting China's GDP growth for the next three years, that is 2016, 2017 and 2018, Goldman Sachs puts it as 6.4 percent, 6.1 percent and 5.8 percent respectively[46].

Fig 11: China's GDP Growth in Percentage 2005-2014[47]

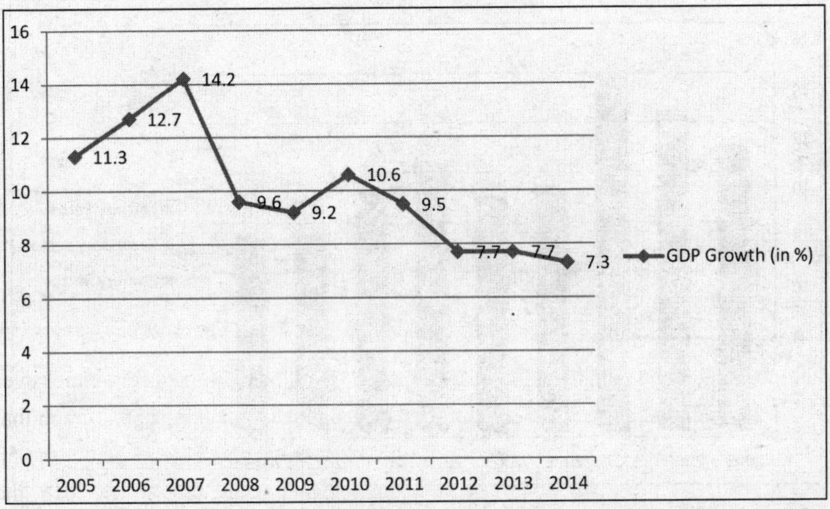

Fig 12 shows the percentage contribution of the three sectors—primary, secondary and tertiary—towards the GDP figure. It is observed that the secondary sector that comprises manufacturing has fallen from a high of 7.1 percent in 2007 to 3.7 percent in 2013. In 2014, the GDP expanded by 7.4 percent with almost half of the GDP growth coming from the services sector. In the first quarter of 2015, the GDP growth continued to taper, with services continuing to remain robust[48]. The decline in the manufacturing sector can be seen more clearly from Fig 13 on the following page, which shows the percentage contribution of the three sectors towards China's GDP. The figure shows clear evidence of a fall in the contribution of the manufacturing sector that is part of the secondary sector towards the GDP, and falling below the tertiary sector that overtook the secondary sector in 2012.

Fig 12: Sectorial Contribution to China's GDP, 2005-2013[49]

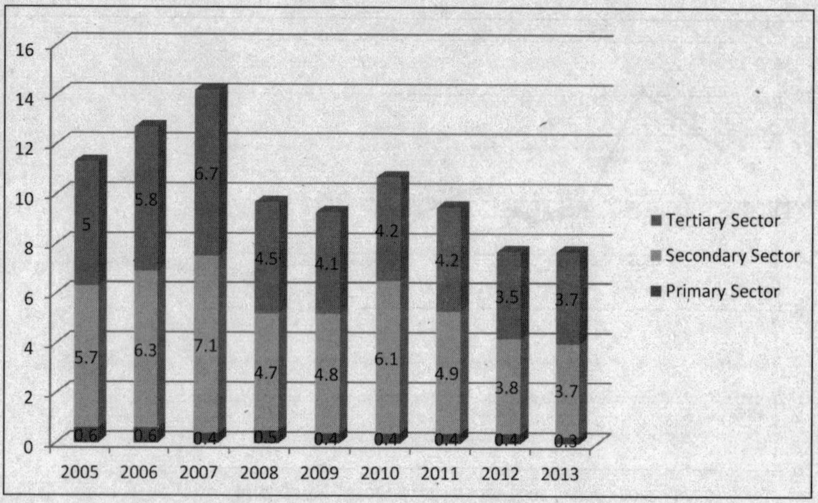

Fig 13: Composition of GDP by the Three Strata of Industry (GDP in percentage)[50]

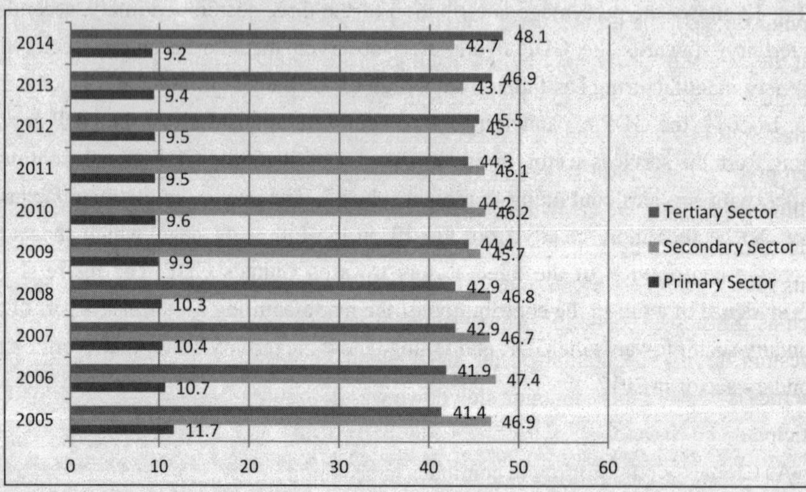

The inference which may be drawn on the basis of these data is that post-2006, China is shifting to a new model of economic growth which is more domestic consumption-led rather than export-led. Through this model of growth, China intends to develop its domestic capacity which is indigenous and less dependent on foreign capital and technologies. Former Chinese President Hu Jintao in his report at the 18th Party Congress on November 17, 2012, stressed on the urgency for this, while stating:

> *...scientific and technological innovation provides strategic support for raising the productive forces and boosting the overall national strength, and we must give it top priority in overall national development. We should follow a path of making innovation with Chinese features and take steps to promote innovation to catch up with global advances....*

On the new model of economic growth, President Hu Jintao stated:

> *...We should adopt policies and measures to better facilitate the development of the real economy. We should make the economy more demand-driven, promote the sound growth of strategic emerging industries and advanced manufacturing industries, speed up the transformation and upgrading of traditional industries, develop and expand the service sector, especially modern service industries, and make the geographical and structural layout of the development of infrastructure and basic industries more balanced....*[51]

Future of China's CNP

Having witnessed the downward spiral of China's economy in 2015, it can be stated that the cause for this cannot be restricted to just external or internal factors. However, the question of whether the Chinese economy has run out of steam may be answered with a definitive 'no', since it has been well established that the Chinese economy has been undergoing reform in its model of economic growth since 2006 and is, therefore, willing to undertake a short-term as well as a medium-term loss, in order to secure a long-term credible growth. No doubt, the Chinese economy has witnessed a curtailment in its growth, and very much so in 2015, but this has been due to various external factors such as the slower economic growth in the West and the nervousness amongst foreign investors due to speculation on the US Federal Reserve rate hike. The question that emerges is whether this economic slowdown was desirable as well as something that was anticipated by China.

As China's economic growth continues to be moderate in 2015, it can be said that the slowdown in its growth is not unexpected and, on the contrary, is desirable from a short-and-medium term perspective. In the short-term, it reflects policies to slow down the rapid credit growth, contain shadow banking, limit the borrowing by local governments and reduce excess capacity in industry. These policies address the vulnerabilities that had built up after the 2008 global financial crisis. Since economic growth prior to 2008 was driven mainly by exports of low value-added, labour-intensive manufacturing goods, this could not be the cause for growth post-2008 economic recession, which has caused a global economic environmental change –with exports no longer being a major driver of growth, as demand has fallen in the West. Over the medium term, lower growth is consistent with a gradual shift in China's growth model, from manufacturing to services, from investment to consumption, and from exports to domestic spending/consumption.[52] Furthermore, the slowdown was something that was anticipated by China's economic policy-makers, who had downgraded the economic forecast and, in most cases, data revealing it to be less than anticipated.

Beijing's economy policy-makers know that even though structural overhauls will moderate growth in the near-term, they will also bolster long-term growth and help avoid a major deceleration. On the issue of its comprehensive national power, it is well established that economics is at the core for Beijing to achieve its goals –since it directly funds its military as well as its defence industries– fuelling Beijing's projected hard as well as soft power. Despite the economic slowdown, according to data from the World Bank on "Military Expenditure (percentage of GDP)", China has had a consistent 2 percent of its GDP going towards its military budget, whereas a country like the United States has reduced its military budget from 4.7 percent in 2010 to 3.5 percent in 2014[53]. The high percentage of the GDP dedicated towards its military expenditure could seem comparatively less when compared with that of the United States. However, it should be realised that the US is militarily engaged globally, which is not the case with China, which till date, has a very limited military foothold globally, with its military concentrated mainly around its vicinity. This would help the PLA to amass enough capacity through the advancement in its military technologies and capabilities, which would push towards its goals of achieving a credible high-tech military that is capable of fighting and winning modern wars.

Beijing has realised that in order to be a global power with an able military, it cannot be dependent solely on technology transfers from the West and, hence, needs to support its defence and military might by undertaking indigenisation of high technologies through domestic research and development. It has also become pertinent for China to innovate and develop its capacity as the country's traditional growth model has shown signs of fatigue in the post-2008 economic recession period. This has enabled domestic investment and consumption to become the main engines of growth.

China is restructuring its industrial growth model by transforming from focussing on labour-intensive sectors to a model driven by advanced technologies. This transformation is forcing Chinese manufacturers to move up their industry value chain by investing more in technology and innovation. China's current Five-Year Plan is in pursuit of achieving this goal and is focussed on developing domestic capacity through huge investments in R&D. According to data on the internal research and development spending in China, it can be seen that from 2006 to 2014, China's expenditure has continued to increase from Yuan 300.31 billion in 2006 to about Yuan 1, 331.2 billion yuan in 2014. The World Bank data on "Research and Development Expenditure (percentage of GDP)" shows that China has increased its expenditure on its internal R&D from 1.76 percent of its GDP in 2000-08 to 1.98 percent in 2010-14[54]. According to the "OECD Science, Technology and Industry Outlook 2014", the squeeze in the R&D budget in the European Union, Japan and the United States, has resulted in a reduction in the weight of the advanced economies in science and technology research, patent applications and scientific publications. China, with its continuous growth in internal R&D spending, is well on track to become the world's top R&D spender by around 2019. According to the United Nation's World Investment Report 2005, there has also been a surge in R&D related FDI inflows into China. These R&D-related FDI inflows have been concentrated in technology-intensive industries such as Information and Communication Industry (ICT), automotive and chemicals. Research from FDI markets and the *Financial Times* data service, revealed that in 2014, China has caught up with the US in attracting foreign investment in R&D. Between January 2010 and December 2014, China attracted 88 greenfield R&D projects from foreign companies, against 91 in the US[55].

China has realised the negative impact of the three decades of its hyper-growth and intends to take corrective measures since it does not want to remain just a manufacturing hub for the West and remain in the "middle-income trap". China's growth, like that of some other countries such as Mexico, Brazil, etc., can be attributed to pairing cutting-edge production technologies with extremely cheap labour. But, in the future, continued rapid growth will require that it develop the capacity to grow based on the quasi-rents of innovation across many sectors. China acknowledges this, as seen in an official goal of moving from "Made in China" to "Innovate in China"[56]. As China's dominance as a manufacturing destination diminishes, with its labour costs in the country rising and its overall FDI inflow rising at a diminishing rate; it has witnessed an offset caused by a successful capturing of higher-value inward investment projects, such as those related to R&D.

However, China needs to realise that investing a mere 2 percent of its GDP into its R&D, would not necessarily translate into growth. Other elements that are necessary to stimulate market growth and reward innovations include reforms in the laws relating to land, labour and environmental issues, and greater emphasis on skill development. Therefore, internal reforms need to be undertaken in order to create a congenial eco-system which would enable the development and growth of its science and technology, which, in turn, will fuel its comprehensive national power.

As highlighted in the paper, despite the visible economic slowdown, China is still clearly a magnet for foreign investment. However, there is also a shift towards more services-related and high-tech investments that are deemed to become the major engines of economic growth for China. This trend is likely to continue as China's overall economy rebalances away from the traditional labour-intensive manufacturing growth towards a services driven high-tech manufacturing and a consumption led growth. Therefore, the entire economic slowdown being witnessed by China will not undermine its goal to achieve its comprehensive national power; not forgetting the fact that despite the big jerk China witnessed in 2015, China's real GDP grew at 6.9 percent – which is a very healthy growth, given the current world economic condition. Furthermore, China still enjoys a favourable balance of trade as well as a very healthy foreign investments inflow through FII and FDI. At the most, the economic turmoil being witnessed in China may be termed as a course correction being undertaken in order to ensure the continuity of a robust economic growth in the long run. Therefore, China's journey towards achieving its CNP could at best be delayed in the short and medium terms; however, it is on the right track given that all international conditions continue to play in its favour. To conclude, it can be stated without a doubt that the Chinese planners are very pragmatic and never consider time to be a factor. For the Chinese, reforms are initiated not with the anticipation of achieving immediate results, rather for positive outcomes after decades or even a century. The current reforms being initiated in its economic and military realms are also long-term ones, during which China is prepared to take on shocks in order to achieve comprehensiveness in its CNP.

Notes

1. "Geopolitical Power Calculations", *China Debates the Future Security Environment,* http://fas.org/nuks/guide/china/doctrine/pills2/part08.htm. Accessed on September 29, 2015.
2. Sean Golden, "China's Perception of Risk and the Concept of Comprehensive National Power", 2013, http://rauli.cbs.dk/index.php/cjas/article/viewFile/4028/4411. Accessed on September 29, 2015.
3. n.1.
4. Greg Autry, "Book Discussion on Death by China", *C-Span,* July 19, 2013, http://www.c-span.org/video/?314071-5/book-discussion-death-china. Accessed on October 5, 2015.
5. Senator Dan Sullivan, "Senate Session on Foreign Relations", *C-Span,* September 25, 2015, http://www.c-span.org/video/?328358-1/us-senate-morning-business&start=5237&transcriptQuery=China. Accessed on October 5, 2015.
6. By this it meant that in case state intervention brought about too many controls in the market, market competition would have to be strongly encouraged. And when the market competition produced a gap between the rich and the poor, there would have to be more emphasis on public guidance.

7. Simei Qing, *From Allies to Enemies: Visions of Modernity, Identity and US-China Diplomacy 1945-1960* (Cambridge: Harvard University Press, 2007), p- 17-20.
8. Satoshi Amako, "China's Foreign Strategy as a Great Power", in Srikanth Kondapalli and Emi Mifune, eds., *China and its Neighbors* (New Delhi: Pentagon Press, 2010), p. 2.
9. Julia Chang Bloch, "Commercial Diplomacy", in Ezra F Vogel. ed., *Living with China: US-China Relations in the 21st Century* (New York: WW Norton & Company, 1997), pp. 186-187.
10. He Jianwu, Li Shantong and Sandra Polaski, "China's Economic Prospects 2006-2020", Trade, Equity and Development Programme, Carnegie Endowment for International Peace, April 2007, http://carnegieendowment.org/files/cp_83_polaski_final.pdf. Accessed on September 15, 2015.
11. "International Trade Statistics 2014", World Trade Organisation, http://www.wto.org/english/res-e/statis_e/its2014_e/its2014_e.pdf. Accessed on October 1, 2015.
12. Phillip C. Saunders, "China's Role in Asia", in David Shambaugh and Michael Yahuda, eds., *International Relations of Asia* (Lanham: Rowman & Littlefield Publishers, Inc, 2010), pp. 128-129.
13. Daniel Blumenthal, "China's Impact on US Economy", *C-Span,* November 18, 2007, http://www.c-span-org/video/?201518-5/chinas-impact-us-economy. Accessed on October 5, 2015.
14. Prof Daniele Schilirò, "Economic Reforms in China: Which Model of Development?" October 14, 2014, http://www.horasis.org/press_releases_all_75.php. Accessed on September 21, 2015.
15. Jianwu, et. al., n. 10.
16. In October 2015, the CPC introduced the "Two Child Policy", in order to overcome its current demographic divide. This policy, if successful, would not only add to the pool of labour force but would also increase domestic consumption and demand – which is part of China's new economic model.
17. "Age Composition and Dependency Ratio of Population", National Bureau of Statistics of China, http://data.stats.gov.cn/english/easyquery.htm?cn=C01. Accessed on October 12, 2015.
18. "China Economic Update June 2015", The World Bank, http://www.worldbank.org/content/dam/Worldbank/document/EAP/China/ceu_06_15_en.pdf. Accessed on September 21, 2015.
19. Jianwu, et.al., n.10.
20. Shanghai Stock Exchange (SSE) Composite Index, http://www.google.com/finance?cid=7521596. Accessed on September 28, 2015.
21. Ibid.
22. "China Foreign Direct Investment", Trading Economics, http://www.tradingeconomics.com/china/foreign-direct-investment. Accessed on October 7, 2015.
23. Matt Schiavenza, "Is China's Financial Crisis Really Bigger than Greece's?", *The Atlantic,* July 9, 2015,http://www.theatlantic.com/international/archieve/2015/07/greece-china-crisis/398066/. Accessed on October 5, 2015.
24. Tom DiChristopher, "The Case for a Single Fed Rate Hike in 2016: Strategist", CNBC, http://www.cnbc.com/2015/12/29/the-case-for-a-single-fed-rate-hike-in-2016-strategist.html. Accessed on December 31, 2015.
25. Ian Talley, "What if the China Panic Is all Wrong?", *The Wall Street Journal,* September 3, 2015, http://blogs.wsj.com/economics/2015/09/03/what-if-the-china-panioc-is -all-wrong/ , accessed on October 5, 2015.
26. "Chinese Yuan", Trading Economics, http://www.tradingeconomics.com/china/currency. Accessed on October 5, 2015.
27. Fixed Asset Investment or FAI is a measure of capital spending. It refers to any investment within the measurement period in physical assets, such as real estate infrastructure, machinery, etc., that are held for more than one year. FAI can be a good indicator for how much investments are occurring in a country or region, but it is not a direct contributor to GDP. See http://lexicon.ft.com/Term?term=fixed-asset-investment. Accessed on October 7, 2015.

28. "China Fixed Asset Investment YOY", Investing.com, http://www.investing.com.com/economic-calendar/chinese-fixed-asset-investment-460. Accessed on October 7, 2015.
29. Ibid.
30. Ibid.
31. Damien Ma, "4 Experts' Predictions for the Global Economy in 2015", *The Atlantic,* December 26, 2014, http://www.theatlantic.com/international /archive/2014/12/4-expert-predictions-for-the-global-economy-in-2015/384061. Accessed on October 5, 2015.
32. The Central Economic Work Conference held in December 2014, sketched out the government's guiding economic policies and priorities for the country for 2015. To reach the desired goal in 2015, the leaders vowed to accelerate reforms, further open up the economy, encourage innovation and improve low-income people's life.
33. Prof Pieter Bottelier, "China's Economy and the US Stock Market", September 1, 2015, http://www.c-span.org/video/?327812-4/washington-journal-pieter-bottelier-chinas-economy-us-stock-market. Accessed on September 16, 2015.
34. "China to Keep 2015 Growth Policy Steady Under 'New Normal'", Xinhua News Agency, December 11, 2014, http://news.xinhuanet.com/english/china/2014-12/11/c-133848770.htm. Accessed on October 5, 2015.
35. "China Economic Update June 2015", The World Bank, http://www.worldbank.org/content/dam/Worldbank/document/EAP/China/ceu_06_15_en.pdf. Accessed on September 21, 2015.
36. Ibid.
37. "Running out of Puff", *The Economist,* October 3, 2015, http://www.economist.com/news/asia/21670084-region-not-crisis-slower-growth-hurting-running-out-puff. Accessed on October 5, 2015.
38. PMI is an indicator of the economic health of the manufacturing and non-manufacturing sectors. The PMI index is based on five major indicators: new orders, inventory levels, production, supplier deliveries and the employment environment.
39. http://www.tradingeconomics.com/china/non-manufacturing-pmi Accessed on October 6, 2015.
40. "China's Non-Manufacturing PMI Improves in July", English GOV CN, The State Council, The People's Republic of China, http://english.gov.cn/archive/statistics/2015/08/01/content_281475158776677.htm. Accessed on October 6, 2015.
41. "Foreign Service Trade Deficit Rises", August 31, 2015, http://english.gov.cn/archive/statistics/2015/08/31/content_281475179802808.htm. Accessed on October 6, 2015.
42. "China Outlook 2015", *KPMG Global China Practice,* http://www.kpmg.com/ES/es/Internacionalizacion-KPMG/Documents/China-Outlook-2015.pdf. Accessed on October 6, 2015.
43. Ibid.
44. http://www.tradingeconomics.com/china/manufacturing-pmi. Accessed on October 6, 2015.
45. n.42.
46. Ansuya Harjani, "Goldman Takes a Knife to China GDP Forecasts", August 31, 2015, http://www.cnbc.com/2015/08/31/goldman-takesw-a-knife-to-china-gdp-forecasts.html. Accessed on September 23, 2015.
47. National Bureau of Statistics of China, "National Data", http://data.stats.gov.cn/english/easyquery.htm?cn=CO1. Accessed on September 23, 2015.
48. "China Economic Update, June 2015", *The World Bank,* http://www.worldbank.org/content/dam/Worldbank/document/EAP/CHina/ceu_06_15_en.pdf. Accessed on October 6, 2015.
49. n.47.
50. Ibid.

51. "Full Text of Hu Jintao's Report at 18th Party Congress", November 11, 2012, http://http://www.china-embassy.org/eng/zt/18th_CPC_National_Congress_Eng/t992917.htm. Accessed on July 30, 2015.
52. n.48.
53. "Military Expenditure (percentage of GDP)", World Bank, http://data.worldbank.org/indicator/MS.MIL.XPND.GD.ZS. Accessed on October 8, 2015.
54. Expenditures for R&D are current and capital expenditures (both public and private) on creative work undertaken systematically to increase knowledge, including knowledge of humanity, culture and society and the use of knowledge for new applications. R&D covers basic research, applied research and experimental development. http://data.worldbank.org/indicator/GB.XPD.RSDV.GD.ZS. Accessed on October 8, 2015.
55. Courtney Fingar, "China Passes US in Race for FDI in Research and Development", *The Financial Times,* July 22, 2015, http://www.ft.com/intl/cms/s/3/241d9366-3058-11e5-91ac-a5e17d9b4cff.html#axzz3nWcGwbcv. Accessed on October 8, 2015.
56. n.48.

6

Becoming a Sea Power in East Asia: China's Quest for Regional Hegemony

Swati Arun

Introduction

Asian geo-politics continues to search for a balance between one country's expanded self-interests and other countries' national security concerns. It is evident from China's behaviour that it will try to employ all its resources to attain what it considers is crucial for its national security, and other countries must understand and comply. Interestingly, the response to such an attitude by the neighbouring countries has been sombre, the reason being that they are free-riding on the US presence and security guarantee. A slight shift was noticed in the region's military expenditure after the US urged the countries to contribute to security in the Asia-Pacific to counter 'other' forces. This move by the US also implied the unwillingness of the US to readily commit to the employment of power under provocation by the revisionist forces. Due to decades of stability, and reliance on the US presence, the East Asian neigbours have a huge gap to fill to be able to stand strong under an attack by China. China has been taken as the centre of conflict due to the disputes it is engaged in under the pretext of 'affecting its core interests'.

China's geography, primarily, makes it a continental power, while it also enjoys a coastline that is approximately 14,500 km long. In the words of Alan Wachman, "Geography... does condition the choices made by policy-makers, presenting both opportunities and constraints, [but it]... does not determine the strategic ambitions or policies of a state".[1] While from this paper one might recognise the importance of geography in subconsciously deriving a long-term strategy for a country, it does agree on how geography can be both an opportunity and a restriction for a nation. For China too, the long continental boundary represents a constraint in its ambition of becoming a sea power, and, given the current maritime environment and boundary, it becomes a necessity.

Map 1: Map of China

If China looks towards maintaining a larger navy which could control its sea boundaries and preserve its interests, the neighbouring countries would lose their strategic autonomy (having China as a regional power). But if China desires to achieve regional hegemony, it must control the seas. The contention here is that China does not enjoy a geographical insularity or a weak neighbourhood to expedite the process. It is also engaged in territorial claims which threaten the security of individual nations that are bound to resist China's approach to the sea and its claims.

This paper argues that given the territorial problems in East Asia, China would find it difficult to achieve sea power status which is the only a means to the end—regional hegemony. The paper also reflects upon the logic of expanding into the sea while having troublesome continental boundaries, whereby China would not be able to sustain its sea power. This is not to say that China would not be able to achieve a sea power status; it is a question of whether it will be able to sustain it. The paper will also present the argument for balancing in East Asia—how China is more likely to get balanced in this scenario. China is not the only continental power to have chosen to expand into the sea, and this is not the first time that China is trying to build its navy – the four voyages of Adm Zheng He during the Ming dynasty in the 15th century are testimony to this. Given the US presence, a hostile maritime environment and China's unfounded territorial claims, the quest for regional hegemony for China is likely to prove detrimental for Asian geo-politics.

The undying puzzle of our time is the evident failure of a balancing apparatus against the US. And it has become increasingly clear that the Waltzian balance of power paradigm suffers from a deficit in the logical reasoning to support the absence of balancing and *lack of motivation* by secondary powers to balance against US 'supremacy'. The US, an insular power, is also the leading sea power and land power. Its annual defence budget surpasses that of the next seven countries combined. But as conventional wisdom states in realist circles, superior 'offence-defence' capabilities (on land or at sea) are resisted by second in line powers. How then has the US managed to keep the world at large weaker and unable to have a coalition against it? Is it the geographical distance from Europe, or its insularity that has helped the US sustain its growth? Is it the maritime power, transitioning into globalisation that has sustained the US growth and dominance in the world? Or the proactive alliance-making, removal of the threat to its national security (creating imbalance of power), and constricting the growth of historically aggressive nations like Russia, Japan and Germany? Objectively, one cannot deny the geographical bonus that the US has enjoyed, easing its road to success and, later, supremacy.

The geographical distance from the European theatre provided the US with an advantageous option that helped it in making good strategic choices: strategic entry in World War II, the North Atlantic Treaty Organisation (NATO), nexus of alliances, military bases all over the globe, etc. The US had the choice to enter the World Wars and participate, as little or as much as it wanted to. The argument stands corrected that *an insular state has an 'unfair' advantage over all other kinds for the basic fact that it is insular and, hence, can maintain strategic autonomy.*[2]

Recent theorisation by Jack Levy and W. Thompson, *that great powers do not intend to ally against the leading sea power* provides an alternate explanation for the lack of balancing in the present system, with two exceptions–China and Russia. But even here, the two countries can only be seen as internally balancing, if at all, against the US. This is not to deny the intensity with which China might be (internally) balancing against the US. However, balancing can only be argued as present if the specific purpose is deterrence by punishment as opposed to denial. But the current political environment in East Asia puts

China in a bad light (a 'belligerent', and 'irresponsible' great power) and strengthens the US' position as the smaller countries are extensively trying to be self-dependent and/or forging and renewing the partnership with the US, elevating the US' legitimacy.

An extensive study has been done over the difference between sea powers and land powers. However, is it true that insular powers are perceived as non-threatening despite an unrivalled naval capability? *Ceteris paribus*, navies are of less utility than armies for destroying a political order, hence, present less territorial threat.[3] But control and denial of the sea both render heavy costs for the lesser powers. Assuming that a leading sea power will depreciate a nation's concern for national security as not being true, but a great power's disability to forge an alliance against such a power is hard to refute.

If a rising power, with both land boundaries and a huge ocean, could accumulate both powers—on land and at sea—how would it define the global/regional power politics? Can China be studied as one such case, as it shares land boundaries with 14 countries, compelling it to accumulate superior land capabilities, and embark upon gaining leverage at sea? China makes for another interesting case study where, in East Asia, an 'alliance' is forming against the 'challenger' to the present regional order (China) and not the 'hegemon' (the US).

China, a continental power, has its most serious national security disputes lying at sea. The threat to the national economy comes from the sea as, statistically, "41 percent of the national population, more than 50 percent of the largest cities, more than 70 percent of the national GDP, 84 percent of FDI, 90 percent of the export-related production are concentrated in regions located within 200 km from the eastern coastline…97 percent of [China's] foreign trade is transported by sea"[4]. The main territorial threat comes from the US naval presence in East Asia and Southeast Asia—the 're-balance strategy' is viewed as the US having tightened "its global military presence…reinforced its military presence in the Asia-Pacific region, and pushed its pawns forward in China's periphery in an attempt to build up a strategic fence around China, particularly at sea"[5] (Tang, Wu; 2002:93-94). The reasons for China's efforts to modernise its naval force can be seen as constraints imposed by the US presence. The modernisation that should have brought 'peace' to Chinese decision-makers, produced counter-productive effects in the region—militarisation by the neighbours at an unprecedented rate, which poses a security dilemma for the Chinese.

Historically, a continental power could not manage to have both maritime and ground (land) capabilities, because it "will leave itself vulnerable by lack of investment in its ground capabilities—an unlikely choice"[6]. Britain never had any stakes in the continental European system, maintaining the stance of an offshore balancer. But great powers like Japan (before 1945), Netherlands (17th century), France (17th-20th centuries) had to choose between keeping one kind of capability, as geographical circumstances played a primary role in outcomes, despite the state's ambition. France and Netherlands were forced to focus on the continent and maintain ground capabilities as the imbalance among the land powers spurted. Such fissures kept these great powers from projecting maritime capabilities as they could not afford to rely on the intentions of the neighbours and ignore the fragile balance of power. On the other hand, Japan, a sea power, ceded control of Liaodong Peninsula and Formosa (Taiwan) in 1894, after the first Sino-Japanese War (1894-95). However, Japan had to give up the Liaodong Peninsula due to the fact that it could not resist the combined forces of Germany, France and Soviet Russia.

During this time period, in 1941, Soviet Russia, owing to its strategic maritime and trade interests, built the Port Arthur fortress[7]. The act provoked Japan while it was still trying to include Korea into the Japanese Empire. Japan attacked the Russian fleet at Port Arthur, securing a complete victory. The historical significance of this victory can be seen in the Japanese attack on Pearl Harbour in 1941. But Japan could not sustain the involvement in a different continent and the cost of conflict (exaggerated due to involvement in two different countries) eventually led to its defeat in World War II.

Balance of Power and Insularity

> *Theory is a process by which we coordinate our ideas, define the meaning of the words we use, grasp the difference between essential and unessential factors, and fix and expose the fundamental data on which everyone is agreed.*
>
> –Julian Corbett.

The chief purpose of a theory is to meet the expectations generated by it. However, in cases where expectations do not correspond to the reality (or some realities), the theory stands weak and inapplicable. In the present scenario, the balance of power theory, once the fundamental in understanding international relations, lacks lustre for the inability and, hence, inapplicability in explaining the current world order. In retrospect, there are several cases where balance of power could not occur and prevent hegemonic instability. Key empirical anomalies, besides the US, are Great Britain during the 19th century, China from the 13th to the early 19th century, and Netherlands in the 17th century.

In *Balance of Power* (Waltz), there is neither a description of alliance behaviour in a situation where there is one superpower, nor a prescription for such situations. Balance of power theorists do not indulge in situations of equilibrium, as the premise maintains that sooner or later, equilibrium will be restored, and the system will always move towards achieving a balance. Lack of explanation for certain times where balance of power could not emerge or be achieved through concerted efforts, has left the theory wanting. And these were empirically *insular sea powers* (maritime powers) against which balancing could not succeed (Levy, Thompson: 2011).

It is true that balance of power theory pleads ignorance when it comes to explaining absence of balancing against maritime powers of the past and present (the US), revealing it to be (arguably) a 'continental' theory. But it cannot be said that because balance of power lacks a descriptive fit, it lacks explanatory value as well. Often, theory is applied much too liberally, and, subsequently, when its abstraction fails to generate appropriate outputs, as per the expectations, becomes obsolete. Balance of power theory is a key element of realism and neo-realism of international relations and it remains so. However, the fractures should not render it useless if they can be remedied through further abstraction and understanding.

Case for China

China did not get balanced from the 4th to the mid-3rd and from the 13th to the 19th centuries. The Qin rulers played a divide and conquer strategy (Victoria: 2005) to counter the strategy of uniting the weaker states (balance of power). Qin was located to the far west of the ancient Chinese system, and the alliance pattern to balance the advancing eastward expansion by Qin was to form a vertical bulwark linking Yan and Zhao in the north, Han and Wei in the centre, and Chu in the south. To break this alliance, Qin sought to form a *lianheng* or horizontal alliance with Han, Wei and Qi. Qin's 51 expansionist wars from 356-221 BC met with only eight allied responses. The alliances under the *hezong* strategy could not manage to block the rise of the Qin Empire. Qi, the hegemonic power of that time, did not consider Qin a threat. In contrast to allies having a unified command, Han, Wei and Zhao chose to fight separate wars, hence,gave a chance to Qin to defeat them one by one. Eventually, the states made 'peace' with Qin, resulting in bandwagoning but not balancing. In the later years, the alliances could not be successfully formed, given the conflict of interest thereby allowing Qin to dissolve the alliance preemptively. By 298 BC, Qin waged a total war of unification marked by military prowess (Lewis: 1999: 638). From the Yuan Dynasty till the Qing Dynasty, China repeatedly suffered setbacks in the maritime domain, even though for a brief period during the Ming Dynasty, China invested in a powerful navy. While it could establish hegemony beyond its boundaries and never got balanced from the 11th to the 19th centuries by any alliance of states, it could not sustain it and shrank during the Qing Dynasty.

The dismal failure of the balance of power strategy in China leaves a gap in understanding as to why the neighbours could not understand that they had a chance of success if they fought a unified war against a not so powerful Qin military (collective security problem).

The balance of power could not emerge against a continental power and led it into hegemony. The Chinese Warring States' behaviour mirrored that of their European counterparts and sought realist methods of expanding and maximising security. However, balance of power could not be restored as the neighbours failed to grasp the essence of balancing, and a united command. Moreover, it removes the mysticism of the ancient Chinese system of a benign power within a unified China and tributary state system outside. And from the 13th century to the 19th century, China did not get challenged by Japan—an insular state. In fact, China could establish a legitimate hierarchical regional order where nations looked for support from China in the face of danger from foreign invaders (security guarantor). However, it was not sustainable as China's power declined and Japan utilised its geographical advantage, being an insular nation.

Having established the lack of balancing in the ancient Chinese order, one might compare it with the current regional situation. At the present moment, a clear balancing coalition is absent. It can be said that the neighbours—Japan, South Korea, Philippines, and Vietnam—are indulging in arms accumulation to remain prepared for any future armed conflict with China. But there is still no clear sign if they will *unite* under any attack on one or all. The presence of the US is an utmost crucial variable in this equation. The speedy growth of the Chinese military and wealth has transformed it into a challenger nation trying to expand its territorial waters. Despite such actions which are detrimental to the sovereignty of the whole region, no coalition has been formed. The threat is now that it might be too late to tackle China if the environment lets it grow further. Deterring China might not gain momentum and fail for the lack of will of the neighbours to come to each other's and (in the absence of the US).

The same imbalance of power that the US created for maximising its self-interest encouraged extreme reliance on the US. However, post-2010, when the China threat became a visible reality, the US started urging the neighbouring nations to contribute to the global security through modernising their own militaries, as opposed to the post ColdWar policy of 'providing' security. Due to this tendency of relying on the US, China has, in effect become the regional power. And if the US fails to keep its commitment to the countries (in any event, of threat or use of force) in the region, it could cause bandwagoning.

One of the reasons why the neighbours are reluctant in 'balancing' China beyond modernising, is the economic benefit provided by China. There is a visible lack of will to balance against China, as it would not be desirable for any party (including the US) to jeopardise economic growth, unless it is under duress, given the extreme threat to national security (and in the US' case, its position as a superpower). However, this is not to deny that nations will forgo economic benefits if there is a threat to their very survival.

Scholars have tried to explain this through the argument that sea powers do not get balanced as opposed to continental powers (Levy, Thompson: 2011; Liska: 1977). The US was first a land power, expanding into the sea gradually, in isolation. From the 16th century onwards, the US built its army and later,its navy, without any balancing from Britain in Canada, Mexico or Latin America. The fight for independence from Britain in the 1700s cannot qualify to be balancing and later, during World War I and World War II, Britain had already relinquished its hegemony to survive the European continental wars. China too, is growing in 'isolation' without any blockade like that on Russia, Japan or Germany in the past. China has almost neutralised its land boundaries and is now moving into the sea. It is possible that the hesitation/ reluctance and confusion among the neighbours in deciding the action policy for China will help it to become a land power as well as a sea power. The argument that sea powers do not get challenged must also take into consideration the proximity and stability of the international order. The US' military maximisation occurred while the rest of the world was starkly unstable. Chinese maximisation might not happen as the regional order is much more stable under the US, and China cannot yet afford a conflict with the US and replace it as a security guarantor. Another anomaly is that sea powers thrive on trade, they promote *laissez faire*, and maintaining freedom of navigation is crucial for their survival. A continental power like China (due to the geographical imposition on policy and ideology) tends to behave like a territorial, expansionist power, looking at the sea also as a territory. It is unlikely for other maritime neighbours of the region to rely on China to keep the sea routes free, and the trade, smooth. An argument has been made that China sees the waters around it as an extension of its land territory, which it must control. In case China succeeds in dominating the seas around it, Taiwan, the Philippines, and Vietnam would suffer greatly as the former would be able to blockade the open seas and, hence, maritime trade, for these countries. In the extreme case, China might want a Sino-centric regional order, as shown in Map 2 below:

Map 2: Trade Routes and Geographical Chokepoints

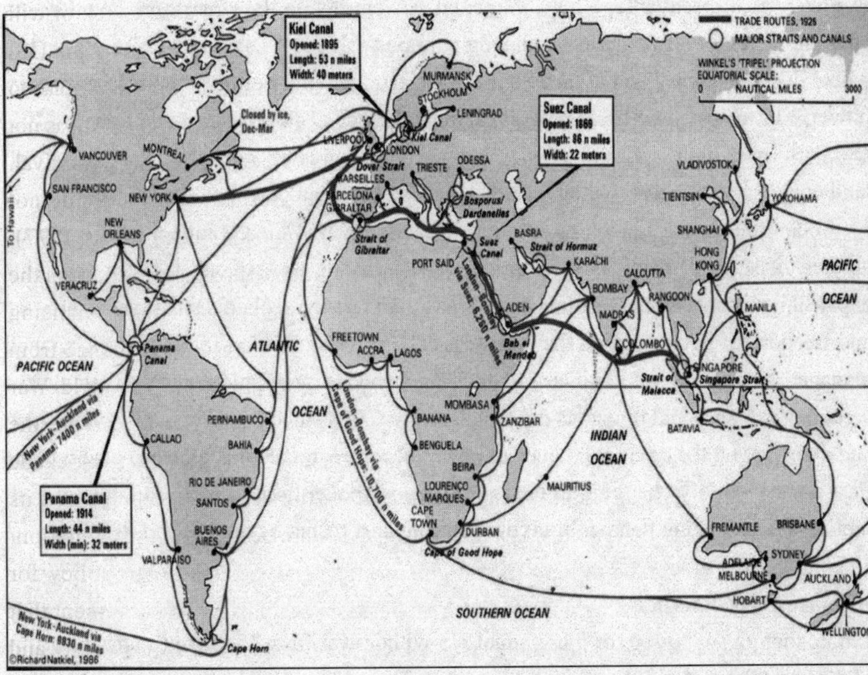

Source: CIMSEC

China does not have access to the open seas and its maritime trade passes through several chokepoints. China's reliance on export of goods and import of oil makes for a disadvantageous situation where sanctions could be used as a weapon, crippling the economy.

Notions of Land Power and Sea Power

Focus on geography provides a comprehensive outlook on a country's foreign policy—how it develops both as a sea power and a land power. For example, a land power will have expansionist tendencies urging it to expand, and a large army to protect the said territory, for that is the only way to maximise security. The differences in the balancing approaches against the sea power and land power also generate from geographical differences. Jack Levy and William Thompson in their essay "Balancing on Land and at Sea" concluded that sea powers do not get balanced. They have attempted to prove the hypothesis that states ally with the leading global power—a sea power—which can also be a land power. George Liska (1977) has attempted to understand a similar concept in his book *Quest for Equilibrium: America and the Balance of Power on Land and Sea,* deducing balance of power as a disadvantage for continental powers, while their maritime counterparts have the leverage of geography, making it impossible for balancing to take place. But where does balancing and alliance behaviour stand when it comes to both land and sea powers? In history, two great powers, namely, France (1495-present) and Spain (1495-1808) enjoyed both land and sea dominance. The degree of capability at both sea and land could suggest balancing against them as against a sea power or land power.

Today, the world is looking at another such power: China. China enjoys a certain amount of security from its land borders and is trying to 'expand' into the sea. This expansion will cost other maritime neighbours their territorial claims on the same territory and freedom of navigation on the high seas. The network of security on the sea, so well managed by the US (superpower) is also threatened if one regional power establishes certain dominance and threatens the establishment. And since China could be both a land and a sea power, the case for balance of power becomes interesting. One can observe that East Asia is rapidly changing in terms of military modernisation and economic growth hinting at a balancing behaviour taking place against China by the US and its allies.

Alliances and Balance

China, though supportive of the gradual US withdrawal from Vietnam (under the terms of the Paris Peace Accord signed in January 1973), was alarmed by the disengagement of pro-US regimes in South Vietnam and Cambodia in 1975. Beijing saw in the unification of an 'expanding' Soviet power with a unified Vietnam that would now fill the power vacuum left by the US danger to its own national security. The Chinese fear urged the US to remain actively involved (militarily, economically, and politically) in Asia and warned the region of the expansionist agenda of the Soviets.[8]

The international system expands or contracts when one or more states decline or rise. Such changes often arise from cleavages in inter-state relations, which are different from regular rivalries. The gaps and differences are qualitative, giving rise to a gradual erosion of checks and balances in the form of incompatible assessment of each other's capabilities, intentions and interests. Such schisms usually end with the fight to control more than just territory, which has universal implications. The source of conflict can be anything from religion or ideology to an alternative international order. At times, such gaps have emerged from the sea, pertaining to its significance for naval power and maritime commerce.[9]A maritime power or a continental power, both have served the purpose of threat or use of force effectively. Thereby, the ambiguity in understanding and, hence,analysing the difference in the effect that a continental power and a sea power has on the international system is of recurrent focus for inter-state relations. However, at times, nations fail to comprehend the above differences that tilt the balance of power in one's favour. An example is the 19th-20th century European system when actors tried to maintain such a balance and failed, resulting in the two World Wars.

Essence of Geography

Land and sea powers (the former surrounded by territorial rivals, and the latter by protective moats) have more than physical geography to set them apart. The essence of geography lies in the advantages it entails, like, for a sea power, it is in the ability to regulate the balance in the mechanics of balance of power, attract alliances and hold a higher bargaining power. Both kinds of powers perceive the 'reality' differently. The understanding of national security threats, sufficient capability, and capability to moderate balance of power come from different rules guiding them.

The alliance system in balance of power works primarily to aggregate power. The discord between land and sea power generates from the latter's ability to restrict the movement of the land power and expansion of the alliance system, making it *insular.*

One of the indispensable qualities of a sea power is 'marinism', the emphasis being on trade, thus, creating an image of a benign power. Economy is the necessity and the incentive to reach further to maximise profit. A maritime power might have a smaller army, with fewer offensive capabilities, because its strategy is not to conquer or expand, not requiring a large army, to trade with other nations. For an island state, it is of utmost importance to trade and, hence, have a merchant navy, and military naval fleet to protect its trade, sea lines of communication, and also,its territory. A maritime power's incentive is in economic growth which comes with the interaction with other nations and exploiting resources, and not from expanding physical territory. The tendency to expand the 'borders' into another continent is rare and impractical for national powers.

There have been very few sea powers, and fewer insular powers throughout history. The rarity of having a sea power (maximum three at any given time) complemented by the geographical advantage, urges land powers to have a different strategic approach, one that does not fear the sea power, rather, benefits from it, allies with it, and treats it as an offshore balancer, while the neighbour with which a state is sharing an actual land boundary will always have a fear of invasion—a perennial national security threat. Insular powers and maritime powers are a handful; fewer patterns have been accounted for their behaviour, hence they remain less researched and theories remain continental in nature.

In 1915, Norman Angell addressed the issue of why the world does not fear British 'marinism',but fears German 'militarism' by arguing that "'marinism' does not encroach on social and political freedom, and militarism does"[10].

Since sea powers have smaller armies, with fewer capabilities to threaten the integrity of land powers, the latter tend to focus on the immediate threat—other continental powers. A land power is associated with large armies, capable of easily crossing borders, invasions and seizing territory. Hence, such a power is capable of destroying political structures and establishing new social systems. The underlying intention is that a land power's territorial security relies on expansion, maintaining minimum threat and maximum security. But the presence of the sea around a state protects the neighbouring states/actors from any expansionist goals. A nation's foreign policy is deeply engaged in its own geography and the environment around it, and the underlying fact that despite having military technology that might nullify the advantage of a sea power, it will still not be perceived as more threatening than a mediocre land power.

Such a notion creates a deficit of incentives to balance against a leading sea power; in fact, it improves the chances for bandwagoning; for a similar reason, land powers suffer a disadvantage by triggering the counter-balancing coalition against them much more easily. Thereby, sea powers, besides the benefit of geography, trade and goodwill, are also less likely to get balanced by other actors (including leading land powers).

The assumption that sea powers do not get balanced by continental powers and that the latter are more likely to ally with the former fits well with the current global order–absence of balancing against the US. But its relations with China do not throw much light on such an intangible pattern. China is predominantly a land power and its sea power status can be debated. China is effectively trying to alter the international order by creating a 'regional power' space for itself, unacceptable to the US.

The international order is perpetually trying to reach re-equilibrium. But the restoration of equilibrium would mean different things to different actors. The power trying only to maintain the balance, which might be in its favour already, would have hegemonic tendencies. And the ones trying to alter the global order, will become the dissatisfied, revisionist powers. Each party trying to maintain such a balance will seek alliances with similar interests. The alliances, therefore, play a major role in deciding which way the order will move, where smaller nations deliberate the advantage of joining either party.

In the case of East Asia, China stands alone, with no official allies (except Pakistan and North Korea as defence partners), while the presence of the US—which has maintained balance in the region and is in favour of peace and stability – is unacceptable to China. The 'threat' from the rise of China has also pressed upon the smaller nations to suspend inter-allied conflicts and tighten their bonds. Japan, the Philippines, Vietnam and the US have been proactively involved in unifying their efforts in maintaining higher levels of maritime protection.

The belief that the neighbours are looking at China as an aspiring sea power, therefore, trying to upgrade their navies, stands valid. The US has re-emphasised on regional security through multiplied efforts to initiate multilateral defence partnerships, and modernisation of individual states for self-defence. It has also rejuvenated the balance of power phenomenon against China, in consonance with its role as prime security provider in the region. The fact that China still remains a major land power trying to become a sea power has introduced new fear in the neighbours, something they didn't have with the 'rising America'. The rise of a secondary power was mostly aided by the senior powers, while trying to restore the balance or upset it. However, what had never happened before was that the US was not empowering any nation to become a regional hegemon, but taking away that power through the security guarantee, the way Britain aided Japan against Russia, helping Japan become a regional hegemon in East Asia, surpassing China. But when the US aided China against Russia, it did not let China project any such military or political influence in challenging US presence overall.

Alliance behaviour towards a sea power and a land power is a topic that has not been dealt with, together with the underlying distinction in behaviour. It can be debated whether the two powers are ever distinct from each other. Several hypotheses have been tested and they can provide a valid reasoning and pattern of behaviour of the states dealing with either of the powers: (1) great powers generally do not balance against the most powerful sea power in the system, even if it is significantly increasing in strength; (2) the stronger the leading sea power's relative capability position, the less likely it is that other great powers will balance against it; (3) the stronger the leading sea power's relative capability position, the less likely that large coalitions will form against it; (4) the stronger the leading sea power's relative capability position, the more likely it is that one or more great powers will ally with it.[11] Hence, if China became a leading sea power, balancing between its land and sea capabilities, it might become difficult for a non-regional power to sustain the costs of conflict with China and the non-regional power would eventually move out of the region. For the regional smaller powers, it would mean severe loss of 'freedom'.

China: A Sea Power?

The increase in the relevance of the Mahanian theory of "whoever rules the waves, rules the world" and supremacy of naval power can be seen over the years, through China's attention to its sea vulnerability and improvement of the People's Liberation Army Navy

(PLAN) to overcome it. China's (official) military budget rose from Yuan 29 billion in 1990 to Yuan 886.9 billion in 2015. However, due to the lack of transparency in the Chinese political system, in the eyes of the world, the figures remain an understatement of the actual spending. The figures are also inaccurate because China does not include Research and Development (R&D) related expenditure or import of weapons. China currently spends about 24 percent of the total budget on the navy, 19 percent and 24 percent on the army and air force, respectively. In the last two decades alone, China launched five classes of destroyers, four new classes of frigates, three new classes of diesel submarines, and a new class of nuclear attack submarine.Among the destroyers, the Type 052C and the Type 052D are the most modern and state-of-the-art platforms. The Type 052C is designed as an air defence ship that could form the air defence component of a battle group. Both destroyers are fitted with the navalised HQ-9, which is the re-engineered variant of the S-300 Surface-to-Air Missile (SAM) system. The platform can be compared to the US Aegis system, though it is not as sophisticated as the Aegis; also, the Chinese system lacks missile defence capability. The Type 052D is designed as a Guided Missile Destroyer(DDG). China will be equipping all of its DDGs with the naval variant of the DH-10 missile. PLAN is also upgrading its submarine force. China's numerous diesel-electric and nuclear attack submarines form the most potent anti-ship component in its Anti-Access and Area Denial (A2/AD) strategy. The new submarines that were inducted are expected to be technologically more advanced in terms of stealth and armaments.

Naval modernisation alone does not label a country as a challenger or a rising sea power. But a close look at China's take on maritime issues in the last decade is a reflection on the change in policy and focus from land to sea. This is not to say that a newly independent China did not have a plan to use the surrounding water bodies to its advantage, but since the threats from land were more significant and imminent, naval modernisation had to wait. One of the concerns for Mao Zedong was "to counter US naval hegemony" in the Western hemisphere (Liu, 2012, quoted in Lim: 2014). The Korean War and Taiwan Strait crisis also brought embarrassment to China when the Seventh Fleet deployment in the Taiwan Strait went unopposed. In response, Mao insisted that "in order to oppose imperialist aggressions, we have to build a powerful navy" (Liu 2007:305). Tracing China's military doctrine has shown gradual change in ambitions, for example, in its first three decades, the doctrine suggested protection of coastal waters only, as China prepared for local land wars. Improvement in *naval capabilities, besides being costly, would have demanded reduction in investment in ground capabilities. China, a continental state, could not ignore improvement in its ground capabilities; hence, it had to give up on its ambitions of becoming a superior naval force for almost forty years.* China did recognise early on that several of the threats to national sovereignty and unity, trade, natural resources are seaborne, and also the US presence in Asia-Pacific. Beijing moved from people's war to local wars under informationised conditions. Under uninformationised conditions, Mao's strategy of luring the enemy deep into the territory played a principle role, "striking and gaining command only after the enemy has struck" and "using the inferior to defeat the superior" could not sufficiently secure the territory. Hence, an informed war tactic was applied where "preemptive strike" (implied) was required. Due to the gap in technological advancement, and informationised systems, waiting for the enemy to strike first would render the state unable to strike at all. And a preemptive strike might deter an attack altogether. Following this principle, China launched into "local war under modern high-tech conditions". The preemptive strike component was valuable because even after excessive efforts, it is probable that China will still find itself technologically inferior in the near future. China's naval doctrine, henceforth, evolved slightly, shifting from "protecting the coasts and rivers to coastal defence". The changes in the doctrine can be validated through China's clash with Vietnam in 1974 for the possession of the western part of the Paracel archipelago. The clash revealed major shortcomings in the Chinese Navy. The changes around China-Russian naval ambitions and modernisation, leading to the clash on the Ussuri, and Vietnam developing the islets for military use, compelled it to"build up a powerful navy with a capacity to fight modern warfare" (Deng Xiaoping 1979, quoted in Liu 2008:304, Lim 2014:62).

In the 1980s, Adm Liu Huaqing gave China its first naval ideology: "China must not only have a 'continental outlook' but also a strong 'oceanic outlook'" (Liu 2007). Liu defined a new strategy in China's naval doctrine as "active defence, near seas operations" (Liu 2007).[12] Though China remained "anti-hegemonic and anti-imperialistic" in its outlook, it understood the need for offence-defence while dealing with a hegemonic US and Russia. 'Local defence' was no longer the operative mode: Liu introduced the concept of offensive with 'Chinese characteristics'. He mentioned, "In the operational and tactical context of China's 'active defence',the PLAN will follow the guiding principles of responding to the enemy offensive by our own offensive. In other words, when the enemy carries out its attack against our shore, we will carry out counter-attack against the enemy's rear" (Liu 2007). In a case of an attack by a greater power, China will incorporate "guerrilla warfare at sea using 'maritime militia forces'; a naval war of movement of offensive-defensive nature to secure the near seas, that is, the Yellow Sea, the East Sea, the South China Sea, the Spratlys and Taiwan, the waters within and beyond the Okinawa Islands chain, and the northern part of the Pacific Ocean" (Liu 2007). This marked a shift in China's view of itself in the world, because naval supremacy entails control and command of the sea, projecting maritime forces, producing ripples of political influence in and around the region. It is also evident that as China's naval outlook and modernisation matured, China's territorial boundary expanded, marking an eastward shift. Interestingly, China's naval ambition left out the Indian Ocean and west of Malacca (Liu 2011), however, China's active participation in developing sea ports around the Indian Ocean, by extension India (String of Pearls theory), rendered China as approaching the Indian Ocean with the same doctrine as "near seas", the second leg of its plan. Until 2010, the PLA Navy remained conscious of the "offshore defence strategy" marking a series of operations conducted in the South China Sea and East China Sea (including the announcement of the Air Defence Identification Zone or ADIZ in the East China Sea). There was a major change in the last Military Strategy White Paper (2015) of China which said, "The PLAN will gradually shift its focus from 'offshore waters defence' to the combination of 'offshore waters defence' with 'open seas protection,' and build a combined, multi-functional and efficient marine combat force structure". The last military doctrine establishes a progressive scope of "near seas" and an undefined limit of the concept. The advancement in technology and "the trend towards longer detection range, higher mobility, quicker reaction time, longer range and higher precision, therefore, increased operational depth of naval theatres… [consequently, Chinese forces] will be able to enhance their ability to repel enemy intrusions and preserve national maritime security *only if it progressively enlarges the space within which China can make use of its naval forces"* (Tang Wang Wang 2011:36). Liu Huaqing's strict adherence to a vague definition of near seas (and active defence) and war under informationised conditions has guided China into more offensive doctrines to achieve command of the sea. The statements made in China suggest the offensive nature of strategies applied for future conflicts. The use of the air force would not be sufficient but crucial when "integrated with surface and submarine forces to carry out wide manoeuvres and create opportunity to annihilate the enemy's vital forces at sea."

China's naval rise has been a matter of concern to all East Asian (including Southeast Asian) nations, extending to the US and allies. The perceptions can be categorised as follows: one, Taiwan and the nearby Spratly and Senkaku/Diaoyu Islands; two, China's peaceful rise/development theory, choice to "embrace economic globalization" (Zheng 2005:20) through the maritime domain, reaching a harmonious world/society through harmonious oceans; three, strategic choice guided by international prestige and local pressure; lastly, the Mahanian view of a naval power, its importance in the growth of the economy leading it to eventually take control over the waters.

China's being a sea power will bring it into the category of powers with both land and sea capabilities, something that is unacceptable to its neighbours. Moreover, a rising China is enough of a threat to the smaller nations and multiplied with the maritime dominance,it will threaten not just the sovereignty of the actors but also the 'free trade system' enjoyed by the rest of the world. Having understood the repercussions of China's entry into the maritime domain, there is ample incentive for the East Asia region to act in unanimity.

Several questions come to mind when looking at China as a sea power: can China be a sea power, having a vast land border of 22,117 km with 14 countries? Even though China has the largest navy in the region, it still is an emerging naval power. The projection of capabilities, so far accumulated, has been done to 'occupy' the disputed territory for resources, and maintain the national unity with Taiwan, and, in effect, eliminate external influence.

Sea Power Problem for China

In World War I, when Germany tried to project power into the sea, it was tackled rightly by Britain. The alliance behaviour reflected balancing. But generation of balancing behaviour against China and not the US contains elements of doubt for the accurate projection of balancing possibilities. The fact that China might never be able to achieve the status of a sea power in the presence of the US complicates the matter further (given its dominant attitude at sea). China's maritime strategy portrays the South China and East China Seas as a matter of national security but forgets the consequences. In a continental set-up like Europe, a state 'A' would get challenged by other states or group of states as soon as 'A' achieved strategic advantage over others. This is a balancing mechanism where each individual's national interest/national security is tied up with curtailing the power of any rising state and, hence, eliminating a challenge leading to an armed conflict. But in the case of China, because the US played security guarantor, China grew powerful without the fear of getting into a conflict. Had it been otherwise, it might have had to fall in line, i.e. get balanced by the rest of the region or tired of managing both land and sea power simultaneously.

As an insular sea power, Britain had the advantage of a favourable balance of power. Land powers or weaker nations allied more readily with Britain against the land hegemon (France or Germany). Being an insular sea power, Britain had a superior capacity to make allies and keep them for as long as necessary. A maritime power has to survive through extensive trade; Britain could afford to provide allies with material gains along with negligible threat to territorial security. The role of proximity downplayed the value and advantage to an insular power—the War of American Independence, wherein Britain could not successfully maintain the balance in its favour as it was dealing with a country across the Atlantic.

"*As a rule, the sea power could invoke the adversity that would befall the balance of power if superior land-based capabilities were combined with matching sea-based capabilities*" (Liska: 1977). According to this hypothesis any continental power (including China) will be at a disadvantage as the insular superpower is capable of adversely affecting the balance of power. **For a continental power engaging in naval modernisation, it will be difficult to maintain the balance between both types of capabilities–on land and at sea, A reduction in investment will render the continental power vulnerable to an attack from bordering nations as it cannot successfully predict the intentions of the periphery at all times.** For China, even if it acquires naval capabilities for maritime projection and sea denial (and, later, sea control), it will be a struggle for it to maintain both legs without stretching its economy to a breaking point. For a continental power such as China, it might have to reduce focus from sea capabilities back to land, ending into a reduced power at sea and reduced influence. The pivot to Asia strategy clearly signifies the importance of the region for the US. The naval deployment of the US made for 60 percent in the Asia-Pacific and 40 percent in the rest of the world.

As was written by George Liska (1977) in the *Quest for Equilibrium: "Similarities strain symbiosis rather than easing it when empire and system function or flounder side by side."* When looked at China and the US through the prism of the same knowledge, it is apparent how 'similar' China and the US are in their ambitions, and notion and use of power. Today, what we see might be a reflection of the US a century ago. China is transforming into a sea power (while it already is a land power). In the world history, only a few countries have had capabilities to defend territory both on land and sea, and maintain such an order. France (1670s and 1680s) and Spain (1500s) were the only two powers that had capabilities to deserve the title of both land and sea power. The US itself started with a miniature army and navy, expanding it in the 1700s and the 1800s in isolation, when it finally emerged as a great power following the naval victory over the Royal Navy in 1815 and later the success of the Monroe Doctrine. The US became *a* superpower after the end of World War II and *the* superpower after the dissolution of the USSR, marking the end of the Cold War in 1991.

The transition in the US' position was primarily due to a strong navy capable of conducting operations from the Mediterranean to the Tasman Sea. However, the US required to expand its navy to continue to be an 'economic power' able to conduct trade with distant countries like China and Japan. But the threat that the Royal Navy posed for the independence of the US put pressure on the government to continue with the expansion of the US Navy. Hence, essentially, the US became a sea power to continue its economic engagement and later realised the importance of the leverage that came along with it. Since the US did not have a competitor, it rose to be a great power (land power) in the region (not a global power or sea power yet).

Conclusion

This paper argues, in conclusion, that for China to become a regional hegemon, it would surely require control and command of the near sea and access to open waters. However, China's drive to achieve this sea power potential is demonstrably problematic and beset by constraints. One, since China is a continental power, it does not enjoy the advantages of an insular power such as the US, primarily, of strategic autonomy coming from geographical isolation.

Two, the chances of Asian states balancing against China are much greater than their bandwagoning with China against the US. This will significantly constrain China's thrust to achieve its desired sea power potential and freedom from time constraints to develop its navy in isolation.

Three, even if these factors do not obstruct China's drive to achieve its sea power potential and move towards regional hegemony, the contradictions rooted in China's continental militarism evidently cast doubts on China's influcnce expanding beyond its regional waters. Will China emerge as a maritime security guarantor?

Lastly, this paper would frame China's sea power potential to be only as achievable as permitted by the regional balance of power politics and not much beyond denying the US its freedom of intervention in China's immediate neighbourhood.

China's naval modernisation is primarily motivated by the immediate security risk, i.e. Taiwan (and by extension, the US). The Chinese coastal region, despite the efforts to open up central and western China, accounts for about two-third of China's GDP (National Bureau of Statistics, 2015)[13]. And four of China's wealthy provinces fall in the vicinity of Taiwan. Therefore, in the case of a conflict, Taiwan would not need to project power deep inside China to incapacitate its economy. Moreover, Taiwan's military has one focus: China. Beijing would have to try and control the island for the security of its economic base. Hence, the Taiwan dilemma bears long-term threats for China, if its ambition is to attain regional hegemony.[14] Consequently, such a desire affects the US and its allies too. As written by Bernard Cole (2006:36), "PLA planners are almost certainly planning to overcome not just or even primarily the Taiwan military, but the US Navy." The strategic importance of Taiwan for China is Taiwan's location in the middle of the first island chain (from the Aleutian Islands to the Japan Archipelago and to the Philippines and Indonesia), providing a gateway to the open seas, allowing the Chinese Navy to sail freely in the Pacific Ocean.

The growth in the Chinese economy had direct consequences for the economy of the region and the world. But due to the weakening economy, the US has urged the regional countries to contribute to the regional security. Therefore, while the countries are trying to pull the weight of the region's security, a stable economy is a prerequisite for such an enterprise.

Deterring China is also difficult as the regional countries see profit (for the short-term) in not containing or provoking China, while also profiting by tilting towards the US (long-term), to maintain the status quo. This balance will falter only if China projects its power to command the disputed territory, or the US (tired of the costs involved) pulls its naval forces all the way back to Australia or the Philippines. The latter move will give a wide berth to China to freely command the adjacent open sea, while the former will test the will and power of the region.

It is in China's favour to build naval capabilities to successfully control and command the seas in future, as asymmetric capabilities can only be used to deny access for the short-term defence from the US Navy.

Realistically, if China's intention is to control the eastern hemisphere, it will be highly difficult, even without the US presence in the region. The growing regional alliances in the region are a clear indication in the shift in perception of China's hard power. The shift suggests balancing rather bandwagoning. Furthermore, as explained earlier, China cannot risk reducing investment in ground capabilities to further its naval ambitions. The insularity enjoyed by the US made it possible for it to project maritime capability without much resistance over the centuries. But since China does not enjoy such a geographical bonus, it will be difficult to achieve and maintain a sea power status.

For the US, a rising China is a direct challenge to the US designed global order. The impact of a loss in Asia-Pacific would not only tarnish the US' reputation, but also devalue its importance as an ally. The presence of the US restrained the regional countries from developing military nuclear capabilities. In the absence of a security guarantor, imposing such a clause would be difficult and, in fact, it will not be in the US' interest.

If China is willing to replace the US as a guarantor of open sea lanes in East Asia, there is little evidence to prove that the Chinese economy can sustain such a cost. Moreover, the neighbouring nations would resist, and hesitate to accept, such a proposal, and might try to collectively fill the vacuum left by the US. Given significant benefits that China has enjoyed due to the US military presence in East

Asia, China might want to keep the arrangement as it is while exempting the US from operating in China's neighbourhood.

Larger questions remain, i.e. would chasing the US away achieve maximum security for China, and would it attain the status of a regional hegemon? In the vacuum left behind by the US, China might find itself more vulnerable and unable to stabilise the region.

References

"China's Military Strategy", White Paper, May 26, 2015, 2014.

US-China Economic and Security Review, 2015, 2014.

"China's Naval Modernization", Pentagon Report, 2014.

Barry R. Posen, "Command of the Commons: The Military Foundation of U.S. Hegemony," *International Security*, vol. 28, no. 1 Summer 2003, pp. 5–46.

Christopher Layne, "The Unipolar Illusion: Why New Great Powers Will Rise," *International Security*, vol. 17,no. 4, Spring 1993, pp. 5–51.

J. Corbett, *Principles of Maritime Strategy*(New York: Library of Congress, 1911).

Erickson Goldstein, *China goes to Sea: Maritime Transformation in Comparative Historical Perspective*(Naval Institute Press, 2009).

G. Liska,*Quest for Equilibrium*(Baltimore: Johns Hopkins University Press, 1977).

Yves-Heng Lim, *China's Naval Power: An offensive Realist Approach*(Ashgate Publishing Co. 2014).

T. Mahan, *TheProblem of Asia*(U.S: Little Brown and Company, 1905).

Stephen G. Brooks and William C. Wohlforth, *World Out of Balance: International Relations and the Challenge of American Primacy* (Princeton, N.J.: Princeton University Press, 2008), p. 1;

Parag Khanna, *The Second World: Empires and Influence in the New Global Order* (New York: Random House, 2008).

Stephen M. Walt, *The Origins of Alliances* (Ithaca, N.Y.: Cornell University Press, 1987).

US-China Security Perceptions Survey, Carnegie, 2013, http://www.chinausfocus.com/wp-content/uploads/2013/12/US-China-Security-Perceptions-Survey.pdf

Notes

1. Alan Wachman. *Why Taiwan? Geostrategic Rationales for China's Territorial Integrity* (Stanford: Stanford University Press, 2007), p. 41.
2. George Liska, *Quest for Equilibrium* (Johns Hopkins University Press, 1977), ch 1, p.4.
3. The applicability of the above statement can be argued as valid in the face of amphibious and strategic lift capability.
4. Yves Lim, *China's Naval Power, An Offensive Realist Approach* (Ashgate Publishing Limited, 2014), ch.3, p.53.
5. Ibid.
6. Blagden,Levy, et al "Sea Powers, Continental Powers, and Balancing Theory", *International Security*, vol 36, no 2, pp. 190-202.
7. Russia needed a warm water port on the Pacific Ocean for its navy and trade, mainly as an anti-British move. Vladivostok was operational only in summer, while Port Arthur was operational throughout the year.
8. Robert Sutter, "China in World Affairs–US Policy Choices", Congressional Research Service, January 31, 1995, pp. 95-265.
9. Liska, n.2.

10. Thompson Levy, "Balancing at Land and at Sea: Do States Ally Against a Leading Global Power", *International Security*, vol 35, Summer 2010, pp. 7-43.
11. Ibid.
12. Speech given at the Academy of Military Science in 1984, see, n.4.
13. National Bureau of Statistics of China, 2015, data.states.gov.cn/english/
14. Also, structural realism states that a state would not stop at the regional level, without trying to expand its influence globally.

7

Possible Detente Among Russia-Pakistan-China: Implications for India

Chandra Rekha

Introduction

The dynamic nature of international relations has brought along with it the realities of the theory of transition of power. In the current international system, it is evident that a 'shift' is taking place in control and influence over global geo-politics that can be outlined in two broad contexts: (a) power and influence in the new world order is no longer monopolised by a single entity but disseminated among several international actors, including non-state actors. However, the established system in the post Cold War era continues to have a dominant player i.e. the United States; and (b) the current international relations are witnessing a power transition which is taking place from West to East or North to South. Strategic thinkers have been presenting their arguments in this regard based on the developments taking place in the Asian region in particular. Many have gone to the extent of defining the current international system as the "Asian Century".

The Asian region has been a key element in the foreign policy interests of the global community. It can be said that the region has played a significant role in determining the policy formulation of many countries, especially those of the West. For instance, Cold War politics saw two superpower blocs aspiring to establish status quo in the region but countries like India took a different path and declared the Non-Aligned Movement (NAM) as their foreign policy principle to halt the impregnation of bipolar politics into the region. Pakistan's tilt towards the US during the Cold War period paved the way for the Soviet Union to penetrate into the Indian subcontinent. In the post Cold War era, India's new economic reforms and growth led to a new slogan, "India Matters" among the political elites, especially in the Washington Administration, as its international relations improved across the board. In the new millennium, the political control of the Taliban in Afghanistan, the rise of militancy and religious extremism, and the "Global War on

Terror" made the Afghanistan-Pakistan (Af-Pak) region the epicentre of international politics. In contemporary world affairs, China, with its economic growth and global outreach, is emerging not only as a global power but an entity which is predicted to replace the US' dominance in international relations.

The economic growth, military modernisation, huge global market potential, infrastructural development and global engagements, especially of India and China have been credited for the rise of the concept of Asian century. In contradiction, the Asian century cannot be confined to these two entities alone as there is also need to mention the sprouting strategic relevance of Pakistan in the regional and international geo-politics in recent times and the role of Russia which is often referred as a 'Eurasian' power, more so due to its links, geographical proximity and involvement in the Asian region's geo-politics. Thus, the region has become a key element in the foreign policy interests of the global community.

Of late, there has been visible development of a strong partnership among Russia, Pakistan and China (RPC). Currently, it is more in the context of the growing trend in the bilateral engagement among these three entities which has, in turn, signalled the conceptualisation of a possible formidable trilateral arrangement in the coming years. This has caused concern among the political elites of many countries such as the US, as the engagement (restricted currently to regional geo-politics) among the three countries may pose a major challenge to the interests and aspirations of other international actors. Unfortunately, this has also caused anxiety among the Indian strategic thinkers and political community as (a) both China and Pakistan have been a potential security threat to India and it was compelled to engage in military confrontation against the two countries; (b) their military doctrines, including that of possession of nuclear weapons, have often been of an offensive nature with hostile intentions; (c) the 'all weather strategic partnership' between Pakistan and China aims to put a check on India's growth and influence in the South Asian region and in international affairs at large; and, lastly (d) the détente between Pakistan and India's long and time-tested traditional partner Russia, has led to anxiety among policy-makers in New Delhi.

Nevertheless, the implications of the détente and strengthening of ties among the three countries—RPC—and more so at the bilateral level, such as China-Russia relations, are seen more in terms of a nexus rather than a benign alliance by the world community, especially the US and its allies. However, is it right to question, even in the Indian context, whether the triple alliance will threaten India's national interests? Under such a scenario, the objective of this paper is to investigate the following aspects:

- What are the prospects of the Russia-Pakistan-China alliance?
- Will the irritants in the bilateral engagements among the three countries impact the future course of RPC?
- Will RPC succeed in becoming a formidable strategic alliance in the future?
- To what extent will Russia's engagement with Pakistan and China impact its bilateral strategic partnership with India?
- Is there any scope for India to join the triple alliance—RPC? If yes, then what comprises the scope and obstacles for India?

These are some of the important questions that the paper intends to answer.

In order to gain a better understanding of these factors, the future prospects of RPC and their implications on India, the paper will analyse the relevance of the growing proximity among Moscow-Islamabad-Beijing through two narratives. Firstly, to understand the relationship that the three countries share at the bilateral levels i.e., it would survey the relations between Russia-Pakistan, Russia-China, and China-Pakistan. Secondly, the paper would lay out a canvas to get a better understanding of the future prospects and implications on India's national interests and global aspirations and more, importantly, the impact on its robust partnership with Russia.

Russia-Pakistan Detente

With regards to the relations between Russia and Pakistan, one may look at the major foreign policy trends during the Cold War politics pursued by both countries, as Pakistan shared close ties with the US and China during this period. This, in turn, led to the emergence of strong Indo-Soviet relations. Hence, it is imperative to investigate the evolution of Pakistan-Russia relations to determine the current trends and the future of the relations in the coming years. The evolution of Russia-Pakistan relations can be understood in three phases:

- Cold War era.
- Post Soviet withdrawal from Afghanistan.
- Post US drawdown from Afghanistan.

Cold War Relations Between Russia and Pakistan

Pakistan began its foreign policy through exploration and friendship with all countries, including the erstwhile Soviet Union, after its partition from India in 1947. Military aid from Russia to Islamabad comprised only $5-10 million as against $600-700 million arms assistance to India.[1]

It follows that Pakistan's eventual membership in the Western security alliances–Southeast Asia Treaty Organisation (SEATO)[2] and Central Treaty Organisation (CENTO)[3]—to acquire substantial economic and military aid and Russia's big swing towards India during the Cold War period made both countries follow a path that failed to accommodate each other in their respective policy goals.[4] In 1960, the American U-2 plane which took off from the airport in Peshawar and made a reconnaissance flight over the Soviet territory created an unfavourable background for Soviet-Pakistan relations. Islamabad's policy tilt towards the West, the Indo-Pakistan armed conflict in 1971 when Pakistan aligned with the US and China, followed by its role in Afghanistan during the Soviet invasion in the region which served as the logistical support for the Afghan Mujahideen made Pakistan a frontline state in the US' proxy war against the Soviet Union in Afghanistan. Pakistan's strong ties with the US were seen by Russia as Washington's strategy to penetrate into the South Asian geo-politics during the Cold War period. Further, Islamabad viewed the emergence of the Taliban in Kabul as an opportunity to penetrate into Central Asia via Afghanistan, especially with the withdrawal of Soviet troops from the region and its implosion in 1990. These are some of the major factors that resulted in the deterioration of the relationship between the two countries, which has been clouded with suspicion and hostility.

Post-Soviet Withdrawal from Afghanistan

After the end of Cold War politics, the US was no longer willing to underwrite Pakistan's economic development and modernisation of its military, more so because the country had lost its strategic relevance for the US' geo-political interests in the region, as the US no longer needed to protect its interests there from the Soviet Union. Hence, a host of factors bolstering this argument are:

- Soviet withdrawal from Afghanistan.
- Break-up of the Soviet Union.
- Emergence of the US as a unipolar power[5]

Despite Islamabad maintaining a focussed foreign policy that was strongly oriented towards the US during the 1990s, Pakistan continued to experience a wave of anti-American sentiment following the suspension of economic and military aid by the US government after the implementation of the Pressler Amendment[6] and Pakistan's continued refusal to join the nuclear Non-Proliferation Treaty (NPT). Even in the military modernisation process, Pakistan's dependence on Western defence markets like France and Britain became an expensive affair, while Russia saw Pakistan with suspicion not only because it shared good relations with India but also for Islamabad's role against the Soviets in the Afghanistan War. Sanctions against Pakistan by Washington during the "War on Terror" had left Pakistan in a limbo. Moreover, the United States made it clear that the SEATO pledge applied only to Communist aggression or subversion. Pakistan's plea to include all kinds of aggression was, thus, not accepted.

An upward trend in the relations between Russia and Pakistan, on the other hand, began to take place in the new millennium. Trade between the two countries started to show signs of expansion. In 2004–05, the bilateral trade volume reached $320 million from $134.24 in 2003–04 and $100 million in 2002. Around 90 percent of Pakistan's exports to Russia were textile items.[7] "During 2012-13, Pakistan exported goods worth $234.91 million against exports of $206.98 million during 2011-12 while Pakistan's imports from Russia were worth $108.01 million against only $87.84 million during 2011-12. Thus, the trade surplus of $126.89 million during 2012-13 favoured Pakistan".[8] As for Pakistan, it identifies two prospective areas for economic engagement: one, textiles, which is the largest export commodity of Pakistan, and two, the oil and gas sector exploration and pipelines in which Russia has the requisite expertise and interest as well.

For Russia, the benefits of improving bilateral relations with Pakistan are well defined, especially for anti-terrorism cooperation as well as Pakistan's interest in buying Russian weapon systems and expanding economic interaction. For Pakistan, having alternative options for its defence needs and technology transfer in the scientific and research fields, including access to the Russian market for its exports and strengthening relations alongside developing closer ties with the Central Asian Republics (CARs) alongwith improved relations with Russia first are the major factors behind Islamabad's growing proximity to Moscow. Hence, the task ahead for Islamabad would be to recraft its image of a nation which has been a hub of religious fundamentalism and terrorist organisations and insurgency, in order to develop strong bilateral relations with international players.

Upward Trend Post-Second US Withdrawal from Afghanistan

The upturn in Russia-Pakistan ties from next-to-nothing is one of the most remarkable shifts playing out in South Asia since the 2001 US-led invasion of Afghanistan.[9] The following factors will help evaluate the Kremlin's tilt towards Pakistan in recent times: (a) Russia wants to protect its interests and hegemony in Central Asia; (b) Russia wants to preserve regional security and stability in the CARs; (c) it needs to protect the Russian ethnics, a major group in Central Asia; (d) underlying Russia's decision to engage with Pakistan is the desire to establish new synergies in the South Asian region in the face of crumbling traditional alliances such as with India.

An upward trend in relations between India and the US and the diversification of its defence markets has been another cause of concern for Moscow. With India diversifying its defence markets and Chinese defence orders starting to decline owing to the growing indigenous capability of China's own defence industry since the mid-2000,[10] Russia is compelled to find defence customers to fund its mammoth defence industrial complex. Hence, Pakistan's desire to upgrade its defence equipment and its need for a reliable defence market and geographical diversification of defence export destinations has led Russia to develop defence ties with Pakistan.The recently concluded agreement on weapons sale such as of the Mi35 helicopters and Klimov RD-93 engines for the JF-17 multi-role fighters to Pakistan by Russia is a step in this direction. Unfortunately for India, Russia will continue its attempt to develop a cooperative relationship with Islamabad as the region is too important to ignore.

The following section will focus on the Russia-China strategic partnership

Russia-China Double Helix

The Sino-Russian relations possess great geo-political weight in international relations. In its nascent stage as a new republic, China was influenced by the Soviet model of governance. Unlike India, Beijing did not opt to stay away from bloc politics during the Cold War period and took the Kremlin as its model for development. This laid the foundation for the future course of bilateral ties between the two countries. However, differences in the ideological approach, border disputes and the 'shift' in their respective foreign policies kept the relationship unsettled. Further elaborating on these aspects, there was the Sino-Soviet split in the late 1960s, as Mao was asserting that there had been a counter-revolution in the Soviet Union, and that capitalism had been restored. Relations between the Chinese Communist Party and the Communist Party of the Soviet Union broke off, as did relations with the Communist Parties of the Warsaw Pact countries.[11] The relations further plummeted when on, March 2, 1969, there was a violent confrontation on the Ussuri river, where dozens of Russian border guards were killed by Chinese soldiers. The Russians retaliated on March 15, with an artillery barrage that left the landscape on the Chinese side of the border looking like the moon's surface.[12]

With Pakistan as the mediator, Mao responded to overtures from President Nixon and turned towards the US for hard balancing against the Soviet Union. In connection with Nixon's visit to China, the Soviet Union severely attacked the "Sino-American rapprochement". Over the next decade, relations faced an implacable confrontation. There was always a danger of renewed border clashes over disputed territory escalating into a more serious conflict. The Soviet Army massively expanded its forces in Siberia and the Far East, posing a continuous threat to Beijing. Soviet intervention in Afghanistan aggravated Chinese concerns about possible Soviet expansion in Asia and kept them on high alert. Until at least the mid-1980s, the official line in Beijing remained the inevitability of war, with the Soviet Union seen as the most likely adversary.[13] Since then, Russia has been concerned with Chinese incursions into its territory, a problem it is unable to deal with.

In the current international milieu, a resurgent Russia and an emerging world power China have posed a major threat to the preeminence of the US and its allies. The policies of the US-led Western allies have mostly signalled curtailing the rise and influence of both Russia and China in global affairs. However, much to the irony of the West, this has only brought the countries closer. The following factors will assist in investigating the growing proximity between the two countries:

- Moscow and Beijing have made efforts to overcome major irritants such as border and security issues which has, in turn, revived the relations between the two countries.
- The countries acknowledge their modernisation paths, hence, have realised that closer cooperation would benefit them both.[14]
- The relations between Beijing and Moscow are of mutual benefit. China needs Russia's raw material (energy) and state-of-the-art Russian weapons, while Russia needs China's economic umbrella and consumer market.
- As China has outperformed Russia in many spheres, especially in economic development, Moscow sees the presence of China in Central Asia more as a 'caretaker' as it is the major economic investor and market in the region. Moreover, both New Delhi and Islamabad are now permanent members of the Russia-China-led Shanghai Cooperation Organisation (SCO), with the prime goal of combating terrorism, extremism and separatism – the main concerns for all member states of the forum. Russia and Pakistan have already started collaborating in the areas of defence and energy resources. Moreover, the "paradigm shift" was motivated by Russia's strategic motivation to balance India and Pakistan and, as a result, make the multipolar world even more cohesive.[15]
- Both countries are concerned with the hegemonic position of the US in international affairs. Hence, their shared interests and concerns have led to strengthening of ties between the two countries.

Elaborating further on this aspect, the Ukraine imbroglio and the international response to Russia's intervention in the crisis have impacted the Russian economy. Much to the dismay of the Western allies, this has resulted in stronger ties between Russia and China. Russia concluded a $400-billion mega gas pipeline deal with China. Two factors emerge from the growing nexus between Russia and China: (a) China's demand for energy resources will enhance Russia's energy security as Moscow is in search of geo-political diversification of energy markets apart from the European Union nations; (b) China's growing infrastructural development and economic prosperity has, in turn, led to a growing demand for energy. The Russian energy market is the key to China's energy consumption.

The Kremlin is in need of a partner that shares similar concerns and has the capability to counter the preeminence of the US in the existing global order. Hence, it has begun reviewing its focus on the South Asian region, more importantly, towards China, which has made remarkable growth in international relations. Similar to Russian worries, Beijing is also concerned about the global supremacy of the US in the Asia-Pacific region and its 'rebalancing strategy', aimed primarily to halt Beijing's global ambitions. This has given way to the inevitable competition between the US and China.

China has actively developed foreign policy concepts to portray its own ascent in the international power standings and has built a coherent literature and narrative to promote the idea of its aspirations. In 2003, China launched its first foreign policy concept "the peaceful rise of China" (*Zhongguo heping jueqi*).[16] China has increased the scale of its economy and military strength. The strategic thinker John Mearscheimer has stated that China cannot rise peacefully as its rise in global politics is seen in terms of establishing a hegemonic status and to challenge the established power (the United States) which may lead to an inevitable conflict of interests, and an intense security competition.

Another argument to bolster Mearscheimer's assessment of China's rise is based on his comparative analysis with the US. According to him, American policy-makers have gone to considerable lengths to keep the United States in an exalted position in world affairs and have worked hard for more than a century to gain hegemony, especially in the Western Hemisphere. After achieving regional dominance, the US has gone to great lengths to prevent other great powers from controlling either Asia or Europe. In a similar fashion, China too is heading in this direction, especially in Asia, and will want to make sure that it is so powerful that no state in Asia has the wherewithal to threaten it.[17] In other words, China in Southeast and Southwest Asia is at a disadvantageous position as it has long standing territorial disputes with many of these states; its aggressive posturing in the South China Sea has caused anxiety among these nations towards China; and the presence of the US and its engagement with the countries of these regions have all led to Beijing looking towards the South Asian region in particular to create a 'comfort zone' to sustain its growth and achieve its perennial goals. The foothold into the region would eventually lead to further access to the Central Asian region—'the heartland'. Access to these pivotal regions will enhance the opportunity to emerge as the hegemonic power, both regionally and internationally.

Therefore, one cannot rule out the possibility of China experiencing a similar fate as the US due to dominance and economic investments in other countries, especially in the CARs. But, the comparison can also be drawn in the context of China's financial investments and foreign policy interests, similar of the Soviet pattern of investment and protection of its interests in the former Soviet space. So here the key question would be, will China's (despite the slowing down of its economic growth) continued financial assistance to the Central Asian Republics in the coming years become a liability rather than an asset?

China-Pakistan Relations

Historically, Pakistan had successfully coordinated with Beijing and Washington during the Cold War politics. India practically stood isolated in the South Asian region during the Cold War period when Islamabad-Washington-Beijing formed the axis in the 1971 War against India. Pakistan acquired nuclear weapons with significant assistance from China. In fact, Islamabad is seen as a surrogate state of China through which the Beijing Administration has achieved its desired goal and aspirations in the region,[18] especially in putting a check on India's growth as a regional hegemon and as a strong international actor. As mentioned earlier, there is a high requirement for economic assistance and infrastructural development in countries such as Pakistan which China has successfully provided. China has been able to meet the demand signal of countries like Pakistan which has, in turn, assisted in preserving Beijing's regional interests.

An important point to be noted here is that the aspiration of the Chinese Administration during the Cold War period was only confined to establishing its hegemony in the South Asian region. However, though China's immediate objective was to become the hegemonic power of Asia, with sustainable economic prosperity and global outreach, China's ambitions in the current world system is no longer confined to the South Asian region but has a global connotation and it is keen to challenge the preeminence of the US and achieve influential status in world politics, in parity with the US.

Ironically, the partnership between Pakistan and China has operated more as a hostile nexus towards India. Pakistan, on many occasions, has offered opportunities for China to encircle India. Its strategic location and China's grand investment has led Pakistan to develop as a nodal point in Beijing's economic corridor vision: the China-Pakistan Economic Corridor (CPEC), and the construction of the deep water port of Gwadar, opened in 2008, with Chinese funding, which offers berthing potential for a growing Chinese naval presence in the Indian Ocean.[19] In 2012, China declared that it would take control of the Gwadar port as it believes that it is a prospective zone to serve as an oil pipeline hub for its growing energy needs and expand its trade relations with the Central Asian Republics.[20] Towards that end, it has to contain the US challenge and presence in Asia, and also contain India's growth. For both these purposes, Pakistan serves as a convenient springboard.[21] The comprehensive robust partnership between China and Pakistan is in the economics, defence, infrastructure, security and nuclear fields. It must be noted that Pakistan is the largest importer of Chinese manufactured defence equipment. Data from the Stockholm International Peace Research Institute (SIPRI) indicates that China was the source of 54 percent of Pakistan's arms imports between the years 2009 and 2013.[22]

Let us now focus on the emerging trilateral engagement that is taking place among a resurgent Russia, the 'zipper' of the pan-Eurasian region,[23] Pakistan, and an emerging global power – China.

Russia-Pakistan-China Detente

South Asian geo-politics has traditionally been marked by the relations between Russia-India, Pakistan-Russia, Pakistan-United States and China-Pakistan. It is also been marked by the traditional hostile relations between India-Pakistan, India-United States, Pakistan-Russia and China-India. Hence, this pattern of relations failed to foresee a Russian-Pakistani strategic partnership until now, due to the restructuring of the region's geo-politics and future possibilities. Russia and Pakistan are clearly moving closer to one another, and this is occurring despite Russia being "India's closest friend". This trend might appear somewhat perplexing to one unaccustomed to the region's happenings, so it's worthwhile to succinctly describe the current state of play in South Asia to better grasp why this development actually isn't all that unexpected, and how it is not motivated by any negative intentions towards India. The burgeoning relationship between the US and India, with extensive trade ties and cooperation on strategic issues in the sphere of defence technology and equipment, does unnerve Pakistan. Since Pakistan's failed misadventure in the Kargil heights, it has lost the support of successive US Administrations on the Kashmir issue and its own relationship with the US has been rocky.[24]

With regard to the strategic trilateral partnership among the RPC, there are several factors that need emphasis in defining the relations among the three international actors. These are:

- Economic prospects.
- Afghanistan and the regional stability.
- The need to contain the rise of Islamist fundamentalism.

- Establishing a security umbrella in the Central Asian Region.
- Energy security.

Economic Prospects: Zipping RPC Together

The Ukraine imbroglio and sanctions politics have not only impacted the Russian economy but have led to a fall in oil prices, that has hampered its energy export markets which is the main source of Russian revenue. Hence, Russia is in search of alternative regions, apart from Europe, to secure its long-term national interests and economic development. As for China, its growing influence in international politics has enhanced Beijing's goal of sustaining its economic performance and military modernisation process. In addition, its aggressive posturing in Southeast Asia and the South China Sea disputes, alongside the US presence in the Asia-Pacific region has threatened China's aspirations and goals. Eurasia, on the other hand, has assisted in the successful execution of China's ambitions.

Pakistan's strategic location in this regard is a key factor for both Russia and China as it brings a system of real-sector trade infrastructure such as roads and railways between Central Asia (the Eurasian Union and the Shanghai Cooperation Organisation—SCO) and Pakistan, intersecting at Xinjiang. The region has, thus, become a significant Eurasian trading hub connecting China, Russia, the Eurasian Union and Pakistan which is also a member of the South Asian Association for Regional Cooperation (SAARC), and connecting the rest of the Asian countries. Pakistan's strategic location and access to the trade corridor have led the region to become a centre of economic gravity that seals key trade and commerce routes together. Hence, in terms of gaining economic efficiency, the overland route transiting Pakistan has provided the platform for Russia and China.[25]

Furthermore, the thinking goes that if Russia were to compensate for its diplomatic 'blind spot' with Pakistan and reinvigorate the bilateral relationship with Islamabad, then it could mirror the role that it plays between India and China in also helping to balance the tension between India and Pakistan. The catalyst for connecting the four blocs together via Pakistan's geo-strategic location is the CPEC, One Belt, One Road (OBOR), SCO, EEU (Eurasian Economic Union), SAARC and, of course, the energy pipeline projects. Despite the strong arguments presented by strategic analysts of the Sino-Russian competition in the Eurasian region and the limited scope in the bilateral ties between Russia and China, President Putin has made it clear that the SCO will operate "actively on convergence between the two big projects"—the China-led OBOR initiative and the EEU. Expectedly, the two projects may become the main driving force for Euro-Asian connectivity and integration,and a top strategic priority for dealing with regional security threats.[26]

Afghanistan and the Need for Regional Stability

Developments in Afghanistan also appear to have played a key role in determining Russia's strategic calculus towards Islamabad. The US drawdown from Afghanistan has created a vacuum which Russia fears will lead to the reemergence of the Taliban and the rise of non-conventional threats such as drug trafficking from the region spilling into Central Asia and the Caucasus. It is likely to have concluded that Afghan instability will persist for the foreseeable future. Therefore, apart from shoring up the defences in Central Asia, there is a growing realisation that Pakistan holds the lever for bringing stability in the Af-Pak region. This is seen as one of the reasons for Russia supporting Pakistan's permanent membership in the SCO and the sale of the Mi 35 Hind attack helicopters for counter-terrorism operations. Thus, developments in Afghanistan play a key role in determining Russia's strategic calculus towards Islamabad. This is likely to be one of the reasons for Russia supporting Pakistan's full membership of the SCO as well. One can also argue that Russia's rapprochement with Pakistan is in response to India's perceived drift towards the West and its weapons diversification programme. However, this would tantamount to perceiving India's and Russia's relationships with other countries as a zero sum game. Against this backdrop, stronger ties with Russia will, in a way, give Pakistan a bargaining chip in its own negotiations with the US.

As for China in the Baluchistan region, the Afghan Taliban has been a major obstacle in China's economic and security interests such as gaining access to the energy rich Central Asia through the Pakistan-China energy corridor and its role in the SCO. In the Xinjiang region, the active presence of the East Turkmenistan Islamic Movement (ETIM) has led to the disruption of overland trade between Pakistan and China. Hence, the two countries are determined to resist the separatist movements on both sides to reap optimum economic benefits. The interests of Russia, China and Pakistan have converged over the evolving Afghan regional security and the three have been working together to find a solution for the same. Moreover, Pakistan is seen as an asset to the Asian security architecture that is shaped, not by the US, but by China and Russia.

Energy Security

Russia has figured out Pakistan's energy requirements and, hence, has offered its support for a string of big ticket energy projects, including the Turkmenistan, Afghanistan, Pakistan and India (TAPI) natural gas pipeline. Russia depends heavily on the energy markets for its economic growth and securing the Eurasian energy resources is an important factor. Russia is also keen on exploiting Pakistan's growing energy demands offering support to energy projects such as the TAPI gas pipeline and also a $2 billion Liquefied Natural Gas (LNG) pipeline plan from Karachi to Lahore.[27]

China, for its part, is much more powerful in terms of its economy compared to the two other countries of the triangle. Pakistan, a developing economy, requires both military equipment and energy supplies from Russia and economic security from China. Some analysts question whether a partnership motivated by external factors could lead to an alliance of countries that formerly distrusted each other. But the old adage, "the enemy of my enemy is my friend" fits well here; the single most important factor that overrides all others is their concurrent perception of the US and its "policy of containment" towards them. China needs allies to change the world order and it begins with Asia.

China which has a strong economy, has invested in huge infrastructural projects and strategic corridors in both Pakistan and Central Asia. Through such economic investments, China is gaining access to the region's energy resources to fulfill its growing energy demands. In the coming future, one can see signs of integration among the three states, as their abilities and requirements complement each other, because Russia is an alternate source for Western military technology and energy supplies, and China and Pakistan's demand for energy resources will enhance Russia's energy market, apart from the European Union. China is economically more potent than the other two, with cooperation in trade and development as its main priority.

The China-Pakistan link is well known and is the most formidable leg of the Russia-China-Pakistan triangle. It is from here that the congruence of interests among the three states of Pakistan, China and Russia stems.

As Pepe Escobar writes, the energy requirements of this grandiose project are expected to be filled by Iran via the larger Iran-Pakistan-China pipeline project, but a supportive component will also be the world's largest solar farm that Beijing and Islamabad are also building as part of the CPEC. In a major sense, the CPEC represents not only a geo-political pivot for China, but also a geo-economic one as well, since it will position the country within easy access to the Mideast oil fields on which so much of its economy depends.

Issues and Challenges in the Trilateral Alliance— RPC

Many scholars in the academic community have surmised the possibilities of a successful trilateral partnership that may be hampered by the issues that exist in their bilateral relations.

To begin with:

- One of the biggest impediments to improving Russia's and Pakistan's relations is the suspicion and hostility that existed during the Cold War period.
- Moscow and Islamabad see their relationship as being mutually beneficial, however, Moscow cannot possibly achieve the status of the US or China in Pakistan's foreign policy interests. The relationship with Russia, in turn, gives Pakistan a bargaining chip in its own negotiations with the Washington Administration.
- Pakistan's strategic interests continue to remain in conflict with Russian interests, especially in Central Asia.
- Russia's strategic partnership with Pakistan is seen by many as a strategic gamble despite being aware of its past behaviour, especially its hostile signalling towards Moscow.
- There is widening disparity in China's global presence and economic progress in the 21st century compared to Russia's current global status.
- Beijing realises that Moscow is concerned about its own fading status as a regional superpower in its sphere of influence. It is believed that it was this trend that led Moscow to cajole India fully into the Eurasian space to prevent losing its hold in the CARs. It is believed that Chinese officials acknowledged that Russia was their major concern during the unveiling of the "One Belt, One Road," scheme, as post the announcement made in 2013, the Kremlin was reluctant to engage in any meaningful negotiation on how Xi's initiative would coexist with the EEU—Putin's pet project. Beijing has realised that Moscow is concerned about its own fading status as a regional superpower in its sphere of influence. However, to Beijing's delight, Igor Shuvalov, Russia's first deputy prime minister, announced at the Boao Forum that the EEU is ready to cooperate with "One Belt, One Road," and embarked on negotiating a framework document with Chinese leaders on Putin's behalf. One of the reasons cited for the Kremlin's conciliation with the Chinese Administration was that it understood that it is inevitable that China will become the major investor in Central Asia and the major market for the region's vast natural resources. The only way that Russia can maintain its influence is to recalibrate its role in the region and accommodate its own ambitions to Beijing's quest for raw materials, and the region's appetite for Chinese money. The document signed by Putin and Xi outlines the possible formula.[28]
- China's habit of reverse engineering of Russian military technology has created a major problem for Russian intellectual property.
- Rapid economic development and successful modernisation of China has made the country much less dependent on Russia. This current trend have led to a 'role reversal'. Over the last decade, Russia has proved increasingly reluctant to provide China

with state-of-the-art military equipment and a supportive investment environment when it found out in 2006 that the Chinese were producing an indigenous version of the Sukhoi SU-27SK aircraft, the Shenyang J-II, under a licence agreement, signed in 1995. Therefore, Russia has apprehensions towards China that it may use reverse engineering to copy Russian military technology. China has made great advances in developing its own military equipment since 2005, with development of indigenisation of its defence industries and is no longer dependent on Russian technology[29] except in aeronautical engineering.

- The Russians are also concerned with the Chinese incursions into their territory. If left unchecked, in a few decades from now, the Chinese will surpass the Russian population in the bordering areas and may cause demographic asymmetry. This has augmented Russia's internal security concerns alongside its external threats.
- Although Russia and China consider the US as an anathema, China would continue to coexist with the US in the international system as long as the US respects Chinese interests and allows scope to its growth in global politics. Due to economic interdependency, China may not collaborate in challenging the preeminence of the US or attempt any military adventurism against it on behalf of Moscow.

Implications for India

With regards to the implications of RPC on India, let us focus at the scope of RPC, if and when it takes a concrete shape, in the coming years.

If one looks at the contemporary foreign policy of India, it mainly focuses on geo-economics. One of the major obstacles to India's access to Central Asia's energy and trade potentials or even the weakest economic ties between India and Russia, has been the geographical distance. Gaining permanent membership in the SCO has enhanced India's chances of addressing its growing energy demands and also its economic prospects. RPC, hence, provides a crucial economic opportunity through economic corridors such as CPEC, OBOR, New Silk Route, infrastructural and energy pipeline projects. Moreover, Indian concerns with Pakistan or China are at the bilateral level and not in multilateral fora. For instance, China and India are involved in multilateral fora such as Brazil, Russia, India, China and South Africa (BRICS) and now in the SCO. In fact, the permanent membership in the SCO is seen as a platform for Russia-Pakistan-China and India to collaborate in a more comprehensive manner that may, in turn lead to the creation of a 'comfort zone' by accommodating each other's interests, as well as overcoming the hurdles that have impacted the interactions among the countries at the bilateral level.

India, alongside Russia and China, has been an ardent advocate of a multipolar world order that stands for anti-Western or non-Western interests. The success of such a vision can only be possible by involving more players, including a long-term Western ally such as Pakistan into the fold. Many in the academic field believe that the Kremlin's greater involvement in the management of Asian security may facilitate favourable conditions for India. Why? Because, Russia is very clear on the intentions of its partnership with China which are not in any way anti-India interests but rather anti-Western interests, and to challenge the preeminence of the US. Russia has a clear impetus to diplomatically and strategically intercede to the best of its capacity in keeping India-Pakistan tensions at bay in order to maximise the economic benefit which can only be possible with their peaceful collaboration. India, however, has more leverage in terms of its relations with Russia than Pakistan. Moreover, Russia has always been vocal in criticising Islamabad's actions that have threatened India's national security. Moscow will continue to extend its support to India as New Delhi will remain Russia's most reliable and trusted ally.

The China- Pakistan nexus will be monitored by Russia, as over time, the alliance between the two countries would entail a diminution of Russia's relative standing in the RPC. Hence, similar to Russia extending its support to India for permanent membership in the SCO, Moscow may cajole India to play a key role in the RPC. Additionally, the last thing that Russia would want is to have to choose between China and India because Russia has a lot at stake and cannot afford to allow a military confrontation between the two Asian giants. The main factors bolstering this argument are: (1) Russia is an export oriented country which depends highly on the energy and defence markets; (2) China and India are two large markets as both these countries are 'imported oriented', especially in terms of energy and defence markets. Any untoward incident between these two countries will impact Russia's 'Pivot to Asia' strategy.

Pakistan's involvement in RPC will be carefully monitored not only by Russia but also by China because both have a lot at stake and, hence, cannot afford to ignore Pakistan's historical record of harbouring terrorist organisations in its territory, supporting the Afghan Mujahideen, recognising the Taliban government and promoting terrorist activities. Russia is concerned about the spread of religious fundamentalism from Afghanistan to the CARs, and China is concerned about Islamist separatists in Xinjiang province, while India is a 'soft target' for terrorist attacks.

Due to the growing security concerns, New Delhi has revamped its national security strategy so that the security response not only attends to the areas of convergence with the international community on terrorism but also the areas of dissonance, stemming from India's own experience, context, identity and strategic environment. The Islamic State of Iraq and Syria (ISIS) and Al Qaeda, have emerged as the principal threats to India, emanating from the base in the Afghanistan-Pakistan border region. These terrorist organisations are compounded by their growing affiliations with Pakistan-based groups such as the Jaish-e-Mohammed (JeM), Lashkar-e-Tayyeba (LeT) and Lashkar-e-Jhangvi (LeJ).[30] Apart from the apprehensions about the rise of Islamist extremism and the intention to create fear among the masses and political leaders alike, the 'spillover' effect of terrorist activities at the domestic level has threatened the very domain of India's national security

Moreover, India not only has security concerns in the Af-Pak region, it needs Afghanistan as a transit to access the energy rich Central Asian region and for a secure execution of the TAPI pipeline project. The security and stability of Afghanistan depends on the tripartite efforts among Russia, China and Pakistan, including India. Another implication of RPC for India is regarding the future prospects of another formidable trilateral arrangement, which is the Russia-India-China partnership.

The geo-politics of the region and the threats from neighbouring countries have, for long, decelerated India's extensive interaction in international relations. In a similar fashion, Russia too has been cocooned in its global prospects as the former Soviet space has markedly been in the policy interests and priorities of the Kremlin. Consequently, close and cooperative ties between India and Russia were forged due to the strategic congruence that dominated the two countries' policy formulations and interests. One such area identified for continuance of closer cooperation is the global participation of both India and Russia based on mutual interests and anxiety, owing to the rise in global security issues, concerns and challenges, from both traditional and non-traditional threats. All in all, with reference to the current geo-political calculus, it stands to reason that the strategic partnership has moved beyond bilateral engagements.

Obstacles

The interesting interplay of several geo-political factors in the evolving RPC trilateral relations has caused anxiety to India. Against this backdrop, the obstacles that exist in RPC for India are as follows:

The lack of trust between India and Pakistan would be the weakest link in RPC as the two countries have engaged in military confrontation in the past. Moreover, Pakistan's policies and military posturing have always been blatantly targeted towards India. Not to forget, Pakistan's nuclear capability is India-centric. Moreover, the hostile relations have stalled the very progress of a forum such as the South Asian Association for Regional

Cooperation (SAARC). The Russia-Pakistan military cooperation agreement is a matter of concern for India as one cannot rule out a more 'productive' defence partnership between the two countries. Nevertheless, Russia will simply be following the business model of the rest of the global defence supplying nations, which indicates that India may no longer enjoy the 'exceptional' status of the past. In other words, due to its robust partnership with India, Russia had for long maintained minimal defence cooperation with Islamabad. Moscow's step is seen as a response to India's diversification of its defence markets.

Another aspect for the growing convergence in RPC is the security and stability of the Af-Pak region. Russia's 'reliance' on Pakistan to combat terrorism has indicated that Moscow may compromise with its previous displeasure and condemnation of Islamabad's role in encouraging and promoting terrorist activities on Indian soil. Though one cannot rule out the fact that Moscow will continue its attempt to mediate in India-Pakistan relations, Russia has eased its stance on Pakistan's behaviour. The thinking also goes that if Russia were to compensate for its diplomatic 'blind spot' with Pakistan and reinvigorate the bilateral relationship with Islamabad, then it could 'mirror the role' that it plays between India and China which mostly is a neutral approach. Russia may, thus, not be as vocal in criticising Pakistan as it has been in the past.[31]

With regard to India's concerns towards China, is the latter's disinclination to resolve the pending territorial border issues with India. Fear of China establishing itself as the 'alter ego' of the United States, especially in the Asian geo-political theatre, is another reason for anxiety among the political elites in India. Beijing's engagement with Pakistan through economic and military assistance will be seen as an attempt to curtail India's growth in the South Asian region.

The China-Pakistan link is well known. Of far greater concern to India is China's South Asia policy, especially its strategic relationship with Pakistan, including generous gifts of nuclear weapon-related technologies and materials, modern conventional weapon systems, and gestures of support for Pakistan in its periodic confrontation or conflict with India. However, it is not only China's all-weather friendship with Pakistan and its advances into the Indian Ocean that comprise a thorn in the side of India; China's extensive political and military relations with its neighbouring countries like Nepal, Bangladesh and Sri Lanka also are of concern to India. China is using aid and investment very astutely.[32]

With the coming of a new government headed by Narendra Modi, the stakes were high with regard to Chinese President Xi Jinping's visit to New Delhi in September 2014. The visit was expected to revamp the strained relations between China and India, especially after signs of de-escalation in Chumar in Ladakh, and an eventual stand-off between the two countries. The People's Liberation Army (PLA) also made a similar incursion earlier by sending its troops into the Indian waters of the Pangong Tso. China has exercised a two-pronged policy towards India which has time and again shaken India's trust in Beijing. The visit of Xi marked a new beginning, with talks held on various issues and aspects, including the idea of the BCIM (Bangladesh-China-India-Myanmar) corridor. But, the display of Chinese muscle-flexing through incursions and transgressions has only cast a shadow on the bilateral relations between India and China, which are still marred by suspicion and hostility.

The outcome of the 1962 War cast a long shadow over Sino-Indian relations and the Indian psyche, in particular, and despite the efforts for substantial improvement over the years, it continues to influence the bilateral relationship. In addition, the war of 1962 has bequeathed China and India the border dispute that triggered the war and has made resolving it a Herculean task. To this day, China continues to claim the Indian state of Arunachal Pradesh, while New Delhi has asserted its legal right over the Chinese-controlled Aksai Chin territory.[33] As for the strategic consequences, the presence of the Dalai Lama and the establishment of a Tibetan government-in-exile in India resulted in the inevitable war with China. Moreover, it impaired the progress of Sino-Indian relations and became the embodiment of the unresolved status of the Tibet issue. For Beijing, the Dalai Lama's government-in-exile in Dharamsala has been a constant challenge to its rule in Tibet.[34]

The growing proximity among Russia-Pakistan-China has caused a certain level of anxiety in the policy circle of India towards Moscow. However, one cannot rule out that the strategic partnership between the two countries continues to share mutual trust and understanding. Ties with Moscow have served India well at critical moments and vice versa. The two countries continue to have a deep understanding of each other's capabilities and concerns. Despite attempts to isolate it, Russia remains relevant on the global stage. A strong partnership with India can also provide Russia breathing space in its evolving ties with China. Therefore, the prevailing trends offer India and Russia challenges and opportunities to find common synergies and engage each other in areas of mutual interest and concern. They cannot afford to dilute the partnership since they both need each other.

Nevertheless, a lot will depend upon the direction of India's foreign policy under the new government and the priority it attaches to the RPC triple alliance. Firstly, improved Sino-Indian relations, to the point where the two do not see each other as threats. Moreover, China's relations with Russia and India are subordinated to two overriding goals of Chinese foreign policy.

- To maintain a stable regional international environment that will allow China to advance its economic development.
- To manage its "peaceful rise" globally so that it does not provoke confrontation with existing major powers as this might thwart its rise.[35]

Simultaneously, Russia, China and India have a number of converging interests that could add substance to the 'triple alliance' talks. All three share concerns of a unipolar world. They still back the primacy of the United Nations in resolving crises and support the principle of non-intervention in the internal affairs of sovereign states. In the long run, it is the mutual confidence which will help these three powers to play a larger role in global politics.[36] Among other factors binding these three states together is a shared concern about Islamic terrorism. Russia faces a secessionist movement in Chechnya, a predominant Muslim territory within Russia; India also faces threats by Islamist militants in Kashmir; while the Chinese are alarmed by Uighur nationalism in Xinjiang.[37]

Yes, there is conflict of interest, hostility and suspicion, irreconcilable issues such as border disputes, military posturing, and lack of trust that will impact how they relate to each other in the decades to come. On the surface, it seems that India, China, Pakistan and Russia are ill-suited to a partnership due to many of these substantive differences among them. But we should not rule out the possibility in the near future as long-term interests such as regional and global security and economic prospects may pave the way for enhancing cooperation among these actors. The process of 'equal participation,' 'mutual benefits' and 'equal opportunities' among the countries may be a good start in this direction.

Notes

1. Adnan Ali Shah, "Pakistan-Russia Relations: Post-Cold War Era", www.issi.org. Accessed on October 10, 2014.
2. In September 1954, the United States, France, Great Britain, New Zealand, Australia, the Philippines, Thailand and Pakistan formed the Southeast Asia Treaty Organisation, or SEATO. The purpose of the organisation was to prevent Communism from gaining ground in the region."Milestones- 1953-1960, South-East Asia Treaty Organisation", US Department of State, https://history.state.gov/milestones/1953-1960/seato. Accessed on September 12, 2014.
3. The Central Treaty Organisation (CENTO) was created as a conventional military alliance in the Cold War climate of the 1950s and served as the central link in the chain of strategic defence pacts against the Soviet Union and its allies established by the Western powers of NATO to the SEATO.http://www.iranicaonline.org/articles/central-treaty-organisation-cento-a-mutual-defence-and-economic-cooperation-pact-among-persia-turkey-and-pakistan-wi. Accessed on September 12, 2014.
4. Consulate General of Russian Federation in Karachi, http://www.rusconsulkarachi.mid.ru/RUSSIA-PAKISTAN.htm. Accessed on November 15, 2014.

5. Susan B Maitra and Ramtanu Maitra, "Pakistan Reevaluates its U.S. Ties after Pressler Amendment Aid Cutoff", *EIR,* vol. 17, no. 48, December 14, 1990, p. 49.
6. Pakistan has signed neither the nuclear Non-Proliferation Treaty (NPT) nor the Comprehensive Test Ban Treaty (CTBT). However, UN Security Council Resolution 1172, which was adopted in 1998 after India's and Pakistan's nuclear tests earlier that year, called upon those countries to "stop their nuclear weapon development programmes, to refrain from weaponization or from the deployment of nuclear weapons, to cease development of ballistic missiles capable of delivering nuclear weapons and any further production of fissile material for nuclear weapons." Paul K. Kerr and Mary Beth Nikitin, "Pakistan's Nuclear Weapons: Proliferation and Security Issues", Congressional Research Service, May 10, 2012. p. 3, http://www2.gwu.edu/~nsarchiv/nukevault/ebb388/docs/EBB035.pdf. It was in this context that the Pressler Agreement was imposed on India and Pakistan by the US Congress that imposed sanctions on both the countries by denying nuclear technology by the Western world.
7. Boonie S. Glaser and Evan S. Medeiros, "The Changing Ecology of Foreign Policy Making in China: The Ascension and Demise of the Theory of 'Peaceful Rise'," *The China Quarterly*, 190, June 2007, pp.298-300. www.ou.edu/uschina/texts/Glaser.Medeiros.2007.cq.PeacefulRise.pdf. Accessed on January 29, 2015.
8. Fazal-ur-Rehman, "Pakistan's Evolving Relations with China, Russia and Central Asia," Slavic Eurasian Research Centre, 2007, p.223, http://srch.slav.hokudai.ac.jp/coe21/publish.no16_1_ses/11_rahman.pdf. Accessed on November 14, 2014.
9. Press Release of Karachi Chamber of Commerce and Industry, PR/ 106, Jumada- al- Sani 16, 1435 A.H, April 17, 2014, http://www.kcci.com.pk/April%2017,%202014.htm. Accessed on November 16, 2014
10. Sanjeev Miglani, "Russia Warming up to Pakistan", Centre for Land Warfare Studies, October 2012, http://www.claws.in/images/journals_doc/SW%20i-10.10.2012.90-95.pdf
11. Sergey Denisentsev and Konstantin Makienko, "The Arms Trade Treaty and Russian Arms Exports: Expectations and Possible Consequences", Centre for Analysis of Strategies and Technologies, p. 8, www.unidir.org. Accessed on October 3, 2014.
12. "Sino-Soviet Split", http://www.ibiblio.org/chinesehistory/contents/03pol/c05s04.html. Accessed on September 25, 2014.
13. Keith Suter, "1969: Russia and China – The War That Did Not Happen", *Global Directions,* http://global-directions.com/Articles/Global%20Politics/China-Russia.pdf. Accessed on September 27, 2014.
14. Peter Ferdinand, "Sino-Russian Relations: An Analytical Overview", Finnish Institute of International Affairs, 2011, pp. 31-34.
15. Arkady Moshes and Matti Nojonen, "Russia-China Relations: Current State, Alternative Futures, and Implicationsfor the West", Finnish Institute of International Affairs, 2011. p.11.
16. Andrew Korybko, "Pakistan is the 'Zipper' of Pan-Eurasian Integration", Russian Institute of Strategic Studies, September, 9, 2015. http://en.riss.ru/analysis/18882/
17.
18. John Mearsheimer, "Why China's Rise Will Not Be Peaceful", September 17, 2004. http://mearsheimer.uchicago.edu/pdfs/A0034b.pdf
19. David Scott, "India's Relations with Pakistan", in David Scott, ed., *Handbook of India's International Relations* (Routledge, 2011), pp. 59 and 65.
20. Ibid., p. 66
21. Gulam Asgar Mitha, "Middle East: The Regional Chessboard", *Oriental Review*, October 20, 2014.
22. K. Subramanyam, "Grand Strategy for the First Half of the 21st Century", in Krishnappa Swamy and Princy George, eds., *Grand Strategy for India 202 and Beyond* (Institute for

Defence Studies and Analysis, Pentagon Security International, 2012), p. 21.

23. Joy Mitra, "Russia, China and Pakistan: An Emerging New Axis?", *The Diplomat*, August 18, 2015.
24. Pakistan is uniquely poised to zip together a variety of economic blocs, taking advantage of both its convenient geography and China's grand investment vision to make it happen. The Russian-led trade organisation also comprises Belarus, Armenia, Kazakhstan and Kyrgyzstan. By bringing the Eurasian Union into contact with SAARC-member Pakistan, a steadfast and growing economy, it can provide a direct trade opening with the rest of the South Asian bloc. Korybko, n.16.
25. Korybko, n.16, p.127.
26. Mitra, n.23.
27. Joy Mitra, "Russia, China and Pakistan: An Emerging New Axis?", *The Diplomat*, August 18, 2015. www.thediplomat.com/2015/08/Russia_china_and_pakistan_an_emerging_new_axis. Accessed on February 10, 2016.
27. P Stobdan, "India's Stakes and Dilemma in SCO", Institute of Defence Studies and Analyses, June 8, 2015. http://www.idsa.in/idsacomments/IndiasStakesandDilemmainSCO_pstobdan_080615.html. Accessed on June 9, 2015
28. Alexander Gabuev, "Eurasian Silk Road Union: Towards a Russia-China Consensus?", *The Diplomat*, June 5, 2015, http://thediplomat.com/2015/06/eurasian-silk-road-union-towards-a-russia-China-consensus/. Accessed on June 9, 2015.
29. Ibid., p. 19.
30. Subrahmanyam, n. 22, p. 6.
31. Dr Subhash Kapila, "Russia's Caliberated Strategic Pivot to Pakistan," South Asian Analysis, Paper No. 6011, September 11, 2015, www.southasiananalysis.org/node/1865. Accessed on January 10, 2016.
32. Roy Medvedev, *China and the Superpowers* (Oxford: Basil Blackwell, 1986), p. 51.
33. Ivan Lidarev, "History's Hostage: China, India and the War of 1962", *The Diplomat*, August 21, 2012, http://thediplomat.com/2012/08/historys-hostage-China-indiaand- the-war-of-1962/, October 21, 2014.
34. Ibid.
35. Moshes and Nojonen, n.15, p. 25.
36. Nivedita Kundu, "Russia-India-China: Prospects for Trilateral Cooperation", *Aleksanteri* (Helsinki), 2004, p. 6.
37. Weitz Richard, "Russia Faces Challenges in India's Arms Market", *World Politics Review*, August 7, 2012, http://www.worldpoliticsreview.com/articles/12236/global-insights-russia-faces-challenges-in-indias-arms-market. Accessed on February 18, 2013, p. 77.

8

Pakistani UAVs: A Case of Indigenising the Arms Industry

RK Narang

On the battlefield of the future, enemy forces will be located, tracked and targeted almost instantaneously through the use of data links, computer-assisted intelligence and automated fire control . . . I am confident the American people expect this country to take full advantage of its technology.....to welcome and applaud the developments that will replace, wherever possible, the man with the machine.

– Gen William Westmoreland
US Army[1]

Introduction

On March 13, 2015, Pakistan's Army Chief Raheel Sharif announced that Pakistan had test-fired the indigenous laser guided missile 'Barq' from the Burraq Unmanned Aerial Vehicle (UAV),[2] which successfully hit stationary and mobile targets.[3] He emphasised that the armed UAVs would help Pakistan in its anti-terrorist operations. Pakistan claims to have simultaneously developed two elusive and advanced technologies through indigenous Research and Development (R&D). Pakistan overcoming the technological challenges associated with the development of UAVs and the miniaturised version of the air-to-ground laser missiles in such a short time, despite limitations in its R&D set-up and funding, has raised a few questions. Pakistan had been earlier trying to acquire armed UAVs from the United States, which was not agreed to by the US government in 2010.

Pakistan had initiated its UAV programme on the request of its armed forces in the early 1990s. The government and the military, over a period of time, had nurtured a group of public and private sector companies which were able to develop and manufacture small to medium UAVs indigenously for both military and civilian use. Its UAVs with civil applications found buyers within Pakistan as well as in other countries due to their low cost, simple design and easy maintenance. Pakistan built its UAV fleet by importing from other countries, manufacturing them in collaboration with other countries as well as indigenously developing them. The path taken by Pakistan in developing UAV capabilities, despite the limitations in funding and technological knowledge base, is interesting and worth analysing.

This paper would look into Pakistan's UAV industry, the acquisition of UAVs through collaboration and import, the challenges faced, and the approach followed, by Pakistan in the indigenisation of UAVs.

Pakistan's UAV Industry

Pakistan was keen to acquire UAVs to meet its defence needs. It was forced to develop an indigenous defence industry due to the Pressler Amendment by the US Senate in 1992 and the associated arms embargo. The indigenisation of the defence industry by Pakistan and the rising demand for indigenous products resulted in the establishment of 20 major Public Sector Units (PSUs) and about 100 private sector companies.

Public Sector

The PSUs involved in the overhaul, design, development and/ or production of defence equipment, including UAVs, have grown with the rising needs of the Pakistan military. These companies are supplying defence equipment and UAVs to the Pakistan armed forces as well as exporting to friendly countries. This is likely to indirectly help them develop a diplomatic leverage. The PSUs involved in the development of defence equipment and UAVs include the National Engineering and Scientific Commission (NESCOM), Pakistan Aeronautical Complex (PAC), Air Weapons Complex(AWC), National Development Complex (NDC) and Global Industrial Defence Solutions (GIDS). The indigenous defence industry is not only providing jobs to the people of Pakistan but also becoming a source of revenue for the country. The details of some of the public sector companies are covered in the succeeding paragraphs.

National Engineering and Scientific Commission (NESCOM): NESCOM was established in the year 2000 in Islamabad and comes under the Strategic Planning Division (SPD) of the General Headquarters (GHQ), Pakistan Army.[4] NESCOM administers defence programmes and is an umbrella organisation for coordinating R&D. The PSUs under NESCOM include the National Defence Complex (NDC) and Air Weapons Complex (AWC). NESCOM is responsible for nuclear, ballistic missiles and military hardware development and production, including UAVs for the Pakistani military and for exports[5]. The Burraq and Shahpur UAVs have been developed by NESCOM. These two UAVs were unveiled at the International Defence Exhibition and Seminar (IDEAS)

Expo in Karachi on November 15, 2012,[6] and inducted into the Pakistan Army and Air Force in November 2013.[7]

PAC, Kamra[8]: The Pakistan Aeronautical Complex (PAC), Kamra, is the ISO-9002 certified factory which is situated 70 km from Islamabad, near Attock city. It was established in 1971[9] with a vision to provide indigenous support to the Pakistan Air Force (PAF) and Pakistan's friendly countries. It houses four aviation factories, namely,the Aircraft Rebuild Factory (ARF), Mirage Rebuild Factory (MRF), Aircraft Manufacturing Factory(AMF) and Avionics Production Factory (APF)[10] and takes care of all operational assets of the PAF. It is spread over an area of 10 sq km and has over 10,000 employees.[11] The MFI-17 (Mushak), a piston engine trainer, is being built here indigenously under licence from the Swedish firm SAABSCANIA since 1975.[12] Its improved version, the Super Mushak, is being exported to some countries which include Saudi Arabia[13] and Iraq.[14] Pakistan is in talks with Saudi Arabia to sell the JF-17 fighter aircraft, which has been co-developed with China[15]. The Falco UAV of the Selex Company of Italy is also being manufactured under licence at this complex since 2009.[16]

Air Weapons Complex (AWC): AWC at the Wah cantonment near Rawalpindi, Punjab, was established in 1992. The Wah cantonment houses the Pakistan Ordnance Factories (POF), AWC and Heavy Industries Taxila (HIT).[17] It is involved in the manufacture of airborne navigation and positioning systems, air-launched weapons and also plays a key role in the development of indigenous UAVs.Its AWC Mk I, a low cost surveillance/ target acquisition UAV, was inducted into service in 1997.[18]The Bravo and Vision-1 UAVs were also developed by AWC.[19]

National Defence Complex (NDC): NDC is located at Fatehganj, Rawalpindi, about 50 km southwest of Islamabad,[20] and was created with the objective of developing an infrastructure of indigenous weapons development, provision for technical services and achieving self-reliance in diverse technologies.[21] It has also been involved in the design and manufacture of UAVs.[22]

Global Industrial and Defence Solutions (GIDS): GIDS is the largest public sector consortium comprising seven PSUs i.e. Advanced Engineering Research Organisation (AERO), Al-Technique Corporation of Pakistan (ATCOP), Integrated Defence Systems (IDS), Institute of Industrial Control Systems (IICS), Marine Systems Limited (MSL), Scientific Engineering and Technology Services (SETS) and Xpert Engineering Services. GIDS manages commercial operations of the companies involved in design, development and manufacturing of defence and electronic systems. These companies are producing air, land, naval and Nuclear, Biological, Chemical (NBC) equipment. GIDS has developed various UAVs, which include Shahpur, Uqab, Huma and Scout mini UAVs.[23] GIDS is the main contractor for military, industrial and technological products and services exports. Maj Gen Syed Guftar Shah, the Chief Executive Officer (CEO) of GIDS, while speaking on the defence industry in Pakistan in 2012, informed that it provides jobs to about 200,000 people, which excludes vendors.[24]

Private Sector

The private sector companies which are playing a key role in the indigenisation of UAVs, include Integrated Dynamics, East-West Infiniti and Surveillance and Target Unmanned Aircraft (SATUMA). A brief description about some of the private sector companies involved in UAV development and manufacture is covered below.

East-West Infiniti (EWI): East-West Infiniti (Pvt) Ltd (EWI) company was established at Islamabad in 1982. It was initially known as the East-West Bridge from 1982-85 and was thereafter renamed as East-West Systems (Pvt) Ltd from 1985-1995 before being renamed as East-West Infiniti (Pvt) Ltd. It has been developing UAVs which include the Heliquad stealthy mini UAV.

Integrated Dynamics (ID): ID is a privately owned, Karachi-based Pakistani company that came into existence in 1997.It has built the Rover, Explorer, Skycam, Spirit and Pride UAVs for civilian use. Its other reconnaissance and surveillance UAVs are the Rover, Explorer, Hornet, Hawk, Vision, Shadow, Vector and Border Eagle.[25] It has also produced decoys, which include the Tornado jet powered decoy, Nishan Mk-II piston engine decoy and Nishan TJ-1000 jet decoy.[26] ID came into the limelight during IDEAS 2008 and it has claimed to be supplying UAVs to the armed forces as well as exporting them to Australia, Spain, South Korea and Libya[27] and the US.[28]ID's 15 kg piston engine Border Eagle UAV, capable of three hours endurance with a 4 kg payload[29] is being used for border/ perimeter monitoring in the US.[30] The reason for the demand for Pakistan's UAVs in other countries has been their low cost.[31] The prices of the UAVs produced by Integrated Dynamics start from $20,000 compared to $200,000 in the West.[32] The export of UAVs by Integrated Dynamics to Australia, Spain, South Korea, Libya and the US was covered in the flight global website, Pakistani media and some sections of the international media. Raja Sabri Khan, while speaking at an event organised in Karachi, Pakistan, on May 27, 2011,[33] discussed the use of his company's drones in the Great Barrier Reef in Australia, to map the ecosystem in the Amazon forest, oceans and Antarctica.[34] However, these claims of export could not be verified from the sources of these countries, except Libya.

Surveillance and Target Unmanned Aircraft (SATUMA): SATUMA started as a small set-up in 1989.[35] It has grown into a private limited company with a wide range of

UAVs. It is located 25 km out of Islamabad, on the banks of the river Soan. The factory has a floor area of 5,000 sq ft and a small airfield to carry out testing and evaluation of the UAVs, ground control stations, and other associated equipment.[36] SATUMA has been involved in the design, development and manufacture of UAVs and supplying these to the armed forces. The UAVs manufactured by SATUMA include the Flamingo, Jasoos (Bravo+), Mukhbar, Stingray UAVs, Full/ Half Scale Trainers, Thunder, Assault and Shooting Star target drones.[37]

Advanced Computing and Engineering Solutions (ACES) Pvt Ltd: ACES was established at Islamabad in 2001 and provides the system integrator, software developer and multi-dimensional engineering products design and development.[38] The company has developed small to medium UAVs for both civilian and military use.[39]

Collaboration and Import of UAVs

China

Pakistan has been using the Chinese ASN 105 and ASN 206 reconnaissance and surveillance UAVs for a long time. These UAVs were built by China's National Aero-Technology Import and Export Corporation (CATIC).Pakistan has been using the UAVs to map border areas to identify routes in order to facilitate infiltration of terrorists into Indian territory.[40]

In 2011, China supplied 75 kg FT-5 small diameter bombs to Pakistan, which are suitable for carriage by UAVs. It had also offered to sell Pakistan the CH-3 armed UAVs, which can carry two AR-1 laser-guided air-to-ground missiles or bombs.[41] However, there was reluctance in the Pakistan armed forces to buy the Chinese armed drones as they were yet to prove their capability.

Selex Galileo (Italy)

Pakistan had collaborated with the Italian company Selex Galileo (SG) in 2009[42] and commenced manufacturing the Falco XN UAV under licence at the Pakistan Aeronautical Complex at Kamra, in Punjab.[43] The production of the Falco Tactical was described by the then Chief of the Air Staff Air Mshl Farhat Hussain as "major step towards the goal of self-reliance in military aviation".[44] According to Air Vice Mshl Aminullah Khan, managing director at PAC, the indigenous production of the Falco would give Pakistan a "quantum jump" in the ability to work with composites and is likely to be used for future projects.[45] The Falco is a versatile UAV, which can be launched from semi-prepared airstrips as well as from a pneumatic catapult, and recovered by either automatic landing or by parachute. It can carry a variety of payloads which include laser designators, maritime surveillance radars and NBC detection sensors upto a range of 200 km.[46]

Turkey

Pakistan has been trying to develop UAVs indigenously as well as through joint collaboration. In 2007, Turkey and Pakistan decided to work jointly on UAVs and signed a Letter of Intent.[47] The Uqab UAV is believed to have been built by the Pakistan Aeronautics Complex (PAC), Kamra,with the help of Turkish Aerospace Industries (TAI) in 2008.[48] According to TAI's GokberkOzturk, Turkey views Pakistan as a prospective buyer of its 'Anka' UAV and gave sub-contracting work to PAC.[49] PAC officials handed over the first batch of the parts manufactured for the Turkish UAV 'Anka' to the CEO of TAI Muharrem Dortkasli, in a ceremony held during the International Defence Exhibition and Fair (IDEF) at Istanbul, Turkey, in May 2013.[50] Pakistan has been seeking access to Turkish UAV technology for improving its indigenous drones and would look to gain from this partnership. However, the weak economic condition of Pakistan could become a hurdle in joint development/ collaboration between the two countries despite their friendly relations.[51]

Germany

The Pakistan Navy signed a contract on June 27, 2012,to acquire eight Luna X-2000 UAV systems and two ground control stations from EMT of West Germany[52]. The UAV was shortlisted by the Pakistan Navy after evaluating offers from eight bidders, including five from China. It is launched by a bungee catapult and recovered by a net or parachute. It has a unique capability to switch off its engine and carry out acoustic signature glide without engine power, and can be restarted on command[53]. EMT is a small firm from Penzberg, Germany, which bagged the contract for the development of short range UAVs for the German armed forces in 1997. Innovation and private entrepreneurship played a key role in the development of the Luna UAV. The first prototype flew in less than a year in May 1998, and by 2000, it was deployed in Kosovo.[54]

Pakistan had earlier procured approximately four or five Luna UAVs for the army in Financial Year (FY) 2005-06.[55] The Pakistan Army has been using the Luna UAVs for intelligence gathering since their acquisition in 2006.[56] At the time of acquisition, reservations were expressed by the Technical Directorate of the General Headquarters (GHQ) of the Pakistan Army about the utility of such a small UAV, which did not fall in the category of a tactical UAV. The Luna UAV procurement, at a cost of $30 million from Germany, has been criticised by local manufacturers due to the high cost[57] as UAVs with similar range and payload manufactured by the indigenous manufacturers were 60-70 percent cheaper.[58]

Rotary Wing UAVs

The Pakistan Navy has been looking for rotary wing UAVs for its ships. The trials for the Camcopter S-100 rotary wing UAV, which is built by the Austrian company, Schibel, were carried out from a Pakistan Navy frigate in 2013[59]. The S-100 can carry out Vertical Take-Off and Landing (VTOL)automatically. It has a service ceiling of 18,000 ft,its maximum air speed to 130 Kts, with speed of 100 Kts[60]. Its main rotor diameter of 3.4 m is just enough to allow shipborne operations. The maximum take-off weight of the S-100 is 200 kg and it can carry 50 kg of payload with 57 litres of fuel. Its endurance can be extended up to six hours. In addition to Pakistan, India, Egypt, Austria, Germany, Italy, French and the US too have indicated their interest in acquiring the versatile Camcopter S-100 rotary unmanned aerial vehicle. However, it has not been confirmed whether the Pakistan Navy has placed an order for S-100 rotary wing UAVs. The interest shown by Pakistan in the S-100 indicates its keenness to acquire the latest technology in UAVs.

Indigenous Development of UAVs

Pakistan's Public Sector Units (PSUs) and private companies, under the guidance of Strategic Planning Division of the Pakistan military, have developed over 34 types of small and medium range UAVs, target drones and UAV trainers with civilian and military applications. The details of the various UAVs are placed at **Appendix 'A'**.The details of some of the endeavours by the public sector as well as private companies to develop UAVs indigenously are covered in the succeeding paragraphs.

Tactical UAV (Uqab)

The Pakistan Army had given a requirement for developing a tactical UAV indigenously in 2007. The requirement was to produce a remotely controlled self-piloted UAV on the modular concept, with low radar signature,which could carry the required reconnaissance sensors. Pakistan had already established a fair network of public and private sector companies which could undertake the design and development of a tactical UAV. Its indigenous industry had sufficient experience in developing small and medium UAVs. Pakistan followed a typical US model for indigenous development of a tactical UAV with three companies competing for the project to come up with a prototype design.[61]

The results of the competition were encouraging with Integrated Defence Systems offering the Huma-I and Huma-II, ACES offering Eagle Eye P-I and Eagle Eye P-II and

Albadeel Technologies offering HudHud II and the larger HudHud III for the tactical UAVs.[62] All the three contenders offered UAVs with a high wing monoplane airframe with twin tail booms and a pusher propeller. The Eagle Eye P-I, which weighed 130 kg, first flew in 2002 and Eagle Eye P-II, weighing 175 kg, followed in 2005. Both its versions operate from runways. The truck mounted Huma-1 was already being used for reconnaissance and surveillance roles since 2003.[63] The Eagle Eye P-I/P-II tactical UAV system of ACES was selected for further modification/ upgradation by the NESCOM and production by GIDS.[64]

Pakistan carried out final test flight of the Uqab on March 20, 2008, prior to its induction into the Pakistan Army.[65] The test was witnessed by Chief of the Army Staff Gen Ashfaq Pervez Kayani, senior armed forces officers and scientists. The Uqab-II, an improved version of the Uqab was subsequently inducted into the Pakistan Navy at the PNS Mehran air base in the presence of Chief of the Naval Staff Adm Noman Bashir in July 2011.[66] This is despite the fact that a day before the Uqab-II induction, one of the Uqab UAVs had crashed at the National Oil Refinery in Korangi after a bird strike. The induction of the Uqab-II was important since the PC3 Orion Maritime Reconnaissance aircraft were destroyed in a terrorist attack on the Pakistan Navy's Mehran air base on May 22, 2011. The Uqab-II was nowhere close to the PC-3 Orion in performance and range, yet it met the short distance reconnaissance needs of the Pakistan Navy.

Shahpur

Shahpur, an indigenous unmanned reconnaissance aerial vehicle was inducted into service in a ceremony attended by outgoing Army Chief Gen Ashfaq Pervez Kayani and Lt Gen Khalid Kidwai (Retd.), director, Strategic Plans Division of the Pakistan Army in November 2013.[67] Shahpur is a medium range tactical UAV with a canard airframe and pusher propellers[68], which has been developed by NESCOM and built by GIDS. Shahpur is powered by the Rotax 912 engine and has automatic take-off and landing capability.[69] The UAV has significantly low radar signature and is equipped with the EO/IR (Electronic Observation/Infra-Red) sensors and laser range finder.

Armed UAVs

US Reluctance and Offer: The US lifted the sanctions imposed under the Pressler Amendment in 2001 after the 9/11 terror strike on its soil,[70] and announced Pakistan as a non-NATO ally, facilitating purchase of military equipment. US UAV operations started in 2004. Pakistan had been tacitly allowing the US to carry out UAV strikes in the Afghanistan-Pakistan border region against the Taliban. It had seen the effectiveness of armed UAVs from close quarters and had demanded them from the US as a *quid pro quo*, on the pretext of undertaking operations against rogue militant groups in 2009-10. The unstated reason for acquiring armed drones was to build a technological edge over India and improve its surveillance and strike capability. The US was reluctant to supply its advanced armed UAVs to Pakistan fearing copying of key technology by the Chinese due to the close economic and strategic relations between Pakistan and China. However, US Defence Secretary Robert Gates, during, his visit to Islamabad, had offered Pakistan 12 Shadow-200 (RQ-7) unarmed surveillance UAVs at an estimated cost of $20 million in January 2010, which were to be paid through its counter-insurgency fund or foreign military assistance[71] and delivered in 36 to 48 months[72]. The Shadow 200 is a catapult launched UAV, which is recovered with an arrester gear. It is being used by the US Navy and US Marine Corps. The US offer was a result of persistent demands from the Pakistan government and the importance of Pakistan as an ally of the US in its Global War on Terror (GWOT).

Opposition to US Offer: The US offer of supplying unarmed Shadow-200 UAV was not viewed favourably by the Pakistan military as well as by the indigenous UAV manufacturers. The military was also not happy with the delayed delivery timeline[73]. The advocates of indigenisation in Pakistan were concerned that the procurement of unarmed surveillance UAVs from the US could adversely impact the fragile indigenous UAV industry. Haroon Qureshi, the pioneer in the field of UAVs and owner of East-West Infiniti Pvt Ltd (EWI), criticised the US for offering an expensive and unarmed UAV. He advocated that Pakistan procure indigenous UAVs, which were equally capable.[74] The high offer price of UAVs in the proposed deal was criticised as being due to the anticipated kickbacks and alleged lure of foreign trips.[75] However, the US-Pakistan relationship soured after the Raymond Davis incident which was followed by the killing of Osama Bin Laden in 2011, and the UAV deal did not go through.

Chinese Link: The reluctance of the US to supply armed UAVs forced Pakistan to explore other options. Pakistan has traditionally been a close ally of China. China had provided Pakistan with crucial missile and nuclear technology in the past. The Chinese offer of supplying armed drones to Pakistan was not confirmed by either side. Since then, Pakistan has been trying to develop armed UAVs indigenously. It carried out trials for firing of rockets from the Italian Falco UAVs in 2012, and arming the Shahpur UAV.[76] Pakistan had faced difficulties in the development of armed UAVs due to non-availability of precision munitions and advanced targeting technology. Pakistani Prime Minister Raja

Pervez Ashraf in a statement in November 2012 had indicated intent for seeking Chinese help in the development of defence equipment, including armed UAVs."Pakistan can also benefit from China in defence collaboration, offsetting the undeclared technological apartheid,"

The statement clearly indicated Pakistan's displeasure at the US' refusal to supply armed drones to Pakistan, which brought Pakistan and China even closer.

Arming the Burraq

Pakistan had inducted the Burraq UAVs into its armed forces in November 2013, claiming it to be indigenous. It had carried out air-to-ground firing of the Barq laser guided missile from the Burraq UAV in March 2015. Gen Raheel, speaking after the success of the missile firing from the Burraq UAV, said, "The newly developed arsenal will increase the military's capacity in fighting terrorism".[77] He congratulated the scientists and technicians for developing state-of-the-art equipment. The Burraq UAV is named after the horse that took Prophet Mohammad to heaven.[78] It is claimed to have the ability to fly in all weather conditions and strike targets with pin-point accuracy.

The video depicting the missile firing by the Burraq demonstrates its ability to strike stationary targets. The video thereafter shows the missile targeting a simulated target mounted on a platform, moving slowly. In a realistic scenario, the actual mobile target could be much more manoeuvrable and moving at a greater speed. Its ability to strike moving targets in a realistic scenario needs to be ascertained.[79]

Benign Media: The missile firing demonstration from the Burraq UAV in March 2015, which was claimed to be indigenous by the Pakistani military, was initially reported without checking the authenticity of the claims by *Jane's*.[80] The unequivocal support of the Pakistani media and military establishment was understandable.[81] The lack of reaction from the Chinese on the Pakistan's claim of indigenous development too was on expected lines. The ignorance of the Indian media was visible from the reporting of this event without ascertaining the facts.[82] The Western media did not take note of the lack of technological expertise in Pakistan, Burraq's similarity with the Chinese armed UAV and simultaneous testing of two different technologies.[83] The lack of reaction from the Western media despite having a large number of professional military experts on their panels was intriguing.[84]

Mysterious Indigenisation

Pakistan claiming to test two vastly different technologies viz. armed UAVs and miniaturised laser-guided missiles simultaneously, is rather unrealistic and raises questions about the authenticity of these claims. These two are leading edge technologies, with each requiring different expertise, extensive R&D, prolonged trials and testing of systems. Any expert who understands the nuances of R&D would take these claims with a pinch of salt.

Pakistan till then had been carrying out R&D to build small to medium range UAVs using low to moderate capability sensors for reconnaissance and surveillance purposes. The designing of the Barq laser-guided lightweight missile by Pakistan appears to be a quantum jump from the known technical and technological capability available within Pakistan. There was no indication of huge investments in these niche technologies and miniaturisation of weapons to facilitate firing from UAVs by the Pakistani R&D agencies in the recent past.

Similarities with CH-3: The Burraq was initially being compared with the Italian Falco UAV. However, the Burraq does not appear to have much similarity in design with the Falco. The Burraq UAV and Barq air-to-ground missile appear to be closer to the Chinese Rainbow-3 (CH-3) UAV and AR-1 missile respectively and could have been either supplied by China or modified to meet Pakistan's specific requirements. *Jane's*, in a subsequent article, had also corrected this anomaly and highlighted the similarities with the Chinese AR-1 missile and CH-3 UAV and also questioned the authenticity of the test[85]. Therefore, in all probability, China appears to have played a key role and provided major assistance to Pakistan in the design and development of the Burraq UAV. The level of assistance could have varied from providing the design or technical assistance to transfer of technology and/ or supply of ready-to-assemble parts. The Barq laser-guided missile could actually be a Chinese (AR-1)missile fitted on the Chinese CH-3 UAV (Burraq) and assembled in Pakistan. However, it still does not take away the credit for developing an indigenous UAV industry and saving valuable foreign currency, which is at a premium for an economy like Pakistan.

The Chinese have been supplying arms to Pakistan and other countries without much publicity and sometimes clandestinely to win contracts, develop relations and to have greater strategic influence. They have been magnanimous in allowing the Pakistan to claim their arms to be of Pakistani origin. This suits both China and Pakistan. China has done it in the past, when it gave nuclear and missile technology to Pakistan and allowed Pakistan to claim them as indigenous. This gives China the manoeuvring space in the conduct of international relations without being targeted as an arms proliferators. Pakistan, on the other hand, can claim it as an achievement for appeasing its domestic audience.

Challenges to Indigenisation

Pressler Amendment

The Pressler Amendment by the US Senate in 1992 came as shock to Pakistan and the associated sanctions had adversely impacted procurement of defence equipment and sourcing of technology for its arms industry. Pakistan chalked out a plan to develop UAVs indigenously to achieve self-reliance. However, it faced enormous challenges in developing its indigenous UAV industry due to the US sanctions, which are covered in the succeeding paragraphs.

Limitations of Indigenous Set-up

At the time of partition, all the ordnance factories went towards India's share since they were geographically located in India and Pakistan did not get even one of them. Therefore, Pakistan had to start from scratch. It had to set up ordnance and defence production factories to undertake repair and overhaul of foreign origin equipment of the Pakistani defence forces. It made slow and steady progress in developing public sector units to undertake R&D in the crucial defence sector. Its armed forces had put up the requirement for a tactical reconnaissance UAV. However, Pakistan had a limited technological base and could not afford huge funding to design and build advanced UAVs.

The public sector units were already committed and could not have taken up mass production of UAVs alone. The private sector filled the void and provided the much needed platform for the production of UAVs for Pakistan and for export to other countries. Pakistan had a few colleges which were providing higher courses in aeronautics and astronautics to support development of high end technology UAVs and defence systems. Therefore, it had to depend on a handful of public sector units and R&D agencies for development of advanced technologies.

Killer Drones or Drones for Peace

The private UAV manufacturers faced a dilemma of convincing their own population since drones were viewed as killers of civilians due to the US drone strikes in Pakistan. The US drone strikes were criticised and viewed as violation of Pakistan's sovereignty. There was a popular perception that drones were only meant for killing humans due to the huge anti-drone campaign in the media. There was reluctance among the Pakistani public to accept UAVs for civilian use and it posed a major threat to the life of indigenous UAV manufacturers.

SATUMA and East-West Infiniti were mostly manufacturing military UAVs and both were based in Islamabad, a relatively safe place. Integrated Dynamics, on the other hand, was located in volatile Karachi and did not want to be associated with the notion of killer drones. It, therefore, came up with the slogan "Drones for Peace" and emphasised the civilian and scientific applications which could change lives.[86] The move was aimed at countering negative perceptions and to ensure that they were not unduly targeted. They aggressively marketed drones for civilian use in order to create acceptability of their products.

A Different Approach to Indigenisation

Pragmatic Goal Setting

Pakistani planners were aware of the strengths and limitations of the technical expertise available within the country. They appeared to have made a conscious decision to design, develop and manufacture small and medium UAVs instead of trying to develop technologically advanced UAVs. It was a pragmatic and sensible approach, which aimed at setting achievable goals, developing indigenous capability and then gradually aiming for higher capability. The endeavour was to develop UAVs which were easy to build, maintain and have a low cost. According to Integrated Dynamics, a key UAV producer, a small civilian UAV in Pakistan cost around $10,000 to $15,000, which was much less than the cost of a UAV of similar capability available in the West, and this became the strength of the indigenous UAVs.[87]

Individuals Matter

Brilliance is not necessarily restricted to certain organisations. The US, Russia, Germany and Britain had made initial progress in niche aviation industry due to the brilliance of individuals. These individuals were dreamers and passionate about their innovative ideas. Pakistan too, riding on the brilliance and passion of a few individuals, proceeded in a systematic manner to build its UAV industry. The Pakistani establishment appears to have encouraged the public sector units as well as individual technocrats, who had undergone higher studies, especially in aeronautics and astronautics, to set up UAV manufacturing units in the private sector under the umbrella of the public sector. Integrated Dynamics is headed by Raja Sabri Khan, who is a graduate from the Massachusetts Institute of Technology (MIT) with a Masters degree in aeronautics and astronautics.[88] He established a drone research centre[89], which is spread over an area of 90,000 sq ft in Karachi. Raja Sabri Khan, while speaking at an event in 2011, had admitted that he was asked by Salim Mehmud, chairman of Pakistan's Space and Upper Atmosphere Research Commission (SUPARCO) in 1998-99 to build UAVs for the government.[90] He also sponsors higher study projects on UAVs in colleges. Haroon Javed Qureshi, an engineering graduate from the University of Engineering & Technology of Lahore had set up East-West Infiniti (Pvt) Ltd in Islamabad.[91] Both of them have been major players in the manufacture of UAVs.[92]

Best Vs Good Enough

The indigenous companies are often pitted against the well-established arms manufacturers of the world that not only have huge finances but also the technical expertise built over a period of decades. The leading arms manufacturing companies/ countries do not tell the stories of the failures, huge investments and long timeframes involved in the development of leading technologies. As a result, the users invariably demand the best from the indigenous manufacturers without giving them the timeframes and funding, as well accepting a few failures, before they are able to establish themselves. Also, while aiming for the "*best*", one at times forgets to take into account some of the requirements which can be met with "good enough". The aspiration to get the best from the indigenous defence industry often results in failures and cancellation of R&D projects, thereby making the country further dependent on foreign suppliers Acceptable Qualitative Requirements (QRs) for initial blocks of equipment could be one way to support the indigenous defence industry. This would give it the time to correct shortcomings and come up with viable solutions. Most countries have obtained self-reliance by supporting their indigenous industry. The US, despite being the leader in the production of defence equipment, has given concession for delays in development and, sometimes,accepted lower performance of equipment in order to encourage indigenisation.

Public-Private Partnership

The Pakistani establishment encouraged and cultivated private sector companies to take on R&D and manufacture in niche defence technologies in order to achieve indigenisation. The cooperation among the government, armed forces, public and private sector units was clearly visible from the way some UAVs were designed and manufactured. The public sector units of Pakistan had carried out R&D and built UAV prototypes and the technology was thereafter transferred to private UAV manufacturers for commercial production.

Uqab Competition: A US Model: Pakistan had called for designing a prototype of the proposed tactical UAV Uqab as per the QRs given by the Pakistan Army. Pakistan had invited PSUs/ private companies to compete for the development of the Uqab UAV. Three companies had competed for the design of the Uqab prototype. All three came up with UAV designs which were better than the current models yet did not meet the QRs for the Uqab. This also highlights the limitations of these companies in undertaking R&D in critical technologies. However, the Pakistani establishment, rather than finding faults in the designs, selected the best among them for further improvement by NESCOM prior to production by GIDS.

Pakistan has been buying weapons as part of the US aid. Its officers have been interacting with, and participating in, training exercises with the US armed forces. They have been undergoing courses in training institutes of the US armed forces for quite some time. The development of the UAV industry has the signature of the US arms development model.

Indigenisation

The only way to create space for the indigenous industry is through innovation and setting realistic, achievable goals. Innovation can overcome challenges with less if organisations and/ or talented individuals are nurtured by the country. The competition for the Uqab did not bring in the best technology but it did provide the basic equipment from which Pakistan's public sector R&D agencies went on to develop the tactical UAV (Uqab). The Pakistani establishment's encouragement to manufacturers resulted in the development of UAVs having similar and even better capability than the Shadow-200 UAV, which was offered by the US.

Balance Between Indigenous Production and Imports: The import of weapons is an expensive business and lack of, or a weak, indigenous industry, puts additional pressure on the economy. As a result, no government is able to spare huge sums and meet all the demands of its armed forces. The planners in Pakistan made an effort to establish a delicate balance between indigenous production and imports, which could be seen from the way Pakistan went about encouraging the indigenous UAV industry. Also, if military equipment is developed and produced indigenously, the government is likely to be more benevolent in sparing additional funds for procurement for the simple reason that it would provide more jobs to its citizens. Therefore, procurement of advanced technology weapons from foreign arms suppliers should only be resorted to as an exception for areas where the indigenous industry is unable to produce. Overall, dependence on foreign suppliers should reduce with time.

Ownership

The Pakistani armed forces have shown initiative and taken ownership of the indigenously designed UAVs. The Strategic Planning Division (SPD) of the Pakistan Army monitors indigenous development of UAVs. It plays an important role in improving coordination among the armed forces, R&D organisations and production agencies. The importance shown towards the development of the Uqab UAV by the Pakistan armed forces highlights the efforts being put in for indigenisation of defence equipment. The following statement by Adm Noman Bashir, chief of the Naval Staff, Pakistan Navy, indicates the ownership of UAV projects by the Pakistani armed forces. "Induction of the UAV is a manifestation of the Pakistan Navy's commitment and resolve towards self-reliance[93]".

Export

The lower scale of production and lack of regular contracts are key impediments to the development of the defence manufacturing sector. The private companies involved in defence manufacturing can become economically viable, competitive and invest in R&D only if they have adequate orders. The Pakistani establishment had focussed on the development of small to medium UAVs in order to develop the space for low cost Pakistani UAVs in the world market as well as to meet the requirements of the Pakistani armed forces. Pakistan had understood this aspect and allowed the private sector companies to export their civilian products. The Pakistani UAV manufacturers could sell their UAVs to organisations, government entities and friendly foreign countries subject to end user certification by the Pakistan government.[94] The end user certification has been made a mandatory requirement in order to ensure that the technology does not fall into the wrong hands.

Export Promotion: Pakistan had set up the Defence Export Promotion Organisation (DEPO) in 2001[95], which is the nodal centre for meeting the requirements of the defence Services and security agencies through a network of R&D organisations, public sector and private sector companies. Maj Gen Agha Masood Akram has been the director general of the DEPO since 2012. These companies have obtained relevant ISO certifications to enhance their acceptability in the international market for export of military equipment. DEPO also organises IDEAS which is held every alternate year. The ninth IDEAS is scheduled to be held at Karachi from November 22-25, 2016. DEPO facilitates customers to interact with defence manufacturing units, identifies markets for indigenous products, promotes Pakistan's defence manufacturers/products, proposes policy options and coordinates between Pakistani manufacturers and prospective buyers.[96]

Pakistan had indicated its intent of exporting UAVs as early as in 2001 during the Dubai Air Show in which the National Development Complex (NDC) had showcased three UAVs, which included the Vector Mk-2, Nishan Mk-2 and Hornet Mk-5.[97] According to NDC General Manager (Marketing), Ijaz Kahn, the Vector is a 200 km range UAV, which can carry a 30 kg payload and operate up to a 14,000 ft ceiling with an endurance of 6-8 hour.[98]

Import Ban

Pakistan has a Ministry of Defence Production,[99] and the Senate Committee on Defence Production recommended a ban on the import of items which can be produced by local industry in September 2015.[100]

Gains

Pakistan has developed its indigenous UAV industry by flirting with various UAV designs. The development of each UAV has strengthened its indigenous industry. The manufacture of UAVs through transfer of technology, licensed production and indigenous development has given Pakistan the ability to manufacture small to medium UAVs indigenously and in large numbers. The experience gained in licensed production of the Falco and production of the Burraq would improve Pakistan's ability to use alloys, as well as in development of indigenous UAVs in the future.

Implications for India

The development of various UAVs has created a wide range of options for the Pakistani armed forces as well as created some confusion about their real capability. Therefore, there is a need to understand the employability of these UAVs against India, based on their capabilities. The battery operated Scout and Sentry UAVs, having an endurance of 45 to 60 minutes, with day/ night operations capability, hand launched and skid/ net recovery, would be difficult to detect. The Stingray, Skycam, Heliquad, Rover and Spirit UAVs with endurance varying between 30 to 60 minutes are also in a similar category. The Pakistani armed forces would have chosen one or two of them to suit their operational requirements. The Helicquad is being operated by the Pakistan Navy probably due to its ability to carry out spot landing. Pakistan's field formations are also likely to have one or two types of UAVs from the Explorer, Hornet, Hawk, Border Eagle, Visions and Huma classes of UAVs, which have an endurance of 3-4 hours and can carry a payload of 4-15 kg, with wheeled and parachute recovery options. All these UAVs could be carrying smaller payloads for day and night surveillance. The indigenous micro, mini and small UAVs could be built in large numbers and provide field formations of the Pakistan Army with the capability to monitor corresponding Indian posts.

The tactical UAVs like the Uqab, Flamingo and Jasoos, with 10,000-12,000 ft altitude of operations, 20-30 kg payload, having a day camera and/or thermal imaging payload for night surveillance could provide the Pakistan Army the tactical reconnaissance capability both by day and night in the plains or areas having hills below 10,000 ft. The EMT Luna X-2000 UAV, despite having an all up weight of 40 kg, carries near

IR (informed) cameras, has 6 hours endurance and ability to operate up to 100 km at 10,000 ft altitude in all weather conditions. Its modular design allows it to be fitted with sensors for detecting NBC contamination, miniaturised Synthetic Aperture Radar (SAR) target illumination or Electronic Warfare (EW) payloads.[101] The catapult take-off and net recovery option gives it a unique capability to undertake tactical reconnaissance missions from restricted areas and could complement the tactical reconnaissance capabilities of the Pakistan Army.

The ability of the Selex Falco and indigenous Shahpur UAV to carry a payload of 50-70 kg up to 17,000 ft altitude up to a range of over 200 km allows them to undertake tactical day/ night reconnaissance and target illumination in the mountainous regions. The Burraq, with 12 hours endurance, ability to fly up to 24,000 ft altitude and carry 100 kg payload, including laser guided missiles or two bombs, is an ideal platform for tactical reconnaissance, target designation as well as armed strike missions in the mountainous regions. The Shahpur and Falco would have limited range in the hills due to their line of sight operations. Whereas the Burraq could have significant range in the hills due to its ability to fly at high altitude. However, the employability of the Burraq at high altitude or in the hills would be limited in adverse weather or turbulent winds, due to its lightweight and slow speed,

Geo-political Implications of Pakistan's Arms Industry

Pakistan is often viewed as a country with a weak economy, which is dependent on foreign aid and does not have a vibrant and strong indigenous industry, let alone a defence industry. Its weak economic condition appears to have been exploited by the USA and China to their advantage. Its alliance with the two superpowers with conflicting interests, is a contradiction in itself. Its dislike for India appears to be the driving force behind the development of military capability and achieving self-reliance in the defence industry. It has left no stone unturned to put India down militarily as well as diplomatically in its existence of over six decades. It has compromised its geographical boundaries by giving away the Aksai Chin area to China to get nuclear, missile and military assistance. It continues to seek military aid from the West, especially the USA, to build military capability as well as to develop its indigenous defence industry.

Pakistan, over a period of time,has made significant progress in developing its indigenous capability to manufacture military equipment, including UAVs. There is reluctance to accept Pakistan's claims of defence equipment manufacture and export to other countries and its programmes are viewed with suspicion and disbelief. However, it is slowly emerging as an arms exporter. The director of the Pakistan Ordnance Factory

(POF) in an interview with *The Express Tribute* on December 4, 2014, had claimed that the POF had exported arms and ammunition to 30 countries, including 400 automatic MP5 carbines to the US.[102] Pakistan is in talks with Algeria, Argentina, Bangladesh, Myanmar, Egypt, Iran, Lebanon, Malaysia, Morocco, Nigeria, Sri Lanka and Uruguay for the sale of the JF-17, which is built by PAC, Kamra, in collaboration with Chengdu Aircraft Industry of China.[103] Four countries have placed orders for one squadron each of the JF-17.[104] Heavy Industries Taxila (HIT) has exported its Al-Zarrar tanks to Bangladesh, Sri Lanka, Myanmar and Nigeria and claims to be close to striking a deal with Saudi Arabia to sell its Al-Khalid tanks.[105] The presence of Russian companies in the Defence Expo in Pakistan in 2014 and possible supply of Mi-35 attack helicopters to Pakistan indicates warming of defence relations between Pakistan and Russia.[106] Pakistan had identified UAVs as one of core areas in the mid-1990s, in which it wanted to indigenise, and manufacture. It has concentrated on the development of small to medium, low cost and easy to operate UAVs to create a space for itself since 2001 in the otherwise competitive world UAV market, dominated by the leaders of the arms industry. Its indigenous UAV industry, combined with UAVs built with transfer of technology and licensed production, has given it the ability to indigenise small to medium UAVs at a lower cost and save taxpayers precious money. It is trying to export indigenously built UAVs which are slowly becoming a source of revenue.

Pakistan's foreign exchange reserves had started recovering in 2014 from the $3 billion level in 2013 due to increased export of defence equipment.[107] Its defence cooperation is increasing with countries like Morocco, Turkey, Malaysia, Czechoslovakia, Poland, New Zealand, Egypt, Myanmar, Sri Lanka, Bangladesh, Nigeria and Thailand. It has been exporting defence equipment to the Middle East, Africa and South America. It lays great emphasis on exploiting areas where there is a void, and targets countries, that cannot buy expensive defence equipment from the West. It views the Central Asian countries as possible markets—these come into existence two and half decades ago, and are in the process of developing their armed forces. Countries from the South and Southeast Asia region are its likely customers.

Takeaways from Pakistani UAV Programme

The Pressler Amendment of 1992 had an immense impact on Pakistan's strategic planners and appears to have played a key role in the indigenisation of defence equipment, including UAVs. Pakistan's establishment had understood the implications of overdependence on foreign vendors and, thus, decided to focus on indigenisation. The indigenous development of various UAVs and the decision not to buy the Shadow-200

UAVs from the USA indicates its willingness to go to any length to encourage indigenisation. The success of indigenisation of military equipment depends largely on three factors, namely, the will of the country, patronage/ ownership by the military, and required R&D set-up. Pakistan's UAV programme had all the three ingredients. The R&D agencies working in close coordination with the SPD Directorate of the Pakistan Army, indicates their desire to take on the ownership of the project from the design stage itself. The Pakistan military's accepting good enough QRs for the Uqab at the initial stage and going for further development by their public sector units shows their intent to encourage indigenous industry. The long-term planning and statements by the Pakistan government functionaries, army and naval chiefs on the UAV programme and nurturing of the UAV industry, reveal the unflinching support to indigenisation. The US and China also follow a similar practice of supporting their indigenous industry and their armed forces are involved from the design stage itself. Their preference for indigenous products is apparent. US law[108] does not permit procurement of weapons from foreign vendors.[109]

The Indian Navy has a Naval Design Directorate, which is involved in the indigenous projects from the design stage itself, whereas the Indian Army and Indian Air Force get involved from the trial and testing stage onwards. As a result, some time is lost in integration and modifications to meet the requirements of the users after the initial design. The indigenous projects are normally initiated as projects of the R&D agencies and the armed forces get involved as users, not as partners. The aspirations of the armed forces to get the best equipment and the reluctance of the public sector units to own up to limitations and failures sometimes results in a mismatch between the two, and the consequent delays, limited production or cancellation. The joint ownership of projects could prove useful in indigenisation as well in understanding each other's requirements and limitations from the beginning. The indigenisation of the arms industry, including UAVs, has helped Pakistan develop military relations with countries of Africa, Middle East, South America, South and Southeast Asia, which also has associated diplomatic and economic benefits. It would improve its standing in the comity of nations as well as help it improve the economic condition of the country.

The indigenously produced UAVs have provided moderate reconnaissance and surveillance capability to the Pakistani armed forces. The realistic goal setting and pragmatic approach has allowed Pakistan to manufacture UAVs,as well as export these to other countries. The existing indigenous UAV capability may not be the best, but is good enough to meet the needs of the country's armed forces, reduce dependence on foreign suppliers and, above all, has saved taxpayers money. Overall, the development of Pakistan's indigenous UAV industry has been an interesting journey despite certain limitations and the exaggerated claims of the Pakistani establishment.

Appendix 'A'

Pakistan's UAVs

Name	Endurance (hrs)	Max Alt (ft)	Range (km)	Max Spd (kmph)	Max Weight/ Payload (kg)	Technical Details/ Remarks
			NESCOM/ GIDS			
Burraq[110]	12	24,606		215	1,000 / 100	NESCOM/ NDC[111]
Shahpur[112]	7-8	17,000	250	150	480/ 50	Zumr1-EP Eqpt with EO/IR, Thermal Imager, Erica-Plus, Low light/ near IR TV& LRF/ Engine 100 hp/ Autonomous T/O &Ldg
Huma-1[113]	4	9,842	100	180	130/ 20	Rocket Assisted T/O & Parachute Ldg/ Engine-22 BHP/ First Displayed 2006 [114]
Uqab-I/Uqab-II [115]	6	10,000	150	120 150	200/20	Day/ Thermal Imager/ Wheeled Version/ Engine 50 hp/ Pakistan Army &Navy
Ababeel Target UAV[116]	25 min		1.5	175	3	Hand/ Wheel T/O/Belly/ Wheel Ldg [117] Pak Army[118]/ Saudi Arabia / Developed by PAC in 1988 [119].
Scout mini UAV[120]	1	1,500	10	60	4.5 [121]	EO/IR Camera/ battery powered/ autonomous ops esp over hills/ Hand/ Catapult Launched & Skid Landing/ Net Recovery
Sentry mini Stealth UAV[122] (Undetected by Radar)	SR 45 min/ LR 1 hr	SR 3,500/ LR 4,500	10-20	20-40	8/0.5	Man portable / Launcher Launched & Parachute Recovery/ Battery Operated *Short Range (SR)/ Long Range (LR)

AWC Mk-I [123]	2		30	110	30/-	Developed by AWC
AWC Mk-II [124]	3		50	130	60/-	Developed in 1999
PAC KAMRA (SELEX)						
Falco XN [125] (has ATOL with STOL performance)	8-14	16,500	2001[126]	215	420/ 68	EO/IR, Thermal Imaging, Laser Designator&Surveillance Radar PAF/ Transfer of Technology from SELEX (ITALY)[127]
SATUMA						
Flamingo [128]	6-8	12,000-14,000	200+	130	245/ 30-35	Wheeled T/O &Ldg
Jasoos-II (Bravo+)[129]	4-5	10,000	80-100	130	145/ 15-25	38 hp Engine/ Day/ Low Lt Camera /Wheeled T/O &Ldg/ PAF[130] / Pakistan Army/First delivered in 2000[131] /Designed by AWC
Mukhbar UAV[132] (Scaled Down Jasoos)	1.5	7,000	30-50	120	40/ 5	Engine 120 CC/ Length -2.86m/ Wheeled/ Non-Metallic Tactical Recce
Stingray Mini UAV [133]				90	7.5/ 1.5	Bungee Launch/ Parachute Recovery
Thunder - Target UAV[134]	1.5		5-10	300	68/ -	Engine 25-30 hp/ 16 Smoke/IR Flares Catapult Launch/ Belly Ldg
Shooting Star -High Speed UAV [135]	1	18,000	200	550	40 / 8	Engine - 2x45 lb-f Turbo jet/ Wing Span 3.5 ft/ Length -9 ft/
Parwaz- UAV Half Scale Trainer (HST for Jasoos II)[136]					40 / 5	120 cc 2 Cylinder 2 Stroke Gasoline engine/ built on Mukhbar airframe Length-2.86 m/3.56m Wingspan
UAV Full Scale Trainer (FST) [137]	4-5			130	110/ -	Trainer for Jasoos-II/ 38 hp Engine/ Wheeled version
Assault Trainer	Wheeled Take Off & Launcher Take-Off/Half Scale Trainerfor Thunder high speed UAVs) [138]					
EAST-WEST INFINITI						
Heliquad Micro UAV [139]	Powered by four motors & equipped with a camera/ Pak Navy/ First displayed in IDAS 2006[1]					

INTEGRATED DYNAMICS						
Vector UAV [140]	8		200	75-208	100 /25	Wheels or Parachute/ GSP-900/1200/ EO/IR/ IFSC-7000/ 22 BHP Engine/
Skycam 1[141] UAV	0.5	1,000	5-10	30	4.5 / 1	Net/ Belly/ Conventional Landing Day camera/ Laptop Ground Station/ Pakistan Army
ShadowMk-1[142] &Shadow Down Under[143] Mk-II[144]	6		160	75-208	90 / 25	EO Payloads for Maritime Research;/22 BHP Engine/ Wheels or Parachute Recovery/ Exported to Australia& Spain
Rover Mk-1 [145]	20-45 min	2,000	2-4	30-100	2//0.5	Hand Launched/ Belly Landing/ Deep Stall/ Day/ Ni EO/IR still camera Exported to USA[146]
Vision Mk-1 Mini UAV[147]	3		50		35 / 10	6.5 BHP Engine/ Wheels or Parachute Recovery
Vision Mk-2 [148]	4		100	75-208	80 /15	Tactical Surveillance/ GSP-900 Camera/ EO/ IR / T/O/ Wheeled or Parachute Landing/ Designed by AWC [149]
Border Eagle Mk-2 (Beagle) [150]	3			30-160	15//4	Wheeled/ Parachute recovery/
Hawk Mk-V Surveillance UAV[151]	6		100	132-240	65 /15	GSP-900 Camera/ EO/ IR / Wheels or Parachute recovery/ Developed by NDC [152]
Hornet Surveillance UAV [153]	4		80	132-240	50/ 15	/ Wheels or Parachute recovery Developed by NDC[154] / GSP-900 Camera/ EO/IR
Explorer UAV [155]	+4				20/ 8	Wheel or Ramp Launched & Parachute recovery/+Enhancable/ GSP-100 Day Camera/IR
Pride UAV [156]	30-45 min		3-5	30-100	4.5/ /0.5	Hand Launched/ Belly Landing/ Deep Stall/ Day/IR
Spirit UAV [157]	45-60 min		10-15	30-100	5 / 0.7	Hand Launched/ Belly Landing/ Deep Stall/ Day/ IR Still camera

Nishan Mk-1 Aerial Target System [158]	30 min	7,000	20-30	250-300	35 / 12	Skid Landing or Parachute recovery 6 smoke flares/ 8 IR Flares/ Developed by NDC [159]
Nishan TJ-1000 Aerial Target System [160]	1	6,500	35	250-300	60 / 12	Skid Landing or Parachute recovery 24 smoke flares/ 16 IR Flares ./ Developed byNDC[161]
Tornado Aerial Target/ Decoy System [162]	20 min		200	130-464	25 / 5	2 xt 20 lbf thrust mini-turbojets Flare/IR/Radar enhancement devices
GERMANY						
EMT Luna X-2000 [163]	6	11,500 [164]	80-100	140/ 35	40/ -	Operated by two persons without flying training/ PN/ Pakistan Army
CHINA						
ASN-105 [165]	7	16,500	150	200	180 / 40	Rocket Booster T/O & Parachute recovery
ASN-206/ 207 [166]	8	16,500	200 LOS	210	220 / 40	Rocket Booster T/O & Parachute recovery

Note

1. Gary Chapman, "High-Tech Warfare is a Losing Proposition", April 26, 1999,http://articles.latimes.com/1999/apr/26/business/fi-31193. Accessed on July 22, 2015.
2. Jon Boone, "Pakistan Military's New Combat UAV is 'Great National Achievement", March 13, 2015, http://www.theguardian.com/world/2015/mar/13/pakistan-military-new-combat-UAV-great-national-achievement. Accessed on July 19, 2015.
3. "Pakistan Tests First Indigenous Armed UAV, Laser Guided Missile", March 13, 2015, http://www.ndtv.com/world-news/pakistan-tests-first-indigenous-armed-UAV-laser-guided-missile-746453. Accessed on July 20, 2015.
4. National Engineering and Scientific Commission (NESCOM), http://www.nti.org/facilities/586/. Accessed on July 22, 2015.
5. Ibid.
6. "Pakistan Developing Armed UAV Technology: Report", November 18, 2012, http://tribune.com.pk/story/467610/pakistan-developing-armed-UAV-technology-report/. Accessed on July 22, 2015.
7. "Pakistan Introduces Fleet of Locally-Developed UAVs", November 25, 2013, http://www.dawn.com/news/1058493. Accessed on July 25, 2015.
8. http://www.pac.org.pk. Accessed on August 5, 2015.
9. http://www.pac.org.pk/history. Accessed on August 27, 2015.
10. http://www.pac.org.pk/complex. Accessed on August 27, 2015.
11. http://www.pac.org.pk/#. Accessed on August 11, 2015.
12. http://www.pac.org.pk/history. Accessed on August 27, 2015.
13. "Pakistan Hands Over 8 Super Mushak Jets to Saudi Arabia", October 6, 2015, http://archives.

dailytimes.com.pk/national/13-Oct-2004/pakistan-hands-over-8-super-mushak-jets-to-saudi-arabia. Accessed on October 6, 2015.

14. Usman Ansari, "Pakistan Sells Trainer Aircraft to Iraq, Seeks Further Contracts", February 11, 2014, http://archive.defensenews.com/article/20140211/DEFREG04/302110026/Pakistan-Sells-Trainer-Aircraft-Iraq-Seeks-Further-Contracts. Accessed on October 6, 2015.
15. "Pakistan to Sell Combat Jets to Saudi Arabia", February 14, 2014, http://www.upi.com/Business_News/Security-Industry/2014/02/14/Pakistan-to-sell-combat-jets-to-Saudi-Arabia/46321392354300/. Accessed on October 6, 2015.
16. Greg Waldron, "Pakistan to Begin Co-production of Falco UAV", August 26, 2009, http://www.flightglobal.com/news/articles/pakistan-to-begin-co-production-of-falco-uav-331492/. Accessed on August 27, 2015.
17. http://fas.org/nuke/guide/pakistan/facility/kamra.htm. Accessed on August 27, 2015.
18. http://uvs-info.com/phocadownload/05_3g_2005/40_Asia-Far_East.pdf. Accessed on August 11, 2015.
19. Air Weapons Complex (AWC), http://www.epicos.com/EPCompanyProfileWeb/GeneralInformation.aspx?id=22773. Accessed on October 06, 2015.
20. National Defence Complex (NDC), http://www.nti.org/facilities/634/, accessed on October 05, 2015.
21. http://www.senatedefencecommittee.com.pk/production-detail.php?pageid=news-detail&pid=MTM=. Accessed on August 11, 2015.
22. "Pakistan Readies Production of UAVs", September 20, 2012. http://www.upi.com/Business_News/Security-Industry/2012/09/20/Pakistan-readies-production-of-UAVs/51871348165951/. Accessed on October 5, 2015.
23. http:// mgids.com.pk/about. Accessed on July 25, 2015.
24. "Global Industrial and Defence Solutions (GIDS) CEO Syed Guftar Shah on the Defence industry in Pakistan", June 11, 2012, http://www.theprospectgroup.com/syed-guftar-shah-ceo-global-industrial-and-defence-solutions-gids-8711/. Accessed on October 12, 2015.
25. Guy Martin, "Integrated Dynamics sells UAVs to Pakistan Armed Forces", November 10, 2012. http://www.defenceweb.co.za/index.php?option=com_content&view=article&id=28471:integrated-dynamics-sells-uavs-to-pakistan-armed-forces&catid=112:ideas-2012&Itemid=254, accessed on July 24, 2015
26. http://www.idaerospace.com/. Accessed on July 24, 2015.
27. Mona Hussain, "Libya Acquires Pakistani Integrated Dynamics Border Eagle UAVs Over Two Year Period", December 12, 2006, https://www.flightglobal.com/news/articles/libya-acquires-pakistani-integrated-dynamics-border-211045/. Accessed on October 7, 2015.
28. http://www.dinarstandard.com/pakistans-defense-private-sector-emerges-with-indigenous-uav-technology/. Accessed on October 5, 2015.
29. http://en.ruvsa.com/catalog/border_eagle/, July 22, 2015.
30. "Pakistan Expands Unmanned Air Force", November 11, 2008, http://www.wired.com/2008/11/pakistans-uav-p/. Accessed July 22, 2015.
31. "Pakistan's Defense Private Sector Emerges with Indigenous UAV Technology", January 30, 2011,http://asiandefence.net/pakistans-defense-private-sector-emerges-with-indigenous-uav-technology/. Accessed on July 22, 2015.
32. Riaq Haq, "Pakistan's Defense Private Sector Emerges with Indigenous UAV Technology," February 12, 2009, http://www.dinarstandard.com/pakistans-defense-private-sector-emerges-with-indigenous-uav-technology/. Accessed on August 19, 2015.
33. Raja Sabri Khan, TEDX Event on Theme "Making the Impossible Possible", at Karachi, May 27, 2011, https://www.ted.com/tedx/events/2617. Accessed on October 6, 2015.

34. https://www.youtube.com/watch?v=v__tRUfKAek. Accessed on October 7, 2015.
35. http://www.satuma.com.pk/Aboutus.aspx. Accessed on August 27, 2015.
36. http://propakistani.pk/2009/05/18/made-in-pakistan-UAVs/. Accessed on August 11, 2015.
37. http://www.satuma.com.pk/Aboutus.aspx. Accessed on August 27, 2015.
38. http://www.aces.com.pk/. Accessed on August 14, 2014.
39. http://www.hellotrade.com/advanced-computing-engineering-solutions/product.html. Accessed on August 14, 2015.
40. http://www.jammu-kashmir.com/archives/archives2001/kashmir20010520a.html. Accessed on August 7, 2001.
41. "Pakistan Successfully Tests First Indigenous Armed UAV", March 13, 2015, http://www.dawn.com/news/1169341. Accessed on July 19, 2015.
42. "Complex at Kamra to Manufacture UAVs", August 21, 2009, http://www.dawn.com/news/880177/complex-at-kamra-to-manufacture-UAVs. Accessed on July 25, 2015.
43. "Pakistan's UAV - UAV Developments", March 7, 2009, http://defence.pk/threads/pakistans-uav-UAV-developments.40550/page-19. Accessed on July 25, 2015.
44. Waldron, n, 16.
45. Ibid.
46. Ibid.
47. "Pakistan Agreement Boosts Turkish Plan", June 18, 2007, http://www.flightglobal.com/news/articles/pakistan-agreement-boosts-turkish-plan-214751/. Accessed on July 31, 2015.
48. Syed Fazl-e-Haider, "Pakistan Moves to UAV Independence", December 3, 2009, http://www.atimes.com/atimes/South_Asia/KL03Df03.html. Accessed on July 29, 2015.
49. Usman Ansari, "Pakistani Turkish Defense Ties Continue to Deepen", January 3, 2015. http://www.defensenews.com/story/defense/policy-budget/industry/2015/01/03/turkey-pakistan-ties-industry/21106293/. Accessed on July 31, 2015
50. "Pakistan Builds Part for Turkey Drones", May 13, 2013, http://tribune.com.pk/story/548713/pakistan-builds-parts-for-turkey-drones/. Accessed on August 27, 2015.
51. Munir Hussain, "Pak-Turkey Relations: On the Common Ties", Summer & Fall 2008, https://www.ciaonet.org/attachments/6319/uploads. Accessed on October 5, 2015.
52. Gary Mortimer, "Luna UAS for Pakistan Navy", June 29, 2012, http://www.suasnews.com/2012/06/17197/luna-uas-for-pakistan-navy/. Accessed on August 2, 2015.
53. Luna, http://www.navalUAVs.com/Luna.html. Accessed on August 2, 2015.
54. Frank Wasgindt, "Luna A Success Story", http://www.emt-penzberg.de/fileadmin/web_data/presse/2007-10-SuT_en.pdf. Accessed on August 2, 2015.
55. MT Butt, "The General in a Hurry Now Buying German Spy Planes for Millions", August 24, 2005, http://antisystemic.org/satribune/www.satribune.com/archives/200508/P1_butt.htm. Accessed on August 2, 2015
56. "Asian Region UAV Capability on the Rise", December 20, 2012, http://www.defencereviewasia.com/articles/195/Asian-region-UAV-capability-on-the-rise. Accessed on August 11, 2015
57. Salman Siddiqui, "The Flawed UAVs Deal", May 4, 2010 http://tribune.com.pk/story/10683/the-flawed-UAVs-deal/. Accessed on July 28, 2015.
58. Butt, n.55.
59. Salman Siddiqui, "Navy Inducts First Fleet of Reconnaissance Drones", July 20, 2013, http://tribune.com.pk/story/213634/pakistan-navy-inducts-drones-into-its-fleet/. Accessed on August 14, 2015.
60. "Camcopter S-100 Unmanned Air System (UAS), Austria", http://www.naval-technology.com/projects/camcopter-s-100-unmanned-air-system-uas/. Accessed on August 18, 2015.
61. http://pakmr.blogspot.in/2011/04/uqaab-tactical-unmanned-aerial-vehicle.html. Accessed on

August 14, 2015.

62. Ibid.
63. Peter La Frenchi, "Pakistan Looks to Develop Indigenous UAV Capability", September 18, 2007 http://www.flightglobal.com/news/articles/pakistan-looks-to-develop-indigenous-uav-capability-216844/. Accessed on August 14, 2015.
64. Siddiqui, n.59.
65. Shakil Shaikh, "Indigenous UAV Test-Flight Termed Successful", March 21, 2015, http://www.thenews.com.pk/TodaysPrintDetail.aspx?ID=13691&Cat=13&dt=3/21/2008. Accessed on August 14, 2015.
66. Siddiqui, n.59.
67. Usman Ansari, "Pakistan Inducts Armed UAVs", November 25, 2013, http://archive.defensenews.com/article/20131125/DEFREG03/311250023/Pakistan-Inducts-Armed-UAVs, Accessed on August 17, 2015.
68. http://gids.com.pk/shahpar, accessed on August 17, 2015.
69. "Shahpur Unmanned Aerial Vehicle (UAV), Pakistan", http://www.airforce-technology.com/projects/shahpur-unmanned-aerial-vehicle-uav/. Accessed on August 17, 2015.
70. "Timeline: History of US-Pakistan Relations", July 4, 2012 03, HTTP://WWW.DAWN.COM/NEWS/731670/TIMELINE-HISTORY-OF-US-PAKISTAN-RELATIONS. Accessed on October 8, 2015.
71. Siddiqui, n.57.
72. "Pakistan Negotiating Shadow 200 UAV with US", January 7, 2011, http://defence.pk/threads/pakistan-negotiating-shadow-200-uav-with-us.87829/. Accessed on August 27, 2015.
73. n.56.
74. Ibid.
75. Ibid.
76. "Pakistan Introduces Fleet of Locally-Developed UAVs", November 25, 2013, http://www.dawn.com/news/1058493. Accessed on July 25, 2015.
77. "Pakistan Develops Armed UAV, Test-Fires Laser-Guided Missile", March 14, 2015, http://www.thenews.com.pk/Todays-News-13-36395-Pakistan-develops-armed-UAV-test-fires-laser-guided-missile. Accessed on July 21, 2015.
78. Tim Craig, "Pakistan Says it will Deploy its Own Armed UAV Against Terrorists", March 13, 2015, https://www.washingtonpost.com/world/pakistan-says-it-will-deploy-its-own-armed-UAV-against-terrorists/2015/03/13/ac0a9008-c98d-11e4-bea5-b893e7ac3fb3_story.html. Accessed on July 20, 2015.
79. "Pakistan Successfully Test-Fires Own Armed UAV 'Burraq," Dunya News Headlines, March 14, 2015, March 13, 2015, https://www.youtube.com/watch?v=wU7rl_XVv7g. Accessed on July 20, 2015.
80. Farhan Bukhari and James Hardy, "Pakistan Successfully Fires Missile from Indigenous UAV", March 12, 2015, http://www.janes.com/article/49938/pakistan-successfully-fires-missile-from-indigenous-uav. Accessed on July 22, 2015.
81. "Pakistan Successfully Tests First Indigenous Armed UAV: ISPR", March 13, 2015, http://tribune.com.pk/story/852698/pakistan-successfully-test-fires-first-indigenous-UAV-ispr/. Accessed on July 21, 2015.
82. "Pak Tests 1st Indigenous Armed UAV, Laser Guided Missile", March 13, 2015, http://zeenews.india.com/news/south-asia/pak-tests-1st-indigenous-armed-UAV-laser-guided-missile_1561262.html. Accessed on July 21, 2015.
83. John Boone, "Pakistan Military's New Combat UAV is 'Great National Achievement'", March 13, 2015, http://www.theguardian.com/world/2015/mar/13/pakistan-military-new-combat-UAV-great-national-achievement. Accessed on July 21, 2015.

84. Bokhari and Hardy n.80.
85. Neil Gibson, "Analysis: Pakistan's 'Indigenous' UAV, Missiles May not be as Homegrown as Claimed", March 25, 2015, http://www.janes.com/article/50212/analysis-pakistan-s-indigenous-uav-missiles-may-not-be-as-homegrown-as-claimed. Accessed on July 23, 2015.
86. Sahar Ahmed, "Pakistani Makes Drones for Peaceful use but Business Risky", June 23, 2011,http://www.reuters.com/article/2011/06/23/us-pakistan-UAVs-idUSTRE75M2BD20110623. Accessed on August 26, 2015.
87. Ibid.
88. "UAV Technology of Pakistan Complete Overview", http://pakarmedforces.com/2014/01/UAV-technology-of-pakistan-complete-overview.html. Accessed on July 22, 2015.
89. Ahmed, n.86.
90. "Selling Drones from Pakistan by Raja Sabri Khan – TEDx", http://whitengreen.com/selling-drones-from-pakistan-by-raja-sabri-khan--tedx-771-video. Accessed on October 7, 2015.
91. https://www.linkedin.com/profile/view?id=ACgAAAoTstQBZJXhX1_5T98-dHUtBX_jTUa9uB0&authType=name&authToken=vSLk. Accessed on August 27, 2015
92. https://www.linkedin.com/profile/view?id=ACgAAAoTstQBZJXhX1_5T98-dHUtBX_jTUa9uB0&authType=name&authToken=vSLk. Accessed on August 27, 2015.
93. Siddiqui, n.59.
94. Betwa Sharma, "Meet Pakistan's UAV Maker, UAVs Have Become Synonymous with the U.S. Attacks Inside Pakistan. But have you Heard about the 'UAVs for Peace' Program?" December 3, 2012, http://www.zdnet.com/article/meet-pakistans-UAV-maker/. Accessed on August 11, 2015.
95. http://www.depo.org.pk/contents.php?section_id=115. Accessed on August 19, 2015.
96. http://www.depo.org.pk/contents.php?section_id=107. Accessed on August 19, 2015.
97. Mohammed Abdul Qudoos, "Export of Pakistan Made UAVs To Begin Soon", November 6, 2001, http://www.rense.com/general16/bes.htm. Accessed on August 27, 2015.
98. "IDEX Show Report- Pakistan to Export Vector by Year End", March 27, 2001, http://www.flightglobal.com/news/articles/idex-show-report-pakistan-to-export-vector-by-year-end-127928/. Accessed on August 27, 2015.
99. http://www.modp.gov.pk/gop/index.php?q=aHR0cDovLzE5Mi4xNjguNzAuMTM2L21vZHAv. Accessed on October 12, 2015.
100. Jon Grevatt, "Bangkok – Pakistan Considering Import Ban on Locally Available Material," September 10, 2015, http://www.janes.com/article/54176/pakistan-considering-import-ban-on-locally-available-materiel. Accessed on October 12, 2015.
101. http://www.emt-penzberg.de/en/produkte/drohnensystem/fluggeraet.html. Accessed on October 12, 2015.
102. Athar Khan, "IDEAS 2014: Pak Defence Exports have Doubled in a Year, Says Minister", December 4, 2014, http://tribune.com.pk/story/801528/ideas-2014-pak-defence-exports-have-doubled-in-a-year-says-minister/. Accessed on October 12, 2015.
103. "JF-17 Fighter Leading Pakistan Defence Equipment Export Success", December 9, 2014, http://www.defenseworld.net/news/11663/JF_17_Fighter_Leading_Pakistan_Defence_Equipment_Export_Success#.Vhsyit-qqko. Accessed on October 12, 2015.
104. Syed Shoaib Hasan, "Pakistan's Ideas Arms Fair Suggests Demand Is Booming", December 5, 2015, http://www.wsj.com/articles/pakistans-ideas-arms-fair-suggests-demand-is-booming-amid-insecurity-1417774357. Accessed on October 12, 2015.
105. "Pakistan Aiming for Jet Boost to Defence Exports", December 7, 2014, http://www.dailymail.co.uk/wires/afp/article-2864097/Pakistan-aiming-jet-boost-defence-exports.html. Accessed on October.
106. Hasan, n.104.

107. n. 105.
108. Valerie Bailey Grasso, "The Berry Amendment: Requiring Defense Procurement to Come from Domestic Sources", February 24, 2014 https://www.fas.org/sgp/crs/natsec/RL31236.pdf. Accessed on September 25, 2015.
109. Alan W.H. Gourley, John E. McCarthy, Jr. and Adelicia R. Cliffe, "Federal Restrictions on Participation by Foreign Investors in Defense and Other Government Contracts," https//www.crowell.com/documents/2009-Federal-Restrictions-on-Participation-by-Foreign-Investors-in-Defense-and-Other-Government-Contracts.pdf. Accessed on September 25, 2015.
110. "NESCOM Burraq Unmanned Combat Aerial Vehicle (UCAV) (2013)", April 24, 2015,http://www.militaryfactory.com/aircraft/detail.asp?aircraft_id=1377. Accessed on July 22, 2015.
111. http://www.dawn.com/news/1169452. Accessed on October 1, 2015.
112. Gunter Endres, "Flying South" [AAD141]. September 17, 2015, http://www.janes.com/article/43193/flying-south-aad141. Accessed on July 23, 2015.
113. Ibid.
114. http://pakmr.blogspot.in/2011/04/huma-1-huma-2-tactical-uav-of-ids.html. Accessed on August 13, 2015.
115. UQAB-II, http://www.navalUAVs.com/UQAB-II.html. Accessed on August 4, 2015.
116. Martin, n.25.
117. http://www.pbaviations.com/downloads/3.pdf. Accessed on August 10, 2015.
118. "Asia/Far East Developing Indigenous Capabilities", http://uvs-info.com/phocadownload/05_3g_2005/40_Asia-Far_East.pdf. Accessed on August 11, 2015.
119. Ibid.
120. http://www.armyrecognition.com/ideas_2014_official_show_daily_news_coverage_uk/gids_presents_complete_range_of_pakistan-made_unmanned_aerial_vehicles_at_ideas_2014.html. Accessed on August 10, 2015.
121. http://gids.com.pk/scout-mini. Accessed on August 5, 2015.
122. http://www.armyrecognition.com/ideas_2014_official_show_daily_news_coverage_uk/gids_presents_complete_range_of_pakistan-made_unmanned_aerial_vehicles_at_ideas_2014.html. Accessed on August 10, 2015
123. Ibid.
124. Ibid.
125. "Burraq: Pakistan's First Domestic Made Armed UAV", December 07, 2011, http://propakistani.pk/2011/12/07/burraq-pakistans-first-domestic-made-armed-UAV/. Accessed on July 23, 2015.
126. Waldron, n.16.
127. "SELEX Galileo Falco Unmanned Aerial Vehicle (2009)," May 24, 2013, http://www.militaryfactory.com/aircraft/detail.asp?aircraft_id=903. Accessed on July 23, 2015.
128. http://www.satuma.com.pk/Detail.aspx?ProdID=1. Accessed on August 4, 2015.
129. http://www.SATUMA.com.pk/Detail.aspx?ProdID=2. Accessed on August 4, 2015.
130. Martin, n.25.
131. n.118.
132. http://www.SATUMA.com.pk/Detail.aspx?ProdID=3. Accessed on August 4, 2015.
133. Ibid.
134. Ibid.
135. Ibid.
136. Ibid.
137. Ibid.
138. Ibid.
139. http://www.dinarstandard.com/pakistans-defense-private-sector-emerges-with-indigenous-

uav-technology/. Accessed on August 10, 2015
140. http://209.198.49.40/products/doc/Vector.pdf. Accessed on August 11, 2015.
141. http://209.198.49.40/products/doc/Skycam1.pdf. Accessed on August 11, 2015.
142. http://209.198.49.40/products/doc/Shadow_mk_1.pdf. Accessed on August 11, 2015.
143. "SHADOW Down Under!", January 1, 2007, http://www.idaerospace.com/ViewNews.asp?nId=2. Accessed on August 1, 2015.
144. August 1, 2015
145. http://209.198.49.40/products/doc/Rover_mk_1.pdf. Accessed on August 11, 2015.
146. http://www.idaerospace.com/ViewNews.asp?nId=8. Accessed on August 11, 2015.
147. n.145.
148. "VISION MK-2, Bound for Italy", May 9, 2007, http://www.idaerospace.com/ViewNews.asp?nId=2. Accessed on August 11, 2015.
149. n.118.
150. "Border Eagle Mk-2, Border Surveillance UAV System", http://209.198.49.40/products/doc/border_eagle.pdf. Accessed on August 11, 2015.
151. http://209.198.49.40/products/doc/Hawk_mk_5.pdf. Accessed on August 11, 2015.
152. n.119.
153. http://209.198.49.40/products/doc/Hornet.pdf. Accessed on August 11, 2015.
154. n.118.
155. http://209.198.49.40/products/doc/Explorer.pdf. Accessed on August 11, 2015.
156. http://209.198.49.40/products/doc/Skycam1.pdf. Accessed on August 11, 2015.
157. http://209.198.49.40/products/doc/Spirit.pdf. Accessed on August 11, 2015.
158. http://209.198.49.40/products/doc/Nisha_mk_ii.pdf. Accessed on August 11, 2015.
159. n.118.
160. http://209.198.49.40/products/doc/Nishan_1000.pdf. Accessed on August 11, 2015.
161. n.118.
162. http://209.198.49.40/products/doc/Tornado.pdf. Accessed on August 11, 2015.
163. Frank Wasgindt, "LUNA A Success Story", http://www.emt-penzberg.de/fileadmin/web_data/presse/2007-10-SuT_en.pdf. Accessed on August 2, 2015.
164. EMT Luna X-2000 Unmanned Aerial Vehicle (UAV) (2000), August 08, 2015, http://www.militaryfactory.com/aircraft/detail.asp?aircraft_id=900. Accessed on April 12, 2016.
165. http://www.catic.cn/indexPortal/home/index.do?cmd=goToChannel&cid=744&columnid=1912&cpid=1651&columnType=102&likeType=view&ckw=FWUAV&lang=US&dataid=429. Accessed on August 7, 2015.
166. http://www.catic.cn/indexPortal/home/index.do?cmd=goToChannel&cid=744&columnid=1912&cpid=1651&columnType=102&likeType=view&ckw=FWUAV&lang=US&dataid=4291. Accessed on August 7, 2015.

9

Challenges to India's Membership of Multilateral Export Control Regimes

Manisha Chaurasiya

The nuclear non-proliferation regime stretches across international treaties, export control institutions, safeguard agreements, and also bilateral nuclear trade arrangements. These international export controls hold an important place in the overall nuclear non-proliferation structure. The four chief export control regimes are: the Nuclear Suppliers' Group (NSG), Australia Group (AG), Missile Technology Control Regime (MTCR), and Wassenaar Arrangement. These have been crafted to overview and regulate trade and transfers of major conventional arms systems and the components for the production of Weapons of Mass Destruction (WMDs) and their delivery mechanisms.

The necessity for an all encompassing and holistic regime structure without leaving any relevant actor outside is crucial for the realisation of the goal of non-proliferation of WMDs. The membership of the export control regimes, unfortunately, doesn't reflect the realities of the century, and requires revision. Accommodation of the actors who (a) adhere and promise their compliance to the norms and principals of the regime; (b) are major actors in trade of goods under the purview of the regime; and (c) have shown compliance with the letter and spirit of non-proliferation of WMDs through their past record, is needed. The case of India in this regard deserves attention. It has been long segregated from the nuclear mainstream in general and export control regimes in particular on account of being a non-signatory of the nuclear Non-Proliferation Treaty (NPT), and the inherent scepticism and mistrust towards it. India has been aiming for a judicious mix of sources for its ever increasing energy requirements. In this light, it perceives nuclear energy as a viable, Green House Gases (GHGs) emission-free, and environment friendly means to achieve the same. Its membership into the export control regimes holds the key to a deserving hassle free nuclear commerce, where there are fewer restraints and comparatively easier arrangements on importing nuclear reactors, materials, technology and components for its growing civilian needs. Inappropriately, less attention has been given to India's clean record of non-proliferation, responsible nuclear behaviour, its share in salient exports to the world, and its compliance with the significant treaties on non-proliferation of WMD guidelines and resolutions, including the United Nations Security Council Resolution (UNSCR) 1540, the Biological and Toxic Weapons Convention (BTWC), Chemical Weapons Convention (CWC), and additional Protocol of the International Atomic Energy Agency (IAEA), to cite a few.

This paper analyses the aspect of membership in each of the four export control regimes. Firstly, it investigates the theoretical concept of international regimes to locate the effect of change in membership on regime survival. Secondly, it looks into the respective criteria for membership in each of the four export control regimes: the Nuclear Suppliers Group (NSG), Australia Group (AG), Missile Technology Control Regime (MTCR), and Wassenaar Arrangement. It analyses the possibility, scope and requirements for new members into the respective institutional structure. The paper then tests the Indian credentials and qualifications on the respective criteria of the four regimes in an attempt to answer a simple yet complicated question: does India deserve to be a member of the export control regimes?

The International Regimes: An Analysis

The international regimes, as known widely, are "implicit or explicit principles, norms, rules and decision-making procedures around which actors' expectations converge in a given area of international relations."[1] The 'like mindedness' and 'shared goals' among members further cements the regimes, which are international processes and collections of rules to limit and overview the exports of technologies and goods related to WMD and some forms of conventional arms that can potentially jeopardise the security of the world. In the particular case of multilateral export control regimes, the underlining belief is on curbing the proliferation of dangerous technologies which strengthen and sustain the regime.

Dissecting the above definition by Krasner, one finds that 'principles' form the hard core, or nucleus, of the aim and conviction of any regime. In the case of nuclear non-proliferation and specifically export control regimes, the principles have been clearly to curb trade and transfers that could be detrimental to the security of the world in general, and in particular are expected to contribute to the production and delivery of WMD. The 'norms' are the accepted standards of behaviour pre-requisite for being part of a regime, usually defined in terms of obligations and rights of being inside the regime. The 'rules' can be definite as exact prescriptions for action. Rules in export control regimes specify the particular technologies that are prohibited from being transferred or traded: these are specified clearly in the respective guidelines, codes of conduct and the related documents of the regimes. Lastly, the 'decision-making procedures' form the practice, structure and bodies inside the regime. They form the usual way of functioning and arrival at a decision by any regime. Krasner has argued that the sustenance of a regime depends on the continuation of the 'principles' and 'norms' embedded in it and an alteration or weakening of either of these two, results in complete breaking down of the overall regime. It is also widely acknowledged that the rules and decision-making procedures often change and get updated without hampering the fabric of the regime. The lessons learnt from the international regimes' definitional analysis are many but the one relevant in the current context is that modifications in principles and norms are unacceptable, but alterations in rules and decision-making procedures are acceptable. As regimes are live entities, they require modernisation as per the requirements of the international system and the confronting of fresh vulnerabilities, therefore, "the rules of international regimes are frequently changed, bent or broken to meet the exigencies of the moment."[2]

Membership and specifically the decision on including fresh members in the regime comes under the decision-making procedures and broadly under the structure of the regime. At different moments in the history of the 20th century, new states have been created and have proved to be active players of the export of salient technologies which fall under the rubric of the export control regimes. The regime theory also complements the fact that alterations in rules, membership and procedures of decision-making do not weaken or break up the regime. Similarly, in the context of non-proliferation and export control regimes too, there is theoretically no reason to believe that expansion in the membership or accommodation of new members is infeasible or counter-productive for the health of these sacrosanct regimes. Instead, the findings suggest that there is both theoretical and practical scope for any structural alteration in the membership aspect of the regimes. The door ought to be kept open.

Multilateral Export Control Regimes

Numerous regimes are ongoing in the world, mostly dissimilar from each other and varying considerably in both scope and size. Some are based on treaties and some are not. The ones on WMD proliferation issues happen to be quite wide. On one side, the NPT prohibits the very possession of nuclear weapons by the majority of member states and pledges eventual elimination of the existing nuclear weapons with the minority member states. The CWC and BTWC, similarly, ban the possession as well as production of chemical and biological weapons respectively. On the other side, the principles and norms of some other institutions concentrate more on restrictions on transfers than bans on possession and production. This makes the former more complicated, in both structure and adherence, than the latter. The norms and rules of the MTCR, for instance, do not prohibit the specific systems of technology but provide guidelines and rules for judicious exports and transfers of missile related technologies. Similarly, the NSG deals with the trade of nuclear fuel or enriched uranium for civilian purposes but with principle of plugging the diversion of the same for military purposes. The chief difference between the former and latter categories is that of "not to possess; and "not to export", where principally the "not to possess" regime prohibits the very existence and possession of that weapon system unlike the "not to export" one undertaking the crucial and very difficult task of monitoring and restricting transfers in a globalised world.

Contemporary Challenges: Placing Membership Therein

Each of the four multilateral export control regimes confronts hurdles to its anticipated success and none can be believed to have successfully and flawlessly achieved what it had aimed for. Any state which shares the core concerns of the regime, extends its faith, believes in its principle and norms, and assures its future adherence to the obligations therein, deserves consideration for becoming a full member. More so, as the export control regimes largely depend on member compliance not through any binding international legislation but through member states tuning their national export control laws to the prescribed ones. In such a situation, expanding membership and enveloping more states, makes perfect sense. Also a relook at the membership aspect holds the possibility to address the contemporary challenges confronted by them in a better manner.

Michael Beck identifies certain challenges that presently undermine the credibility of the export control regimes. His analysis hints towards an eternal battle between the member's self-interest and the collective interest of the organisation. One of the major problems is the lack of consensus on proliferation threats regarding whom to target and how to avoid destabilising transfers.[3] The control of dual use sensitive technologies has expanded with the rise of international exports and the ubiquity of dual use technologies in a global economy has made it even harder to track and control them.[4] There has been an ever increasing competition among international technology suppliers that also happen to be co-members of these regimes.

Another contributor to contemporary challenges emerges from the informality of regime provisions and the freedom of interpretation. "The regime guidelines are often so vague that disputes arises over what exports are contrary to regime provisions."[5] The greatest challenge to non-proliferation and export controls comes from non-state actors. The rise of non-state actors' audacity and reach has increased multifariously, be it the

2001 terrorist attacks in New York, the London bombings of 2005, the attacks in Mumbai in 2008 or these in 2015 in Paris. "The fear of nuclear proliferation has increased manifold with the probability of transfer of these weapons (WMD) or related technologies to rogue or terrorist entities."[6] The fresh vulnerabilities emerging out of the threats from Al Qaeda and the Islamic State in Syria and the Levant (ISIL) compel the export control regimes and also the parental nuclear non-proliferation regime to monitor even more keenly the transfer elements and the buyers. Terrorist groups could operate using front companies in non-threatening states to access coveted and restricted technologies. The bitter lessons learnt from Iraq which acquired most of its technology for a weapon programme in the guise of civilian use, and Pakistan which developed its overall weapon programme and the delivery mechanism missiles through blatant theft and illicit transfers, calls for plugging of the loopholes in the institutions and the multilateral regimes on export controls.

The export control regimes in the 21st century find themselves firmly placed in the midst of challenges. In such a pessimistic environment, with serious hurdles, shying away from membership expansion makes little sense, that too when (a) it holds the potential for better universalisation of the principal and norms of non-proliferation of WMDs; (b) it could help in disentangling the regimes from the present web of challenges; (c) it could provide the regimes with greater compliance of a variety of state actors and discouraging dangerous adventures by the non-state actors; and (d) it would be limited to an alteration in the structure, which, as mentioned in the regime theory would remain "a change in the regime and not of the regime."[7]

Membership Criteria of the Four Export Control Regimes

The four export control regimes form an important means to ensure and further the goal set by the parental nuclear non-proliferation regime. "The need for having control over the transfer of nuclear technology, the export of fissile materials, or the missiles themselves, has been a priority for the advocates of non-proliferation."[8] The export control regimes are distinct from each other and have played their respective roles in restricting the availability of technology essential for various ghastly weapon systems and missile programmes, which come under their purview. The package on export control works as follows: the Nuclear Suppliers' Group (NSG) works for controlling crucial nuclear materials and technology, nuclear fuel being a chief component, under their auspices. The Australia Group is designated to curb the chemical and biological weapon potentials and related exports. The Missile Technology Control Regime (MTCR) is designed to curb proliferation of the delivery mechanisms of nuclear weapons like ballistic missiles. The Wassenaar Arrangement looks into the aspects of conventional arms and some dual use goods that have the potential to destabilise and jeopardise security. These four are often counted as "the additional approaches to controlling the spread of nuclear weapons (whose) emphasis, scope of application, and potential achievements vary greatly."[9] Their respective membership criteria are discussed below.

Nuclear Suppliers Group (NSG)

The Nuclear Suppliers Group (NSG) is a group of nuclear supplier countries that seeks to contribute to the non-proliferation of nuclear weapons through the implementation of two sets of guidelines for nuclear exports and nuclear-related exports. The 48-member body was established in 1975 with the purpose to prevent the proliferation of nuclear weapons through controls on nuclear and nuclear-related material, equipment and technology.

The factors taken into account, as per the NSG, for participation in the regime broadly depend on the prospective party's (a) adherence to the NSG Guidelines and action in accordance with them; (b) ability to supply items (including items in transit) covered by the Annexes to Parts 1 and 2 of the NSG Guidelines; (c) enforcement of a legally-based domestic export control system which gives effect to the commitment to act in accordance with the NSG Guidelines; (d) international support efforts towards non-proliferation of weapons of mass destruction and of their delivery vehicles; and (e) adherence to one or more of the NPT, the Treaties of Pelindaba, Rarotonga, Tlatelolco, Bangkok, Semipalatinsk[10] or an equivalent international nuclear non-proliferation agreement, and full compliance with the obligations of such agreement(s).[11]

Australia Group (AG)

The Australia Group is an informal multilateral body formed in 1984 to address concerns about proliferation of chemical and biological warfare capabilities. The regime controls chemical substances and biological agents and related equipment that could be used in the production of chemical and biological weapons. The Australia Group mentions the criteria for participation as (a) commitment to prevent the spread of Chemical and Biological Weapons (CBW) proliferation, including being a party, in good standing, to the Biological and Toxic Weapons Convention and the Chemical Weapons Convention; (b) being a manufacturer, exporter or trans-shipper of the Australia Group (AG) controlled items; (c) adopting and implementing the AG Guidelines for Transfers of Sensitive Chemical or Biological Items; (d) implementing an effective export control system which provides national controls for all items on the AG common control lists and is supported by adequate licensing and enforcement regimes; (e) creating relevant channels for the exchange of information including: accepting the confidentiality of the information exchange; creating liaison channels for expert discussions; and creating a denial notification system protecting commercial confidentiality; and (f) agreeing to participate in the AG in a way that will strengthen the effectiveness of the AG in preventing CBW proliferation.'[12]

Missile Technology Control Regime (MTCR)

The MTCR is an informal non-treaty association of states established in 1987, sharing common interests in the non-proliferation of missiles, Unmanned Air Vehicle (UAVs) and related technologies. The regime reaches decisions based on consensus but lacks a verification and enforcement mechanism for compliance. The MTCR partners are called "to exercise extreme vigilance to prevent the transfer of goods and technology, which could contribute to WMD missile programmes, in accordance with their national legislation and consistent with international law."[13] The MTCR depends on the established Guidelines and Equipment and Technology Annex. Category I of the annex restrains transfers of items like complete rocket systems and unmanned air vehicle systems capable of delivering a 500 kg (1,100-pound) payload to a range of 300 km (186 miles) or more, and complete sub-systems of such missiles and vehicles. Category II of the annex prohibits transfer of UAVs also with the abovementioned range.

On the issue of membership, the decision to admit a new partner is taken by consensus, as it is the accepted way to reach decisions in the MTCR. The regime presently has 34 member states, of which seven are founding members, namely, Canada, Germany, France, Japan, Italy, Britain and the United States of America. The broad considerations while making membership decisions are: (a) whether a prospective new member would strengthen international non-proliferation efforts; (b) whether it demonstrates a sustained and sustainable commitment to non-proliferation; (c) whether it has a legally-based effective export control system that puts into effect the MTCR Guidelines and procedures; and (d) whether it administers and enforces such controls effectively.[14] The group does not have an observer category but invites adherence to the MTCR Guidelines.

Wassenaar Arrangement

The aim of the regime is to promote transparency and responsibility in transfers of conventional arms and dual-use items (i.e. those having civil and military uses), and to prevent transfers of arms and technology to states and regions of concern, thus, to prevent destabilising accumulations. The regime started in 1996 with 28 members, a majority of whom were members of an erstwhile organisation on similar lines called the Coordination Committee on Export Control (COCOM) which was a Cold War relic.

Presently, the Wassenaar Agreement has 41 members. The organisation establishes lists of items to which member countries are expected to comply through their respective national export control systems.[15] Member governments implement these controls to ensure that transfers of the controlled items do not contribute to the development or enhancement of military capabilities that undermine the goals of the arrangement. The membership in the Wassenaar Arrangement is based broadly on the following criteria: the prospective member should (a) produce/export arms or associated dual-use goods and technologies; (b) implement national policies that do not permit the sale of arms or sensitive dual-use items to countries whose behaviour is a cause for concern; (c) adhere to international non-proliferation norms and guidelines; and (d) implement fully effective export controls. In 2012, Mexico entered the regime as the 41st member. The Wassenaar Arrangement will mark its twentieth anniversary in 2016 with a special commemoration.

Analysing the Indian Case: Practical and Political Hurdles

After discussing the eligibility criteria for membership of the four export control regimes, this section would test the Indian credentials. Out of the four regimes under discussion, the NSG and the MTCR deserve greater attention as these two have already considered the Indian case and are expected to discuss it further in 2016. A breakthrough, however, is on the horizon in a couple of years or so. The Australia Group and the Wassenaar Arrangement, however, would probably follow up through the experience of the former two in regard to the Indian inclusion.

MTCR

"The intensity of change is dependent on the dynamics of the international strategic situation. There is hardly any sector or aspect of MTCR which has remained untouched over the years."[16] There has been remarkable modernisation and modifications in both cruise and ballistic missile technology as they continue being among the most reliable means of delivery of nuclear weapons. Yet, the scepticism and reservations on the issue of new entrants in the MTCR continue to prevail. The membership aspect becomes crucially important, more so in the present context, as four countries with long range missiles or space launch vehicle capabilities are presently outside the regime, with practically no obligation therein, namely India, Iran, Israel, and Saudi Arabia. One also cannot discount the capabilities of Pakistan and North Korea in regard to missile technology. The ones inside the regime are not insulated either as there have been instances of members pursuing transfers which challenge the spirit of the regime. Weaknesses make the regime vulnerable to future misadventures. A revisit to the membership with special reference to India, holds deserving attention.

Practical Hurdles

Testing the Indian case on the requirements of the MTCR reveals that there are actually very few practical hurdles in adding India to the regime. As per the MTCR, the first and second requirements for a prospective new member are that it strengthens international non-proliferation efforts and demonstrates a sustained and sustainable commitment to non-proliferation. India has had prolonged adherence to the cause of non-proliferation. It has been a member of the IAEA since 1957. It has constantly supported the international efforts, resolutions and regimes on the cause of non-proliferation of WMDs. On the domestic front, it has a legally-based, effective export control system that is in consonance with the MTCR Guidelines and procedures. India has administered, and enforced, both the rules and norms effectively as it has never indulged in transferring the technology, goods and expertise of its indigenous missile and space capabilities and dual use technologies to any other state. India's adherence to the prescribed transfer limits of the MTCR has been quite remarkable without a single event of violation. Above all, India is destined to emerge as a greater defence equipment manufacturer soon, as many countries, including Vietnam, Indonesia, South Africa, Egypt, Oman, and Brunei, Venezuela have expressed interest in its (BrahMos) missiles.[17] India overall appears eligible for MTCR membership as tested on the practical cligibility criteria, more so as, in the near future, it has planned for dedicating greater attention to defence exports. However, the political hurdles in the process appear to be daunting.

Political Hurdles

The MTCR recently considered the Indian case for membership. In the Plenary Meeting, 2015, Italy blocked the consensus on India's inclusion into the MTCR owing to a recent unpleasant incident involving two of its marines who are detained in India on charges of murdering two Indian fishermen. The exposure India received after submitting the formal application for the MTCR in June was worthwhile and the application was "received well and remains under consideration" as per the Indian Ministry of External Affairs. The chairman of the regime also tweeted that there was "broad support for India's membership in the MTCR, but, regrettably, no consensus yet. I remain optimistic."[18] After the MTCR Plenary Meeting, 2015, Ambassador Roald Næss, the chairman of the regime, while updating on the last plenary meeting, spoke on "emphasising the observance of the MTCR Guidelines by as many states as possible (with) the continuation of efforts to assist non-member countries and other interested parties in implementing missile-related export controls as required under UNSCR 1540."[19] The next plenary meeting of the MTCR is expected to hold high hopes for India's membership.

NSG

Indian membership into the NSG has been one of the most heated contemporary debates in non-proliferation circles. On one side, the NSG's establishment was prompted by India. The immediate cause for the formation of the NSG was further claimed to be "the explosion in 1974 of a nuclear device by a non-nuclear weapon state, which demonstrated that nuclear technology transferred for peaceful purposes could be misused."[20] On the other side, India is the only country which has received an NSG waiver,[21] that waived the full-scope safeguards requirements and brought India into the coveted and restricted nuclear commerce.[22] The "heightened sensitivity to environmental concerns emphasises the need for compatibility between the methods of electricity generation and ecological sustainability"[23] is a fact that India has well acknowledged. But it needs to further push through its facilitation and integration in nuclear commerce to achieve the requirements of both an ever increasing energy demand and a GHG emission free clean source of energy generation.

Practical Hurdles

The practical positioning of India on the 'requirements' laid down by the NSG for membership is as important as the intricacies of politics. Where is India placed on the broad eligibility of NSG, is an important question. An analysis of the Indian case reveals that India falls safely inside the crease demarcated on the pitch by the NSG on the first requirement of adherence to the guidelines and action in accordance. On the other criterion of being able to supply the materials under the purview of the NSG, the Indian case holds hope. India's Special Chemicals, Organisms, Materials, Equipment and Technologies (SCOMET) list, updated in March 2013, is in accordance with the multilateral export control guidelines and the current NSG control lists.[24] Other "key legislations that cover India's legal export control system are the Foreign Trade Development and Regulation Act or FTDR of 1992, the Atomic Energy Act of 1962, the Customs Act of 1962, and the Weapons of Mass Destruction and their Delivery Systems (Prohibition of Unlawful Activities) Act of 2005, also referred to as the WMD Act."[25] The Indian nuclear non-proliferation record has been clean, and certainly its national export control laws have long been in accordance with the internationally prescribed ones. The state itself regards the proliferation of WMDs as a serious concern as it has often been a victim of sponsored terrorism. Situated as it is in a proliferation prone neighbourhood, this reality is more apparent to New Delhi and it fully comprehends the dangers of unbridled nuclear proliferation.[26] India has been an adherent to the UNSCR 1540, the Additional Protocol of the IAEA[27]. The last point of eligibility for NSG membership requires two aspects simultaneously: adherence and compliance with major non-proliferation treaties like the NPT, the various Nuclear Weapon-Free Zone (NWFZ) treaties, etc. The very uniqueness of the Indian case lies in the fact that even after being a *de facto* nuclear weapon state, outcast and, thus, not bound by the export controls regimes, it has still followed the spirit of non-proliferation. It unilaterally adhered to the principles and guidelines of various non-proliferation regimes quite diligently. It has proved the virtue of 'restraint' and significance of stable deterrence through its nuclear behaviour as well as its nuclear doctrine. The NSG, previously known as the London Club, unfortunately, continues to operate like a club[28], and the features of opacity of proceedings and a conservative attitude in membership, are its continuing realities.

Political Hurdles

The political hurdles appear greater and more opaque to decipher. The country achieved the 2008 waiver through consensus from the NSG after tough rounds of negotiations. The element of politics was explicit even then and continues till today. The US support proved decisive in this regard. But, presently, there has been uneasiness on the decisions around India's entry into the regime, voiced particularly by China and Pakistan, the two interlinked political hurdles.

- Pakistan

  Pakistan aims for an "India style" relationship with the NSG. A waiver for itself has been on its wish list since 2008. Its desire to be inside the regime has led it to creating all types of diplomatic noises where it has tried to prove that India's 'exception' in this regard is invalid, and unhealthy for the regime. Worth noting at the same time is the fact that it brushes away the same 'invalidity' claims by asking for a similar exception for itself. Pakistan has argued that the creation of an exception for India in the NSG would be counter-productive for the non-proliferation regime and regional peace and stability. On the other hand, it argues for an 'India-like' treatment for itself from the NSG, including entry for itself. It projects serious concerns on the loosening of the credibility of the non-proliferation regime[29] which according to it, would happen if India enters the NSG. Pakistan is seriously pursuing this agenda diplomatically and has also engaged China to facilitate its entry into the NSG, irrespective of its history of non-proliferation. Pakistan's non-satisfactory record and its illicit trade in WMD technology is a known secret in the world. Any consideration of nuclear export control membership or even plain nuclear cooperation for Pakistan begins and ends with the not so old story of A.Q. Khan, the head of Khan Research Laboratories, who ran a 'nuclear Wal-Mart' and proliferated WMD technologies to Iran, Libya and North Korea. Iran and Libya themselves have disclosed the Pakistani hand in providing them with WMD related technology. "The IAEA inspectors determined that Iran had received classified designs and components for uranium-processing gas centrifuge machines from Pakistani scientists."[30] Also, the IAEA has strong evidence that North Korea was able to overcome numerous hurdles in the path of achieving WMD technology courtesy Pakistan. In such a backdrop, Pakistan audaciously claims an 'exception' for itself in nuclear non-proliferation regimes, in general, and the NSG, in particular. Apprehensions regarding Pakistan's nuclear intentions, lack of faith in its promises and a lack of consensus for it among the members of the NSG and MTCR comprise a reality from which the state is shying away. As George Perkovich argues, the proliferation damage done by the Khan network is an enormous fact. At some point, the question arises whether and when to learn from this fact and try to create new facts that are more propitious.[31]

- China

  China, unlike Pakistan, is inside the regime, and has the privilege of being better heard than the latter. China extended conditional support for India's Nuclear Suppliers Group membership in January 2015. It added that "prudence and caution" are needed on the issue: "We support India to take further measures to meet the requirements for the inclusion in the group."[32] However, India might possibly face hurdles soon from China on the matter of full Indian membership. Pakistan, an ally of China, would play its cards to gain entry into the NSG despite its bad track record on nuclear proliferation. A Pakistani daily[33] reported that the matter of NSG membership was discussed at length between Pakistani President Mamnoon Hussain and his Chinese counterpart during his recent visit to China. Here, **China presumably assured Pakistan of its support to its membership bid in the NSG if India is let in.**

Most members of the NSG presently are actually accepting of an Indian entry but remain sceptical about Pakistan. They trust India but are worried regarding the precedent of special treatment to India as it could become an excuse for the non-member states, with pathetic non-proliferation records and credentials, like Pakistan, to argue for a similar undeserving exception. The Pakistan-China nexus remains at the foundation of the political hurdles faced by India in the NSG membership. The plenary meeting scheduled for June 2016 would be crucial for India as the pending Indian application would come up for consideration. Despite its clean non-proliferation track record, India has had, and continues, to struggle long and hard on the NSG membership.

On the eligibility issue laid down by the Australia Group and Wassenaar Arrangement, the Indian case deserves a brief scrutiny. India is a signatory of both the CWC and the BTWC, making its testimonial further authentic. In 1997, it declared a stockpile of 1,044 tons of sulphur mustard[34] whose promised destruction was completed in 2009, that made India the third state to completely destroy its chemical weapons stockpile. "India also plays an expanding role in global non-proliferation norms by providing extensive support to the Organisation for the Prohibition of Chemical Weapons (OPCW) and seeking greater participation in international export control regimes."[35] On biological weapons too, India has cleared its stance. Indian President A.P.J. Abdul Kalam had asserted that India "will not make biological weapons. It is cruel to human beings..."

Why India Deserves Membership

Testing the Indian case on the practical and political hurdles helped to build a case for the Indian membership into the four export control regimes. The necessary practical components for supporting its candidature in the regimes largely appear to have been met by the country. This leads to re-phrasing of the *de facto* politically driven accepted agenda: "why India does not deserve the export control regimes' membership," into a more robust and factually backed one, "why India deserves membership of the export control regimes." The following are broad five factors that are self-explanatory on the Indian membership issue.

The Indian Nuclear 'Exceptionalism'

The hallmark of difference between the Indian nuclear journey and that of others outside the non-proliferation regime lies in the fact that it possesses a crystal clear record of nuclear non-proliferation. This has been acknowledged broadly by the world, combined with the fact there has been no case of illicit trade and transfer of nuclear technology and goods from the country. The well-known clean track record of India in adhering to non-proliferation even while being outside the compliance framework of the NPT and its continuation of being self-restrained in the proliferation of WMD technology and materials, is worthwhile. Thomas F. Dorian and Leonard S. Spector in their work, "Covert Nuclear Trade and the International Non-Proliferation Regime," list the cases of critical weaknesses in the international non-proliferation regime, and the covert and illicit nuclear trade by states since the 1960s. They mention Israel, South Korea, South Africa, Iraq and Pakistan as "episodes of covert nuclear trade"[36]. India is missing from an intense academic work like this, the reason being an absence of a history of the nuclear black market or clandestine transactions of nuclear technology in India. India, in letter and spirit, has had the utmost respect for, and responsibility towards, the international nuclear non-proliferation regime norms. India's nuclear doctrine reflects restraint. Credible minimum deterrence, No First Use (NFU) and a unilateral moratorium on nuclear testing are some of the highlights of the country's responsible nuclear behaviour.

India's nuclear mainstreaming into the nuclear non-proliferation regime with its recognition as a state with advanced nuclear capabilities took place in the last decade. The credentials of the country were realised post-2005 Indo-US Civilian Nuclear Cooperation Agreement. A "responsible nuclear actor connotes a wide range of acceptable non-proliferation behaviour like denying nuclear materials and technology to non-Nuclear Weapon State (NNWS) for military purposes, non-use of nuclear weapons against NWS under any circumstances, cooperating with international authorities for enforcing non-proliferation rules and such other practices.'[37] Dr. Manpreet Sethi had proposed a "country specific" framework for the NSG Guidelines way back in 2004 wherein she argued for the need to comprehend the issues that make India an exceptional case. This would ensure that "the twin goals of nuclear non-proliferation and flow of technology and materials for nuclear power for developmental purposes are fulfilled."[38]

The Elephant is Already Half Way

Presently, the diplomatic positioning of the giant Indian elephant is such that though it has crossed the Rubicon, through the 2005 nuclear deal, it remains stuck, unable to proceed further into the terrain ahead. India awaits the deserving, promised and much delayed complete merger into the nuclear non-proliferation regime. Membership of the four export control regimes in this regard is crucial, more so because presently, India has 'partial presence' in the nuclear non-proliferation regime, with complete segregation from its salient wing on export control. Export control regimes lie at the heart of the umbrella structure of the non-proliferation regime. The Indian merger and full membership into these export control institutions become more important in the present context as the 'otherwise' hanging status is sending wrong signals to a broad spectrum of actors in the international system. Firstly, there is curiosity and lack of clarity regarding the actual positioning of India in the nuclear non-proliferation regime, leading to apprehensions and roadblocks in nuclear commerce and trade for India. And, secondly, the hawks of the non-proliferation regime and politically motivated actors who are against India being a case for exception, are strengthened to deprive India of full acceptance by the regime.

The Indian elephant which was largely misunderstood and mistrusted in the past decades, post the deal, is in a better position and it is bound to proceed further, completing its journey into the regime. The Indian foreign policy has actually proceeded already half way after the nuclear deal with the US, and membership of these export control regimes would complement and complete the process. The nuclear deal and the statements in 2005 by President Bush and Prime Minister (PM) Manmohan Singh,[39] and then in 2008 by the then Indian Foreign Minister Pranab Mukherjee[40] signalled an optimism and a beginning of a new chapter for the Indian foreign policy. India made significant disarmament and non-proliferation commitments.[41] In a decade, from 2005 till 2015, it has delivered on most of the promises, a feat performed both surprisingly fast, and thereby, impressive. India has already placed the Separation Plan on the IAEA table as it has voluntarily agreed to separate the civilian nuclear facilities from the military ones. The US has for long regarded the need for building "a framework for participating governments to combat multilaterally problems related to export control and WMD proliferation."[42] India has agreed to a policy of "refraining from the transfer of enrichment and reprocessing technologies to states that do not have them, and supporting international efforts to limit their spread."[43] It is ready to assume the same responsibilities "...as other leading countries with advanced nuclear technology"[44] in this regard.

Present Indian Stature in the World and Rise as a Technological Power

PM Manmohan Singh on the adjustment of the NSG Guidelines to enable full civil nuclear cooperation with India in 2008, had said that the day "marks the end of India's decades' long isolation from the nuclear mainstream and of the technology denial regime (and) a recognition of India's impeccable non-proliferation credentials and its status as a state with advanced nuclear technology. It will give an impetus to India's pursuit of environmentally sustainable economic growth."[45] The present century is certainly the Asian century. The progress India has achieved has been remarkable. In a six-decade journey, it has transformed itself from a poor, dependent, decolonised entity into a flourishing economy, and a trade and technological heavyweight. India's access to nuclear reactors, technology, and materials is significant, as nuclear energy holds a prominent place in the energy mix of the country. The nuclear energy infrastructure is booming, and so are the investment opportunities. The indigenous capabilities of the state have also supported it to become both a major importer and also exporter of the materials that come under the purview of the export control regimes. The Mangalyaan or the Mars

Orbiter Mission[46] last year gave another proud moment to India to display its advanced technological capabilities. The Mangalyaan mission also made the world's space leaders take note of the capabilities of the Indian Space Research Organisation (ISRO). Prime Minister Modi has also announced a South Asian Association for Regional Cooperation (SAARC) satellite for the neighbouring countries to help them in areas such as tele-medicine, weather forecasting and communication. India has been an active developer of several dual use goods and technologies. The BrahMos, a joint venture between India and Russia for production as well as joint defence designing of the supersonic cruise missile, has also attracted international attention for its cost-effectiveness, technological sophistication and deterrence competence. A full merger of India as an emerging technological leader into the multilateral export control regimes seems evident.

Indian Adherence to the Regimes Through National Legislations

The four export control regimes are informal multilateral bodies providing guidelines and codes of conduct to member states. The export control regimes *per se* do not dictate an overarching international rule on export control to member states, but rely on their adherence to the prescribed controls through their respective national legislations. The Indian export control laws appear to be well in tune with the requirements of the multilateral export control mechanisms. India's full adherence to UNSCR 1540 is well known. Its scientific, technological and industrial capabilities have matured to a stage where it is presently a major user and producer of a range of dual-use materials, equipment and technologies. Being a responsible member of the international community, India has realised the gravity of the threats that proliferation of these dual-use products and technologies poses. "India has, therefore, instituted a domestic regime to prevent the illegal export of dual-purpose items and technologies through the creation of laws and an inter-departmental administrative mechanism."[47]

India adheres to the Australia Group Guidelines in its domestic legislation; in addition, India has been a party to both the BTWC and CWC. India's signature to the CWC in January 1993 was followed by a public notice, effective from March the same year, in which the director general of foreign trade specified a list of dual-purpose chemicals, the export of which is either prohibited or permitted only under licence. In the year 2000, a list of Special Chemicals, Organisms, Materials, Equipment and Technologies (SCOMET) was published that specified all dual-use items and technologies within 8 categories.[48] Australia, along with the Australia Group, realises and recognises the importance of India[49] to be inside the club owing to the country's large chemical and bioscience industries, trade flows and the large volume of exports it provides to the world. Presently, India is a major stakeholder and supplier to the chemical industries, hence, it becomes more important for it to be closer to the regime and its members, to gain further expertise.

India, the sole recipient of a waiver from the NSG, has finalised the Separation Plan, harmonised its export regulations with the NSG Guidelines and also ratified the IAEA Additional Protocol, as promised. The country's current export control system[50] from the legal point of view, is well established and governed. To quote former Foreign Secretary Mr. Rajan Mathai, India has "a law-based export system, covering about nine different legislations (and that) the nation's export controls are in line with the highest international standards."[51] According to Saira Bano, "India is likely to be a nuclear exporter and it would strengthen the regime to have a responsible nuclear state in the group."[52]

In the second decade of the 21st century, India occupies a position where, firstly, it is hard to overlook its global presence and positioning; secondly, the volume of its exports in the world is expanding, with trade booming. The Indian BrahMos supersonic cruise missile, which it has developed in collaboration with Russia, adheres to the MTCR. India has been a developer of missile technology, but has a zero record for proliferation and transfers exceeding the MTCR Guidelines. Instead of assuming that it will go against the spirit of the regime, the MTCR, with India on board as a member, would gain assurance that all supplies of sensitive missile and related technologies under the ambit of the regime that India exports, will adhere to the MTCR Guidelines in the future too.[53] With India poised to become an active trading partner and prospective exporter of a wide range of dual use sophisticated technological products, it would be a rational move to incorporate it, through mainstreaming it into the export control regimes without delay.

Appreciation, Recognition and Acceptance for India

Decisions in the export control regimes, including those on membership, are taken by consensus, and it is obvious that building a consensus takes time. All the four regimes are separate in institutional structure and decision-making procedures, thus, a 'package deal' approach seems less likely and more injurious to the sovereignty of the decision-making of the respective members and organisations. It will be much more salient if India gains and retains the support and confidence of various states. The Indian nuclear diplomacy, with dedicated efforts, has tried to erase the prevalent misunderstandings and misinterpretations regarding India, including the issue of its not joining the NPT and CTBT. Interestingly, "a strong section of the strategic and policy-making communities of the multilateral export control regimes have been demanding inclusion of technologically emerging countries like India into these regimes to strengthen them."[54] There has been a high level of recognition and support for the Indian nuclear non-proliferation record and the Indian nuclear doctrine.

The Chinese too have acknowledged that "such an inclusion (India) should be conducive to the integrity and effectiveness of the regime and the decision should be made on consensus. We notice India's commitment to relevant issues"[55] Kelly Wadsworth has argued that "India should be given membership to the NSG on the basis of its compliance with the spirit of these regimes and in demonstrating responsible non-proliferation behaviour as per the US-India Civil Nuclear Agreement."[56] The United States has also communicated its intent to support India's full membership in all the four multilateral export control regimes in a phased manner, which "includes consultations with the partners of the regimes to encourage the needed evolution of membership criteria."[57] India has pledged its adherence to maintain the core principles and full adoption of the export control regimes' requirements to reflect its prospective membership. The White House also believes that India should qualify for membership in the Australia Group and Wassenaar Arrangement (too) as it is ready to impose export controls over all the items on these regimes' control lists into its national laws. The appreciation, recognition and acceptance for India can be noted from "shifted requests for export of sensitive technologies to India from 'presumption of denial' to 'presumption of approval'."[58] The US has expressed its concerns regarding the absence of a country of India's stature from the multilateral export control regimes, claiming this is counter-productive and a cause of ineffectiveness therein. The UK, along with lending full support for India's permanent membership in the United Nations Security Council (UNSC), also has a positive opinion on the Indian membership into the export control regimes. On the other side, the Russian Federation, in 2010, communicated its belief in multilateral export control regimes as an important component of nuclear non-proliferation, identical to the Indian belief and expressed its "readiness to assist and promote discussion and positive decision in the NSG on India's full membership...and welcomed India's intention to seek full membership."[59] Russia has also communicated faith in India's full membership in the MTCR and Wassenaar Arrangement. The responsibility and restraint in the Indian approach towards nuclear weapons has been widely acknowledged and appreciated. The nation continues to be firmly on the same path, without getting stirred by provocations, which is embedded in "no first use" and the credibility of minimum nuclear deterrence. Above these valid reasons, an additional fact that cannot be discounted is that India's rising profile and the efforts it has undertaken in the recent past to prove its credentials and case, are impressive. The last decade has been really exciting for India, in the sense that it reaped the fruits of its hard work, investment and responsibility in nuclear diplomacy. The US has highlighted that it is "very important that India be brought on, and participate in, these (multilateral export control regimes)...it's going to enhance the international strength of all of these regimes, and it's a high priority for us."[60] The joint statement of 2010 between India and the United States is enshrined in President Obama's call and "the need to 'evolve' a criterion to make India's entry possible… (and added that) while a country fulfils all the criteria, the politics of the regime may prevent a country from taking the membership."[61]

The Way Forward

In the recent past, it has appeared that water (the non-proliferation regime) has become more conducive for the fish (new members with high non-proliferation credentials and clean records, like India) to survive and be better accommodated. In regard to the multilateral export control regimes and Indian membership, the second decade of the 21st century seems positive and hopeful. On one side, the Indian leadership and diplomatic fraternity are enthusiastically working towards facilitating and furthering India's engagement with the non-proliferation regimes. On the other, the Indian nuclear non-proliferation journey and record are receiving global appreciation and acceptance, suggesting that "long-term adherence to regime guidelines will be indiscriminately rewarded."[62] The potential Indian membership of the export control regimes will complete the circle that was initiated with the Indo-US civilian nuclear cooperation, with India being accepted as a full member of the regime. It would "help in mainstreaming the country (and) also assist in further image building and confidence building."[63]

Apart from the gain in status as a great power, with membership of the export control regimes, India is also bound to do away with the repeated tiresome diplomatic process of explaining to the world bilaterally every now and then, the details of the Indian nuclear 'exceptionalism', the Indian record of non-proliferation, its responsible nuclear behaviour, and its prolonged and voluntary adherence to the regime's rationale and guidelines. With membership of the export control regimes, India would get a "single window clearance" to nuclear commerce which is urgent and essential for its growing civilian energy needs, and multinational investments for the construction of nuclear plants.

India has long been eligible on the core criteria-based rules of a prospective member laid down by the NSG. The 'NSG membership would also bring India into a well established international nuclear market where finances and transactions operate along sound economic traditions, reaping optimal benefits.'[64] Admitting India into the NSG would do away with the doubts of the major exporter states about trade and investment with India, and entering the Indian nuclear market. This "would be another step in elevating the civil nuclear energy cooperation that Obama and Modi envision."[65] The prime minister's call for "Make in India" pays attention to, and lays emphasis on, the long neglected defence sector. India is also inclined to export defence items to friendly countries. PM Modi, in a meeting with his Vietnamese counterpart, Nguyen Tan Dung, emphasised, "Our defence cooperation with Vietnam is among our most important ones. India remains committed to the modernisation of Vietnam's defence and security forces."[66]

Already a key player in the export of some crucial items under the purview of the export regimes, with defence exports, India will become a player, too big to be pushed to the sidelines of the international system. The consensus-based Indian entry, particularly into the MTCR, is also imminent.[67] Most pundits on the export control and non-proliferation regime regard the entry of India in the MTCR as being on the horizon, probably followed by the NSG in the coming five years.[68] India's much awaited merger with the regimes, specifically the MTCR and the NSG, is predicted to be "a landmark development for India, opening doors to trade in high technology systems like cryogenic rockets, so urgently required for the country's space programme."[69] India has emerged as a rising economic power and a responsible nuclear power as well. The way forward from here will certainly transcend the days when India was the target of these regimes. India's entry into the regimes, especially in the four export control regimes, is of utmost importance not just for its own good but for maintaining the overall health of the regimes, as well. Indian membership would make the regimes better represented and complete. Contrary to the belief of some that the export control regimes are hastening the Indian case for membership, the fact of the matter is that it is actually a long delayed and deserving addition to the regime of non-proliferation.

Notes

1. Stephen Krasner, "Structural Causes and Regime Consequences: Regimes as Intervening Variables", *International Organization*, 36 (2), 1982, pp. 185-205.
2. Robert O. Keohane, "The Demand for International Regimes", in Stephen Krasner ed., *International Regimes* (New York: Cornell University Press, 1983), p. 147.
3. Michael Beck, "Reforming the Multilateral Export Control Regimes", available at: http://cns.miis.edu/npr/pdfs/72beck.pdf. Accessed on November 15, 2015.
4. Ibid.
5. Ibid.
6. Pervaiz Iqbal Cheema, "Missile Proliferation and Export Control In South Asia: MTCR And Beyond", *South Asian Survey*, 11 (2), 2004.
7. By "change in the regime," Stephen Krasner refers to those alterations which a regime can resist without falling back. They are designed to be strong enough to withstand alterations into the 'rules' and 'decision-making procedures' without weakening or breaking up. On the other

hand, 'change of the regime' signifies the replacement of the present regime with a new one. Clearly, when the 'principles' and 'norms' of a regime change, the regime breaks up and ceases to exist, thus, it becomes a change of regime.

8. Cheema, n.6, p. 243.
9. Thomas F. Dorian and Leonard S. Spector "Covert Nuclear Trade and the International Non-Proliferation Regime" in Fred Holroyd, ed., *Thinking About Nuclear Weapons: Analyses and Prescriptions* (London: Routledge, 2001), p.298.
10. The Treaties of Pelindaba, Rarotonga, Tlatelolco, Bangkok, Semipalatinsk stand for the establishment of five Nuclear Weapon-Free Zones (NWFZ) in the world. According to the United Nations, their establishment is a regional approach to strengthen global nuclear non-proliferation and disarmament norms, and consolidate international efforts towards peace and security. The parties to the treaties agree to ban the use, development, or deployment of nuclear weapons in a given region. The Treaty of Tlatelolco prohibits nuclear weapons in Latin America and the Caribbean. The Treaty of Rarotonga does the same for the South Pacific. The Treaty of Bangkok establishes the Southeast Asia nuclear weapon-free zone. The Treaty of Pelindaba establishes the African nuclear weapon-free zone and, finally, the Semipalatinsk Treaty established a nuclear weapon-free zone in Central Asia.
11. Nuclear Suppliers' Group (NSG), "NSG Participants", available at: http://www.nuclearsuppliersgroup.org/en/participants1. Accessed on December 5, 2015.
12. Australia Group (AG), "AG Membership", available at: http://www.australiagroup.net/en/membership.html. Accessed on December 5, 2015.
13. MTCR, "Public Statement from the Plenary Meeting of the Missile Technology Control Regime (MTCR)", Oslo 2014, available at: http://www.state.gov/documents/organization/232825.pdf. Accessed on November 25, 2015.
14. "MTCR Membership," available at: http://www.mtcr.info/english/partners.html. Accessed on November 10, 2015.
15. In addition to that, every six months, members exchange information on deliveries of conventional arms to non-Wassenaar members that fall under eight broad weapon categories: battle tanks, Armoured Combat Vehicles (ACVs), large-calibre artillery, military aircraft/unmanned aerial vehicles, military and attack helicopters, warships, missiles or missile systems, and small arms and light weapons. In 2003, members also added the ACV, aircraft, and helicopter categories, including models designed to perform reconnaissance or conduct command of troops missions.
16. Rajiv Nayan, "Trends in the Missile Control Regime", *Strategic Analysis*, 1998, 22(6), pp. 867-881.
17. Debidatta Aurobinda Mahapatra (2014), "BrahMos Missile Exports a Challenging Proposition", available at: http://in.rbth.com/economics/2014/11/10/brahmos_missile_exports_a_challenging_proposition_39615. Accessed on December 20, 2015.
18. Roald Naess, available at: https://twitter.com/roald_naess/status/652489223971454978. Accessed on December 10, 2015.
19. MTCR, "The 22nd Asian Export Control Seminar, Tokyo: Statement by the MTCR Chair, Ambassador Roald Næss", 2015, p.3.
20. Nuclear Suppliers' Group (NSG) "History", available at: http://www.nuclearsuppliersgroup.org/en/history1. Accessed on December 5, 2015.
21. In 2008, the NSG waived the full-scope safeguards requirement of paragraph 4 and expressly allowed ENR exports, subject to paragraphs 6 and 7, for India. The NSG waiver, in simplest terms, meant that India now had a right, under the regime, to trade in civilian nuclear fuel and technology.
22. Nuclear commerce, as Brahma Chellany quotes, is the most "politically regulated commerce in the world". The regime of non-proliferation has held a tight grip on commerce in nuclear technology and commodities.

23. Manpreet Sethi, "NSG Guidelines: Need for a Country-Specific Approach" in Jasjit Singh, ed., *Nuclear Power and Non-Proliferation: Conflict or Convergence?* (New Delhi: Knowledge World, 2004), p.29.
24. Ministry of External Affairs (MEA), "Meeting between India and the Nuclear Suppliers Group(NSG) Troika Held in Vienna", available at: http://mea.gov.in/press-releases.htm?dtl/21888/Meeting+between+India+and+the+Nuclear+Suppliers+GroupNSG+Troika+held+in+Vienna. Accessed on December 10, 2015.
25. Arka Biswas (2015) "India in the Missile Technology Control Regime", available at: http://www.observerindia.com/cms/export/orfonline/modules/occasionalpaper/attachments/Occasional Paper_70_1441699467117.pdf. Accessed on December 10, 2015.
26. Sethi, n.23, p.29.
27. The Additional Protocol (AP) to the Safeguards Agreement between the Government of India (GOI) and the IAEA for the Application of Safeguards to Civilian Nuclear Facilities was ratified in July 2014.
28. As pointed out by Sethi, n.23, p.31.
29. Pakistani Foreign Office (FO) Spokesman Qazi Khalilullah while addressing the weekly press briefing, said this, in November 2015, available at: http://economictimes.indiatimes.com/news/defence/india-nsg-membership-to-impact-regional-peace-stability-pakistan/articleshow/49940484.cms. Accessed on December 10, 2015.
30. Sethi, n.23, p.39.
31. George Perkovich (2015) "Civil Nuclear Cooperation with Pakistan: Prospects and Consequences", available at: http://carnegieendowment.org/2015/12/08/civil-nuclear-cooperation-with-pakistan-prospects-and-consequences/imv3. Accessed on December 15, 2015.
32. Chinese Foreign Ministry Spokesperson Hua Chunying, at a media briefing in January 2015, available at: http://articles.economictimes.indiatimes.com/2015-01-26/news/58470148_1_south-china-sea-wassenaar-arrangement-nsg. Accessed on December 10, 2015.
33. "China Assures Pakistan of Help to Join Nuclear Suppliers Club", *The Express Tribune*, November 2015, available at: http://tribune.com.pk/story/999286/china-assures-pakistan-of-help-to-join-nuclear-suppliers-club/. Accessed on December 10, 2015.
34. Sulphur mustard, commonly known as mustard gas, is a class of related cytotoxic and vesicant chemical warfare agents with the ability to form large blisters on the exposed skin and in the lungs. Mustard agents are regulated under the 1993 Chemical Weapons Convention(CWC).
35. Nuclear Threat Initiative (NTI), "Country Profile- India, Chemical", available at: http://www.nti.org/country-profiles/india/chemical/. Accessed on December 10, 2015.
36. Dorian and Spector, n.9, pp. 137-165.
37. Jayanna Krupakar, "Assessing India's Case for NSG Membership", January 2015, available at: http://www.indiandefencereview.com/assessing-indias-case-for-nsg-membership/. Accessed on October 6, 2015.
38. Sethi, n.23, p.34.
39. White House 2005, Joint Statement by President George W. Bush and Prime Minister Manmohan Singh, July 18, 2005, available at: http://2001-2009.state.gov/p/sca/rls/pr/2005/49763.htm. Accessed on September 15, 2015.
40. Pranab Mukherjee, Statement by the External Affairs Minister of India Sri Pranab Mukherjee on Civilian Nuclear Initiative, September 9. Accessed on September 15, 2015, available at: http://mea.gov.in/in-focus-article.htm?18806/Statement+by+External+Affairs+Minister+of+India+Shri+Pranab+Mukherjee+on+the+Civil+Nuclear+Initiative
41. n.39.

42. United States, "A Resource on Strategic Trade Management and Export Controls: Non-Proliferation Regimes", available at: http://www.state.gov/strategictrade/resources/c43178.htm. Accessed on November 13, 2015.
43. n.39.
44. Ibid.
45. Manmohan Singh, "Statement by the Prime Minister on the Final Outcome of the Meeting of the Nuclear Suppliers Group", 2008. Accessed on November 15, 2015, available at: http://www.mea.gov.in/in-focus-article.htm?18804/Statement+by+the+Prime+Minister+Dr+Manmohan+Singh+on+the+final+outcome+of+the+meeting+of+the+Nuclear+Suppliers+Group
46. ISRO, "Mars-Orbiter-Mission," available at:http://www.isro.gov.in/pslv-c25-mars-orbiter-mission. Accessed on December 20, 2015.
47. Ministry of External Affairs (MEA), Government of India, "India's System of Controls over Exports of Strategic Goods and Technology," available at: http://mea.gov.in/in-focus-article.htm?18843/Indias+System+of+Controls+over+Exports+of+Strategic+Goods+and+Technology. Accessed on December 5, 2015.
48. See Guidelines for Export of SCOMET Items, available at: http://dgft.gov.in/exim/2000/scomet/scomet2011.pdf. Accessed on December 5, 2015.
49. Rory Medcalf and Amandeep Gill, "Unconventional Partners: Australia-India Cooperation in Reducing Nuclear Dangers", Policy Brief, Lowy Institute for International Policy, 2009. The authors believe that Australia is well placed to begin soundings within the Australia Group about possible Indian admission, and building the consensus that would be required and an Indian addition would benefit the Group to achieve practical coordination of export controls with multiple security partners.
50. A comprehensive regulatory framework has been long in place in India on export controls. To cite a few, the Explosive Substance Act, the Chemical Weapon Convention Act, the Atomic Energy Act, the Customs Act, etc. are in place. The Weapons of Mass Destruction and their Delivery Systems (Prohibition of Unlawful Activities) Act being one of the most recent domestic legislation on export control in India.
51. Gulshan Luthra (2015) "India Fails to Get MTCR Membership, But Wins Wide Support". Available at: http://www.indiastrategic.in/topstories4124_India_fails_to_get_MTCR_Membership.htm. Accessed on December 5, 2015, p.20.
52. Saira Bano, "India's Nuclear Supplier Group's Membership and the Nuclear Non Proliferation Regime", *Irish Studies in International Affairs*, 25, 2014, pp.117-135.
53. Biswas, n.25.
54. Rajiv Nayan, "Integrating India with Global Export Controls System: Challenges Ahead", *Strategic Analysis*, 2011, 35 (3), p. 442.
55. Hua Chunying, Chinese Foreign Ministry spokesperson, http://www.thehindu.com/news/national/pakistan-resents-us-concession-to-india/article6827381.ece
56. Kelly Wadsworth, "Reward India's Nonproliferation Good Behaviour," August 2015, available at: http://csis.org/publication/pacnet-52-reward-indias-nonproliferation-good-behavior. Accessed on October 5, 2015.
57. The White House, "Joint Statement by President Obama and Prime Minister Singh of India", November 8, 2010, available at: https://www.whitehouse.gov/the-press-office/2010/11/08/joint-statement-president-obama-and-prime-minister-singh-india. Also available at: http://www.mea.gov.in/bilateral-documents.htm?dtl/5081/Joint_Statement_of_Prime_Minister_Dr_Manmohan_Singh_and_President_Barack_Obama. Accessed on October 5, 2015.
58. Jyoti Malhotra, "Out of Pokharan Shadow, India, US to Sign Hi-Tech Deal", *Indian Express*, December 13, 2003.
59. Government of India, Ministry of External Affairs, "Joint Statement: Celebrating a Decade of

the India- Russian Federation Strategic Partnership and Looking Ahead", 2010, available at: http://mea.gov.in/outoging-visit-detail.htm?5118/Joint+Statement+Celebrating+a+Decade+of+the+India+Russian+Federation+Strategic+Partnership+and+Looking+Ahead. Accessed on November 15, 2015.

60. Thomas Kelly, acting assistant secretary of state for political-military affairs, in April 2013, said this in response to a question from Congressman Steve Chabot, available at: http://articles.economictimes.indiatimes.com/2013-04-25/news/38817228_1_export-control-regime-defence-relationship-wassenaar-arrangement. Accessed on December 10, 2015.
61. n.57.
62. Kelly Wadsworth (2015) "Reward India's Non-proliferation Good Behaviour", available at: http://csis.org/publication/pacnet-52-reward-indias-nonproliferation-good-behavior. Accessed on December 10, 2015.
63. Nayan, n.54.
64. Krupakar, n.37.
65. Ibid.
66. Mahapatra, n.17.
67. Luthra, n.51.
68. Dr. Toby Dalton predicted Indian entry into the export control regimes as member in the next five years during the joint workshop organised by Carnegie Endowment, Stimpson Centre and the Institute of Peace and Conflict Resolution on November 4, 2015, in New Delhi.
69. Luthra, n.51, p.20.

10

Offensive Potentiality of Cyber Attacks: A Multifaceted and Multivariate Analysis

AK Gupta

The fundamental underpinning of the present-day conflicts is information and the outcome of any conflict is largely decided by the ability to generate, distribute and manipulate information with appropriate temporal and spatial relevance. Exchange of information facilitated through information technology, computers, networks and telecommunications is considered as the ontological keystone of war in any domain. The dynamism, sustainability, survivability and mission accomplishment of a functioning war-fighting entity is directly linked with reliable, secure, resilient and survivable information infrastructure. Much erudite discourse and lucid expositions have been made and a great deal of attention has been paid to the problem of how to defend information technology systems and networks against debilitating cyber attacks in both military and non-military contexts. However, the possibility of a sovereign state, leveraging and engaging the cyber assets and capabilities for perpetrating cyber attacks for the protection and furtherance of its national interest is rarely discussed in public. From a cyber warfare perspective, the dangers of cyber attack are so imminent across a multitude of national interests that it deserves wide-ranging, robust and open debate to exploit all the tenets of military, intelligence craft and international law without prejudice or reservation.

The overarching dependence of many societal functions on information technology and cyber infrastructure has made the growing challenges of defending the cyber space against a multitude of threats emanating from various sources, a top national security priority. The national security and the national interests of a sovereign nation are intricately linked to, and inextricably dependent upon, its ability to maintain a strong cyber security posture with proportionate emphasis on defensive strength and offensive capabilities. In other warfare domains, both defensive and offensive components add up and synergistically combine to provide comprehensive national security. The principle conventional military doctrinal exposition primarily focusses on the offence-defence balance that determines the relative efficacy of offensive and defensive security strategies. In the realm of cyber security, the primary focus of attention remains deeply skewed towards defence. As states become increasingly involved in cyber space for military purposes, the cyber domain has emerged as a critical component of the overall security paradigm.

Passive defensive measures in the cyber warfare context facilitate attainment of a *strong defensive posture* capable of thwarting a cyber attack. Nevertheless, these measures offer only enhanced deterrents, not a *foolproof defence*. An adversary pays no penalty for failed attacks and an attack needs to succeed only once out of numerous attempts to shatter the credibility of passive defensive posturing. This defensive posture often weighs heavily on overall preparedness and puts it at an asymmetric disadvantage. This bring to the fore the question of exploring other approaches which might bolster the defensive posture. One approach advocates elimination or degradation of an adversary's ability to successfully prosecute an attack. In that case, the severity of a malevolent cyber attack perpetrated by an adversary would be much diminished due to taking a lot of wind out of the sails of the attack as a consequence of lost or degraded capabilities. The equally effective possibility would be to make the cost of undertaking a cyber attack *prohibitive and overwhelmingly* deleterious such that anticipated gains from a cyber attack far exceed the expected costs. A cyber attack will be inhibited or deterred because of the threat of punitive reprisal and if a deterrent threat is created before the proscribed cyber attack is even contemplated.[1] In that case, the motivation, severity, magnitude and frequency of cyber attacks will be much more diminished even when undertaken by a determined and capable adversary. In general, there are many options for imposing costs on an adversary, including economic penalties such as sanctions, diplomatic penalties like breaking off of diplomatic relations and even kinetic military actions. In-kind military action—a counter-cyber attack—is also a possibility.[2] The initiation of these possible actions can be construed as part of the 'active defence strategy'. But some of the actions undertaken in the realm of active defence are often captured under the rubric of offensive acts.[3] The limitation of passive defence necessitates consideration of evaluating attack options for defensive purposes. An acquired attack capability bolsters the active cyber defence posture with the possibility to use this for other non-defensive purposes. Attack capabilities also give teeth to the nation's credible deterrence posture.

Strategic and Political Dimension of Cyber Attacks

Cyber attacks are increasingly being used as instruments and agents of conflict enunciation, resolution and reconciliation both as independent entities and in conjunction with broader military operations. The effects and implications of such attacks on variegated targets may be large or small, ephemeral or permanent; cyber attacks have shut down networks, cut off access to essential information and services, damaged industrial infrastructure, and disrupted banking services. Even if the needle of suspicion points to state-sponsored cyber attacks, the relative anonymity under which actors operate in cyber space makes definite attribution a distant possibility. This highlights the importance of a measured and nuanced professional debate on this unequivocally important issue and interweaving the tenets of offensive cyber attacks into the concept of operations.

- **Empirically Supported and Efficaciously Applicable National Policy on Cyber Attacks**: The nation should have a declaratory policy on the use of cyber space for offensive cyber operations. A befitting analogy that highlights the veracity of public discourse on 'potentiality of cyber attacks' is the debate during the initial enunciation of India's nuclear doctrine. Initially, the shroud of secrecy was drawn over all nuclear policy issues, preventing an animated public debate about them. However, some of the seminal works undertaken by prominent thinkers mobilised the public opinion and their subsequent incisive work outside the precinct of government organisations had a real impact in formulation of the nuclear doctrine. The potential relevance of a cyber attack across the whole spectrum of national interests in both war and non-war situations makes it imperative to constitute a study committee, mandated to closely examine various aspects of cyber attacks, factoring in perspectives from members with very diverse backgrounds. The amalgam of expertise of domain practitioners with acquired domain-specific competence through experience will fructify in the emergence of a national policy on 'cyber attack', capable of addressing and responding to issues from a national security perspective. The study committee may provide guidelines for setting up of an organisational framework for planning, managing and evaluating offensive cyber capabilities. Based on the dynamic and qualitative assessment of acquired capabilities and evaluation of their 'deterrence quotient' against present, potential and perceived threats, the committee may decide the quantum and extent of the offensive cyber operations after identifying situations warranting such use.

  A comprehensive policy framework in this area will enable various stakeholders to weigh accrued advantages vis-à-vis risk potentiality of cyber attacks in their concept of operations and will *establish functioning guidelines*, operational precincts and appropriate yardsticks. An overarching policy framework will guide the armed forces, intelligence agencies and others in a domain which is still not adequately governed by national and international laws. The existing laws are ambiguous in expression and lend themselves to idiosyncratic interpretations leading to fragmented understanding of impact and ramification of cyber attacks across the whole range of national issues.

- **National Decision-Making Apparatus with Strategic Priorities for Offensive Cyber Operations:** The establishment of an informed, clear and inclusive decision-making structure capable of deciding on the quantum, timing and risks associated with the perpetration of a cyber attack will accelerate the decision-making process due to the enhanced overall effectiveness and contextual relevance of *actionable decisions*. The decision-makers should include or at least ensure consultations with all stakeholders that might directly or indirectly be involved and affected by the use of a cyber weapon. The decision to undertake a cyber attack should be made by weighing in various military, diplomatic and economic compulsions. For example, if the stakes are high enough to justify the associated risk, the use of a preemptive cyber attack will amount to a *well-thought out and timely* action.

  As such, in the military realm, preventive measures taken to mitigate hostile actions against own resources, personnel, facilities and critical information are standing rules of engagement. However, if a cyber attack, conclusively, presumptively or speculatively, appears to be emanating from a known adversary, a response action may lead to escalation, especially if the incident occurs during times of strained relations and the effects of retaliatory cyber attacks post execution far exceed the effects anticipated during the planning phase. For such reasons, the decision to launch a cyber attack should be taken after weighing the various equities (military, diplomatic, economic) by appropriate competent authorities.
- **Support to the Enactment of International Laws/ Treaties with Enforceable Mechanisms:** The understanding of key issues on cyber attacks among most of the nations has yet to reach a level that can address a broad range of related issues. The far-reaching manifestations and consequences of cyber attacks will only grow in severity and invasiveness, with potential to cause financial crisis, social upheaval and political instability. Enacting laws with enforceable mechanisms and creating international standards or rules for abidance by all states may rein in the *malevolent* use of cyber attacks. The efforts in this direction will evoke common understanding for policy formulation and quantification of the degree of international outrage consequent to a cyber attack. This will foster better coordination and information sharing and will avoid misunderstandings. At the very least, it will help in developing mechanisms for coordinating cyber attacks to avoid collateral and unintended consequences. It is equally important to engage with ambiguous and perfidious allies as well as with

existential and conceivable adversaries on these issues. Though such consultations could prove be inconclusive, contentious or *politically fraught,* these would at least help in mutual understanding of the stakes involved and the expectations from their perspectives.

- **Acquisition, Maintenance and Consolidation of Effective Cyber Attack Capabilities**:[4] The nation must have credible, potent and flexible cyber attack technologies at its disposal with the requisite intent to wage cyber war. The methodologies should be consistent with the potentiality of the situation, with the necessary command and control. The *type, quantum and period* of cyber attacks should be based on intelligence garnered through various sources with assured mission success and minimum collateral damage. Such capabilities, while providing operational advantages also act as credible deterrence against cyber adversaries.
- **Extent, Causes and Consequences of Cyber Attacks**: Cyber attacks, in the realm of cyber warfare have been relegated to *footnotes* rather than being incorporated and assimilated into the *main* narrative, thereby denying a template to base a conceptual framework. It is difficult to categorise some activities as constituting a cyber attack and their subsequent quantification of damage or harm in definite terms of economic loss, loss of strategic assets, disruption of critical information infrastructures or suffering to the civilians. The losses as a result of cyber attacks can reasonably be construed as a threat to national security. Some of the consequences after a cyber attack may constitute a "use of force" and an "armed attack" and can invoke a state's right to use force in self-defence.
- **Severity, Extent, and Duration of Planned Cyber Attack to be in Conformity to Moral and Ethical Standards:**[5] The laws of armed conflict governing cyber attack, both *jus in bello* (the law of armed conflict) and *jus ad bellum* (the set of rules to be consulted before engaging in war), should have moral and ethical underpinnings even when cyber weapons are used covertly. The computers and networks that make up cyber space are so intricately linked and inextricably interconnected that, if attacked, infiltrated or blocked, as part of a strategic or tactical move, may have far-reaching spillover effects on people, establishments and institutions likely to enjoy immunity in a conventional war. The basic rule of the law of armed conflict that "during war between similarly matched armies, civilians and other non-combatants enjoy *immunity from direct* or intentional harm"[6] needs to be followed in the case of cyber attacks also. Even during war, adherence to established ethical benchmarks in the context of cyber attacks, though difficult to implement, will provide the moral compass for guiding actions *righteously***.**

- **Creating a Pool of Trained Personnel with the Requisite Skills:** Understanding of strategic, conceptual and operational complexities associated with cyber conflict requires specialised expertise in operations, intelligence and technology. Similarly, policy understanding and formulation related to cyber attacks requires integration of domain experts from the defence, industry, academic, diplomatic, intelligence and corporate communities. For the planning and execution of cyber attacks to achieve the intended results, an involved workforce rigorously trained, with a high premium placed on professionalism is a mandatory prerequisite. These needs are in consonance with the history of how cyber attacks have evolved, from being innocuous endeavours to pernicious enterprises. The personal computers and later the World Wide Web are at the forefront of the information technology revolution, ubiquitously impacting the way sectors of society, including the military interact, engage and operate. The notion of attacking an adversary's networks and computers as an instrument of warfare is burgeoning and growing, with the senior military leadership embracing the potentiality of such possibilities seriously. Against this backdrop, there needs to be full realisation of the challenges, opportunities and consequences of cyber attacks by the entire spectrum of personnel involved. Because cyber conflicts are interdisciplinary in nature, a comprehensive and *integrated human capital development programme focussed on establishing* cross-linkages between different entities, promoting cross-fertilisation of ideas and furthering cross-disciplinary interactions will be able to meet the variegated challenges of cyber attacks.

Technical and Operational Considerations in Cyber Attack

The complexity, implications and nuances of a cyber attack cannot be captured within a simple formal definition. Activities in cyber space do not have a comparable template vis-a-vis principles that govern armed conflict under the conventional laws of war. The analysis of the potential consequences of a cyber attack has yet to emerge in a definitive form from speculative accounts. The US National Research Council defines cyber attack as "deliberate actions to alter, disrupt, deceive, degrade, or destroy computer systems or networks or the information and/or programs resident in, or transiting, these systems or networks."[7]

The Shanghai Cooperation Organisation (SCO), a security cooperation group which includes India as an observer, has adopted a much more expansive means-based approach to cyber attacks. The organisation has "express[ed] concern about the threats posed by possible use of [new information and communication] technologies and means for the purposes [*sic*] incompatible with ensuring international security and stability in both the civil and military spheres."[8] It defines an "information war" as "mass psychologic[al] brainwashing to destabilize society and state, as well as to force the state to take decisions in the interest of an opposing party."

The approach towards the use of cyber weapons in an offensive role needs to be goal-based rather than means-based. The emphasis needs to be put on the results and their significance. In cases, where methods become a priority over results, the unbounded ramifications might be calamitous. A goal-based approach requires capabilities across the spectrum of present, potential and perceived threats and not on a limited number of threats. Depending upon the intent, opportunities and envisaged results, the corresponding capability suitable for achieving the objective with minimum collateral damage may be used. Any of the means—hacking, logical bombing, *malware infection*, forceful intrusion and advance persistent attack—can be leveraged for perpetuating cyber attacks to undermine, disrupt or destroy the adversary's cyber assets or *using* them as a *conduit to* attack dependent physical assets. The means and weapons for carrying out cyber attacks have the following distinct characteristics:

- **Incidental and Collateral Effects of Cyber Attack are Indiscriminatory and Unpredictable:**[9] A cyber attack targeting a particular computer system or network, in addition to causing system specific degradation, causes indirect or follow-on effects on interdependent systems and devices and on the people who depend on these for numerous societal functions and sustenance needs. The cyber attacks, in effect, neither satisfy, the 'principle of proportionality' nor are in conformity with the 'principle of discrimination'. The cascading and spillover effects, consequent to a cyber attack will be unpredictable and unquantifiable and may be well above the planned and intended objective.
- **Post Cyber Attack, Effects Quantification is Uncertain due to Complex Determinative Mechanisms**: The outcomes post cyber attacks are often highly uncertain as cascading effects rapidly cut across societal sectors, critical infrastructures and vital institutions, causing disruption across a wide array of domains. The incidental and collateral damage may far exceed the intended effects. A holistic assessment of a cyber attack across the entire spectrum of infrastructure and operations will be challenging due to the risk of uncertain and unforeseeable consequences. In some cases, the results will be tangible and immediate; in others, more subtle, with a long gestation period before their manifestations.
- **Cyber Attack Planning is Often Associated with Obliquity and Complexity:** An offensive *cyber attack carried out* against a chosen military, economic or societal target, *in addition to* interrupting, destroying, or limiting the capabilities of the

primary target, may also try to elicit and exploit effects on interdependent secondary targets. It makes the pre-attack prediction and evaluation of outcomes an extremely arduous and subjective task. The temporal scales of a cyber attack may stretch from a few seconds to years and the spatial ranges may be anywhere from the immediate neighbourhood to distant places.

- **Identification, Acquisition Maintenance and Consolidation of Cyber Attack Capabilities:** In the military domain, identification and acquisition of effective capabilities to dissuade, deter or defeat potential adversaries and existential enemies, is a fundamental and crucial necessity for offence and defence. On the assimilation of newly acquired capability into the 'Concept of Operations' (CONOPS), this needs to be seamlessly dovetailed with existing capabilities to bring in a significant enhancement in overall operational efficiency and capability. For preserving its operational viability, potentiality and potency, comprehensive and constantly evolving maintenance support is also a prerequisite. For acquisition of cyber attack capabilities, a thorough analysis of potential targets, their strengths and vulnerabilities, weapon to target ratio, possible retaliatory response, collateral and spillover effects, time and duration of attack, will fructify in making congruent qualitative and quantitative projections. The technical sophistication required to develop a potent and credible cyber attack capability exists and is only limited by resources and motivation. A cyber weapon once developed, and added to the repository of other cyber weapons ready for deployment needs to be constantly evaluated, updated and improved to ensure its effectiveness and potency, if employed.
- **The Problem of Attributability and Accountability Associated with Cyber Attacks:** The perpetrators of a cyber attack can *conceal their* true *identity behind the 'technological fog' and 'digital thicket'*. Besides, the follow-up process to assign attibutability and establish accountability to an organisation, group or individual is marred by unfathomable complexities specific to cyber space. Cyber attacks are often called bloodless, non-violent attacks, in stark contrast to kinetic attacks which are invariably accompanied with high visibility explosions, violence and body counts. However, cyber weapons have undeniable capacity to achieve kinetic effects, when used by a determined adversary with the requisite technical sophistication and unwavering intent. By exploiting vulnerabilities in the information systems and processes, cyber attacks can cause direct, incidental or collateral physical damage, injury or death.

Comparison of Key Characteristics of Cyber Attack Versus Kinetic Attack[10]

The use of a weapon of any kind is for attainment of a strategic, tactical or operational objective over an adversary by disrupting, damaging, destroying or disabling some capability of the adversary. On an adversary, the effects elicited by the action of a weapon system can be direct or indirect, with perceptible gains in terms of asserting dominance, forcing behavioural changes or diminishing belligerent posturing. Weapons are largely perceived as military solutions to belligerent, contentious and complex problems. In the case of kinetic weapons, the immediate targets bear the brunt of the devastation, while other physical entities bear the follow-up consequences and experience indirect effects such as temporary or permanent disruption, disablement, dislocation or destruction. Cyber attacks are easy to conduct with plausible deniability and are reasonably suited for being instruments of conflict enunciation and resolution. A significant cyber attack can be concealed with relative ease, compared to a kinetic attack. The exponential proliferation of Information and Communications Technology (ICT) devices has expanded the list of possible targets. An assessment of the multivariate characteristics of a cyber attack versus a kinetic attack provides a comparative understanding.

- **Quantum and Significance of Attack**: Kinetic attacks largely rely on achieving physical destruction, decimation, death and injury, with high visibility and conspicuousness. The 'shock and awe' is considered to be one of the main objectives of a successful kinetic attack. The indirect effects resulting from a kinetic attack are not significantly factored into the overall objective. Cyber attacks try to elicit maximum efficacy by relying on indirect effects as follow-up consequences of an attack on an information system or network.
- **Consequences of Attack:** The recovery and reconstruction process post a kinetic attack may be time-consuming and resource-intensive and, in some cases, even irreversible. Cyber attacks have limited effects on physical entities and are often targeted against peripherally located assets, as core assets are generally well secured and protected with firewalls, *encryption*/authentication algorithms and need-based access. The restoration, consequent to a cyber attack, is relative less time consuming and the effects may be reversed, depending upon the consequential manifestations of damage.
- **Associated R&D and Acquisition Cost:** The R&D and acquisition as well as operational costs of a kinetic weapon system are high compared to a cyber weapon. Besides, a cyber weapon can be designed, tested and used within the close confines of a work station without elaborate infrastructure spread over a large area, teeming with skilled and unskilled labour and resources The low entry cost of acquisition

of cyber weapons acts as a catalyst for states and terrorist groups, inimical to the sovereignty and integrity of a country, to acquire these with relative ease.

- **Technical Knowhow and Systems Required**: The technical knowhow to develop effective cyber weapons is readily available and a new crop of developers entering the arena for monetary gains and notoriety make it possible to stockpile cyber weapons with ease, away from the prying eyes of international observers.

Offence/Defence Balance in Cyber Space

In strategic thinking and planning, the 'Offence-Defence Balance (ODB)' is a major determinant of the relative efficacy of offensive and defensive security posturing. The tipping of the balance of one of the two, the theory suggests, affect the patterns of international relations and foreign policy. The offence-defence theory contends that international conflict and war are more likely when offence has the advantage, while peace and cooperation are more probable when defence has the advantage.[11] When it is believed by one side that its offensive capabilities *far exceed* the other side's *defensive capabilities*, it will be tempted to perpetrate preemptive attacks. On the other hand, when defence is easier than offence, states are more likely to mutually cooperate, embark on confidence-building measures and even take initiatives toward slackening the *pace of the arms race*.

Heuristically, the viability of the 'offence-defence balance' focusses on *identifying important causal variables* that are contemporaneous and modifiable. Military prowess *alone*, however, does not usually suffice as a variable capable of securing lasting peace.[12] For practical purposes, the major issue with the ODB theory is how to measure this balance. While assessing the ODB in cyber space, one is compelled to accommodate the peculiarities and idiosyncrasies of cyber space. The existence of cyber space in the real and virtual realms, populated by real *and amorphous* mass of faceless individuals makes it a peculiar battlefield. Secondly, and equally peculiar, is the centrality of the 'Internet' for both military and non-military actors. While there are differences between civilian and military networks, they mostly use the same hardware and software. In cyber space, the main objective of an offensive action is not to seize and control a geographical entity but to compromise/deplete the effectiveness of a system or network.

The seemingly exponentially growing spate of cyber attacks and resulting multi-dimensional losses has led to a movement among strategists towards creating a deterrent factor embodied in the use of "counter-offensive strategies".[13] These mechanisms encompass a range of activities that go beyond active cyber defence. Several analysts have succinctly compared the deterrent offered by offensive technologies to the nuclear deterrent. In the early stages of the nuclear era, an attacker with a monopolistic hold on nuclear technology could annihilate an opponent without fear of reprisal. It is worth reiterating that India's nuclear doctrine is based on the notion of 'massive retaliation' to a first strike, designed to inflict 'unacceptable damage'. During the period of the Cold War, when the Soviet Union developed its own nuclear capabilities in response to America's burgeoning nuclear arsenal, the dynamics of the world order changed. Attacks could now be carried out remotely and destruction on a scale unparalleled in human history would surely occur soon after the initiation of an attack. The defensive mechanisms, which evolved against a nuclear attack were either untested or speculative. The realisation of this new reality motivated the formulation of the "Mutually Assured Destruction" (MAD) strategy. The threat of mutual obliteration emerged as a strong deterrent reining in the war-mongering stance of both superpowers.

There are a few striking commonalities between cyber and nuclear warfare. Like nuclear warfare, cyber warfare is of an asymmetric nature, with no conventional battlefield and no foolproof mechanism for protection of targets. To make deterrent threats credible, and credible threats have a strong deterrent effect, in both cases, the defenders need to respond within a very limited period of time. In the case of cyber warfare, if a response is not initiated almost immediately, the traces of the attack will be lost and the attacker will disappear in the apparently fathomless *labyrinth* of *cyber space* and remain untraceable. For an effective deterrence posture, it must be communicated to the adversaries in no uncertain terms that the costs of an attack would be prohibitively high and reprisals would be swift and severe.

Possible Objectives of Cyber Attack[14]

Whether a cyber attack is conducted as part of an offensive strategy or an active defence measure, attainment of some objectives, in sync with the overall strategy, the possessed capabilities and the envisaged degree of severity, is central to their orchestration. In the larger context of warfare, some types of warfare are characterised by the 'employed mean', which, in most cases, happens to be a weapon. For example, in the case of nuclear warfare, the 'employed mean' would be a nuclear weapon. Other types of warfare focus on 'objective' in the form of a target-based approach for neutralisation. In the mean-based approach, the result is an outcome of a specific weapon's capability, lethality, and survivability. In the objective-based approach, the objective accomplishment, by any means at one's disposal, is the priority. In the context of cyber warfare, an objective-based approach *captures its nuances* and complexities more fittingly than the means-based approach.[15] The orchestration of cyber attacks is invariably linked to the attainment of objectives in furtherance or pursuance of some military, political or economic goals.

- **Manipulation Through Information Exploitation:**[16] In the present scenario, our society can be termed as an ubiquitously interconnected information society in which the creation, distribution and manipulation of information have become the most significant drivers for most of the societal activities. In an information society, the social, political and economic underpinning is primarily exchange of information facilitated through information technology, computers, networks and telecommunications. The inclusive growth, continuity and dynamism of the information society are directly linked with a reliable, secure, resilient and survivable information infrastructure. In effect, securing information has become a major challenge for national security. Cyber attacks directed against critical information systems for stealing, altering, modifying or deleting crucial information will undermine the adversary's capability to respond to threats across a broad spectrum of military, economic and political contingencies.
- **Cyber Attacks in Conjunction with Kinetic Attacks:**[17] Cyber attacks may be carried out in conjunction with, or as an adjunct to, conventional kinetic armed attacks intended to maximise the cumulative war-waging efforts for neutralisation of the adversary's defensive and command and control systems.[18] A potent cyber attack can create *widespread pandemonium and confusion in the rank and file of the enemy, disrupting the command,* demoralising the forces and taking the winds out of the sails of *the war efforts. The state of disarray is exacerbated manifold when cyber attacks are used in conjunction with kinetic attacks.*
- **To Destroy Data on a Network or a System Connected to the Network:**[19] A cyber attack might be conducted to delete and permanently erase data files or to wipe clean all memory storage devices that it can find. Moreover, destruction of a network will have an adverse *cascading effect* on other interdependent systems connected to it. For example, power generation facilities controlled and operated by a network will come to a grinding halt if the controlling network is disabled.
- **Donning the Guise of a Bona Fide User for Propagating Spurious Information:**[20] A cyber attacker might masquerade as a senior official or agency and issue bogus orders or pass fake intelligence information. This virtual impersonation of someone who calls the shots and is on a high rung of the hierarchical ladder, will facilitate a cyber attacker to take over control of a trusted machine. By obtaining the authentication and encryption keys, the malicious activities will be interpreted as legitimate by other machines/ persons.

- **Clandestine Data Manipulation in Data Repository:**[21] The military relies on detailed planning, resource management and allocation of tasks to achieve its objectives. The central repository for such information in the form of data is used in the entire course of the operation. For example, the logistical support to the armed forces, such as deployment of weapons, replenishment of ammunition, repairing of weapon systems and delivery platforms or the management of complex technological systems, is driven by data manipulation that apportions responsibilities, manages spares and produces coherent and *appropriate sequences of tasks.* A corrupted database may compromise the intended effectiveness or efficiency of the mission.
- **Degradation and Denial of Service on a Network:**[22] A cyber attacker might try to degrade the quality of the services available to network users by overwhelming communication channels with a huge influx of bogus traffic. A cyber attacker with intent to degrade the quality of service may overwhelm communication channels with a huge influx of bogus traffic. A denial-of-service attack on a network controlling factory floor operations and other interconnected activities might shut it down. By taking control of a telecommunications exchange, a cyber attacker may acquire the ability to wreak havoc with the functioning of an organisation, with anomalous calls and wrong or random cross-connections. A denial-of-service attack on a communication system might force an adversary to resort to the use of a less secure method which could be easy prey for cyber exploitation.
- **To Wrest Control of a Network and Modify Interconnects, Services or Privileges:**[23] An attacker might wrest control of an Internet service provider in an adversary nation and, depending upon its strategic objectives, deny or curtail services and privileges to the extent deemed essential for mission success. By intentionally and clandestinely limiting the bandwidth to key users, the transmission of large files (e.g., images or videos) would be made agonisingly slow to rob them of their real time relevance. Delays in transmission might cause time lags between decision-making and communication of decisions to the forces for tactical action, thereby missing important deadlines.

Attacks on Cyber Physical Systems

The inextricable conjoining and interdependent interplay between the cyber domain and physical resources has accelerated the convergence and integration of computer systems with the physical realm over a wide spectrum of industrial and military endeavours. The economic and societal potential of such systems is vastly greater than what has been realised and major investments are being made worldwide to develop the technology.[24]

The Cyber Physical Systems (CPS) technologies are ubiquitously used in devices, systems and sectors, including critical infrastructure control systems, defence systems, avionics, automotive systems, medical devices, automotive systems, industrial processes and research laboratories. The use of CPS is only limited by the innovation of the technology and by the demand, willingness and acceptance on the part of the users or consumers. It is not difficult to envision the future in which the cyber systems will be used with such prolificacy that they will permeate and proliferate into all the societal, industrial and military domains. Unfortunately, unbridled proliferation of CPS will also act as a catalyst for unrelenting creation of, and inexorable search for, new vulnerabilities. While the possibility of widespread mayhem and apocalyptic destruction through cyber attacks targeted at CPS, which have been vividly and convincingly conjured up by so many screenwriters and novelists, currently appears far-fetched, the possibility of physical damage, superficial or grievous injury and intentional death through the exploitation of vulnerabilities in information systems, either inherent or introduced, is no longer an imaginary threat. In the past, a number of cyber attacks have caused physical damage to physical entities, disrupted physical systems and sabotaged physical processes.

Kinetic cyber attacks, on the one hand, are a menacing and growing threat to national and international security. On the other hand, they offer a potential opportunity to be exploited by interweaving their transformative potential with the doctrinal framework of offensive cyber operations. Cyber attacks do not fit neatly into the conventional paradigm of warfare in terms of violence, death and destruction. Nonetheless, the effects consequent to a cyber attack on CPS can be comparable to an actual kinetic attack causing intentional, incidental or collateral damage to physical resources and claiming human lives as casualties. In 2010, Iran faced the full wrath of a kinetic cyber weapon when the 'Stuxnet' worm ravaged its Natanz nuclear facility. Though not as spectacular as Stuxnet, the example of numerous other cyber attacks, with varying success, has unwittingly compelled many states to throw their hats into the ring, ushering in a new and more insidious phase of an already diabolical cyber arms race. In October 2011, the discovery of 'DuQu' jolted the security agencies across the world as it shared a code similar to that of the Stuxnet but differed in functionality. It was designed to clandestinely acquire information about the industrial control systems for planning and executing potential future attacks.[25] In June 2012, it was reported that the Iranian oil industry had been a the victim of the sinister malware 'Flame', which, while masquerading as an innocuous and routine Microsoft software update, penetrated the computers of senior Iranian officials and allegedly stole a treasure trove of sensitive data in preparation of a cyber attack.[26]

Cyber physical attacks aimed at severing the interactions between the cyber and physical components within a CPS have been used many times. Conversely, it is also possible to cause disruption, incapacitation or destruction of cyber assets by carrying out attacks on physical assets and infrastructure. Computers and network devices connected to one another using some common protocols for exchange of data are the building blocks of cyber space. These devices themselves are physical objects with inherent vulnerabilities similar to those associated with other physical assets. In effect, both cyber and kinetic attacks can be used against cyber and physical assets, and the choice is largely determined by the possessed capability, the *target's vulnerabilities* and the ability to absorb a retaliatory blow.

Cyber Attacks as Force Multipliers for Military Operations

Today, military operations have become much more complex, geographically dispersed, and often represent lightning temporal and spatial transitions from minor *skirmishes to* full campaigns. Against this backdrop, defence policy-makers have to tackle challenges which have substantial contextual differences from those of the past. Even if a single, large military engagement may seem a distant possibility, the potential for multiple and disparate operations of varying intensities calls for capacity building that entails bolstering numerous tangible and intangible military resources. There is also a need for putting in place mechanisms and corresponding tools across the diplomatic and military space to respond to challenges arising from rogue states, state sponsored terrorist organisations and radical religious groups. Traditional military systems will have to continuously evolve and redefine their roles in meeting the challenges of the future. Compressed timelines, amorphous mass of enemies, high tempo of operations, remote and unfamiliar battlefields are all leading to the development of highly specialised niche platforms and military systems.

Cyber attacks are *endowed with some attributes* that are well aligned with this evolving threat landscape. From a life cycle cost perspective, though cyber weapons have comparable research and development costs; the production and deployment costs of cyber weapons are relatively low. Cyber attacks can be applied across a wide gamut of military activities, *either as stand-alone* systems or integrated into information operations. In addition, missions outside the realm of military prowess may also be successfully accomplished by using cyber exploitation.

- **Cyber Attack in Support of Defence and Other Information Operations:**[27] Offensive cyber capabilities, as a preemptive weapon, have the potential to neutralise an eminent threat emanating from a belligerent adversary. Some of the nations, including the US, have declared cyber attacks as acts of war due to the increasing realisation that measures of functionality and severity consequent to a cyber attack are comparable to those of kinetic attacks. Even so, the problem of traceability, attributability and accountability makes cyber attacks a more lucrative and preferred option in comparison to kinetic attacks.

- **Psychological Operations:**[28] A cyber attack designed to inundate adversary decision-makers with bogus e-mail messages or insinuating telephone calls could disrupt their cohesion and derail their decision-making process. The contents of e-mail messages may include disturbing and incriminating information in order to create distrust, disharmony or dissension among members of an organisation. Fanning the *fear psychosis with threats of public exposure of aberrant behavioural traits may force some decision-makers to tweak or modify their decisions. Another way of leveraging Psychological Operations (*PSYOPs) is by launching a small and easily manipulated cyber attack with a very high degree of visibility, with the intent to undermine the adversary's confidence in its systems and networks.
- **Military Deception and Operations Security:**[29] Cyber attacks can be used against specific adversary sensor systems with an aim to either render these inoperative or to flood them with fabricated information to manipulate the adversary's decision-making capabilities and thereby elicit decisions and actions that can be accurately anticipated or favour own operational plans. Cyber attacks directed against the command and control centre of an adversary may render it incapacitated of taking viable operational decisions. Injecting misinformation regarding capabilities, intentions, force deployments and favourable courses of action of friendly forces may undermine the adversary's war-fighting efforts.
- **Electronic Warfare:** The ubiquitous proliferation of software defined and hardware dependent devices such as radio communication, radar, satellite links have added *vulnerabilities* that were non-existent just a few short years ago. Cyber attacks against the adversary's software-defined radios may degrade wireless battlefield communications, air defence radars and other systems. In fact, Electronic Warfare (EW) capabilities could be leveraged to support cyber attacks. For example, the computer systems connected through wireless links may be rendered useless if these links are jammed using EW capabilities. In effect, jamming may be construed as a denial-of-service cyber attack against such networks.
- **Cyber Attacks Augmenting Traditional Military Operations:**[30] Cyber attacks could also be used to augment a variety of military operations. Targeting Command, Control and Communications (C3) with cyber attacks will diminish the ability of an

adversary to manage and dominate the battlefield, achieve the requisite degree of situational awareness, and exploit information for operational missions. By using cyber attacks to invoke denial of service, render communication links unusable, impersonate high ranking decision-makers or spoof the identity of a legitimate device, the adversary's planning could be disrupted or altered. With severed tactical links, the forces in the field will be deprived of operational guidance and direction from the higher command authority. Secondly, in air defence operations, monitoring and lateral sharing of information are the core elements of mission accomplishment. The air defence systems are made up of a set of sensors and a set of kill vehicles, collectively called a weapon system. A networked air defence system uses sensors to detect incoming targets and the information is communicated to kill vehicles for the destruction of targets. Disruption of communication links for information sharing in real time can considerably degrade the performance of the overall system. With clandestine insertion of spurious signals and the adversary's total incomprehension, the adversary may be led to believe that the distorted air picture is the true picture of an unfolding situation. Thirdly, spurred by technological advancement, the so-called dumb munitions have been transformed into sophisticated smart munitions with enhanced lethality, precision, stealth and sustainability. The on-board sensors of smart munitions are linked with computers which, in real time, guide these munitions through the course of their flight for the most efficient way of engagement and subsequent damage. To guard against such munitions, a cyber attack targeting on-board programmable circuit boards and ground computers for in-flight control of smart munitions may degrade their precision strike capabilities.

Cyber Jurisprudence to Tackle Emerging Issues

Article 51 of Chapter VII of the United Nations (UN) Charter acknowledges the inherent right of individual or collective self-defence against an armed attack. [31] It is pertinent to dwell at some length on the issue of an armed attack, especially in the context of cyber space and its consequential effects on national interests. *Webster's Dictionary* defines weapons as "as an instrument of offensive or defensive combat; something to fight with; anything used, or designed to be used, in destroying, defeating, or injuring an enemy, as a gun, a sword, etc."[32] The weapons achieve their intended goals through perpetration of particular damage, destruction or injury, commensurate with their functionality and lethality. Although, the essence of the purpose and functionality of traditional weapons might be captured under the rubric of kinetic warfare, it remains empirically inadequate for capturing the idiosyncratic nature of cyber warfare. A cyber weapon may be used to achieve objectives which may, or may not, be measured against, or compared with, outcomes listed in the definition. The term 'cyber attack' has been used generically to refer to activities ranging from penetration of a network, insertion of malicious codes, implantation of software Trojans, stealing of information, unauthorised downloading of sensitive contents or disrupting the services provided by these networks with a focus upon the consequential impacts without any inquiry into the legality or the ethicality of these acts. The consequence and effect of a cyber attack determine whether or not, the act is in contravention of, or compliance with, the laws of armed conflict. It is both the offensive capability of the malicious code and the intended outcome or effect produced by that code that transforms it into a weapon that would be governed, as with any conventional weapon, by the laws of armed conflict.[33]

To encapsulate the belligerent acts committed in cyber space within the definition of "threat or use of force" is not easy. The phrase "threat or use of force," has been used in Article 2(4) of the UN Charter which states, "All Members shall refrain in their international relations from the threat or use of force against the territorial integrity or political independence of any state."[34] The logical entailments and empirical evidence require that the international legal norms and the laws of armed conflict, either customary or treaty-based, which apply to the other domains are applied to activities in the cyber domain. A determination of what is a "threat or use of force" in cyber space needs to be made in the contextual backdrop that led to the occurrence of the event, the purpose of the actions in question and its consequences on national interests. In the face of compelling evidence that a particular cyber attack has been perpetrated in conjunction with, or as an adjunct to, a larger military operation and its political and/or military attribution to malevolent intent, a state may invoke its inherent right to self-defence.

International laws have been articulated to provide a rationale for waging war for legitimate and righteous purposes. The *jus ad bellum* (the set of rules to be consulted before engaging in war) defines the rightful reasons for use of force by states, focussing on fulfilling certain criteria that legitimise the war as "just and necessary". In the context of cyber space, the key question is whether a cyber attack constitutes a use of force or an armed attack, invoking the inherent right to self-defence. Governing the belligerent cyber attacks under such rules proves difficult because of enunciation of these rules in the context of domains, without any overlapping linkages with cyber space. For example, the lack of consensus in determining whether or not the "Stuxnet attack" was an "armed attack" or "use of force" brings to the fore the various issues and problems that emanate from subjective interpretations of various provisions of the UN Charter. The interpretation may differ, as the same event, depending upon the interpreters' perspective and interest, could be termed as an armed attack, an unlawful intervention without a use of force or a use of force not amounting to armed attack. [35]

Conclusion

Warfare is no longer a sum total of capabilities of putting more personnel, capital and technology on the battlefield, but of better situational awareness, contextual knowledge, discerning disposition and homogenised actions. Technological breakthroughs have profoundly altered and shaped the doctrinal, organisational and strategic contours of warfare. Information technology has revolutionised the way warfare is conducted. Once comprising solely mechanical and electrical parts, military hardware has evolved into complex systems, by a combination of various components and functionalities of sensors, microchips, microprocessors, hardware, software, data storage and connectivity in myriad ways. These "smart, connected products", bolstered by advancements and improvements in processing power, device miniaturisation and by ubiquitous wireless connectivity, have put warfare on the cusp of an epochal shift from conventional to an information-based virtual age. Embedded sensors, intelligent processors, sophisticated software and seamless connectivity in these products, coupled with data analysis and algorithmically induced decision-making capabilities, are driving unfathomable improvements in product functionality and performance. This wave of cyber-driven transformation is radical, sweeping and innovating, demanding a relook at the established strategic plan and direction for operational enhancements and improved tactical efficiency. Cyber space and cyber systems offer a whole new set of technological solutions to some of the challenges in modern warfare.

The policy and organisational issues which need to be tackled in the wake of acquisition and use of cyber attack capabilities have strong and integrated linkages across the whole spectrum of conflict from all-out war to small skirmishes to situations below the armed conflict threshold. Outcomes of cyber attacks can vary across an enormous range and they can affect military, intelligence, diplomatic, economic and law enforcement equities.[36] The acquired capabilities to wage offensive operations in cyber space greatly expand the list of options available to policy-makers and practitioners of warfare. A major issue which hinders all aspects of policy formulation for offensive cyber attacks is the collateral nature of effects consequent to a cyber attack which may be unintentional, incidental direct or indirect. Although, during cyber attacks, computer systems and networks are primarily targeted, the consequential effects on other systems due to interdependence significantly influence other entities such as people, critical infrastructure, banking, machinery, etc. The consequences of a cyber attack may vary in severity, lethality, intent or geographic distribution and can *manifest in complex, dynamic and unpredictable ways having far-reaching tactical and strategic implications. Moreover, the absence of an appropriate publicly stated policy framework for guiding and regulating the use of cyber attacks has further exacerbated the complexities involved in the possible use of cyber attacks in support of national interests.*

Notes

1. Robert J. Art and Kelly M. Greenhill, *The Use of Force: Military Power and International Politics* (Lanham: Rowman & Littlefield,2009), p.25.
2. U.S. National Research Council of the National Academics, William A. Owens, Kenneth W. Dam, and Herbert S. Lin *Technology, Policy, Law, and Ethics Regarding U.S. Acquisition and Use of Cyberattack Capabilities* (Washington, D.C.: The National Academies Press, 2009), p.9.
3. Herbert Lin, "Escalation Dynamics and Conflict Termination in Cyberspace", *Strategic Studies Quarterly*, vol. 6, no. 3, 2012, p.47.
4. Owen, et. al., n.2, p.69.
5. Ibid., p.68.
6. Leslie C. Green, *The Contemporary Law of Armed Conflict* (Manchester: Manchester University Press, 200), p.124.
7. Herbert S. Lin, "Cybersecurity Symposium: National Leadership, Individual Responsibility: Offensive Cyber Operations and the Use of Force," *Journal of National Security Law & Policy,* vol.4, no. 1, 2010, p.63.
8. Agreement between the Governments of the Member States of the Shanghai Cooperation Organisation on Cooperation in the Field of International Information Security (61st plenary meeting, December 2, 2008).
9. Owen, et. al., n.2, p. 19.
10. Derek S. Reveron, *Cyberspace and National Security: Threats, Opportunities, and Power in a Virtual world*, (Georgetown: Georgetown University Press, 2012), p. 38.
11. Seam Lynn Jones, "Offense- Defense Theory and its Critics," *Security Studies*, vol. 4, 1995, p. 660.
12. Andrea Locatelli, "The Offense/Defense Balance in Cyberspace", *ISPI Analysis,* no. 203, October 2013, p. 4.
13. Ibid., p.7.
14. Owen, et. al., n.2, p. 114.
15. Oona A. Hathaway et al., "The Law of Cyber-Attack" *California Law Review, 2012*, p.828.
16. Myriam Dunn Cavelty, *Cyber-Security and Threat Politics: US Efforts to Secure the Information Age* (Oxon, Routledge, 2007), p.45.
17. Reveron, n. 10, p. 42.
18. Terry D. Gill and Paul A. L. Ducheine , "Anticipatory Self-Defense in the Cyber Context," *International Law Studies* (US Naval War College), vol. 89, 2013, p.438.
19. Ibid., p.114.
20. Owen, et. al., n.2, p.115.
21. Ibid., p.117.
22. Ibid., p.118.
23. Ibid.

24. E. A. Lee, "Cyber Physical Systems: Design Challenges," (11th IEEE International Symposium on Object and Component-Oriented Real-Time Distributed Computing (ISORC)), May 2008, pp. 363–369.
25. Symantec Security Response, "W32.Duqu The Precursor to the Next Stuxnet," https://www.symantec.com/ content/en/us/enterprise/media/security_response/whitepapers/w32_duqu_the_precursor_to_the_next_stuxnet.pdf. Accessed on November 10, 2015.
26. Ellen Nakashima, Greg Miller and Julie Tate, "U.S., Israel Developed Flame Computer Virus to Slow Iranian Nuclear Efforts, Officials say ," *The Washington Post* , June 19, 2012, https://www.washingtonpost.com /world/national-security/us-israel-developed-computer-virus-to-slow-iranian-nuclear-efforts-officials-say/2012/06/19/gJQA6xBPoV_story.html. Accessed on November 10, 2015.
27. Owen, et. al., n.2, p. 117.
28. Jason Andress and Steve Winterfeld, *Cyber Warfare: Techniques, Tactics and Tools for Security Practitioners* (Massachusetts: Elsevier, 2011), p.156.
29. Owen, et. al., n.2, p. 178.
30. Ibid., p.179.
31. The United Nations, "Charter of the United Nations Chapter VII: Action with Respect to Threats to the Peace, Breaches of the Peace, and Acts of Aggression," http://www.un.org/en/documents /charter/ chapter7.shtml. Accessed on November 10, 2015.
32. Webster-Dictionary online, s.v. "weapon," http://www.webster-dictionary.org/definition/Weapon. Accessed on November 10, 2015,
33. L. Arimatsu, "A Treaty for Governing Cyber-Weapons: Potential Benefits and Practical Limitations ," (Paper presented at the 4th International Conference on Cyber Conflict, Tallinn, Estonia, June 5-8, 2012).
34. The United Nations, "Charter of the United Nations Chapter I: Purposes and Principles," http://www.un.org/en/documents /charter/ chapter1.shtml. Accessed on November 10, 2015.
35. Reveron, n. 10, p. 243.
36. Owen, et. al., n.2.

11

Inevitable Warfare Technologies: Pragmatic Role of Robotics, 3D Printing and Supercomputers in Future Wars

E Dilipraj

In the not so distant future…

Emergency alarms in the joint forces Command Headquarters create panic in the building in the early hours of the day following reports of a border town being heavily bombed by the enemy. Everyone in the command goes back to their respective seats to attend to their duties. Eventually, signals and orders started flowing to the tri-Services units across the country, preparing them for an offensive action.

Following which, in a border region, small mine sweeping ground robots are let loose to scan a section of the land for identifying the location of landmines planted by the enemy and transmitting the exact coordinates to the demining robot vehicles following them.

Mini drones, fitted with air quality check kits and guided by the Global Positioning System (GPS) are left to fly around in a suspected region to sniff out the presence of toxic agents in the atmosphere. The data about the air quality is transmitted live to the base station and is constantly monitored.

Reconnaissance drones, equipped with high definition cameras with the ability for thermal imaging as well as night vision capability, are flown to infiltrate enemy air space to gather real time intelligence of their movements, troop deployment and other information of the enemy. This information is transmitted live through the base station to the joint Command Headquarters to help the analysts formulate a strategy.

At the same time, on the naval front, a submarine returning from a successful reconnaissance mission deep inside enemy waters, suddenly experiences an engine failure and becomes a sitting duck. The captain of the submarine is informed by the engine crew that due to an anti-submarine homing torpedo explosion near the vessel, that was randomly dropped by the enemy's low flying aircraft, a few critical parts of the engine have broken down, for which they have no spares and it is highly impossible for other ships to come to their aid as the submarine is well within enemy waters. To avoid being sunk to the bottom of the ocean, the captain immediately dishes out two orders to his crew: (a) start 'printing' those small components which can be printed in the submarine; (b) send a emergency message to the Naval Headquarters regarding the submarine's situation and coordinates.

Meanwhile, in the joint forces headquarters' war room, military analysts and specialists are explaining all the updates about the war, including the emergency signal from the submarine with the engine failure, to the three chiefs of the armed forces and the defence minister. They are also briefed about various war strategies, with visual simulations about the implications of every strategy which are generated with the help of supercomputers based on the intelligence and updates arriving directly from the war zones.

Simultaneously, a few kilometres away from the border, in a mountainous region, evacuation of civilians is underway as this region has earlier previously faced heavy bombing from the enemy. The army and a team of specialists from the disaster management agency are working together in order to evacuate the people to a safe location before the next round of the offensive begins. Their efforts are slowed down mainly due to the mountainous terrain and more so because of the debris created as a result of the bombings. In view of the situation, the army commander and his counterpart from the disaster management agency order their respective teams to unleash all their robots to assist the evacuation process. A team of robots of various sizes—micro, mini and medium size—is activated and deployed on the field, guided by their operators.

In the meantime, the submarine which suffered the engine failure receives a reply signal from the headquarters. The reply lists out a number of spare parts which are being sent to help it through the Unmanned Submarine Vehicles (USVs) at a stipulated time, and the submarine crew is asked to confirm their coordinates again. This reply from headquarters is conveyed to the captain who immediately orders his diving crew to prepare themselves to receive the supplies at the stipulated time.

The various robots at the mountainous evacuation scene are effectively assisting the evacuation team to their utmost potential. Small crawling robots with cameras that mimic the movement of a snake are being used to navigate through the holes in the debris to identify survivors underneath. Medium sized robot mules, fitted with high sensitivity sensors carry old and wounded people, and descend the hills to the plains. Due to the inaccessibility of large cranes in the terrain, medium sized mobile industrial arms mounted on robotic mini tanks are used to remove the rocks and debris for clearing the way and saving the survivors who are stuck under the debris. Mini surveillance drones, fitted with cameras, are flown over the region and the live feed from these drones is monitored from a van stationed in the plains operating as the mobile control room in order to effectively coordinate the whole evacuation process.

Within a few hours, on the naval front, the sinking submarine's diving crew ecstatically receives their spares which were dragged into the coordinates by the USVs. After a few hours of swift work by the engine crew, the submarine's engines regain power to navigate the vessel to safety.

Around the same time, with the help of various robots, the mountains area has been evacuated successfully, well before another offensive attack from the enemy. This also allows the armed forces to set up their defences.

At the same time, the minefield has been sanitised thoroughly by the demining robots and the surveillance drones have also gathered enough intelligence of the enemy positions and their movements, which are sent to the high command. After thorough analyses and deliberations regarding the different war scenarios, simulated by the supercomputers, based on all the inputs and intelligence collected from different sources, including weather reports generated by supercomputers, the high command prepares the offensive strategy. Orders start flowing to the respective units stationed battle ready. Receiving the signal from the headquarters, the field commanders prepare for their tactical offensive to proceed and, eventually, the infantry starts moving into the enemy territory in full strength, following a swarm of gun mounted robots leading the way.

A careful study of the above hypothetical scenario would lead to a realisation of how high end technologies like robotics, Three Dimensional (3D) printing and supercomputers have the potential to change the nature of warfare and also play an influential role in future wars.

Background

Wars have been an integral part of the process of human evolution and nation-building. Wars have also been instrumental in the development of many new technological inventions and innovations, which, when applied on the ground, have transformed the very nature of warfare. A few of the revolutionary technologies have, in fact, created new domains of warfare while others have upgraded the existing defensive and offensive capabilities of a country by a few notches.

In the ancient days, wars were mostly fought on land, then gradually ventured into the naval sphere and for a long time, these two were the only domains of warfare. However, in the early 20th century, after the invention of aeroplanes, warfare stepped into the third dimension i.e. air space. Very soon, with the invention of rockets, the domain called outer space, and after the invention of computers and widespread access to the internet, the 'cyber' domain joined the league of warfare domains in the second half of the 20th century and the early 21st century respectively, thus, increasing the number of warfare domains to five.

As mentioned earlier, it is not necessary for all inventions or innovations in the defence sphere to lead towards the establishment of a new domain of warfare—rather, they can create a superior capability in the existing domains to enable a country's defence forces to gain an upper hand over its adversary. For instance, Alexander's employment of the Phalanx formation, Genghis Khan's raids with an army of cavalry mounted archers, Babur's deployment of artillery guns, Tipu Sultan's firing of crude rockets, Nazi Germany's deployment of V1 and V2 flying bombs and, of course, the explosion of the atomic bombs by the US, all changed the nature of warfare and, in due course, the history of mankind. When one looks into the future to identify and analyse a few technologies that would have a similar effect in revolutionising the future warfare scenarios, a few promising technologies stand out, like robotics, 3D printing and supercomputing.

Supercomputers are the giants of the computing world which occupy enormous space and perform millions of calculations per second. In general, a supercomputer can be defined as a machine with a high computing performance and extremely fast processing speeds which is employed for specialised applications that require immense amounts of mathematical calculations and logical analysis. A supercomputer may either be built as a single machine or can be a cluster of computers that process data simultaneously.

Robotics by definition is a branch of engineering that involves the conception, design, manufacture, and operation of robots. This field overlaps the technological luxuries of fields like electronics, computer science, artificial intelligence, mechanical engineering, nanotechnology and bioengineering. In fact, while the concept of robots had existed as a hypothetical thought in the minds of people for a long time, the coining of the terms robot and robotics, and the arrival of a practical robot model took place only in the 20th century. Coining of the term 'robot' is widely credited to Karel Čapek, a Czech writer, who borrowed it from his brother Joseph Čapek[1], and coining of the term 'robotics' is credited to Isaac Asimov, a science fiction writer.[2] From such humble beginnings, robotics and robots have grown to become a phenomenon in the modern world. Due to the technological advancements in the fields of electronics, computer science, mechanical engineering, and bioengineering in the later part of the 20th century and in the 21st century, the field of robotics acquired a huge boost which, in turn, has resulted in the development of advanced robots of various sizes, models and functions.

3D printing or "additive manufacturing" is the process of layer by layer manufacturing/printing of 3D physical objects virtually of any shape of their digital models. Unlike the conventional form of manufacturing an object, which relies on removal of material with methods like cutting, drilling and scraping that are subtractive methods, the process of 3D printing only involves the additive method of adding layers of material, one above the other. Therefore, in the process of 3D printing, wastage of material is minimal, which helps in cutting costs. Also, 3D printing does not require large scale factories to manufacture an object but can be produced in a small space. Interestingly, the ability of 3D printing to print complex parts regardless of the geometric complexity, opens up new frontiers for design flexibility, which are otherwise constrained by traditional manufacturing technologies.[3]

It is evident that the three technologies discussed above have immense potential in the evolutionary process of warfare and, therefore, a deeper study would help understand the pragmatic possibility for these technologies to play a crucial role in future wars.

Robotics and the World of Automation

Robotics has fascinated humanity for centuries and many people belonging to different civilisations have made efforts either in the form of literature or as practical models to achieve this fantasy. However, it was not until the 20th century that a breakthrough was achieved in this field, and the concept, which had remained a fantasy for a long time, started becoming a reality. This was made possible not because of one individual's invention or work but due to the contribution of several individuals and simultaneous development of many technologies like remote access, computer technology, miniaturisation, electronics, etc which collectively resulted in achieving this feat.

Even during the early years of their creation, robots were utilised in war-fighting mainly for aiding equipment. For instance, during World War I, a robot called 'Electric Dog' was utilised for carrying supplies. The robot was nothing more than a converted tricycle which was able to move following a light source carrying the load.[4]

Fig 1: The 'Electric Dog' Following its Illuminous Master and a General Setting of the Inside.

Source: http://cyberneticzoo.com/precyber/1914-seleno-the-electric-dog-hammondmiessner/. Accessed on October 12, 2015.

Over the years as various technologies like electronics, radio signals, computer technology, artificial intelligence, nanotechnology, etc developed, these started reflecting in the field of robotics too. As a result, multifarious robots of various sizes, models and purpose are now in operation around the world. Therefore, classification of the robots based on different taxonomy is as follows[5]:

- **Control Taxonomy:**
  - Pre-programmed (autonomous)
  - Remotely controlled (telerobots)
  - Supervised autonomous
  - Fully autonomous
- **Operational Medium Taxonomy:**
  - Space
  - Air
  - Ground
  - Water
  - Hybrid
- **Functional Taxonomy:**
  - Military
  - Industrial
  - Household
  - Commercial

Unlike the traditional thinking and the widespread belief that a robot is a mechanical human (humanoid/ android) that would overtake the human species in the future as and when it achieves enough artificial intelligence, in reality, a robot, in simple terms, is a machine which reacts to the situation or command based on its programmed mechanics. In more scientific terms, a robot is a machine with sensors, processors, and effectors which have the ability to perceive the environment, make appropriate decisions and act upon the environment either autonomously based on its preloaded programmes or with consistent human interaction through remote commands.[6]

In the age of information, due to the developments in computer technology and information technology, smarter robots are being created across the world. These are also created with the latest electronics and mechanics with advanced sensors, processors and effectors which make them more agile and responsive. It is mainly due to these characteristics, that modern day militaries are recruiting more robots to their ranks. For instance, the United States has a military modernisation programme called "Future Combat System" worth $200 billion, under which robots were to replace one-third of armoured vehicles by the end of 2015.[7]

In the military sphere, a number of robots of varying sizes and models are entrusted with numerous tasks ranging from surveillance, reconnaissance, espionage, disaster management, logistics, active combat, etc. Even with the current advancements in the field of information technology and artificial intelligence, these military robots, though they are mostly pre-programmed, operate under the constant supervision of humans in order to avoid untoward accidents and collateral damage. It can be said beyond doubt that this situation will remain unchanged for a few more decades at least, as humans do not want robots to accidently start a war.

Military Robots Around the World

While the topic of the paper is vast, the focus here is on a few popular military robots from around the world, as preparing a database of all the existing military robots of the world would be an elaborate and tedious exercise.

United States of America

The US has a plethora of robots at various levels of development and operations in the military sector. In fact, it is the only country, which has successfully deployed military robots in modern wars: the US' military robots performed their missions in Iraq and Afghanistan during the country's military presence in these two countries during the first decade of the 21st century. Some of the popular military robots of the US are as follows:

Predator: This Unmanned Aerial Vehicle/ System (UAV/ UAS) manufactured by General Atomics Aeronautical is one of the few famous military unmanned systems/

robots operational in the world due to its active role in combat over Afghanistan, Pakistan, Bosnia, Serbia, Iraq, Yemen, Libya, Syria, and Somalia. Although this family of UAS is primarily used for the reconnaissance and forward observation roles, it has been upgraded over the years to carry and fire two AGM-114 Hellfire air-to-surface missiles or other munitions. The latest version of this unmanned aerial robot called Predator XP has a maximum operational endurance of 35hrs and can fly at a maximum altitude of 25,000 ft.[8]

SWORDS: The Special Weapons Observation Reconnaissance Detection System (SWORDS) is a weapon mounted Unmanned Ground Vehicle (UGV)robot manufactured by Foster-Miller, a US-based company. 'SWORDS' is the weaponised version of Foster Miller's TALON family of remotely operated tracked military robots which were exclusively built for the US Army. The SWORDS robots fall under the category of telerobots category which would be operated by controllers from a safe distance from the actual combat zone. In 2007, SWORDS gained much media publicity when three robots were inducted into active operation and rolled alongside human combatants in the Iraq operations. However, the US Army did not deploy these robots for further action and even went to the extent of discontinuing the funds for the SWORDS project, the reasons for which are still not clear.[9]

X-47B: The X-47B is an advanced Unmanned Combat Aerial Vehicle (UCAV) developed by Northorp Grumman, specially for the US Navy. The X-47B is a tailless, strike fighter-sized unmanned aircraft designed for operating from the US Navy's aircraft carriers. In 2013, these aircraft were successfully tested for carrier-based launches and recoveries by an autonomous, low-observable relevant unmanned aircraft. In April 2015, during another test, the X-47B successfully achieved the first ever Autonomous Aerial Refuelling (AAR) of an unmanned aircraft. The X-47B is touted to be the beginning of the future carrier-based unmanned aviation.[10]

Micro Aerial Vehicle: Also known as the Micro Air Vehicle (MAV), this is a category of a miniature UAV which has the potential of being used for remote observation of hazardous environments inaccessible to ground vehicles, and for aerial reconnaissance, surveillance and aerial photography of inaccessible places. There are multifarious numbers of MAVs in operation with the US military and more are under development in different agencies for future use. The US military used many models of MAVs during the operations in Iraq and Afghanistan, mainly for the purpose of aerial surveillance.[11]

Big Dog: Claimed to be the most advanced rough terrain robot on earth by its manufacturing company Boston Dynamics, Big Dog is a logistics robot which has the capability to walk, run, climb and carry heavy loads. This robot is almost the size of a small mule with dimensions of 3 ft length, 2.5 ft height and weight around 108 kg. Initially funded by the Defence Advanced Research Projects Agency (DARPA) and later by the Army Research Laboratory's RCTA programme, the Big Dog is considered to be a successful programme as the robot can run at a speed of 4 mph, climb slopes up to 35 degrees, walk across rubble, climb muddy hiking trails, walk in snow and water, and can carry a load of up to 150 kg.[12] There is a high possibility for this robot to become the load carrier of future infantry units.

Fig 2: (Left to Right) Predator, SWORDS, Micro Aerial Vehicle (RQ-16 T-Hawk), X-47B and Big Dog

Source: Google Images

Russia

Unlike the US, Russia has a limited number of military robots but it is fast catching up with this technology after realising its importance post analysis of the United States' Afghan and Iraq Wars. A few highlighting military robots of Russia are as follows:

Uran-6: The Uran-6 is a multi-functional demining system that can do the work of 20 sappers. The machine, equipped with bulldozer blades and trawls, moves across the dangerous terrain, searching for mines and unexploded ordnance and neutralises them on the command of its operator, who operates it from a safe distance of 0.6 miles. This device is claimed to have the ability to neutralise an explosive object with a potential of 130 lbs of TNT equivalent. As of early 2015, the Uran-6 was under the testing stage in Chechnya, in the mountain ranges of the Vedensky region.[13]

Platform-M: The Platform-M is the latest robotic combat system, created to fight without coming into contact with the opponent. It is capable of carrying out reconnaissance and patrol missions, as well as guarding important sites. The Platform-M can also act as gun support and its aiming mechanism works automatically, without human assistance. The robot is armed with four grenade launchers and a Kalashnikov machine gun. After having proven itself during the drills in Kaliningrad in 2013, the robot platform was inducted into the armed forces in mid-2014.[14]

Wolf-2: The Wolf-2 is a similar robot like the Platform-M; however, it is more powerful and heavier than the latter. The robot is controlled via radio from a distance of three miles and has an off-road tracked chassis which enables it to roll over rough terrain at high speeds. The robot is armed with Kalashnikov machine guns and large-calibre Utes and Kord machine guns, and it can fire while moving at a speed of 22 mph in any weather and at any time of the day. Also fitted with an imager, a laser rangefinder and a gyrostabiliser, the robot is claimed to fire with precision and the whole machine is said to be protected by a layer of special armour. The robot is touted to be used in the strategic missile forces as a guard for the Topol-M and Yars missile systems.[15]

Shooter: The Shooter is a simple tracked chassis mounted with a machine gun. This machine is designed for urban warfare during low intensity operations as it can be used for storming buildings in dense urban areas, thereby, helping to avoid military casualties. The robot, in spite of its slow speed (2.5 mph), can ascend staircases, and is claimed to be irreplaceable during urban warfare or a counter-terrorism operation.[16]

Gnom: The Gnom is an underwater robot which carries a video camera for surveillance. The Gnom is controlled by an operator with the help of a joystick from the surface and the robot searches for, and aids in neutralising, dangerous objects such as mines under water. It is equipped with an omni-directional locator and can see objects at a distance of 110 yards. This feature helps the robot to perform search and rescue tasks, as well as underwater reconnaissance missions. After having been tested in 2005 in the Baltic region, the Gnom was inducted to serve in the Russian Navy.[17]

Fig 3: (Left to Right) Platform-M, Wolf-2, Uran-6, Shooter and Gnom

Source: Russia Beyond the Headlines

Israel

Along with the US, Israel is another country which has a good number of military robots in its possession. In fact, the Israeli Defence Forces are one of the most sophisticated forces in the world whose ground forces train side by side with "advanced ground robotics". Its 7th Armoured Brigade achieved this feat in early 2015, as was revealed to the public by Maj Gen Eyal Ben Reuven during his speech at the International Ground Forces Conference held at Tel Aviv.[18] Some famous military robots of Israel are as follows:

Heron: The Heron is a multi-role strategic Medium Altitude Long Endurance (MALE) Unmanned Aerial System (UAS) developed by Israel Aerospace Industries (IAI). Currently, there are three operational variants of this machine, namely, Heron, Super Heron and Heron TP. The UAV is equipped with different types of advanced radars and data link facilities, with an operational endurance of more than 35 hours. The Heron has a payload capacity which ranges from 250-1,000 kg depending on the variant. Also being a medium altitude model UAV, all the variants of Heron operate below 45,000 ft.[19] While surveillance and reconnaissance are the main operations of the Heron, different variants of this UAV family are in operation in more than 14 countries, including Israel, India, the US, etc, playing an active role in their respective armed forces operations.

VIPeR: The VIPeR is a ground robot created by Elbit Systems of Israel and it was unveiled in March 2007. These robots are extremely lightweight, one-person, portable system, weighing approximately 3.5 kg, equipped with advanced sensors that allow full operation in various adverse terrains, as also allow ground forces to survey structures before entering into action. It is claimed to be highly suitable for land warriors in today's low intensity conflict situations. Being portable, these VIPeR robots are configurable for multiple types of missions by using add-on sensors, modules and payloads, tailored for specific tasks. These remote-controlled robots are currently being used in situations which are considered extremely dangerous for humans like exploring tunnels and caves.[20] Another important advantage of this machine is that it is fitted with the "Galileo Wheel", a patented system developed by Galileo Mobility Instruments Ltd. that allows automatic back and forth conversion among a wheel configuration, a track configuration and a special stair climbing configuration[21] Although the robot is utilised exclusively for surveillance and reconnaissance purposes, it can also be mounted with small arms for combat operations.

Fig 4: (Left to Right) Heron, Super Heron, Heron TP and VIPeR

Source: IAI and Defence Update

Robotics in India

Robotics in India is an upcoming sphere which involves people from research institutions, universities, government research centres and industry. The Robotic Society of India, a non-governmental academic society was established on July 10, 2011, to promote Indian robotics and automation activities. Almost all the Indian Institutes of Technology (IIT,) and many educational campuses across the country have a robotics study centre and many students from different universities and even schools are actively involved in developing micro and mini robots mainly for academic as well as entertainment purposes. There are occasional robotic competitions conducted at university level where crude robots created by students are displayed and demonstrated. Many private industries, mainly Micro, Small and Medium Enterprises (MSMEs), are involved in the manufacture of industrial and other commercial robots in the civilian sector.

In the military sector, robots are still on the periphery as not many of these smart machines are actively deployed by the armed forces in spite of their being inducted in the Services. The Defence Research and Development Organisation (DRDO) is the nodal agency in the government sector that is involved in the creation and Research and Development (R&D) of military robots. An Unmanned Ground Vehicle (UGV) programme, which forms part of mobile robotics, has been conceived by DRDO to evolve a family of mobile platforms for the armed forces for use in hazardous conditions and hostile environments. Out of the 50 odd laboratories functioning under DRDO, four labs are responsible for the research and development of ground robots of various sizes (see Table 1 for more information).

Table 1: Classification of UGVs Development Programme of DRDO

S. No.	Category Nomenclature	Category Weight	Laboratory Responsible
1	Micro UGVs	<500g	CAIR, Bengaluru
2	Miniature UGVs	<50 kg	CAIR, Bengaluru
3	Small UGVs	<500 kg	R&DE(Engrs), Pune
4	Medium UGVs	<25,000 kg	VRDE, Ahmednagar
5	Large UGVs	>25,000 kg	CVRDE, Chennai

Over the years, along with the UGVs, DRDO has also succeeded in developing a number of military robots of various sizes and purposes, with or without collaboration with private industries. A few of the military robots of India are discussed below:

Robot Sentry: The Robot Sentry is a surveillance robot which has the ability to provide continuous video feed via a pan-tilt-zoom network colour camera for three hours. The robot has an in-built WiFi link for command and control which can be remotely controlled from a laptop.[22] The robot is claimed to be suited for surveillance duties at entry and exit points of buildings.

Netra: The Netra is the famous intelligence, surveillance and reconnaissance UAV robot primarily conceived by IdeaForge, a private company, which later collaborated with DRDO for further enhancement and production of the product. This robot can be launched from anywhere and made to fly over the area of interest up to an altitude of 400 m. While flying at its peak height, it is claimed that the UAV has the visibility to cover a radius of 4 km and can zoom up to 500 m. This user friendly robot has both day and night vision cameras and can even function in the complete autonomous flight mode. The video feed from the UAV can be monitored live which can also be set to target mode in order to follow a particular target in a crowd. The vehicle has a battery endurance of around 40 minutes and is suitable for counter-insurgency, border management, hostage situations, disaster management or simply crowd monitoring/ control.[23] The UAV is currently in operation with the Central Reserve Police Force and Border Security Force of India.

Rustom: There are three Rustom variants currently under various stages of development namely Rustom-1 (prototype flight testing), Rustom-H High Altitude Long Endurance (HALE) UAV (under development), and Rustom-2 UCAV (Prototype flight testing). The Medium Altitude Long Endurance (MALE) UCAV would add more firepower to India's aerospace sector after its induction into the Services. The Rustom 1 MALE UAV is expected to have an endurance of 24 hours, with an operational altitude of 35,000 ft., and will be capable of autonomous take-off and landing, wheeled undercarriage and will have a single (Rotax) piston engine. It is claimed that all the variants of the Rustom would have high stealth capability. The machine is being developed by the Aeronautical Development Establishment (ADE), a Bengaluru-based DRDO laboratory.[24]

Takshak: The Takshak is a Remotely Operated Vehicle (ROV) which is claimed to have a good cross-country mobility, and can be remotely driven from 200 m. This swift moving six-wheeled robot was designed to diffuse Improvised Explosive Devices (IEDs) and suspicious objects and, therefore, it is equipped with three cameras for taking visuals of the suspected explosive for assessment and two recoilless water jets which can be fired individually. The purpose of the water jets is to shoot water at the explosive device like a bullet to diffuse the IED and water is used as it would be able to diffuse the explosive without triggering a blast. The accessories like the power supply, battery and communication system can be mounted on a back pack which comes associated with the ROV.[25]

Daksh: Like the Takshak, the Daksh is also an ROV primarily used to locate, handle and destroy hazardous objects safely. This remotely controlled, battery operated ROV is equipped with a robotic arm, portable X-ray device, water jet disrupter and a shot gun. The Daksh can be controlled by its operators from a safe distance of 500 m and can be used to scan a suspected location for hazardous objects using its X-ray device, and, if needed, the water jet and shot gun can also be used. The Daksh can also climb stairs, negotiate steep slopes, roll over through narrow corridors and tow vehicles to the hazardous objects. The Daksh has been in active service in the Indian Army since 2011. Another variant of the Daksh known as the Gun Mounted Robot (GMR) which is also in the testing phase is nothing but a Daksh ROV mounted with a gun in place of the robotic arm.[26]

Fig 5: (Left to Right) Robots Sentry, Netra, Rustom, Takshak and Daksh

Source: Google Images

Thus, the above overview of military robotics around the world, including India, shows that robotic warfare is still in its nascent stage will many robots in the development and testing stages. Although a few countries are progressing rapidly in this sphere, hoping to achieve a breakthrough in the near future, it would take at least a few decades for the robots to get fully inducted into the armed forces at par with human soldiers.

Supercomputer Capabilities

High capacity supercomputing machines are used for various types of scientific research like recreating the Big Bang, understanding earthquakes, protein folding, blood stream mapping, modelling of new diseases, oceanographic modelling, predicting climate change, weather forecasting, recreating brain patterns, finding the God's particle and various other atomic and subatomic researches. While supercomputers are constantly relied upon for performing the above mentioned high end complex civilian scientific researches, they are also used at almost the same magnitude by different countries around the globe for defence related missions and research.

Role of Supercomputers in Defence

The use of supercomputers enhances a country's national defence in the field of R&D by imbibing the capabilities that these supercomputers possess. Countries employ these computing giants in the development of various weapon programmes, simulations of weapon systems and in designing and modelling of high end technologies for different weapon systems. This process of using the supercomputer capabilities for defence related research makes research less time consuming, more efficient and also helps in boosting the technology of weapon systems.

Around the world, countries possessing supercomputers are employing this superior technology in the field of defence for various purposes, of which a few of the major uses are as follows:

- Simulation of nuclear weapons testing.
- Biological warfare testing.
- Missile and space programmes.
- Submarine programmes.
- Simulation of war games.
- Weather forecast for military operations.
- Data mining and information espionage,

Although all the supercomputers are designed to be extremely fast and capable of handling complex tasks, as listed above, the general practice is to make mission specific machines to assign them for a precise task.

Simulation of Nuclear Weapons Testing

The Comprehensive Test Ban Treaty (CTBT) which bans countries from conducting nuclear tests has been signed by 183 countries around the world.[27] Under such conditions, simulating the tests of nuclear weapons by using supercomputers is seen as a safe method for any state that wishes to pursue its nuclear weapon programme. It is also seen as a preferred option for countries to clandestinely test nuclear weapons through simulations to avoid any international criticism. A supercomputer also helps a country to keep its nuclear stockpile safe, secure and effective without the need for underground testing and gives increased confidence in the nation's nuclear deterrence as the weapons stockpile changes under treaty agreements. Supercomputers also allow nuclear scientists a better understanding of the weapons' performance by simulating and predicting what happens to materials at very high/ low pressure and temperature points. They also help to anticipate and prevent problems that come as a result of the ageing of nuclear weapons through simulations. The weapons are assessed and modified in order to make them last longer with the life extension programmes using supercomputers.[28] For instance, the US' supercomputer 'Sequoia' was used by the National Nuclear Security Agency of the USA for monitoring the country's nuclear stockpile and also to conduct simulated nuclear tests.

Biological Warfare Testing

Although biological warfare is recognised as one of the most dangerous forms of warfare and the international community has banned the use or even production of any biological weapons, a few countries still use covert methods to keep their biological weapons production alive. The supercomputers come in handy in this process by aiding in the research to develop genetically modified biological weapons in the labs which can be used against a rival state. The supercomputers help in reducing the time and money spent on research and, at the same time, increase the possibilities and efficiency of these hazardous weapons. It is believed that China has an active biological warfare programme with the aid of its supercomputers and has exported its biological warfare technology to Iran.[29]

Missile and Space Programmes

The missile and space programmes involve a lot of complex arithmetic calculations combined with theories and formulas of physics and, therefore, supercomputers are seen as a boon for scientists who undertake research in this field. These mega machines are used in all possible ways to conduct studies in aerodynamic modelling, missile trajectory simulation, missile testing (simulation or real-time), missile defence programmes, design and analysis of delivery vehicles, and to solve complex aeronautical problems. In November 2012, India conducted its Ballistic Missile Defence (BMD) test, in which, for the first time, two incoming missiles were intercepted simultaneously, and destroyed successfully.[30] Of these two incoming missiles, one was simulated and the simulated missile was destroyed by a simulated interceptor. This simulation testing was made possible by the supercomputers used by DRDO, the defence research organisation of India. On the space front, the Satish Dhawan Supercomputing Facility located at Vikram Sarabhai Space Centre (VSSC) in Thiruvananthapuram, built a supercomputer called "SAGA 220" in 2011 based on Graphic Processing Unit (GPU) Architecture-220 TeraFLOPS for solving complex aerospace problems.[31]

Submarine Programmes

Regarding research of submarine programmes, supercomputers are mainly used to undertake computational fluid dynamic studies to increase knowledge and assist the evaluation of the technical risks associated with the hydrodynamic performance of future naval platforms. They are also used to analyse the risk factors associated with the newly designed model by conducting simulated tests, especially with the designs of nuclear powered submarines. In July 2013, the Australian Department of Defence had purchased a supercomputer from CRAY Computers[32] for $2.2 million in order to conduct research for their future submarine programmes.[33]

Simulation of War Games

Conducting war games is always important for a country to understand war-fighting and to explore the various possibilities in a battlefield. The advancements in technology and the induction of supercomputers in the field of defence have enhanced the quality of war games that countries can conduct. The supercomputers help in creating simulated complex war scenarios which help the country's armed forces to understand the battle situations much better during peace-time. They also help in simulating complex war scenarios in order to train soldiers to effectively overcome such odds. Almost all the major countries of the world use this method of simulation of war games with the help of supercomputers to keep their forces alert and prepared for all possible situations. Even a small territory like Taiwan, which is claiming sovereignty over its territory and is at loggerheads with the mighty People's Republic of China (PRC), is using supercomputers bought from the USA for the purpose of simulation of war games.[34]

Weather Forecast for Military Operations

In military operations, accurate weather predictions can mean the difference between success and failure – life and death. Accurate forecasting by military meteorologists provides situational awareness for the field commanders in order to make wise and timely military decisions. A supercomputer plays an overall role in this work in accurately predicting the weather for the military to operate in the field. Especially, air force weather specialists use the capabilities of supercomputers in tandem with satellites in order to predict the weather more accurately for their fighters. Almost all the countries of the world follow this method to make their armed forces' operations successful.

Data Mining and Information Espionage

The digital age has become an advantage for the intelligence agencies of various countries as they are able to use the technology to tap into the communications and other information, whichever they prefer to acquire. All the digital data collected are stored in bulk data deposits located in safe houses and are processed using the massive supercomputers to trace out the enemy of the state. The high processing speed and storage capacity of the supercomputers are very useful for this purpose. Also loaded with some trawling software, these supercomputers can be converted into spying giants which can trawl into millions of sites on the internet, especially the posts in the social networking sites in order to identify a possible terrorist. In mid-2013, Edward Snowden revealed various covert mass digital surveillance programmes of the US like Prism[35], X Keyscore, etc. These programmes were made possible due to the existence of various high powered supercomputers and cognitive computers in the possession of the National Security Agency (NSA).

Supercomputer Capabilities of the World

The capacity of the supercomputers used for both civilian and defence related purposes varies amongst nations. The need to have such capable supercomputers for a country is directly proportional to its national interest and also the country's technological capability. While the history of supercomputers dates back to the 1960s, every year, the number of countries mastering the technology and their capabilities is increasing drastically. This is evident from the 'List of Top 500 Supercomputers of the World' published twice a year by the website www.top500.org. This list of the top 500 is compiled by Hans Meuer of the University of Mannheim, Germany, Erich Strohmaier of NERSC/Lawrence Berkeley National Laboratory, Jack Dongarra of the University of Tennessee, Knoxville, Horst Simon of NERSC/Lawrence Berkeley National Laboratory and Martin Meuer of Prometeus.[36] It is speculated that apart from the machines in the list, there are many other faster machines possessed by various countries which are kept hidden from the world community due to their use in secret missions.

According to the list published in November 2015, out of the top 500 fastest supercomputers, the United States of America has 199 machines which is the highest number possessed by any country, followed by China with 109 machines. Other countries like Japan, Germany, the United Kingdom, France, India, South Korea and Russia follow with 37, 32, 18, 18, 11, 10 and 7 machines respectively in their possession.[37]

The capabilities of these computing mammoths are also huge. In the same list, the fastest supercomputer of the world is topped by China's Tianhe-2 with a speed of 33.86 petaflops per second which is equivalent to 33,860 trillion calculations per second or in simple terms, the Tianhe-2 is 338,600,000 times faster than a normal desktop computer. Next in the list is the USA's Titan, with a speed of 17.59 petaflops per second. The Chinese indigenously built Tianhe-2 surpassed the USA's Titan with its superior technology and almost double its speed.[38] It came as a huge surprise to the world community when China unveiled its Tianhe-2 in 2013, as the project was actually scheduled to be operational only by 2015. Other countries like Japan, France, the United Kingdom and Germany are also in the competition—all have at least one supercomputer in the rank list of the fastest 20 supercomputers of the world. Another surprise entry into the list of the 10 fastest supercomputers of the world is Saudi Arabia at 9th position with its machine called "Shaheen II", which is set up at the King Abdullah University of Science and Technology.[39]

However, countries which are unable to make their own machines are either opting to purchase the machine from abroad or to transfer the technology from their friendly countries. For example, Iran buys its supercomputers from China, while Taiwan purchases these from the USA. In fact, the Shaheen II of Saudi Arabia is also an outright purchase from the USA's famous supercomputer manufacturing company, CRAY Inc. In the supercomputing technology, apart from the hardware components, the capability to create compatible software also plays an important role so as to conduct accurate research.

Supercomputing Capability of India

The history of supercomputing in India started way back in the 1980s although it was denied import of CRAY supercomputers, the leading supercomputers developing company of the US during that period, due the fact that these supercomputers can be used to develop nuclear technology. In spite of such an embargo on India to acquire the technology and components for developing a supercomputer, India managed to develop its own supercomputer, with help from Russia. The first supercomputer of India was called PARAM 8000 which was the first in the PARAM series and it was developed by the Centre for Development and Advanced Computing (C-DAC) in Pune, India. The development was made possible due to the cooperation established between India and Russia in the field of science and technology. The C-DAC is collaborating with the Institute of Computer Aided Design (ICAD), Moscow, Russia, for making its first supercomputer.[40]

The C-DAC has designed and assembled six other supercomputers belonging to the same PARAM series and the latest, PARAM YUVA II, is in the 251st position in the listing of fastest supercomputers in the world, according the website www.top500.com, in the recent report. Including PARAM YUVA II, 11 supercomputers from India have been ranked in the top 500 list of fastest supercomputers of the world. These supercomputers occupy the ranks of 96, 119, 145, 166, 251, 286, 300, 313, 316, 380 and 397 in the list. According to the November 2015 update, the fastest supercomputer of India is a CRAY computer, which is being used in the Supercomputer Education and Research Centre (SERC) of the Indian Institute of Science. This supercomputer functions at a speed of 901.506 TFlops per second.[41] Although India ranks 7th in terms of the number of fastest supercomputers possessed by a country, according to the list of top 500 supercomputers, it lags behind in speed and technology that the other countries possess in the field of supercomputing. This is evident from the fact that the position of Indian supercomputers is descending in the subsequent ranking lists.

However, the supercomputers of the BARC ANUPAM series, DRDO DHRUVA series and SAGA 220 which do not appear on the list of fastest 500 supercomputer are part of India's defence related supercomputing programme. The supercomputer ANUPAM, developed by BARC, functions at a speed of 202 GFlops per second at peak performance, and is used to solve large complex problems in the research of molecular dynamics simulation, crystal structure analysis, laser-atom interaction computation, gamma ray simulation, neutron transport calculations, etc. It is also used for weather forecasting at the National Centre for Medium Range Weather Forecasting, Noida, and in the research of the computational fluid dynamics at the Aeronautical Development Agency, Bangalore. Moreover, DRDO's DHRUVA which was the product of the Advanced Numerical Research and Analysis Group (ANURAG) is placed at the Centre for High Performance Computing and Research (CHITRA). The DHRUVA is used in aero-modelling to design airborne or waterborne systems. Also, as mentioned earlier, the SAGA 220, operating in the Satish Dhawan Supercomputing Facility, located at the Vikram Sarabhai Space Centre (VSSC) in Thiruvananthapuram, is believed to be used in designing future space launch vehicles.

Supercomputers have become an integral part of the defence system in the field of research and operations. The use of these machines in the modern world which is becoming increasingly digitalised and virtual, can have serious repercussions if they fall into the wrong hands or countries with malignant intentions. Supercomputers have already become the battleground for the information war that is going on in the world. On the whole, the increased use of supercomputers in the field of research for defence would undoubtedly enhance the defence capabilities of a country but, at the same time, make the offensive capabilities more fatal than ever.

What is 3D Printing/ Additive Manufacturing?

3D printing started in the 1980s with Chuck Hull being the pioneer in the technology: however, the widespread commercial use of this technology gained momentum only in the 21st century.[42] Within a short span of time, the technology was adopted into various fields due to its high capacity and flexibility. Today, 3D printing is used globally in the following fields: construction, industrial designing, automobile industry, aerospace industry, defence production, medical industries and fashion industry, mainly for prototyping and small volume production.

In recent years, this technology has reached a level where scientists claim to have developed a 3D concrete printer that can be used to print a house within 24 hours.[43] More interestingly, in the UK, BAE Systems have used 3D printed parts in one of their Tornado fighter jets and conducted a successful test flight. The parts printed include the cockpit radio cover, plastic window breather pipe and components in the landing gear.[44] Although these are the least risky parts in the aircraft, the practical utility of this technology has opened new avenues in the aerospace industry.

Promising Aspects of 3D Printing

As mentioned earlier, 3D printing at present is mainly used for making prototypes and for small volume production. With this technology, the producers are enabled to skip the stage of fabrication of tools after designing and go straight to the production of finished products. This aspect helps the manufacturer in saving time and money to create a prototype of any product, and helps in the overall development of the product. Particularly, this aspect would be of great help to the defence industries for making prototypes at less cost.

Moreover, products that are produced on a very small scale or for dedicated purposes like satellites, missiles and launch vehicles, are suitable applications where 3D printing is a boon. Since satellites, missiles and space launch vehicles need intricately designed parts, the traditional method of producing by fabricating tools to make the moulds is very expensive, whereas printing the parts directly is cost-effective and less time consuming. In addition, a product printed in a 3D printer is much lighter than the same product produced by conventional methods even though both exhibit relatively similar qualities. This aspect would be very beneficial in the aircraft manufacturing industry as for every one kilogram reduction in weight, fuel cost of US$35,000 can be saved by the airlines over an aircraft's life.[45]

The supply chain and logistics comprise the backbone of any country's defence forces. The ability to supply goods to the forces at the right time is the ultimate challenge. The ability of a 3D printer to directly convert a digital design into a finished product is the aspect which would attract the defence forces to use 3D printing in their supply chain and logistics department. (Remember the printing of spare parts by the crew of the submarine whose engine had failed, as described earlier.)

Another more innovative aspect of 3D printing technology is its ability to print products of any size, irrespective of their complex geometric shape. While a whole house can be printed using this technology, it can also be used to print a small product like a coffee mug. Since making digital designs for big complex structures is a big challenge for the designers, this technology can also be used to create simple sub-assemblies of interconnected parts.

Expertise of USA and China in 3D Printing

In view of the salient features of 3D printing technology, global powers such as the USA and China have started incorporating the technology in various fields, including the defence sector. The Government of the USA has invested $30 million in setting up a national 3D printing centre in Youngstown, Ohio, for civilian purposes. For the purposes of defence, the state's Future Warfare Centre at the Space and Missile Defence Command in Alabama, has been involved in developing cheaper 3D printers which would cost less than $700. On a trial basis, the 3D printers produced in this centre were supplied to the American troops on the front and used by the Rapid Equipping Force (REP) that was deployed in Afghanistan and Iraq.[46] Moreover, a study conducted by the Centre for New American Security, an American think-tank, reported that in the future robotic warfare, the USA would use fleets of unmanned 3D printed drones along with the cyber warfare tools and guided munitions.[47] The National Aeronautics and Space Administration (NASA), the nodal space agency of the USA, is also conducting research on the possibility of printing food for space missions and future space settlements through 3D printing which also has implications for future missions to the planet Mars.[48]

Following in the American footsteps, China started experimenting with 3D printing technology in its military aviation industry towards the end of the 20th century and gained a lot of benefits from this technology. The Chinese aerospace industry and the outer space sector have seen drastic development in the past three decades. An important factor which helped China to keep up the momentum was the capability to produce the aircraft, missiles and launch vehicles indigenously well in advance, before the expected deadlines. It is claimed by a few reports that China has used its expertise in 3D printing technology in the production of its indigenously built fighter aircraft projects, the J-15, J-16 and J-20.[49] The Chief Engineer of the J-15 project, Mr. Sun, said during an interview to the Chinese news media:

> After nearly 20 years of research and development, [3-D printing technology in China] can produce…products that can replace metal structures made by complicated traditional manufacturing processes. We have applied the technology to [the aviation] industry, including sizeable titanium alloy structures and aircraft engine renovation, as well as some other high-end components.[50]

Therefore, it can be speculated that China may be using the expertise in 3D printing in its missile development programmes and outer space research also. This may be one of the reasons why China is able to deliver all its aerospace projects, including the fifth generation fighter aircraft, the J-20, its various missiles projects, and build advanced space launch vehicles before the expected time.

Fig 6: Large Titanium Alloy Fighter Jet Part Made with 3-D Printing in China

Source: http://mil.huanqiu.com/

Building a successful prototype is the biggest challenge in an aerospace project, and the ability of 3D printing to convert a digital design directly into a finished product helps a country save time and also avoid the hassles of making the moulds for making the prototype as in the traditional manufacturing process. Therefore, through this technology, China has achieved results sooner, as well surprised the world with its advanced capabilities in the defence manufacturing sector.

Risks and Drawbacks of 3D Printing

Although 3D printing technology seems to be promising and fascinating in its own way, the technology is still in its nascent stage and, therefore, it has its own drawbacks and risks. The first and foremost major risk associated with this technology would be the widespread access to 3D printers in the future that could increase the risk of counterfeit products being introduced into the market, in competition with the real ones, which would not only be detrimental to the original products but also aggravate the issue of intellectual property rights violations. This risk factor is much higher in the defence sector as it is more profitable and advantageous. Laser imaging technology or any low cost 3D scanners can be used by counterfeiters to scan the original product and create the digital image, which can then be reverse engineered and printed, to result in counterfeit products.[51] Any such event of counterfeiting would lead to the question of intellectual property rights violations, as 3D printing technology deals with digital designs that are owned either by the designers or by the institutions they belong to.

Especially in the defence industrial sector, as 3D printers operate on Computer Aided Design (CAD), they are easy to be copied and circulated which would lead to the proliferation of weapon systems.[52] Since these CAD designs would be stored in virtual locations, they could become vulnerable targets for hackers who wish to copy, change or delete the entire information. Furthermore, states might even go to the extent of fighting cyber wars to get their hands on each other's digital designs, making cyber space an intense battleground.

In addition, digital designs of weapon systems being freely available in the open source internet comprises another major challenge for global security. For instance, the digital designs of the AR-15 semi-automatic rifle were published in 2012 in a website, www.defdist.org, with the option to download the designs.[53] Another website, www.defcad.com, can be accessed for digital designs of weapons and other products.[54] Apart from these websites, there are numerous other pages and video hosting sites in the deep web which give guidelines and step by step tutorials for building a 3D printer at home, giving free digital designs for making various pistols and rifles. Therefore, access to such open source digital designs of weapon systems would be of great interest to the non-state actors and other anti-social elements, who will, in turn, use them to terrorise the global society. In addition, the non-state actors getting their hands on digital designs of advanced weapon systems like missiles and drones would be a frightening situation. Therefore, the cyber vaults which contain the digital designs can become one of the national critical information infrastructures and also the states would be forced to enhance their level of cyber security.

Other minor drawback is the high cost of making the 3D printers. Despite the availability of cheaper versions of 3D printers, the fact remains that different products needs different models of 3D printers in various sizes; hence, the cost of acquiring/manufacturing them would be high although it is a one-time expenditure.

Another drawback is the number of materials that can be used in the 3D printers. At present, 3D printers in commercial use are restricted to use a limited number of materials which includes a plastic, a few metals and alloys. Although, a few countries like the US and China possess advanced 3D printers in their defence industries that are capable of using hundreds of materials, including cement concrete, the end products produced by these printers with the available technology face a problem of structural integrity. Nevertheless, in the future, advanced melting technologies like electron beam melting can come in handy to melt the materials to achieve fully dense, void-free parts that could, in turn, be used to print high quality and more lasting products.

3D Printing in India

The 3D printing technology in India is restricted to a few quarters and is being sparsely used in jewellery, fashion, food and a few other industries which are not critical to the nation-state. However, as the popularity and usage of 3D printing technology has increased on the global stage, the realisation of its importance has emerged in the country, and, as a result, the premier academic institutions of India like the National Institute of Design, National Institute of Fashion Technology (NIFT) and Indian Institute of Technology (IIT) have included 3D printing in their curricula which would help the future generations to understand and effectively use the technology.[55]

Nevertheless, it is unclear as to how much inroads this technology has made into India's defence and aerospace production sectors. India's geo-strategic location, with a hostile neighbourhood, has made the country the world's largest importer of arms. Every year, a major chunk of thc country's budget is spent on procuring arms and advanced weapon systems. While it has been a long prevailing dream for India to attain self-reliance in defence production which has led to policies like "Make in India" originating from the country's highest political establishment, the Prime Minister's Office, the question that arises is whether 3D printing technology could be a viable and pragmatic solution for India in this direction

With the identified potentials of this technology, it can well provide a solution for India's efforts for indigenous defence production, provided the country is ready to utilise the technology in the right way. With the availability of expertise in the fields of engineering and information technology in the country, dedicated Research and Development (R&D) in the 3D printing technology would enhance the capability of the country in the manufacturing sector with the ability to print complex products with various kinds of materials.

Conclusion

In the future, when warfare would be network-centric, non-contact warfare would become the trend where robotic operations, cyber operations and missile operations would take centre-stage, and human involvement in the war would be limited to decision-making, command and control, pre-war preparations, battle management and occasional swift and precise commando operations. It is in this scenario that the countries of the world, especially the ones which are aiming to be at the top in the global decision-making hierarchy should adapt to the latest changes in the different warfare domains so as to retain/ attain their desired position in the world order.

Under these circumstances, and considering the nature of futures warfare, robotics, 3D printing and supercomputing would act as force multipliers for a country's armed forces by enabling them to fight short, decisive wars. Advancements in these technologies would also help in reducing the risk of collateral damage. However, in order to achieve this level of expertise, the countries of the world have to put in their individual and collective efforts in the development of these technologies in tandem with their national interests. At present, all three technologies are in the exploratory stages; therefore, their full potentials have to be identified at the earliest. The existing knowledge about these technologies is still limited to a small group of experts, and there is a need for this expertise to spread to a larger audience. Focussed research and development, and planned growth towards achieving the county's vision should be the approach followed in order to achieve success in these technologies.

With regards to India, robotics and supercomputing are in a more developed position compared to the 3D-printing technology of the country. In order to enhance the 3D-printing technical capabilities of the country, focussed R&D has to take place, in both the public and private sectors, with appropriate funding. The armed forces could take the initiative in this technology by starting 3D-printing fabrication labs in their servicing facilities for production of small, commonly available parts. As 3D-printing can also be used in the medical field for printing human organs, the armed forces medical corps should also be involved in R&D of this technology, in collaboration with the appropriate agencies, public and private alike, in order to master the technology.

India's supercomputing capability is yet to catch up with the capabilities of its not so friendly neighbour China and even other Western countries. In spite of the claims about the country's expertise in the information technology sector and its human resource, as of now, supercomputing is not India's forte. However, dedicated R&D, appropriate funding and an effective public-private partnership could turn the tables in favour of India.

Military robotics in India is gaining momentum with both the public and private sectors actively involved in the development of various robotic systems. Therefore, the robotic policy guidelines are the need of the hour, and should come from the government, in order to set the rules and regulations for robotic systems development in the country, as well as to avoid overcrowding of the robotic market in the future. Another major challenge in this sector is for the armed forces to prepare themselves for the future robotic battles in a networked scenario where many robots have to be deployed simultaneously in various theatres, and both men and machines have to be coordinated with cohesion. Although it would take a few decades for such a situation to arise, it would be prudent to start the preparations at the earliest. Finally, irrespective of the growth in technologies,the real strength of a nation's armed forces does not rest in its machines rather, in the minds of its people.

Notes

1. "Science Diction: The Origin of the Word 'Robot'", http://www.npr.org/2011/04/22/135634400/science-diction-the-origin-of-the-word-robot. Accessed on November 12, 2015.
2. Russel A. Faust, *Robotics in Surgery: History, Current and Future Applications* (Nova Science Publishers, 2007).
3. "3D Printing: A Potential Game Changer for Aerospace and Defence", *Gainingaltitude*, Price Water House Coopers, 2013 at www.pwc.com/us/gainingaltitude. Accessed on January 27, 2014.
4. Gerald Mies, "Military Robots of the Present and the Future", *Technology*, vol 9, no 1, 2010, pp 125-137.
5. Dr. Robert Finkelstein, "Military Robotics: Malignant Machines or the Path to Peace?", paper presented at the Military Robotics Conference, Institute for Defence and Government Advancement, Washington, DC, 2010.
6. Ibid.
7. National Defence Authorisation, Fiscal Year 2001, Public Law 106-398, 114 STAT. 1654, October 30, 2000, p 40.
8. "Predator XP RPA", General Atomics Aeronautical, http://www.ga-asi.com/predator-xp. Accessed on October 19, 2015.
9. "The Inside Story of the SWORDS Armed Robot 'Pullout' in Iraq: Update", *Popular Mechanics*, September 30, 2009, http://www.popularmechanics.com/technology/gadgets/a2804/4258963/. Accessed on October 19, 2015.
10. "X-47B UCAS Makes Aviation History…Again!", Northorp Grumman, http://www.northropgrumman.com/Capabilities/X47BUCAS/Pages/default.aspx. Accessed on October 19, 2015.
11. Thomas K. Adams, "Future Warfare and the Decline of Human Decision-Making", *Parameters*, Winter 2001-02.
12. "Big Dog - The Most Advanced Rough-Terrain Robot on Earth", *Boston Dynamics*, http://www.bostondynamics.com/robot_bigdog.html. Accessed on October 19, 2015.
13. "Military Robots to Shine at 2015 Russian Army High-Tech Expo", *Russia Today*, April 21, 2015, https://www.rt.com/news/251645-russia-army-robots-expo/. Accessed on October 20, 2015.
14. Alexander Korolkov, "New Combat Robot is Russian Army's Very Own Wall-E", *Russia Beyond the Headlines*, July 2, 2014, http://rbth.com/defence/2014/07/02/new_combat_robot_is_russian_armys_very_own_deadly_wall-e_37871.html. Accessed on October 20, 2015.

15. Tatyana Rusakova, "Automatons with Epaulettes: Russia's New Generation of Military Robots", *Russia Beyond the Headlines*, January 22, 2015, http://rbth.com/defence/2015/01/22/automatons_with_epaulettes_russias_new_generation_of_military_robots_43071.html. Accessed on October 20, 2015.
16. Ibid.
17. Ibid.
18. "IDF Begins Integrating Robots Into Ground Forces", *Israel Today*, May 7, 2015, http://www.israeltoday.co.il/NewsItem/tabid/178/nid/26564/Default.aspx. Accessed on October 21, 2015.
19. "Heron", Israel Aerospace Industries, http://www.iai.co.il/2013/18900-en/BusinessAreas_UnmannedAirSystems_HeronFamily.aspx. Accessed on October 21, 2015.
20. "Elbit Systems Launches Two New Robots, Creating a VIPeR Family", Press Release from Elbit Systems, August 9, 2010.
21. "Elbit Systems Unveils VIPeR a Portable Combat Robot", *Defence Update*, March 8, 2007, http://www.defense-update.com/newscast/0307/news/080307_viper.htm. Accessed on October 21, 2015.
22. VS Mahalingam, "Mobile Robotics – A DRDO Perspective", Paper presented in 1st US-Asian Technology Demonstration and Assessment of Micro-Aerial and Unmanned Ground Vehicle Technology, Agra, March 10-15, 2008.
23. "Netra UAV", Idea Forge, http://www.ideaforge.co.in/home/products/. Sccessed on October 22, 2015.
24. Ravi Sharma, "India Joins Select Group to Develop UCAV Technology", *The Hindu*, August 27, 2007, http://www.thehindu.com/todays-paper/tp-national/tp-karnataka/article1899911.ece. Accessed on October 22, 2015.
25. "Case Study – Design of Takshak Disruptor Mounted Robot", Onio Design Pvt. Ltd., 2010.
26. "Daksh", Research and Development Establishment, Defence Research and Development Organisation, http://www.drdo.gov.in/drdo/labs/RDE(E)/English/index.jsp?pg=homebody.jsp. Accessed on October 22, 2015.
27. Preparatory Commission for the Comprehensive Nuclear Test Ban Treaty Organisation, "Status of Signature and Ratification", https://www.ctbto.org/the-treaty/status-of-signature-and-ratification/. Accessed on October 26, 2015.
28. Edward Tessen Tanaka, "IBM's Sequoia and the Politics of Dual-Use Supercomputers", June 21, 2012, http://www.patexia.com/feed/ibm-s-sequoia-and-the-politics-of-dual-use-supercomputers-20120621. Accessed on October 20, 2015.
29. Charles R. Smith, "Chinese Germ Warfare Ignored by State Department", http://www.freerepublic.com/focus/fr/584818/posts. Accessed on October 15, 2015.
30. "India Proves Capability of Missile Defence System", *The Hindu*, November 23, 2012.
31. "ISRO Builds India's Fastest Supercomputer", *The Economic Times*, May 2, 2011.
32. CRAY Computers is one of the oldest and the leading supercomputer manufacturing company headquartered in the US.
33. Trevor Clarke, "Defence to get New Supercomputer", June 11, 2013, http://www.smh.com.au/it-pro/government-it/defence-to-get-new-supercomputer-20130611-2nzxr.html. Accessed on October 20, 2015.
34. Brian Hsu, "Military to Buy New Supercomputer", *Taipai Times*, December 8, 2003, http://www.taipeitimes.com/News/taiwan/archives/2003/12/08/2003078791. Accessed on October 21, 2015.
35. PRISM is a clandestine mass electronic surveillance data mining programme known to have been operated by the United States National Security Agency (NSA) since 2007.
36. "About Us", www.top500.org, accessed on November 20, 2015.
37. "Top 500 Supercomputers List", November 2015, www.top500.org. Accessed on November

23, 2015.
38. Ibid.
39. n.36.
40. Marvin V Zelkowitz, *Advances in Computers* (Academic Press, 1997).
41. n. 36.
42. "3D Printing", http://en.wikipedia.org/wiki/3D_printing. Accessed on January 27, 2014.
43. Bushey Ryan, "Researchers Are Making A 3D Printer That Can Build A House In 24 Hours", *Business Insider*, January 9, 2014, http://www.businessinsider.in/Researchers-Are-Making-A-3D-Printer-That-Can-Build-A-House-In-24-Hours/articleshow/28601182.cms. Accessed on January 28, 2014.
44. "Successful Test Flight for Tornado Jet Containing BAE Parts Made on 3D Printer", *The Telegraph,* January 05, 2014, http://www.telegraph.co.uk/finance/newsbysector/industry/10552462/Successful-test-flight-for-Tornado-jet-containing-BAE-parts-made-on-3D-printer.html. Accessed on January 28, 2014.
45. Jewell Catherine, "3-D Printing and the Future of Stuff", *WIPO Magazine*, April 2013, http://www.wipo.int/wipo_magazine/en/2013/02/article_0004.html. Accessed on January 29, 2014.
46. "US Military Invests in 3D Printing on the Frontline", *dezeen Magazine*, November 12, 2012, http://www.dezeen.com/2012/11/12/us-military-invests-in-3d-printing-on-the-frontline/. Accessed on January 29, 2014.
47. Robert O. Work and Shawn Brimley, *20YY - Preparing for War in the Robotic Age* (Centre for New American Security, January 2014).
48. "3D Printing Food in Space", http://www.nasa.gov/directorates/spacetech/home/feature_3d_food_prt.htm. Accessed on February 5, 2014.
49. Minnie Chan, "3-D Printers Help China Jet Development Take Off", *South China Morning Post*, May 29, 2013, http://www.scmp.com/news/china/article/1248385/3-d-printers-help-china-jet-development-take. Accessed on January 31, 2014.
50. Ibid.
51. "3D Printing: A Potential Game Changer for Aerospace and Defence", *Gainingaltitude*, Price Water House Coopers, 2013, www.pwc.com/us/gainingaltitude. Accessed on February 1, 2014.
52. Catherine Jewell, "3-D Printing and the Future of Stuff", *WIPO Magazine*, April 2013,http://www.wipo.int/wipo_magazine/en/2013/02/article_0004.html. Accessed on February 1, 2014.
53. www.defdist.org. Accessed on October 2, 2015.
54. www.defcad.com. Accessed on October 5, 2015.
55. "3D Printing in India", October 25, 2011, http://3dprintingindia.com/. Accessed on February 3, 2014.